ICE AXES FOR FROZEN SEAS

ICE AXES FOR FROZEN SEAS

A BIBLICAL THEOLOGY OF PROVOCATION

WALTER BRUEGGEMANN

Edited by Davis Hankins

BAYLOR UNIVERSITY PRESS

Waco, Texas 76798-7363

Cover Art and Design by Hannah Feldmeier
Book Design by Diane Smith

Library of Congress Cataloging-in-Publication Data

Brueggemann, Walter.
[Works. Selections]
Ice axes for frozen seas : a biblical theology of provocation / Walter Brueggemann ; edited by Davis Hankins.
430 pages cm
Includes bibliographical references and index.
ISBN 978-1-4813-0218-0 (hardback : alk. paper)
1. Theology. 2. Bible. Old Testament – Criticism, interpretation, etc.
I. Title.
BT15.B69 2014
230–dc23

2014010725

Printed in the United States of America on acid-free paper with a minimum of 30% post-consumer waste recycled content.

CONTENTS

PART III
Legal Covenants that Coalesce

PART IV
Imaginative Provocations that Compel

INTRODUCTION

I
THIS BOOK

In a 2011 interview on Krista Tippett's NPR show, *On Being*, Walter Brueggemann alluded to the following passage from one of Kafka's letters that reflects on the practice of reading and the capacity of words to change lives. In that 1904 letter to a friend, Kafka wrote:

> Altogether, I think we ought to read only books that bite and sting us. If the book we are reading doesn't shake us awake like a blow to the skull, why bother reading it in the first place? So that it can make us happy, as you put it? Good God, we'd be just as happy if we had no books at all; books that make us happy we could, in a pinch, also write ourselves. What we need are books that hit us like a most painful misfortune, like the death of someone we loved more than we love ourselves, that make us feel as though we had been banished to the woods, far from any human presence, like a suicide. A book must be the ax for the frozen sea within us. That is what I believe.[1]

In his research and publications over the last half-century, Brueggemann has offered a theoretical account of how language can have the kinds of capacities Kafka describes. He has explored the implications of language's ability to affect our lives and lead our realities for both our understanding of biblical literature and for contemporary forms of cultural practices, including the religious, and he has done all that through oral and written texts that brilliantly illustrate the point. As my professor in my first year of seminary and often since, Brueggemann and his words have been for me as they have for many others ice axes breaking frozen seas, enabling new ways of thinking and being to flow freely into the world. I remain grateful to him for that, and of course for the opportunity to edit and introduce this book.[2]

I have organized the volume into four parts according to both thematic and generic coherence. For Brueggemann, of course, the two are related. A text's capacities depend at least in part on its genre, and different genres tend toward different thematic functions.

Part I, "Poetic Cadences that Create Hope," begins with analyses of poetry and hope. As is especially clear in chapter 4, "Poem vs. Memos," Israel's poetry is often wild and playful, at times soft and elusive, and always potentially subversive of settled certitudes and generative of new realities where human dignity, worth, freedom, and responsibility thrive. Brueggemann opposes poetry's surprising, life-giving power that creates to our dominant, memo-writing culture that wants no more than to collect and calculate. The poems might just sing us to freedom from our flattened calculations aimed merely at "no child left behind."

Part II, "Narrative Complexities that Challenge," focuses on similar alternatives made available by Israel's ancient narratives, especially the paradigmatic story of the exodus and the following covenantal traditions. Part III, "Legal Covenants that Coalesce," shifts focus from the narrative alternative between Israel and Egypt to the policies for the covenant community that issue from the choice and pursuit of the Israel option over the Egypt option. So chapter 11, "From Narrative to Policy," delineates five texts where Deuteronomy transforms "the old narrative memory into a workable practice of policy."

Finally, part IV, "Imaginative Provocations that Compel," includes several interventions into matters of contemporary concern. Chapter 14, "Testimony," offers a programmatic articulation of what is at stake in and what possibilities are created by interventions such as those that follow in part IV. Chapter 15 casts in a new light the standard historical account of Martin Luther King Jr.'s legacy by creatively telling his story alongside Moses'. In chapter 16 Brueggemann offers his thoughts on what is crucial in education and socialization in the twenty-first century. Chapters 17 and 18 offer short interventions aimed at two particular socioeconomic issues that serve as bookends for the period in which Brueggemann wrote these texts: the 2008 bail out and the 2012 resurgence of the labor movement. This movement included many Walmart employees and happened to coincide with Walmart's fiftieth anniversary—a perfect time, says

Brueggemann, for a Jubilee that would more evenly distribute among employees the wealth generated for the company through their labor.

Each chapter and part of this book reflects, on the basis of different foundations and in the interest of various concerns, on a set of common ideas that dominate Brueggemann's thought in the first two decades of the twenty-first century. In what follows I introduce these central ideas, their various expressions in this book, and matters of context and background that are necessary for a full understanding of Brueggemann's engagements with the Bible, biblical interpreters, and the contemporary world.

II
BRUEGGEMANN IN SOCIOPOLITICAL CONTEXT

One prominent feature of all the chapters in this volume is an explicit, sometimes more sometimes less, directly expressed critical opposition to many of the United States' social, economic, political, and military policies (for one example, see chapter 16, "Slow Wisdom").[3] To understand the political nature of Brueggemann's interpretive practice, one should be mindful of the context of its development in the 1970s, 1980s, and 1990s, the period of liberal capitalism's transformation into neoliberal corporate (or, as he often calls it, postindustrial) capitalism. Following the widespread social movements that sought universal access to the political, economic, and cultural wealth made available and created after World War II by massive public works and publicly subsidized development, in the last forty years the racially diversified, technologically advanced, and economically productive majority has declined in influence and access to wealth. This period of expanding markets, stagnate wages for the majority, and declining energy reserves can be thought of as beginning with the peaking of domestic oil production in the United States in 1970 and the concurrent dominance of free-market policies developed and unleashed on the world by disciples of Milton Friedman from the 1970s to the present.[4] During this period the United States expended massive amounts of resources aimed at ensuring its future access to wealth and energy, the ideological justifications for which depicted the world as a hostile space of global scarcity. Such anxiety over scarcity fueled overwhelming concentrations of wealth and excesses of consumption in rich nations. All of this has culminated in the impoverishment of most of the planet's population and the onset of the global slump in 2008, which saw further redistribution of wealth from the poor and middle class to the rich.[5] On the other hand, 2008 also included the successful presidential campaign of Barack Obama, which was due in part to the resonances of its fusion politics with large social movements seeking less economic stratification, increased access to jobs and social services, and more representative politics. Each essay collected here was written in or after 2008, and each more or less directly responds to the ensuing experiences of both ongoing crisis and hope for change.

Brueggemann's work has consistently opposed the reactionary resurgence of liberalism that privatized and redistributed wealth from workers to corporate elites, developed a market society in place of a market economy, and effectively created the conditions for an increasingly isolated, anxious, and alienated individual experience—without thick relations and disseminated across thin technological networks of postmodern media and marketing.[6] Yet his work has also been at odds with the concurrent rise in identity politics and the conservative sectarianism that have proved incapable of countering the erosion of sociopolitical solidarity.[7]

Brueggemann's political interventions characteristically avoid both apolitical resignation and cynicism, which have at times marked postmodernism, and reactionary tactics aimed at safeguarding tradition, which often mark religious political thought. Instead he roots his political hope in the fragmented, internally differentiated, and contradictory content of the Bible. The Bible's power and potential resides in its capacities to supply words that voice our pain; analogues that reflect our struggles for peace, justice, and human development; and visions of peoples joining together in solidarity around the struggles, wounds, and joys thus perceived and proclaimed in order to foster a general flourishing of life in all of our worlds.

III
BRUEGGEMANN'S CRITICAL BIBLICAL HOPE

While Brueggemann draws deep hope from the Bible, he knows all about the various politically problematic uses and abuses of and in the Bible. Yet Brueggemann is primarily interested in imagining how the biblical text summons its reading communities to a way of life alternative to the coercive demands for endless productivity and the seductive comforts that pacify the laborers and marginalized and that entrench the world's acquisitive and exploitative powers. To be sure, Brueggemann is not naive about the difficulty, threat, and conflict that face any attempt to pursue such alternatives. In places such as chapter 9, "The Antidote to Amnesia,"

Brueggemann courageously recognizes the violence that at times erupts in the struggle to achieve "life beyond Pharaoh." About Moses' act that killed the Egyptian who was beating a Hebrew slave in Exodus 2:11-12, he writes, "Someone had to act. You might call him a 'terrorist,' for he killed a government agent. Or you might call him a 'freedom fighter.' Call him what you will. The kids need to know that life beyond Pharaoh does not come by innocence. It comes by risky engagement with public power. The story of this killing is a rich didactic moment that sets the community of faith over against the force of empire." Against the liberal Christian temptation to let the narrative of Jesus' nonviolent facedown of Pilate (John 18:28–19:16) "override the old one of violence," Brueggemann provocatively proclaims, "life in the presence of forced labor and all its exploitation under any kind of regime is no moment for timidity."

Brueggemann is also aware that the Bible contains plenty of ideological content alongside radical content. Indeed, his publications often analyze and oppose competing, antagonistic ideological tendencies and operations in various biblical traditions.[8] The present volume offers a parade example in chapter 6, "Food Fight."[9] Not only does this chapter identify and oppose two antagonistic and "competing ways to think about food and hunger" in the Bible, the struggle between them is clearly rooted in class antagonisms that implicate readers no less than the text:

> The struggle for food between those who have advantage, resources, markets and leverage with those who lack those advantages is a long-term fight that is waged in many modes. . . . The Bible is a map of profound contestation that turned up in public practice and that was given theological rationale and eventually came to be taken as authoritative. That tension in the Bible itself is a counterpoint to the tension we ourselves know about. Thus I suggest that each of us is variously involved in a food fight concerning the legitimacy of our own hungers and the pressure of the hungers of others that impinge upon our cache of food. In the midst of that struggle that is grandly biblical and acutely personal, we carry on an enquiry about what is right and what is true, what is permitted and what is required.

This quotation exquisitely displays Brueggemann's deft ability to make subtle, dialectical moves between ideological analyses of biblical texts and ideological analyses of their interpreters, without either separating or confusing texts and readers.

Yet Brueggemann does not simply recognize, identify, and extrapolate from the Bible's inherently dynamic and antagonistic character. While true in some respects, one would be mistaken to view his analyses as diagnostic of conflicts between different perspectives that exist in a zero-sum relation of exclusion of each other. Things are far more complex, as is evident in his reading of the Songs of Zion in chapter 3, "Misbegotten Hope." While linking "the illusionary faith of these psalms to the cadre of the privileged elite in the Jerusalem establishment," as well as to "contemporary Zionism that is fed and authorized by that ancient Zionism," he also attends to these psalms' subversive capacities in the belated colonial context of exilic life under Babylonian rule. When, in Psalm 137:3, the captors ask the captives to sing one of the songs of Zion:

> They did so for purposes of mocking contempt. In doing so, however, they unwittingly permitted the deported, in their very presence, to perform their alternative world that offered *mythological rootage* beyond the reach of empire, that entertained *new historical possibility*, and that mediated *long-term hope* against the empire. Thus the tormenters created a venue for counterpossibility to their own brutalizing mastery. The performance they required was itself an act of hope that contained dangerous seeds of revolutionary imagination.

Far from isolating a distinct perspective—say, of royal ideology—that is simply opposed in an external relation to another—say, of prophetic theology—Brueggemann attends to how the same set of claims can be as readily harnessed to a liberating as to a dominating cause. Thus his advocacies and repudiations are never either secured by some guaranteed foundation or universally valid apart from historical particularities; they are instead proffered as strategic interventions made possible by this very lack of an integrated foundation for political action. How then does this conflicted, dysfunctional ground make possible transformative sociopolitical action?

IV
BRUEGGEMANN IN THEORETICAL CONTEXT

As Brueggemann regularly demonstrates, at the heart of the Bible is neither a unified ideological program nor even a diverse array of variously different, externally related perspectives. The disjunctions that lie at the Bible's center are not at all the same as such extensive differences. This point is crucial for understanding how Brueggemann deploys these fissures to open new possibilities for thought and action that readers can pursue and use to form new social links. That is, this point is crucial for grasping why Brueggemann engages the Bible as a source of real sociopolitical hope and emancipatory energy. To explain this point I attend in what follows to some of the theoretical and philosophical background to my analysis of Brueggemann's work.

The twentieth-century French philosopher Gilles Deleuze may not appear in many of Brueggemann's wide-ranging bibliographies, but Brueggemann shares Deleuze's concern to maintain a distinction between what the latter calls extensive versus intensive differences.[10] Extensive differences exist between two or more opposed entities and are measurable according to some external criteria.[11] "Intensive differences cannot be located in space in the same way, and do not depend upon oppositions between static entities. Intensive differences often concern the internal variations within a single entity. One example of an intensive difference is the differential pressure within a given air mass that can produce wind—the greater the pressure differential, the stronger the wind—and even storms."[12] Brueggemann's analyses privilege such intensive, nonoppositional, and generative difference in the Bible, and it is in such difference that he often grounds his hope.[13]

A clear example is found in chapter 2, "Conflicted Divine Agency." In Isaiah 54:7-8, the first line of each verse is separated from the second by a huge chasm, and so each verse presents a deep, conflictual fissure. In the first line "God concedes that God has been fickle," and so human faith in a time of crisis "comes to the abyss of theological absence." But then, "The second line in each verse contradicts the first. It is as though YHWH has reversed field in mid-sentence. . . . I propose that the poet daringly gives us access to the internal life of God, which is profoundly conflicted." From such conflictedness stems newness: "It is as though God, in that moment, discovers something about God's self that God had not known before. And while we may take this as a measure of God's wondrous love, we may also take it as a measure of the limit of God's freedom, for God cannot slough off this endless vexation." Obviously these two interpretive options—God's love versus God's endless vexation—are not on equal footing. In fact, the difference between them corresponds precisely to the difference between intensive and extensive differences. To take this new discovery as a measure of God's love would subordinate the true difference that generated the compassion (God's profound, intrinsic conflictedness) to the extrinsic difference that it produced (God's love as opposed to some other attribute, e.g., hate or justice). Reading this passage as an indication of such an extrinsic, oppositional sense of identity, that is, as an indication of God's love, obscures and thus misrepresents the internal forces and intensities that underlie such a passing moment of identity. The vexation is, as he says, endless. In other words, Brueggemann's hope is not grounded in the identity of God—as fixed and opposed to some other identity as one might oppose mercy and justice. Brueggemann's hope is rooted instead in the intrinsic differences that are constantly shifting, never fixed, and responsible for generating the extensive differences that have tended to interest and satisfy traditional theological discourse.

Although he frequently acknowledges the non-necessity of theological language,[14] Brueggemann's interest in an intrinsic difference that is not subordinate but superior to identity is at least in part what motivates his retention of theological categories and references to divine agency.[15] He tends to follow the text by identifying the agency responsible for the text's generative capacities with YHWH:[16] "*The substance of Israel's testimony concerning Yahweh, I propose, yields a Character who has a profound disjunction at the core of the Subject's life*. This disjunction, moreover, is the engine that drives Israel's testimony; it is the splendor of Israel's odd faith and the source of the deep vexation that marks Israel's life."[17] From a theoretical angle, what is crucial here is that the source and consequence of Israel's testimony about YHWH, as well as of the social links that create and mark Israel as a people, is not an organic or substantial tie that binds the whole, but rather a disjunctive interstice. Thus neither Israel nor YHWH ever achieve any sort of stable unity or fixed coherence even though, through performative and affective articulations and actions, they crystallize into various formations that have specific effects.

For Brueggemann the rhetorical act of naming these fissures is essential for generating their productive capacities. The productive capacity of naming sites of contestation is the primary subject of chapter 14, "Testimony." He writes, "The very utterance of . . . pain, dignity, and hope in a context that generates pain, overrides dignity, and nullifies hope *puts establishment truth in contestation*." The witnesses to such utterances, he continues, "do not get to decide the outcome of such articulation and such adjudication. Rather they set in motion processes that run well beyond their own utterance. Their work is to break the silence, to mount a contest, and to insist upon openness to a possibility not heretofore entertained." The agency behind the utterance and the consequences of the naming exceed our capacities for understanding or controlling. "In ways that we do not understand, the silence is broken. The poet, 2 Isaiah, broke the silence in daring, lyrical ways that contest the truth of Babylonian claims. The silence is broken, says the poet, by the instigation of the holy God." He continues, "In this utterance based on hidden experience, the poet as witness opens up a large, lyrical alternative world in which Jews are invited to recover enough of their identity in order to act, according to their destiny, against the will of the empire. The sequence of *hidden experience, poetic utterance*, and *engagement in contestation* with imperial truth becomes paradigmatic for Israel's faith." Brueggemann delights in showing how the utterance of a condition that is unsayable or inconceivable within the dominant social rationality can generate a truth that can be affirmed only by breaking with existing social languages.

Here again Brueggemann's work resonates strongly with that of a contemporary critical theorist. Ernesto Laclau has uncovered a precisely analogous sequence shared by all genuinely political movements in his extension to the political realm of Jacques Lacan's concept of a Master Signifier—an emptied signifier whose lack of meaning enables it to "suture" meaningful relations among various elements, thus constituting identities among what are otherwise merely different particularities.[18] And yet social identities are never fixed, both because "all identity is relational . . . [and] the system of relations does not reach the point of being fixed as a stable system of differences" and because "all discourse is subverted by a field of discursivity which overflows it."[19] Laclau calls the political operation that forms a people out of dispersed, floating particularities "articulation," which "consists in the construction of nodal points which partially fix meaning; and the partial character of this fixation proceeds from the openness of the social, a result, in its turn, of the constant overflowing of every discourse by the infinitude of the field of discursivity."[20] In short, an utterance that "represents" what is absent—that is, a people participating in a political movement—constructs nodal points that reshape the social field, deforming it and constructing new differences and relations. This corresponds precisely to the capacity that Brueggemann attributes to biblical rhetoric, particularly as voiced in poetry. A sequence identical to Laclau's is clear in the last quotation in the previous paragraph: an initial *hiddenness* (of social life and political practice), followed by a *poetic utterance* (necessary for aggregating social relations out of concrete historical forces), which leads to *engagement in contestation* (by forging new differences and identifications among social relations and political demands).

In my opinion often underappreciated, the theoretical interests, resonances, and background to Brueggemann's work are quite sophisticated.[21] One can trace out the lines of an evolving, shifting dynamic in the shape of Brueggemann's work on the basis of this background. In the late 1960s, 1970s, and 1980s he was primarily concerned with working out the inherent connections between two emerging approaches to biblical literature that were at risk of diverging: rhetorical criticism and sociological analysis. From Brueggemann's generation the two primary representatives of rhetorical criticism and sociological analysis are Phyllis Trible and Norman Gottwald, respectively. For his part Brueggemann showed how they could and indeed should always be at work together.[22] Brueggemann's explorations of the social and historical capacities of rhetoric, as well as of the rhetorical character of social life, have led him consistently to affirm the dialectical interconnectedness of rhetoric and reality. This conviction advanced in the late 1980s, 1990s, and 2000s when Brueggemann's work drew heavily on the resources of postmodern philosophy for Old Testament theology.[23]

One of the most curious features of Brueggemann's work is how he both identifies as an Old Testament theologian, insisting on the importance of preserving theological categories in biblical criticism, references to divine agency, and so on, while embracing many insights that emerged with postmodernity, which is generally considered the time in biblical criticism when the entire biblical theological enterprise became increasingly contested, uncertain, and unpopular. By reinventing and reviving critical biblical interpretation under the auspices of Old Testament theology, Brueggemann became one of the most innovative thinkers in the field. He has made various efforts to respond to the many criticisms of the basic concepts and conclusions of biblical interpretation—many of them raised or echoed by him—not by returning to the old categories and practices but by reconceiving biblical theology in the wake of the failure of the Enlightenment project, that is, the failure of the Enlightenment to carry out its efforts at eradicating the theological by expanding the rational. Brueggemann has vigorously advanced and upheld various valid historical, theoretical, and political critiques of biblical theology and religion. And yet, in line with various postmodern currents, he has tirelessly insisted that rhetoric and rhetorical devices, including theological claims, are not secondary to and do not transcend self-contained conceptual structures, externally given realities, or social relations. Instead, every logical structure, every construction of reality, and every social bond require appeals to and uses of both rhetorical devices and faith in what is impossible to perceive or verify empirically.[24] So too has he critically sought and constructed theoretical support for his belief that biblical interpretation is difficult if not impossible without reference to the agency of the God about which the texts speak. As will be made even more clear in what follows, Brueggemann's loosely speaking "postmodern" biblical theology is far from sheep's clothing for old theological wolves. Instead he has labored hard to reformulate the meaning and function of the God with which biblical criticism deals.

On the one hand, and in line with postmodernism's general interest in writing (écriture, *graphé, trace*, etc.), the God hosted by Brueggemann's interpretive endeavors is an unequivocally "paper god."[25] Brueggemann (in)famously stakes his theological program on the claim that no critical biblical theology can credibly contend that it deals with a God that is in any way present outside the text. "Speech constitutes reality, and who God turns out to be in Israel depends on the utterance of the Israelites or, derivatively, the utterance of the text. . . . *The God of Old Testament Theology . . . lives in, with, and under the rhetorical enterprise of this text, and nowhere else and in no other way*."[26] In this sense Brueggemann's theology is thus vehemently antagonistic to traditional ideas of transcendence.[27]

On the other hand, and in line with postmodernism's general interest in the social-symbolic nature of power, the reality of the virtual, the critique of ideology, and so on, this biblical (paper) God operates with real agency within lived social reality.[28] Brueggemann stridently insists on the need for a biblical theology that can affirm both that, when it comes to God, there are only texts, and simultaneously that this God, once textually rendered, enigmatically operates in ways that interpreters cannot simply pin down to specific, stable referents. This conviction sets Brueggemann at odds with proponents of certain other postmodern approaches to biblical theological interpretation, not only those that reject any assertion of divine agency as a priori untenable or incomprehensible[29] but also those that are oriented by a different set of categories. Here Brueggemann's differences with Terence E. Fretheim prove instructive and illustrative of what sets Brueggemann's work apart from other biblical theologies.

V
BRUEGGEMANN'S UNIQUE CRITICAL BIBLICAL THEOLOGY

A. Brueggemann's Unique Biblical Theology

In the wake of the publication of *Theology of the Old Testament*, Fretheim's review critiqued Brueggemann's theology, especially his insistences on God's sovereign freedom. Brueggemann develops the concepts of sovereignty and freedom to describe the capacity of the biblical God to exceed God's history, God's relationships, and the terms of those relationships.[30] For Fretheim, however, "The biblical God is transcendent *within* relationship (never 'above' it). . . . This God is so committed to full participation in a genuine relationship with Israel and the world that God no longer has the option of finally pulling back from it. . . . God will make surprising, unsettling, and sharply judgmental moves. . . . But all such divine moves occur *from within* this resolve."[31] For Fretheim the biblical God is free to act, but this freedom is constrained both by God's unwavering resolve to act "*always* in the service of God's loving and saving purposes . . . in the service of God's *absolute* will for life and blessing"[32] and by God's unbreakable, "once-for-all decisions that implement that will."[33] Fretheim concludes that "God's *ongoing* ambivalence," which Brueggemann locates at YHWH's very essence, is related only to "various circumstantial decisions."[34] While for Fretheim God's essence is in process, not static, the process occurs within the unambivalently fixed framework of an unwavering will that is tied to unbreakable promises. For Brueggemann, on the contrary, the Bible testifies against the idea that anything—person, world, or God—could be immune to destruction or transformation.[35]

Fretheim's position is not only suspect from the practical standpoint of its failure to correspond with biblical testimony but also from its failure to take into account theoretical issues that Brueggemann's position does consider. First, how can the "once-for-all" decisions that supposedly represent God's resolve emerge "from within" such resolve? If God possesses the agency to make such decisions (that is, if they really are worthy of being called decisions), then in some way God must be capable of operating beyond them. "Yahweh's connection to the partner is undertaken as sovereign, unfettered choice. . . . Because this commitment of fidelity to the partner is undertaken in sovereign freedom, it follows that Yahweh can indeed withdraw from the relationship and cancel the commitment."[36] If God's decisions in fact inaugurate God's resolve, then this resolve must remain incomplete and violable, haunted both by the specter of the decision point and, as I will elaborate below, by the lack of any ultimate guarantee that the judgment will turn out to be, for example, just or loving.[37]

To understand why it is necessary to posit such an inherent corruptibility to God's decision to be in relationship and thus to the relationship itself, it will help to take a detour through the French philosopher Jacques Derrida's discussion of justice. Derrida is one of the most important philosophers informing Brueggemann's thought, and Brueggemann's proximity to him is clear in the following passage, worth quoting at length.[38]

> The very emergence of justice and law, the instituting, founding, and justifying moment of law implies a performative force, that is to say always an interpretive force and a call to faith. . . . Justice—in the sense of *droit* (right or law)—would not simply be put in the service of a social force or power, for example an economic, political ideological power that would exist outside or before it and that it would have to accommodate or bend to when useful. Its very moment of foundation or institution, besides, is never a moment inscribed in the homogeneous fabric of a story or history, since it rips it apart with one decision. Yet, the operation that amounts to founding, inaugurating, justifying law, to *making law*, would consist of a *coup de force*, of a performative and therefore interpretive violence that in itself is neither just nor unjust and that no justice and no earlier and previously founding law, no preexisting foundation, could, by definition, guarantee or contradict or invalidate.[39]

There is too much in this quotation to unpack here. Most important for my purposes is the sense in which the founding of any law—say, the founding act whereby God commits to covenantal life in relationship with Israel—is an act that is necessarily outside of the law and so indicates a place where the law remains open to a force that exceeds it. Or, in Brueggemann's words, "Yahweh makes a commitment of care, fidelity, and obligation to the partner that Yahweh did not need to make. In the end, Israel can give no reason for this act of Yahweh's freedom. It is simply a given."[40] The commitment is, in Derrida's words, "a performative and therefore interpretive violence" that cannot be accounted for by any preexisting foundation. Furthermore, this unaccountable, forceful performance keeps the commitment unresolved and always under threat: "Israel's text and Israel's lived experience keep facing the reality that something like Yahweh's self-regard keeps surfacing in demanding ways. This self-regard may emerge as unsurprising moral claim, or it may emerge as a kind of wild capriciousness, as sovereignty without principled loyalty. It is this propensity in Yahweh . . . that precludes any final equation of sovereignty with covenantal love or with pathos."[41] Such a precluded "final equation" is the precise substance of Fretheim's unsustainable insistence on God's unalterable will.

The theoretical problems with Fretheim's position go deeper and are worth considering because they also demonstrate the nature and value of Brueggemann's. How could there be any decision or resolve without this inherent openness to transformation or corruptibility? That is, if it exists at all, the divine capacity to decide requires a lack of any assurance about the deciding will or the decision's outcome. If the future were known and certain, what need would there be for decisions?[42] Why would we call it a decision? It is because the future is unknown and the outcomes incalculable that decisions have to be made.

Again Derrida clearly and concretely makes this point about inherent corruptibility that requires us to view fidelity as inherently capable of betrayal. In his major engagement with democracy Derrida uses the 1992 Algerian elections to illustrate democracy's autoimmune condition.[43] An antidemocratic majority was expected to win and then curtail democratization, so the government suspended the democratic elections, thereby abolishing democracy for the sake of democracy, attacking democracy to avoid an attack on democracy. There is no avoiding such a situation, argues Derrida, because being democratic requires democracy's openness to antidemocratic contamination, both from an inherent emergence or election of antidemocratic forces and from protective measures that may threaten it no less. The basic point here is the same as in the argument about justice: the conditions for the possibility of democracy are simultaneously the conditions that make it impossible. These are necessary but autoimmune conditions that open the phenomenon in question to the risk of transformation or even annihilation. I hope that the connections between Derrida's arguments and Brueggemann's theology prove as easy to perceive as the problematic nature of Fretheim's critique. Brueggemann's God is no less afflicted by such an autoimmune condition. God's sovereignty refers for Brueggemann to God's ability both to honor the commitments established by the once-and-for-all promises that the Bible calls "covenants" and to dishonor those commitments, which thus opens God to the possibility of annihilating God's character as God.[44]

B. Brueggemann's Uniquely Critical Biblical Theology

Brueggemann's theology is a clear outgrowth of his text-immanent ontology. The former emerges out of the latter's unfinalizably conflictual character. The text is simultaneously the condition of possibility and the condition of impossibility of the reader's access to the divine and other subjects to which it testifies. The foundational plane of immanent-textual substance is open, cracked, internally differentiated, and incompatible with itself. It is, in short, constitutively weak and essentially nonfoundational.[45] In Brueggemann's words, "The text is 'unreadable.' "[46] And, therefore, so is its God: "the subject and character [YHWH] who dominates the plot does not conform to our flattened reading propensity, theological or critical."[47] The text's fingerprints are always already all over its God, and it does not provide access to any God that would be free from its conflictually dynamic character. In another engagement with Brueggemann's work, Norman Gottwald complains about Brueggemann's neglect of ontological concerns in his rhetorical critical enterprise.[48] While Gottwald's complaints are well-founded, it is also true that Brueggemann says little about his ontology because it is weak, internally conflicted, and nonsystematic. And as Gottwald recognizes, I think that Brueggemann's oeuvre provides the material necessary for unleashing a theoretically sophisticated, interpretively productive, and politically liberative approach to biblical criticism. This approach could be called a dialectically materialist, critical biblical theology.[49]

By this I intentionally allude to the question, which has been asked before, is a critical biblical theology possible?[50] The prevailing consensus remains, I believe, that it is not. But unlike other biblical theologies of which his work is critical, this is precisely what Brueggemann's approach makes possible.[51] Note first that Brueggemann's perspective stems in part from his rejection of the hidden, metaphysical presupposition infecting and pervading even the most seemingly secular and objective biblical criticism.[52] Brueggemann's critiques of historical criticism testify to the immense difficulty of reading texts apart from distorting metaphysical commitments, whether theological or philosophical. He moves effortlessly from critiques of a Christian or Jewish scholar's reduction of the text to some article of faith to critiques of a secular scholar's pretense to objectivity as constituted by, if not supportive of, Western, patriarchal, individualistic, or even capitalist commitments.

The positive basis for what makes Brueggemann's biblical theological enterprise critical lies in at least two points. First, the God to which the Bible attests is emergent in relation to the texts and the human beings who engage the texts. Second, the texts out of which this God emerges are internally conflicted and antagonistic. It is because of this weak, inconsistent character that the more-than-material subjects such as Israel's God can emerge from the texts and achieve agential capacities that exceed determination by their textual ground. Once generated, these subjects continue to be marked by the same internally conflicted character of their anterior ground, yet they also become irreducible to their sources, which they are in turn capable of affecting even as they continue to be dialectically related and susceptible to influence by their textual-material grounds. This enterprise is critical in part because it remains thoroughly bound to the dialectical relationship between texts and more-than-textual forces, including those of historical reality.[53]

In the field of biblical studies, the label "critical" has often been reduced to mean "historical" in a flat, static, positivistic sense that Brueggemann has tirelessly shown to be far from critical. By calling his biblical theology critical, I intend a quite different meaning, yet one that has no less venerable a tradition.[54] Brueggemann's biblical theology is critical in the way that critique operates in the German philosophical tradition from Kant through Hegel, Marx, and up to the Frankfurt School. I am instructed by the way that Wendy Brown and Janet Halley have attempted "to reinvigorate and revalue the tradition of critique as vital to what the intellectual left has to offer."[55] As they write,

> What critique promises is not objectivity but perspective; indeed, critique is part of the arsenal of intellectual movements of the past two centuries that shatters the plausibility of objectivity claims once and for all. In the insistence on the availability of all human production to critique, that is, to the possibility of being rethought through an examination of constitutive premises, the work of critique is potentially without boundary or end. . . . Critique offers possibilities of analyzing existing discourses of power to understand how subjects are fabricated or positioned by them, what powers they secure (and disguise or veil), what assumptions they naturalize, what privileges they fix, what norms they mobilize, and what or whom these norms exclude.[56]

Those who know Brueggemann's expansive corpus can attest to the many resonances of this description with his theological analyses. Brueggemann's work focuses on the functions of ideology and power in the production of social, political, theological, and economic possibilities. But the text's characteristic testimony attributes to God responsibility for the internal limit that keeps the work of critique endless, and so this God naturally becomes the primary subject of Brueggemann's analyses. His critical theological enterprise is a restless, impassioned operation that yields much enjoyment but refuses the possibilities of full satisfaction or of ever finally arriving at a formulation of Israel's God outside of the vagaries of historical particularity.[57] His recurring critiques of Enlightenment rationality and modernist pretenses to autonomy and objectivity are rooted in his approach's antiteleological and historically particular character. Brueggemann repeatedly shows how theology functions as one of the contradictions of whatever forms the prevailing social, economic, and political landscape of a time. Of course, as many others including Brueggemann have shown, theology has also been used ideologically to legitimate a system's claims to coherence. Yet it also, because of its references to a God that will not be abstracted either from history or into a stable identity, inherently challenges and destabilizes such claims.

The example of this critical character that repeatedly appears in his work is his treatment of the relationship between theology and socioeconomic history. As Gottwald also indicates in the review mentioned above, Brueggemann at times neglects the role played by historical concerns in his focus on the rhetorical capacities of the text. This is in part because the field was so dominated by simplistic positivism and idealistic ontologies at the moment he developed his perspective that he naturally focused on the capacities of rhetoric to exceed determination by its social and historical contexts and indeed to constitute reality.[58] However, he is certainly aware of and accounts for the capacities of sociohistorical circumstances to affect speech.[59] His great sensitivity and attention to the ideological nature and function of theological language rests upon his awareness of how sociohistorical interests can shape and be served by discursive regimes. For example, in one place he writes, "the splendor of Yhwh has to do with social power and economic relationships."[60] In another he refers to the "inalienable connection between the character of God and the shape of community."[61] His work as a whole adopts a dialectical approach to the relationship between rhetoric and all more-than-rhetorical forces such as history that impinge upon and inflect rhetoric even as they are affected by and can emerge from that rhetoric.

Brueggemann's uncompromisingly dialectical approach to the relationship between theology and socioeconomic history lies behind his conviction that, if references to God as an agent were omitted from constructions of Israel's history, then essential aspects of that history would be lost. Thus, while Gottwald's critique that Brueggemann at times neglects historical concerns is correct, this neglect is an unnecessary consequence of his attempt to develop an approach to history that would correct for the inadequacies pervading prevailing biblical interpretations. Brueggemann's work thus consistently challenges not only the interpretations but also the topics and questions that interpreters have tended to treat as appropriate, objective, and comprehensive.

VI
THE FUTURE OF BRUEGGEMANN'S CRITICAL BIBLICAL THEOLOGY

At this point there opens what is to my mind a prominent space for future work in the wake of Brueggemann's path-breaking career (which, thankfully, continues). Whereas his work is clearly based on such a dialectic, this approach is not always sufficiently described, and certain thorny problems remain unaccounted for. So long as this situation remains, his work will continue to be susceptible to significant misuses and misunderstandings. I conclude this introduction with a brief account of my take on this point of departure and some lingering questions left by Brueggemann's oeuvre.

First, if Brueggemann's perspective can be taken seriously in the way I have argued here—that is, as a dialectically materialist, critical biblical theology that provides a genuine alternative to the standard options available in biblical studies—then more work is required to formulate in clearer theoretical terms the relationships between text and ontology and theology and history.[62] What remains clear is that Brueggemann does not follow the prevailing options that aim in one way or another to bridge the gap between theology and history. The standard secular approach has been to treat theological claims as historical data without agency. The confessional approach, on the other hand, has tended to treat God as a historical agent that is, although unique, nonetheless akin to other historical agents. The uniqueness of Brueggemann's approach has been to insist upon the gap itself as inherent to both and unbridgeable. There is a fundamental disruption in history and human society that blocks one from directly experiencing oneself, that prevents words from directly referring to their social contexts, and that enables and even requires certain nonsubstantive points of reference to operate with a causality of their own.

Brueggemann's persistent refusal to speculate about or search for a God "behind" or "beyond" the text is thus not a mere effect of his intellectual humility. There is no hidden, true substance or inner kernel of a God operating behind the scenes. Even still, while correct from Brueggemann's perspective, the materialist reductionist who claims "there is no God" misses the point, which is that God nonetheless operates as a surface effect in the life of a community whose discourse employs various ways of speaking about God. There is nothing behind such testimony save various social, political, economic, and other interests, the meaning of which depends upon the functioning of a discourse that may be, as it was in ancient Israel, theological. What remains in need of explication is thus an account of how the appearance of a God, for example, can (1) nonreductively emerge from the substance of which society consists and (2) function with an agency of its own while (3) remaining fully immanent to this same social substance.

Collected here are some of Brueggemann's essays, public lectures, and provocative interventions conceived between 2008 and 2012. The content of the essays varies, often in accord with the initial contexts and original audiences, which included academics, church leaders and laypeople, and the broader public. Yet, the thread of his provocative biblical theology runs within and throughout. Ultimately, while it is by no means perfect and at times needs clarification, elaboration, or even correction, Brueggemann's theology has provided the most theoretically sophisticated and politically effective approach to Israel's literature and the God that Israel takes to be central to its life and the life of the world. To return to Kafka, Brueggemann's work provides the best account of how ice axes can, from time to time, here and there, break the frozen seas of our Gods, our worlds, and ourselves. Thankfully Brueggemann has not yet ceased producing such axes. Hopefully we, his students and collaborators, will mobilize the possibilities that surge forth from his explosive expositions for more true and just ways of thinking about and being in the world. Much is at stake, so let us continue hacking away at it!

Davis Hankins
Appalachian State University
November 2013

PART I

POETIC CADENCES THAT CREATE HOPE

1

CONFLICTED HUMAN AGENCY

My invitation from Walter May to address you was a suggestion that I focus on an "Old Testament narrative of hope and faithfulness" in the service of a larger "narrative of hopeful, inclusive ministry."

I

I think I understand the double accent on *hopeful* because we live in a society (and church) that is overwhelmed by the "data of despair" all around us, with no one knowing where to turn next. The facts on the ground, moreover, are situated in *a narrative of despair* that I have termed "military consumerism," a preoccupation with satiation and self-indulgence about commodities that is reinforced by a military muscle that aims to protect our entitled advantage in the world. It is clear that that narrative, which dominates the imagination among us, is not hope-filled, because it cannot make us either safe or happy. It is clear that the world generated by the narrative of "military consumerism" holds no human future for us. And it is unmistakable among preachers of every ilk that that dominant narrative cannot be easily critiqued because it functions in our society as an unquestioned religious totem. We are pressed elsewhere for hope; that, however, is not so clear, given the powerful combination of *the facts on the ground* and *the narrative of despair* that converge in concrete ways among us.

I am, moreover, impressed that Walter May's mandate to me twice used the word "narrative," "*narrative* of hope and faithfulness in the Old Testament" in the service of a "*narrative* of hopeful, inclusive ministry." It is clear against both Enlightenment reason and fundamentalist reductionism that there is no tight settled edict that could yield sustainable hope. Rather hope arises precisely through the narrative process in which we tell and retell our lives.[1] Thus narrative has privilege as a mode for the substance of faith because we tell a story in which newness emerges specifically and concretely in a way that cannot be explained or controlled. Thus the question among us is, "What story shall we tell?" given that the dominant story we tell allows for no news to emerge, precisely because we are bent on explanatory control. A controlled story, one in which we know the end before we start telling, is no venue for hope.

When a Christian preacher or teacher asks about narratives of hope, we are drawn to the big narratives:

"My father was a wandering Aramean" as the defining story of ancient Israel, a story that culminates with gratitude for the new land.

The Pauline summary of faith grounded in Scripture:

> For I handed on to you as of first importance what I in turn had received: that Christ died for our sins in accordance with the scriptures, and that he was buried, and that he was raised on the third day in accordance with the scriptures, and that he appeared to Cephas, then to the twelve. Then he appeared to more than five hundred brothers and sisters at one time, most of whom are alive, though some have died. Then he appeared to James, and then to all the apostles. Last of all, as to one untimely born, he appeared also to me. (1 Cor 15:3-8)

The eucharistic mystery of faith:

Christ has died,
Christ is risen,
Christ will come again.

And eventually we come to the creeds that pivot on that awesome phrase, "and was made man."

But of course the big narratives, in order to be pastorally compelling, emerge in small pastoral venues that well up in the concrete lives of the faithful. I submit that in all of these small venues, widely variant as they are, the defining connection is between *bodily reality* (of life, suffering, and death) and *holy mystery* that we cannot articulate with any precision but that matters decisively to us. It is the wonder of our faith—and of the stories we tell—that *bodily reality* and *holy mystery* make contact, not unlike that instant of contact between God and Adam sketched by Michelangelo in the Sistine Chapel. To tell a surprising, compelling interaction of bodily reality and holy mystery, we situate our *immediate narrative* and shape it according to the *remembered narrative* of that same interface that we cannot explain but to which we bear witness. Thus I assume that in telling and in hearing such a tale that yields newness, we inescapably move back and forth between what *we remember* from previous tellings and what *we know* in the present tense of our own bodily contact with that holy mystery. So I take my assignment to tell a tale of hope that is a remembered story in which newness emerged at the mix of body and holy. As we tell and hear such a remembered story, we let the memory become present tense among us and find the pulse of new possibility that is in part God-given and in part humanly felt and discerned.

II

I have decided to focus on Psalm 30:6-12, which I suggest is a narrative of hope that can sustain and support a hopeful, inclusive ministry.[2] I will return to vv. 1-5 later on but will begin my reflection with v. 6. This psalm belongs to the genre of Song of Thanksgiving that Claus Westermann has identified as a "narrative psalm."[3] In this genre the psalmist returns to tell a story of a completed act of divine transformation that issues in gratitude. For all of its concreteness, this psalm is paradigmatic and exhibits all the moves that faith makes in the process of hope. Like all such psalms, it is immediately concrete but is transferable to other contexts, so that it may be used repeatedly by different people in different circumstances of despair and hope.

1. The story has as *its premise* vv. 6-7a in which the psalmist describes a situation of well-being. I take this as a premise and not as the first act in the narrative because nothing happens. The speaker reflects a happy occasion of stasis:

> As for me, I said in my prosperity,
> "I shall never be moved."
> By your favor, O Lord,
> You had established me as a strong mountain . . .

Verse 6, taken by itself, sounds like a statement of smug self-sufficiency. It begins with a double "I, I," the independent pronoun plus the pronominal suffix. This is indeed self-announcement. The term for "prosperity" is derived from *shalom*, and the word rendered "not moved" means "not destabilized," not to "totter" or "stagger"; it is the same term used three times in the familiar Psalm 46 (vv. 2, 5, 6):

> Though the mountains *shake* . . .
> It shall not be *moved* . . .
> The kingdoms *totter.*

The word is variously rendered as "shake, moved, totter," as the psalmist ponders the force of chaos against the city. The statement in our psalm (30:6) reflects confident stability. Calvin takes v. 6 alone in that way:

> This carnal confidence frequently creeps upon the saints when they indulge themselves in their prosperity, and so to speak, wallow upon their dunghill.[4]

But as is so often the case in his commentary, Calvin has it wrong. Verse 6 does not stand alone. It belongs with v. 7a, which acknowledges, "By your favor, O LORD." The speaker recognizes that this moment of serene stability is a gift from God; there is nothing in it of self-congratulation. This is the creation as the creator intended it, "Very good." YHWH is the source of well-being! That is the premise of what follows.

2. Just as quickly, however, without any explanation, serene stability is disrupted. God is promptly acknowledged as the source and cause of that destabilization. There is no hint of guilt or judgment or punishment. The speaker belongs fully and willingly to a world defined by YHWH. And now that world yields dismay:

> You hid your face;
> I was dismayed. (30:7b)

As God has guaranteed well-being "*by your favor,*" so God by *hiding* brings the world to disruption. It does not occur to the psalmist to take the loss as punishment or that it may be his fault. The trouble happens because God hides. The world moves from stability to acute loss because God hides.[5]

3. But the speaker knows what to do. Now we get immediate, direct address to YHWH. In the affirmation of v. 7, the psalmist addressed YHWH, but now the matter has become intense. It is "To You."

> To you, O LORD, I cried,
> and to the LORD I made supplication: (v. 8)

The word order is properly inverted in the NRSV so that the indirect pronoun comes first. The verb in v. 8 is a reflexive form of *ḥanan*: "I present myself for mercy." The speaker does not grovel nor does he repent. He simply positions himself before God in his need.

4. But what follows in v. 9 is not yet a cry for help, as we have been led to expect. Now the psalmist quotes himself, what he said in his dismay. The words are rather a dispute in the form of three demanding rhetorical questions:

> What profit is there in my death
>   if I go down to the pit?
> Will the dust praise you?
>   Will it tell of your faithfulness?

The questions come very close to being an act of defiance. The questions assume that God wants and needs and loves to be praised. The purpose of the "supplication" (if that is what it is) is to show that God has something at stake in protecting the suppliant. It is not just for "my sake" that God should act but for God's own sake, for God's honor and reputation. The tone is one of chutzpah in which the suppliant assumes a certain position of covenantal leverage and entitlement. That same defiant urgency is voiced in Psalm 88 and is characteristic of Israel's prayer:

> Do you work wonders for the dead?
>   Do the shades rise up to praise you?
> Is your steadfast love declared in the grave?
>   or your faithfulness in Abaddon?
> Are your wonders known in the darkness?
>   or your saving help in the land of forgetfulness? (88:10-12)

The answer in every case is "no." No, there are no miracles for the dead. No, the dead do not praise you. No, your steadfast love is not talked about in the grave. No, your faithfulness is not championed in the pit. No, your miracles are not known in the darkness. No, your saving help is not recalled in death. No, on all counts. The conclusion is that if I die, YHWH will lose a witness; the choir will lose a tenor and God will be diminished.

In our psalm the speaker will drop out of the choir and cause the loss of one voice in the praise brigade, to the diminishment of YHWH. Calvin comes close but cannot finally bring himself to see the leverage that is voiced here:

It highly concerned the glory of God that he should be preserved alive, until by obtaining his desire, he should be able to bear witness to God's faithfulness in completely fulfilling his promise to him.[6]

Thus the answers to the three rhetorical questions are implied:

There is no gain for anyone to let the speaker die, so why let it happen?

No, the dead cannot praise God.

There will be no one to attest God's faithfulness.

Ergo . . . better to let me live! The covenant means that the death of the speaker or the well-being of the speaker is a matter of acute interest to both parties. This God is no disinterested observer to the processes of death, but stands at risk among the gods. The psalmist can remember having said this. He calls it a plea for mercy (*ḥanan*); but we note that it is an insistent plea that provides God reason to respond.

5. After the plea in Psalm 30:9, v. 10 issues a triple imperative petition:

Hear O LORD,
be gracious to me!
O LORD, be my helper!

The three imperatives are intermingled with the double use of the divine name, so that the double use here matches the double use in v. 8. The four recitals of the divine name bracket the challenge of v. 9:

To you, O LORD . . .
to the LORD. (v. 8)

Hear O LORD . . .
O LORD. (v. 10)

The petition of the speaker strategically quotes what he said, so that the questions to YHWH serve to remind YHWH of YHWH's proper function as a deliverer toward the covenant partner who prays. That is what it means to be YHWH, so be YHWH! The speaker does not doubt that he is entitled to such divine attention, nor does he doubt YHWH's capacity to deliver a good future. Thus the supplication that includes a challenge is in itself an act of hope. The speaker knows where to turn and how to speak, and fully expects (hopes!) that God is ready and willing and able to do what is asked and needed.

6. After v. 10 comes a long pause. Then in v. 11, a threefold acclamation in which the "I" of the speaker is only the acted upon object. The subject is grandly YHWH. YHWH as subject is gladly and fully acknowledged in a way that places "me" on the happy receiving end of divine engagement:

> You have turned . . .
> You have taken off . . .
> You have clothed . . .

It is all about "you." The speaker has no option or wish to take YHWH as any less than a full character in the drama, and so no reluctance about direct address and no embarrassment about crediting divine transformative activity. Thus "I" received from YHWH what I needed and asked for:

> You have turned my mourning into dancing;
> you have taken away my sackcloth,
> and clothed me with joy.

You as senior partner, *me* as glad, needy recipient. The verse in three lines is a doxology of resolution. The dismay of v. 7 has been answered. It has only been answered, however, because this speaker knew how to mount a cry, had the nerve to pose rhetorical questions that goaded YHWH, and summoned the daring confidence to use imperative petitions. God is portrayed as one who did indeed hear and answer, but only because the psalmist could initiate the exchange. It is *the voice of bodily need*, pain brought to speech that has mobilized holy mystery. The transformative resolution that God has wrought is an evangelical mystery. But that mystery is enacted only in response to a human self-presentation that is full bodied as an unapologetic determined force in the very life of God.

7. The narrative ends in v. 12 with a curious "so that." The term makes it sound as though God has performed the three verbs of v. 11 "in order that" there should follow praise and thanks in v. 12. But that clearly is what we should expect from the half-taunt of v. 9. The speaker had parleyed with YHWH to gain recovered well-being. And God has taken the offer. God wants praise that cannot come from the dead. God wants witnesses to God's own faithfulness.

And now the psalmist declares what was tacitly promised in the rhetorical questions:

> So that . . .
> my soul may praise you and not be silent.
> O Lord my God, I will give thanks to you forever. (v. 12)

The outcome is praise, not the silence that death would have yielded. Now it is thanks, forever and ever; and it is, for the first time, "my God." The doxological outcome that enhances YHWH sandwiches a final utterance of the divine name. It is YHWH my God who is praised and thanked. The speaker has turned full attention and full voice, and we may imagine full life, to the gracious, defining reality of God. God has not remained hidden. God has come out of hiding at the behest of the speaker. God has become, so to say, visible in the reclamation project. The speaker is no longer self-preoccupied if that is what v. 6 indicates. Now everything is yielded in glad confidence and gratitude.

That is, as they say on NPR, "the story." That is the story of one particular person. It is, at the same time, the story we keep retelling and reperforming. It begins in *a premise of well-being*, though not every performance begins there. It moves, step by step, through *dismay*, desperate *cry*, defiant *questioning*, urgent *imperative*, glad *affirmation*, and finally on to yielding *praise and thanks*.

This is, I submit, pervasively and in every element a narrative of hope. Every step in the narrative is an act of hope because every step assumes a defining, empowering linkage to the holy God. It is not as though hope turns on one facet of the narrative; the whole is a dramatic performance of imagined possibility. My conclusion is that this dramatic sequence is an act of hope because it is an exhibit of *dialogical freedom* granting full priority to the Holy One, but exhibiting at the same time audacious passion for one's self in the face of the Holy One. It is not abdication before God in a passive voice; it is not autonomous freedom apart from God. Rather this third option exercises engaged freedom in the insistent utterance of the divine name, an honest address to "you," and an uncompromising insistence on "me, a 'me' who can be positioned as the 'I' of the verbs." Every step of the narrative depends upon this interactive dyad that witnesses against a reductionist abdication before God as if God were honored by self-denial. It also witnesses, at the same time, against an arrogance that imagines that God could not be the subject but only an adored object. This hope is participation in a narrative in which both parties are at risk and in which either party, at the right moment, can be the dominant party in the engagement. God is at risk because the loss of a tenor will diminish praise. The psalmist is at risk because he might, in the end, remain God-abandoned and does not know, in the utterance of rhetorical questions and petitions, if there will be a response from the other side. God in the end holds initiative and acts out the great work of transformation. But the entire plot depends upon the speaker to speak up, to name God, to summon God, to petition God, and finally to praise and thank God.

I propose that this psalm is indeed a narrative of hope and that this sequence of moves is an indispensible dramatic pattern for a life of health:

initial *self-acknowledgment*;

honesty about dismay;

freedom about a shrill cry;

nerve about rhetorical questions;

passion in petition;

self-forgetting focus on "You, you, you";

buoyancy in praise and thanks.

What an inventory of possibility! The narrative of the psalm matters because it evidences that we know what to say, we know when to say it, and we know to whom to say it. That is why we have these old texts that we sense with contemporary immediacy.

III

I want now to pause in my exegetical reflection to consider the theoretical formulation for hope as I believe it to be voiced in this psalm that I propose is a paradigmatic text for us. I do so by appeal to three Jewish thinkers, for it is surely true that hope is *a Jewish gift* to the world. While the Greeks make the contribution of reasoned order (*logos*) to the world, it is Jews who have set out for a new land, who have witnessed that God is doing a new thing, who wait yet for the Messiah. And when we recite the eucharistic "mystery of faith" that Christ will "come again," we are appealing to the great Jewish dimension of our evangelical faith.

1. First I appeal to *Karl Marx*, the nineteenth-century political economist who upended Euro-American thought and who continues to do so. The phrase of Marx that seems poignant for our purposes is that we "become subjects of our own history."[7] By that Marx means to assert that the self must assert the self, to be conscious of one's own life, one's own body, and one's own pain, and to act for the freedom, healing, and well-being of one's self. In such an imperative, Marx wanted to refute the passive propensity of conventional law-and-order types who wait and receive what is given to them from above. Marx calls for nothing less than the announcement of self, the utterance of "I," the willingness to take an initiative against a deficient present tense for the sake of a new possibility.

My judgment is that this readiness to be the subject of one's own history is reflected in the cry of the psalmist in 30:8, "To you, O LORD, I cried." I do not wait in silence, but I take an initiative and address you. I suggest that the capacity to be "subject" is as old in biblical faith as the initial cry of the slaves in Egypt:

> After a long time, the king of Egypt died. The Israelites groaned under their slavery and cried out. (Exod 2:23)

That moment when Pharaoh died and pain came to speech is an awesome moment in the Bible and an awesome moment in the history of the world. It is a moment that is replicated whenever folks speak up to honor pain and to embrace it, to insist that it is no longer bearable and must be relieved. It is the self-announcement of African Americans who have waited too long, and feminists who refuse to be second class, and gays and lesbians who will not bear the silence any longer. That initial cry is confirmed by the self-announcement of YHWH in response to the slave cry. YHWH is full of promissory resolve toward Israel:

> I have observed the misery of my people who are in Egypt; I have heard their cry on account of their taskmasters. Indeed, I know their suffering, and I have come down to deliver them from the Egyptians, and to bring them up out of that land to a good and broad land, a land flowing with milk and honey. . . . The cry of the Israelites has now come to me; I have also seen how the Egyptians oppress them. (Exod 3:7-9)

But then, YHWH interrupts YHWH's own self-resolve with a mandate to Moses: "You go to Pharaoh." *You go* as human agent. *You go* insist upon your future. *You tell* Pharaoh that I said . . . you can quote me: "Thus saith the LORD God, 'Let my people go.' " But *you run* the risk.

The same readiness to be subject of one's own history is evident in the narrative of Mark 5:25-34. The woman with twelve years of hemorrhaging is insistent in her resolve: "If I but touch his clothes, I will be made well": she did touch him! She extended her hand. She took the initiative. She was healed. And Jesus concludes, "Your faith has made you well." So also with the blind Bartimaeus (Mark 10:52): He cried out. "He threw off his cloak. He sprang up. He came to Jesus." The narrative is overrun with his active verbs. Jesus asks him, "What do you want me to do for you?" He answers, "Let me see again." And Jesus says to him, "Your faith has made you whole."

From Moses to the woman to Bartimaeus, these characters act for a future on which they insist. They will not wait. They will not be passive. They will act. Among the company of those who will not wait are those who come to AA who begin with their self-announcement, "My name is Bill; I am an alcoholic." And in less stylized venues, it is the same self-announcement of every hope-filled person who seeks a counselor, yearning for transformation, knowing that there is nothing "normal" about present pain or servitude. It takes a Jew like Marx to authorize such hoping!

2. The second Jewish scholar I mention is Martin Buber, who is best known for his I-Thou thesis. Buber has taught us that there is no "I" without a prevenient "Thou." He might have taken our psalm as his text. The psalm reverberates with "I":

> I said . . . "I shall never be moved" . . .
> I was dismayed . . .
> I cried . . .
> I made supplication. (30:6-8)

And in the end,

> I will give thanks. (v. 12)

But the "I" alone is inadequate, as this speaker learns. And so the psalm turns to "You":

> *To you*, O LORD, I cried . . .
> *You* have turned my mourning to dancing;

> *You* have taken off my sackcloth . . .
> I will give thanks *to you* forever. (vv. 8, 11-12)

There is no confusion between the two of them. The speaker never compromises his identity. He does, however, come to understand in his dismay that his "I" is driven back to "you" who has the capacity to transform. But this capacity of the "you" depends upon the courage of the "I" to issue the imperatives based on need, expectation, and hope. The petitions, "Hear, be gracious, be my helper," are all premised on the conviction that dismay is not my proper habitation. Thus the "thou" can move from dismay; but it is the task of the "I" to move the "thou" to act by self-insistence.

Buber first contrasts prophetic-covenantal faith with apocalyptic, which he regards as decadent. He says of the latter:

> Everything here is predetermined; all human decisions are only sham struggle. The future does not come to pass; the future is already present in heaven, as it were, present from the beginning. Therefore, it can be "disclosed" to the speaker and he can disclose it to others. His innermost question, accordingly, is not concerned with what poor man shall undertake but why things happen to him as they do.[8]

By contrast, serious hope, which Buber champions, goes like this:

> The question is: do I dare the definitely impossible or do I adapt myself to the unavoidable? Do I dare to become other than I am trusting that I am indeed other and can so put it to the test, or do I take cognizance of a barrier in my present existence as something that will eternally be a barrier? Transposing the question from biography to history: does a historical hour ever experience its real limits otherwise than through undertaking to overstep those limits it is familiar with?[9]

Hope is the capacity to "overstep the limit" in urgent insistence:

> The depth of dialogical reciprocity between heaven and earth is brought to its strongest expression by the prophets of Israel—from the early period to the postexilic epoch. . . . What view of the ruling of the Ruler underlies all this? Clearly a view that preserves the mystery of the dialogical intercourse between God and man from all desire for dogmatic encystment. The mystery is that of man's creation as a being with the power of actually choosing between the ways, who ever again and

> even now has the power to choose between them. Only such a being is suited to be God's partner in the dialogue of history. The future is not fixed, for God wants man to come to Him with full freedom, to return to Him even out of a plight of extreme hopelessness and then to be really with Him.[10]

The accent on the Thou might suggest that Buber is a counter to Marx. If we read carefully, however, we can see that both of them insist that human leverage and human freedom culminating in human self-announcement are decisive for the mystery of God's transformative response in one's life and in the life of the world.

3. Finally, I mention the Jewish philosopher Ernst Bloch, who provided the elemental suggestion for Jürgen Moltmann that led him to his *Theology of Hope*.[11] Bloch acknowledges a horizon concerning bread for the poor. But then he says:

> The other hunger, the unassuaged, explosive hunger of the life-force, presents itself as the continual Not-yet of true human possession. It is an aspect of the quest of meaning, and, far from drugging the hunger for meaning (and with it the non-meaning of death) with any opium of the people in the form of dreamed-up compensation in another world, it fills it with the food of restless labor, working away, unswerving and incorrupt, to gain a true awareness and genuine satisfaction of man's Utopian needs. Only in this way—not in the ideological apologias of any ruling class, nor in the remorseless morality and finality of the Utopia of missing expectations which echoes through the pages of a homeless, twisted history—only in this way can that other dream come into being: the radical subversive dream of the Bible which, far from being rooted in a haze of opium, stems forth as proud wakefulness to the future, to the great dimension of light with which the world is pregnant.[12]

Bloch quotes Marx's phrase, "the world possesses something of a dream," and then he writes:

> The ultimate concrete awareness of all true hunger, and its concrete activity, is directed toward possession of this "something" in its Not-yet-being.[13]

Bloch's articulation of the human future is deeply infused by his Jewish reading of the Hebrew Bible. But Bloch is also profoundly aware of the way in which the church—notably the European church—has been on the side of the status quo. And so he writes:

> The forward-look has replaced the upward-look. Feelings of humility and obeisance vis-à-vis the prince and lord are no more than memory, as are prayers of supplication and all the rest of the baptized beggary. Even the Bible's ownmost emotion of hope is unworthy of us whenever it makes man a servile retainer, waiting only for manna from on high. Hope cannot at the same time raise itself from the ground in a transcending sweep and bow down humbly to take alms, conscious only of the so-called Fall behind it as the symbol of human frailty, and of the imperious, unmerited (if you follow Luther) realm of grace above it. Where there is hope there is religion, but where there is religion there is not always hope: not the hope built up from beneath, undisturbed by ideology.[14]

The upward look has been toward authority figures who control the bread supply. The upward look—in terms of social power—generates despair. Bloch goes further to indict the upward look to heaven as well.

By contrast the forward look is not servile and refuses passivity. Bloch knows very well that this forward look has a religious impetus; it is, however, a religious impetus that has been too often coopted by controlling religion allied with the status quo of worldly power. And it need not be so! As an addendum to my discussion of Bloch, I mention the exodus exposition of Michael Walzer, who has seen that the exodus narrative has provided the subtext for all the great revolutions in modern history. Walzer quotes Bloch about the "ineradicable subversion" of the exodus narrative.[15]

Well, perhaps I labor the obvious. Marx, Buber, and Bloch, each in a distinct way, have seen that the Jewish practice of hope is the capacity to act in freedom for the self for the sake of a future that summons to shalom. Among them, Buber is the most explicit about the Thou who occupies that future, but even Marx and Bloch will not deny that dimension of reality. I have taken the trouble with these more theoretical perspectives because they help us to read the text. In the end, however, it is the text that matters. For in the text we see not critical reflection on hope but *the actual practice of hope* that brings pained, grief-infested life in the world before the Holy One who has the power to transform.

We are left with the question of how we may live faithfully in a society, and to some extent in a church, that is held in thrall to the "upward look." The upward look, taken theologically according to Bloch, is to abdicate present reality Before Jehovah's Awful Throne. That theological posture, moreover, is readily associated with a political-economic upward look that relies excessively on the rich, the powerful, and the learned who dispense the goodies for social well-being according to their own unexposed interests. But hope refuses that arrangement. We can see that refusal in Psalm 30. The psalmist, in his dismay, his cry, his questions, and his petitions, is not deferential. His many repetitions of the divine name—once in v. 7, twice in v. 8, and twice in v. 10—are not deferential. Such speech is rather a calling to account, a summons, and an insistence. The whole of the drama is characteristically Jewish and flies in the face of both fundamentalist scholasticism, which assumes that the Thou of God is fixed and settled, and Enlightenment rationality, which assumes the Thou of God is irrelevant. Covenantal hope—against fundamentalism and Enlightenment perspective—is a willingness to engage dialogically in a life-or-death interaction with the Holy One, taking the Holy One seriously but taking the self and its yearning with equal seriousness. Hope of this sort, so faithfully biblical and definingly evangelical, requires the recharacterization of God and ourselves in a dialogical casting.[16] Faith is the capacity to participate in the drama and to see it through. It is, I submit, not unlike faith one may have in an AA group or in pastoral counseling. It is not blind confidence that the counselor can solve matters for me. It is rather resolve to see the drama through to the end of fifty minutes, over and over and over, because the drama requires endless reperformance. Without such intentional reperformance, the drama ends in a despairing status quo.

IV

I turn now to ask, "Who hopes?" I do so because Walter May's invitation ended with an accent on "a narrative of hopeful, inclusive ministry." That means, I assume, an expectation that all may be invited to hope with us. I will identify five candidates who may be the speaker of this psalm.

1. We do not know who first spoke this psalm. It is obviously highly stylized; but it is also exactly what an honest hoper might say. We may thus imagine that its first voicing was by an anonymous Israelite who had learned the way to practice hope. The NRSV, in its superscription, speculates that it is a speaker who had been sick, thus giving thanks for recovery from grave illness. Perhaps so. People do get healed; often at least 10 percent of the time they return to give thanks. We may then

imagine that this psalm is a script for the active hope of a sick person or one who has been sick. If so, we notice that the prayer implicates God in the illness. It does not accuse God of causing the illness, but the rhetorical questions claim that God has a stake in the healing, for the healing will enhance the healing of God; such people do actively hope! But so also do unemployed people and those with wayward children and with abusive priests and "all sort and conditions of men" and women. There is no specific evidence for the crisis voiced here.

2. But the psalm has been coopted in the canonical process. Now it is "of David." No critical scholar thinks this is a Davidic song. But we may read it so. The psalm sounds like the grief of David over the death of the child of his lust (2 Sam 12:16), or the death of Absalom (2 Sam 18:33; 19:4), or the death of Jonathan (2 Sam 1:19-27), or the truth of old age when he "could not get warm" (1 Kgs 1:1). Even the king knew about being dismayed, by the economy, by military reversal, by advisors who lied or betrayed. The poem opens out to all of royal life because there is no circumstance in which we may not hope. The movement from "not being moved" in v. 6 to "dismay" in v. 7 reminds us that nobody, not even the king, is immune. Dismay comes everywhere; but all may hope.

3. But of course we read and pray this script as Christians. We may, in precritical fashion with Augustine and Bonhoeffer, hear this psalm on the lips of Christ.[17] Because he dares to pray Psalm 22, "My God, My God, Why have you forsaken me?," we may believe he could also pray Psalm 30 and ask God hard questions. We can imagine the drive of the psalm from the triumph of Palm Sunday to the dismay of the Thursday arrest. Given the way of the cross, we can hear the cry of v. 7 on his lips as well. It is a cry of dismay; that cry, however, is an act of hope. It is an address that insists that the present is unbearable and that a new future from God should be given now. We do not know that Jesus uttered such defiant rhetorical questions; but clearly the suffering and death of the Son puts much at stake for the Father.

4. If the psalm could be an act of hope in the life of Jesus, we can readily see how it could be a prayer of the people clustered around Jesus. The ones who gather around him for healing do not need to be so stylized. The woman in Mark 5 and the blind man in Mark 10 and the importunate widow in Luke 18 are all hopers. They all believe newness can indeed be given. They all cry out. They all cry out in hope, making a connection between their urgent need and the Holy One who hears.

And if those who clustered around Jesus and prayed so were answered, it is not a surprise that the contemporary church clusters around Jesus and prays in the same way.[18] Our prayers are, to be sure, more domesticated and our petitions are less intense. And when the church is domesticated, it cringes from such prayers, and it eliminates such psalms from its lectionary. Consequently we pray only polite prayers and express polite grammar and practice polite hope. Except of course, in desperate emergency, we may get down and dirty and be glad for such a psalm.

It occurs to me that all of these hopers, *the ancient Israelite* who spoke first, and then *King David* and then *Jesus* and then *those who came early to him* and then we *who come later to him* . . . we all have in common that we know the name of the one who hears the prayer. We are like the initial psalmist, repeatedly sounding the divine name. We may set it as a judgment that in order to hope, there must be God, and in order to practice hope, we must know and name the name with incessant repetition. Such hope is practiced in a tradition of hope, and those outside the tradition do not know or name the name, and so their hope is feeble.

5. Except . . . hope is not a property of the traditioning community. Hope is a broader, deeper intractable human action. We may imagine,

> a school teacher who prays passionately when a kid pulls out a knife in a classroom; or
>
> a young man who prays eagerly amid the threat of a bully who knows no curb to violence; or
>
> a frantic mother in Baghdad who prays desperately, aware that her son is caught in "the clash of civilizations," a clash that concerns him not in the least.

Some of those may know the name and so pray. But many of them do not know the name or the tradition, and they hope anyway. Thus I propose, as we ponder this strange truth, that whereas some *know the name*, some by their bodily honesty *evoke the name* they never had known. The easy case of such a judgment is the way of the slaves in Exodus 2:23-24. The text does not say that they cried out to YHWH. In that regard they are unlike our psalmist; they do not utter the name. They precede the psalm and the tradition. The text says only, "They cried out." They did not cry out to anyone. They named no name. But it is a prayer. It is an act of hope. It is a bodily declaration that it must be made better than this. It must be, because this is unbearable.

The cry is uttered by those slaves become "subjects of their own history," something Pharaoh has precluded, until he died.

The cry is toward a "thou" who is unknown and may not be there, but such speech imagines one who listens.

The cry is not addressed to Pharaoh, but it is forwarded to the one who waits for us.

And the wonder of that narrative is that the next verse affirms,

> God heard,
> God remembered,
> God looked,
> God knew them.

God knew them because they cried, because they hoped, because they voiced their bodily truth without compromise.

Thus we may judge that inclusive ministry has as its second moment the engagement of the "thou" who generates relief and transformation. The first moment for inclusive ministry, however, the moment that precedes the engagement of the "thou," is the honest, bodily declaration of the needy self, not the unmoved self, the needy self who waits and hopes and expects with eager longing. If this is right, then hope requires a safe venue for that bodily utterance of the self, an arena for breaking the imposed silence of dominant society, the truthful engagement of the true story of the world that moves, not in guilt, but in pain and dismay. Such an exercise makes clear that God can not only be *known and named* but also *evoked* by those who do not know the name.

Those who do not know the name may stand alongside that company of the ancient Israelite who cried out, and King David, and Jesus, and Bartimaeus, and the whole church. Being an insider yields no special claim for hope. All hope . . . unless they are caught in the silencing ideology of Pharaoh. Pharaoh does not want hope and so stifles the cry. Not unlike those ancient slaves, we live amid a silencing ideology that wants or permits no cry. In the narrative of Bartimaeus, moreover, Jesus is surrounded by people, his disciples among them, who try to silence the needy blind man (Mark 10:48). Hope can be silenced and is often silenced, by force, by seduction, by law, by manipulation. Except that every silencer finally learns that silence cannot prevail. It is the bodily truth of the human creature that hope will break beyond silence. And when the silence is broken, newness begins to emerge in more ways than we can anticipate or explain.

V

I return now to the first five verses of the psalm, which are highly stylized. These verses sound much like the conclusion of v. 12 that culminates in praise and thanks. In vv. 1-3, the "I" of the psalmist speaks:

> I will extol,
> I cried out.

The "I"—who may be any one of the candidates I have nominated—utters the name of God three times:

> I will extol you, O LORD.
> O LORD, my God.
> O LORD.

The "I" and the divine name move summarily toward the "you":

> You have drawn me up;
> You do not let my foes rejoice;
> You have helped me;
> You brought up my life from Sheol;
> You restored my life from the pit.

The speaker has sounded the "I" but does not need to dwell on it because the "I" has been made secure in God's regard. Thus the "I" gladly cedes time over to the "thou." The self who has been claimed in honesty is now the self who can be ceded to this other.

In vv. 4-5 the now satisfied speaker of the psalm addresses the congregation. This hoper is not alone but dwells in the company of fellow hopers. We can imagine that when the one who prays is answered, the isolation is broken and "we can get back to church." The congregation of "his faithful ones" is addressed and summoned. The speaker needs companions to help get thanks said and sung. The address to the congregation is in two imperatives:

> Sing praises,
> Give thanks.

The indirect object of the imperatives is YHWH: "Sing to YHWH, give thanks to YHWH." The double imperative, as in every such doxology, is followed by reasons for thanks and praise, introduced by *kî:*

> Sing praise,
> give thanks,
> *For* his anger is for a moment,
> his favor is for a lifetime.

This is the first time in this psalm that we have heard of divine anger. There is no speculation or explanation, no suggestion about merited anger or whether God has been arbitrary. The only important point is that the mention is over with quickly. The trouble did not last. What endures is God's "favor," YHWH's ready, generous acceptance. The term "favor" is reiterated here from v. 7, "By your favor, O LORD." The psalmist is willing to allow an instant of divine rejection because the psalmist wants to credit long-term good to God.

The move is from weeping to joy. The weeping does not linger, and the psalmist does not linger over the weeping. Weeping must be full and honest and acknowledged. Only so can it be brief. If not full and honest and acknowledged, it will last much longer. Unwept weeping lasts forever. But not here! Now it is a memory in Israel. It is now, with the sunrise, a new day of creation. It is Easter day past Friday. Hope does not disappoint!

VI

It will be evident that hope, as I have sketched it, is a determined act of subversion that intends always to counter a culture of despair. In the Old Testament, that subversion reflects the peculiar sense of being Israel that is derived from the peculiar character of YHWH. In its acts of hope, Israel sustained its distinctiveness amid a series of empires that were, as all empires are, hostile to hope in a resolved maintenance of the status quo.

I propose that every move in the drama of hope that I have traced in Psalm 30 is inherently subversive:

1. The act of dismay in v. 9 is counter to the seduction of denial and the pretense that all is well. And for that matter, the hiding of YHWH, Luther's *Deus Absconditus*, is itself subversive, for dominant culture always requires an "available God."

2. The capacity to cry is an exposé of the brokenness and dysfunction of life "as usual." The cry is a subversion of the continual assurance of well-being so well managed by the "happy" church. Indeed Jesus' warning against laughing now is a profound subversion:

   Blessed are you who weep now,
   for you will laugh . . .
   Woe to you who are laughing now,
   for you will mourn and weep. (Luke 6:21b, 25b)

3. The rhetorical questions with a note of defiance constitute a subversive act on two counts. First, those below are not supposed to question the power people, on earth or in heaven. And second, it is subversive to suggest that God's interest is at stake in such a transaction because the high God is known to be beyond such enmeshment. To have such an "interest" is to suggest that God is not a settled absolute but, like the petitioner, an agent under way.
4. The imperative petitions of v. 10 are deeply subversive. How dare a needy person address an imperative to the high God! The God of dominant culture thrives on praise, and does not expect that praise to be interrupted by insistent demand.
5. Finally, thanks is subversive, because a show of gratitude militates against self-sufficiency. As John Updike famously said of Ted Williams when he refused to tip his cap at his retirement, "God does not write thank you notes." Nor do members of the dominant culture need to write thank you notes, since it is all self-achievement.

So consider the sequence:

Dismay, *not denial*;

Cry, *not silence*;

Question, *not acceptance*.

Petition, *not submissiveness*;

Thanks, *not self-sufficiency*.

These elements of hope are in sum and in each particular subversive. The reason they do not seem subversive to us is that we have not, in my judgment, properly delineated or exposed dominant culture for what it is.

But consider the totalism of the U.S. system of military consumerism, an ideological totality that is all devouring and that needs and wants only a God as object and not a God as subject:

> It is *a culture of denial* where never is heard a discouraging word. We are sure to return very soon to normalcy.
>
> It is *a culture of silence* in which honest speech is trivialized by talk shows, endless exposure, and tittering that eschews thoughtful honest sensibility.
>
> It is *a culture of buoyant confidence* with a hedge of billionaires around it, so that the disadvantaged are permitted no voice to question or to suggest that the system is a collage of not-very-well-hidden interests.
>
> It is *a culture of immunity* in which the urgent bodily truth of those who ache in their powerlessness is dismissed.
>
> It is *a culture of self-sufficiency* in which the best we can say is "no problem," which does not really give voice to either gratitude or acknowledgment.

The nurture of military consumerism with heavy doses of market ideology is, in principle, a culture of despair. It intends and allows no serious transformative possibility, but intends to keep an eternal present tense going for the benefit of those on top of the heap.

And then, into this culture of despair,

> comes *the God* who makes all things new,
>
> comes *the text* in its abrasive disruptiveness,
>
> comes *the community* of the text in dialogue with this unsettled God.

And from God, text, and community, emerge

> new practices that refuse despair;
>
> new songs that refuse the silence;
>
> new prayers that refuse submissiveness;
>
> new truth that refuses denial.

The newness is carried by the ones who have known the name of this God and of his messiah. These carriers, however, welcome others who do not yet know the name but who know the bodily reality that will not be denied or immobilized. That remarkable company, always gathered in subversive possibility,

> But as it is, they desire a better country, that is, a heavenly one. Therefore God is not ashamed to be called their God; indeed, he has prepared a city for them. (Heb 11:16)

That journey, since Abraham and Sarah, has been *by faith* because sight alone ends in despair.

2

CONFLICTED DIVINE AGENCY

In chapter 1, I explored hope on the basis of Psalm 30. I was led to three conclusions about the covenantal practice of hope:

1. Hope is not a *flat propositional premise* from which faith can proceed;
2. Hope is not a *certain and settled outcome* of thought or belief that once established can be counted on as absolute; and
3. Hope is a *dramatic process* that must be *continually reperformed* in active ways that may draw God into our matrices of despair where God can respond in transformative ways.

Thus it was a dramatic process that led the psalmist to the wondrous conviction that,

> Weeping may linger for the night,
> but joy comes in the morning. (Ps 30:5b)

That affirmation, moreover, has been reached through a demanding dramatic process that the psalmist portrays. Surely in the next night of weeping, the drama must be reperformed in all of its parts.

That performance of Psalm 30 of course is human speech. The psalmist reports to the congregation on how the process has gone so that it has come to a good outcome. In that described process, however, God never speaks. God is, to be sure, the subject of active, transformative verbs. But it is all human experience and human testimony.

In this chapter I propose to explore how that same dramatic performance is offered in biblical faith from God's side. In doing this, we face two hindrances. First, the data about the work of the performance in God's life is scant, and we must imagine much of it. Second, what is given us of God's process of hope is all given us in human voice. In a postcritical way, however, I take what is surely human voice as revelatory of God's life and character. Thus in the end, I will suggest that the dramatic performance of hope in human life has a symmetrical counterpoint in the dramatic performance of hope in God's life. I will focus on three texts from Isaiah, for the oracular utterances of 2 Isaiah are as close as we get to divine self-announcement, which is surely how the church has honored and responded to the poetry of 2 Isaiah.

I

Second Isaiah is set in an exile of despair in which God is seen to be absent and defeated by the gods of Babylon. It is in this context that the poetry of the book of Lamentations can conclude that hope is gone:

> He has made my teeth grind on gravel,
>   and made me cower in ashes;
> my soul is bereft of peace;
>   I have forgotten what happiness is;
> so I say, "Gone is my glory,
>   and all that I had hoped for from the LORD."
> The thought of my affliction and my homelessness,
>   is wormwood and gall!
> My soul continually thinks of it
>   and is bowed down within me. (Lam 3:16-20)

The Old Testament is filled with various interpretive responses to the crisis of destruction, deportation, and displacement in the sixth century.

First, there is the conclusion of Realpolitik that Babylon is simply an aggressive superpower. Even if YHWH had mandated Babylon to chasten Jerusalem, the empire has grossly overstepped that mandate:

> I was angry with my people,
>   I profaned my heritage;
> I gave them into your hand,
>   you showed them no mercy;
> on the aged you made your yoke exceedingly heavy. (Isa 47:6)

There is also the daring thought that Israel had been faithful to the covenant but that YHWH was fickle and had punished Jerusalem gratuitously. Thus in the seldom-used Psalm 44, Israel can declare:

> *Yet* you have rejected us and abased us,
> and have not gone out with our armies.
> You have made us turn back from the foe,
> and our enemies have gotten spoil.
> You have made us like sheep for slaughter,
> and have scattered us among the nations.
> You have sold your people for a trifle,
> demanding no high price for them.
> You have made us the taunt of our neighbors,
> the derision and scorn of those around us.
> You have made us a byword among the nations,
> a laughing stock among the peoples.
> All day long my disgrace is before me,
> and shame has covered my face
> at the words of the taunters and revilers,
> at the sight of the enemy and the avenger.
> All this has come upon us,
> yet we have not forgotten you,
> or been false to your covenant.
> Our heart has not turned back,
> nor have our steps departed from your way,
> *yet* you have broken us in the haunts of jackals,
> and covered us with deep darkness. (Ps 44:9-19)

These verses are framed by "yet" in vv. 9 and 19, both of which assert that God has acted negatively toward Israel, contradicting the expected divine actions that would have been appropriate toward a covenant-keeping people. The claim of Israel's innocence pushes to an accusation against YHWH.

But of course the overwhelming claim of the Old Testament, largely fueled by the theology of Deuteronomy, is that destruction and exile are the proper and inescapable outcome of Israel's disobedience. YHWH responded to that waywardness, according to prophetic speeches of judgment, with wrathful vigor. But there are also texts that indicate that God is fundamentally sad, and not angry, that Israel has chosen a path of self-destruction.[1] It is as though there are inexorable connections between deeds and consequences, and YHWH is powerless to intervene to break that connection. As a result, YHWH is reduced to grief:

> O that my head were a spring of water,
> and my eyes a fountain of tears,
> so that I might weep day and night
> for the slain of my poor people!
> O that I had in the desert
> a traveler's lodging place,
> that I might leave my people
> and go away from them!
> For they are all adulterers,
> a band of traitors.
> They bend their tongues like bows;
> they have grown strong in the land for falsehood,
> and not for truth;
> for they proceed from evil to evil,
> and they do not know me, says the LORD. (Jer 9:1-3)

The lament in God's mouth is a quotation from Psalm 55. It portrays God as grief-stricken because of Israel's falsehood and evil and refusal to "know me." God wishes that God had bigger tear ducts to cry more, or that God had a refuge place in the wilderness to escape all the turmoil and suffering. That is, God wishes to be absent from the unbearable pain of a willfully broken relationship.

Those various interpretive responses lead me to the first text that I want to parse at some length in Isaiah 54:7-8. In this quite remarkable text, YHWH speaks in poetic parallelism in order to make this two-fold acknowledgment:

> For *a brief moment* I abandoned you . . .
> In overflowing wrath *for a moment*
> I hid my face from you.

The time frame for that negation is a "moment," a beat, an instant. The word echoes from Psalm 30:5:

> For his anger is *for a moment.*

But that "moment" is forever when it is abandonment, like that instant of marital betrayal or that instant of a small child lost from his or her mother in a big store. More than that, the instant may stretch from poetry to historical experience, so that in this case it is for fifty years until the emancipatory action of Cyrus against Nebuchadnezzar. Thus the time of bereavement is quite open-ended, as every pastor knows. And while "time may heal," there is no reliable timetable for such healing.

What occupies us in this poetic parallelism, however, is YHWH's own acknowledgment of YHWH's willful absence from Israel. For a time Israel and Jerusalem were left to their own inadequate resources and without the sustaining presence of YHWH. The key term is *'azav*, to "abandon, forsake, divorce," to depart the vows of covenant and violate the most elemental promises of fidelity. Israel of course can, on occasion, accuse YHWH of such abandonment, as in the familiar words of Psalm 22 that are famously reproduced in the passion narrative of Matthew 27:46 and Mark 15:34. Because biblical covenantal faith is passionately relational, abandonment is on Israel's mind. In the psalms Israel exhibits confidence that God is faithful and reliable in every time of need:

> And those who know your name put their trust in you,
> for you, O LORD, have not *forsaken* those who seek you. (Ps 9:10)

> For you do not *give me up* to Sheol,
> or let your faithful see the Pit. (Ps 16:10)

But that confident poetry from the Psalter is interrupted by the ominous tone of covenantal demand:

> My anger will be kindled against them in that day. I will *forsake* them, and hide my face from them; they will become easy prey, and many terrible troubles will come upon them. (Deut 31:17)

This threat, moreover, comes to fruition in the historical process:

> You have *abandoned* me, so I have *abandoned* you to the hand of Shishak. (2 Chr 12:5)

And so Israel can accuse God of infidelity, in the face of which every bad thing can happen:

My God, my God, why have you *forsaken* me?
Why are you so far from helping me,
from the words of my groaning? (Ps 22:1)

Why have you forgotten us completely?
Why have you *forsaken* us these many days? (Lam 5:20)

But Zion said, "The LORD has *forsaken* me,
my Lord has forgotten me." (Isa 49:14)

These relational categories of covenant of course fly in the face of much conventional theology about the omnipresent God. Israel could of course also talk *that* way:

Where can I go from your spirit?
Or where can I flee from your presence?
If I ascend to heaven, you are there;
if I make my bed in Sheol, you are there.
If I take the wings of the morning
and settle at the furthest limits of the sea,
even there your hand shall lead me,
and your right hand shall hold me fast.
If I say, "Surely the darkness will cover me,
and the light around me become night,"
even the darkness is not dark to you;
the night is as bright as the day,
for darkness is as light to you. (Ps 139:7-12; see Amos 9:2-4)

But now, in crisis, YHWH comes and goes. And now, even God concedes that God has been fickle. This is the sort of theological extremity that comes to shrill voice in Job:

Oh that I knew where I might find him,
that I might come even to his dwelling! (Job 23:3)

This is the rhetoric of last resort. If, however, we are to process the despair, hopelessness, and futility around us as theological data, then we are led to this rhetoric as Israel was led to it. In the end, in our two verses in Isaiah 54:7-8 YHWH concedes the point. Faith does come to the abyss of theological absence. It is my judgment that we have this abyss of absence because we now entertain, in our scary candor, wonderment about our deepest certitudes as the world we have trusted runs amok.

II

But the poetry of Isaiah 54:7-8 makes a dramatic turn. So we take a deep breath and come to the second line of each of vv. 7 and 8:

> but with great compassion I will gather you . . .
> but with everlasting love I will have compassion on you,
> says the Lord, your Redeemer.

The movement from the first to the second line in each verse, from abandonment to compassion, is accomplished with rhetorical ease. In both cases it is a waw-consecutive that does not call attention to itself that we translate as an adversative "but." In each verse, the second line contradicts the first line. It is as though YHWH has reversed field in mid-sentence to move beyond abandonment. The second line in the two verses includes a double use of the word "compassion," as a plural noun ("compassions") and as an active verb, plus the reassurance of "everlasting fidelity" (*ḥesed 'ôlām*), plus the active verb "gather" that assures homecoming to well-being. These two last lines in the two verses summarize all the prophetic promises and say everything that needs to be said to the displaced. They are indeed a full and adequate summation of evangelical hope. Thus we can see the parallel to Psalm 30:

> Weeping may last for a night . . .
>
> > For a brief moment I abandoned you . . .
> > In overflowing wrath for a moment
> > I hid my face from you.
>
> but joy comes in the morning . . .
>
> > but with great compassion I will gather you . . .
> > but with everlasting love I will have compassion on you.

The contrast between the psalm and the oracle, of course, is that in the prophetic oracle YHWH is the active agent to abandonment, whereas in the psalm there is no such culpable agent.

But the compelling question is how to get from line a to line b, because the waw-consecutive does not tell us enough. Clearly something happened to YHWH in mid-verse that evoked the adversative "but." To illuminate that abrupt transition from abandonment to compassionate restoration, I appeal to two other texts.

In Jeremiah 31:20, in the midst of promissory poetry, we have a verse that portrays YHWH in a soliloquy, as though God were thinking out loud in order to process a transition in God's internal life, a process that I will call a "performance of hope." This verse begins with two rhetorical questions:

> Is Ephraim my dear son?
> Is he the child I delight in?

The answers to these questions are not unambiguous. No, Israel is not my delight, because I have rejected Israel in its disobedience. Well, yes; Israel is my beloved son, because here I am in my rejection of him, still thinking about him. Broken relationships lead us to an ambiguous "yes and no."[2] We want to have done with the offending party . . . but cannot. So it is with YHWH. YHWH wants to be done with this endlessly vexing son. YHWH speaks against him. It is as though there is another adversative "but." "But . . . I still remember him." I cannot get my mind off of him. I still care about him . . . even against my first inclination. I find that behind that first inclination there is this residue of mercy and fidelity that I cannot shake. I propose that the poet daringly gives us access to the internal life of God, which is profoundly conflicted. It is the conflictedness that everyone faces who knows about broken fidelity in primary relationships. It is as though God, in that moment, discovers something about God's self that God had not known before. And while we may take this as a measure of God's wondrous love, we may also take it as a measure of the limit of God's freedom, for God cannot slough off this endless vexation.

And so YHWH arrives at a conclusion, perhaps a reluctant, bittersweet conclusion:

> Therefore [in spite of myself] I am deeply moved . . .
> Or, alternatively:
> "Therefore my bowels are troubled for him." (KJV)
> "Darum bricht mir mein Herz gegen ihn." (Luther)[3]
> "Therefore, my womb trembles for him";[4]
> I will surely have mercy on him, says the LORD.

The final verb is an absolute infinitive, a deep intensification of the verb. Phyllis Trible stresses this double use of "mercy" or "compassion" that is linked to the same Hebrew consonants for "womb," which thus obliges us to understand this as an emphatic, motherly compassion for a vexing son.[5]

If we take this verse as pivotal for our consideration, we see that God's fresh resolve for Israel is a powerful attentiveness that compels God to act toward Israel even against God's own aching judgment. Every parent of a teenager knows about this requirement, and every spouse in a broken relationship knows the experience of facing a conflictual demand that may (but need not) evoke fresh positive regard. That is, hope arises for Israel because YHWH has an almost biological, bodily regard for Israel that YHWH cannot deny or evade.

The imagery of Jeremiah 31:20 points us to the dialogic exchange between Israel and YHWH in Isaiah 49:14-18. In v. 14, the poet quotes the lament of Israel:

> The LORD has forsaken me,
>   my Lord has forgotten me.

That lament is surely a quotation from Lamentations 5:20:

> Why have you forgotten us completely?
>   Why have you forsaken us these many days?

The key words in both cases are "forget" and "forsake." The lament is an accusation against YHWH.

The divine response of vv. 15-18 moves to refute that accusation. No, God has not forgotten and not forsaken, no matter how it has been experienced by Israel. Then God poses a question to Israel: "Can a nursing mother forget her suckling child?" Well, no, because the mother's breast would hurt if the child did not nurse. Well, yes, in an extreme case such a mother might forget. But the poet offers YHWH's self as more reliable than all other nursing mothers. And so there is, as Trible has seen here as well, a play on the words "womb/compassion" because the two words have the same consonants; YHWH's reach toward Israel is nothing less than womb-like mother love that the mother cannot avoid and that therefore the child can count on.[6]

As a fallback assurance, moreover, God anticipates Sarah Palin by having the name of the child written on God's own hand:

> See, I have inscribed you on the palms of my hands;
>   your walls are continually before me. (v. 16)

Just in case YHWH is negligent, God can look down and remember. The outcome is that God has looked down, has seen the name, and has remembered.[7] As a result, there will be a gathering (homecoming, v. 18). Israel will be adorned as bride. Thus the imagery shifts from Jeremiah 31:20 to Isaiah 49:18, from child to spouse, a bride who is celebrated, joyous, and adorned. But the point is the same; the linkage is elemental, nearly biological, and intrinsic to God's own life.

We can now return to the two lines in Isaiah 54:

> but with great compassion I will gather you . . .
> but with everlasting love I will have compassion on you,
> says the LORD, your Redeemer. (vv. 7b, 8b)

The move from harsh rejection in the first lines of vv. 7 and 8 to the adversative assurance in the second lines might look rhetorically smooth. In fact it has come about and been made possible only by a deep wrenching in the internal life of God. In the depth of the abyss where God's preferred conduct is abandonment, God discovered, with the aid of the poets, that God is so bound to God's people that God must, perforce, enact deep newness. That newness is intrinsic, familial, and bodily.

The exhibit of that newness as historical restoration and rehabilitation is highly visible in the world. Hope of an evangelical kind requires this linkage between *internal rootage in poetic idiom* and *socioeconomic, political reconstruction*. The spectrum of God's new resolve moves from the *most intimate* to the *most public*. God is so bound to this historical reality that it cannot be otherwise. I submit that if we seek a ministry of hope, faithfulness, and inclusiveness, we find its grounding in God's own performance of hope as God moves from willful abandonment (that matches Israel's despair) to mandated compassion (that matches Israel's hope). Given the womb-like mother love of Jeremiah 31:20 and Isaiah 49:14-18, it is no wonder that Isaiah 54:7-8 cannot avoid the double use of "compassion" (as a verb and as a plural noun) that is grounded in everlasting love and enacted as gathering. The themes converge because God exhibits the readiness and freedom to go deeply into conflict and find truth there. The poet exhibits courage commensurate to that of God in order to exhibit for us this vexed internal life of God—given only poetic idiom—that holds a future for Israel and eventually a future for the world. The world is bound in God's compassion even as God is bound to enact compassion toward that world.

III

From the two positive lines of Isaiah 54:7-8, rooted in divine compassion, the more extended poetry of Isaiah 54 exhibits a wide imaginative spectrum of the agenda of Israel's hope, and commensurately, the reach of God's promise.

1. In vv. 1-6, the lead up to our vv. 7-8, the poet appeals to two familial images in order to portray the deep intimate linkage of YHWH to Israel. In vv. 1-3, the image concerns a barren woman, an image that reaches back to the barren women in the Genesis narratives, Sarah, Rebekah, and Rachel. Only now the barren woman is Israel in exile who has produced no heirs and so has no future. But like the burst of new birth in the Genesis narratives, God's new resolve in exile overrides barrenness; God invites mother Israel to sing and shout because births of futures are about to occur. The poem issues a series of imperatives to mother Israel:

> Enlarge . . . your tent;
> let the curtains . . . be stretched out;
> do not hold back;
> lengthen your cords;
> strengthen your stakes. (Isa 54:2)

This is like preparing a nursery for the time when the baby comes home for the first time. Except there are many babies, many heirs. The place will swarm with birthed futures. They will crowd the tent and pull it down, unless it is reinforced. Barrenness now teems with futures.

The imperatives are supported by two "reasons" introduced by the particle "for":

> *For* the children of the desolate woman will be more
>   than the children of her that is married, says the LORD . . .
> *For* you will spread out to the right and to the left,
>   and your descendants will possess the nations
>   and will settle the desolate towns. (vv. 1, 3)

The old promises of Genesis are about to be fulfilled. Israel will "possess the nations," that is, experience a dominant place in public affairs (see Gen 22:17).

2. The second image is of an abandoned wife who, in that ancient culture, was fated to live in shame and isolation (vv. 4-6). The imperatives that match those of vv. 1 and 2 are direct and simple:

Do not fear . . . do not be discouraged. (v. 4)

That is all! The words are a generic salvation oracle; they are, however, poignant in context when addressed to a shamed, rejected woman. The two imperatives are supported by a remarkable cluster of five "reasons," each of which is introduced by "for":

For you will not be ashamed . . .
For you will not suffer disgrace;
For you will forget the shame of your youth,
and the disgrace of your widowhood you will remember no more.
For your Maker is your husband,
the LORD of hosts is his name;
the Holy One of Israel is your Redeemer,
the God of the whole earth he is called.
For the LORD has called you
like a wife forsaken and grieved in spirit,
like the wife of a man's youth when she is cast off,
says your God. (vv. 4-6)

The imagery offers a full acknowledgment of desolation. It then reverses field and imagines full, joyous, fruitful restitution. The agency of God is prominent and decisive for the restoration. Not only is God the Lord of hosts and of the whole earth. More than that, this is "our redeemer," surely a figure not unlike Boaz in the Ruth narrative, a redeemer who restores the honor of a bereft woman in a patriarchal society. More poignant than any of that is the fact that YHWH is "your Baal" (your husband), the one who makes pregnant with new children and therefore new futures. Thus all the blessings of creation, abundance, and well-being are anticipated, grounded in the work of the redeemer who will restore a scorned woman.

I have two observations about this imagery. First, it is intensely patriarchal; for good reason feminist criticism focuses on the risks of such rhetoric.[8] More important to the internal life of the poem, YHWH is not mentioned as the one who has disgraced or abandoned wife Israel. YHWH is celebrated as the restorer, but no agent of abandonment is named. Perhaps it is to be inferred. Perhaps YHWH could not bring YHWH's self to admit as much . . . at least not until vv. 7-8. Thus the abrupt rehabilitation of the one forsaken (*'azûbâ*) is credited to YHWH. It is as though the poetry so wants to credit YHWH with restoration that it could not speak the negative antecedent. But of course the silence cannot be sustained; in vv. 7-8 YHWH is known to be the perpetrator, so that YHWH enacts a reversal that becomes the ground of hope for hopeless Israel.

The imagery of marital reversal is reiterated in the grand promise to Zion in Isaiah 62. Here the marital imagery concerns the land in its abandonment and restoration:

> You shall no more be termed *Forsaken*,
>   and your land shall no more be termed *Desolate*;
> but you shall be called *My Delight Is in Her*,
>   and your land *Married*,
> for the LORD delights in you,
>   and your land shall be married. (62:4)

Of the four titles applied to Israel and to the land, two negative (*Forsaken, Desolate*) and two positive (*My Delight Is in Her, Married*), two directly concern us with reference to our two verses. The title "Forsaken" renders *'azûbâ*, and "Married" is *be'ûlâ*, a feminine form of Baal, thus fructified. The same two terms occur in Isaiah 54:5-6, for YHWH is Baal and Israel is abandoned (forsaken, *'azûbâ*); thus we have a parallel between land and people. In both cases, YHWH is the one who has abandoned and generated hopelessness. In both cases YHWH is the one who will restore and enact all the hopeful possibilities that Israel can conjure.

3. In the verses after our vv. 7-8, the poetry of Isaiah 54 utilizes two other images of assurance and well-being. In vv. 9-10, the chaos of exile, which is the poem's concern, is likened to the chaos of the flood in Genesis. The opening "this" refers to the sixth-century crisis of being abandoned. The analogue between flood and exile, both of them modes of chaos, is that as YHWH promised "never again" concerning the flood (Gen 9:15), so YHWH now promises "never again" concerning exile. The world may be destabilized, but the committed fidelity of YHWH toward Israel, expressed in a triad of phrases, is more reliable than the cosmos:

> steadfast love (as in v. 8),
>
> covenant of *shalom*,
>
> compassion (as twice in vv. 7-8).

The ground of hope is committed fidelity, and that fidelity is on the part of the one who had abandoned but who now voices new, deep resolve for the well-being of Israel.

4. The final extended imagery of the chapter concerns the rebuilding of the city and its guaranteed security (vv. 11-17). Israel will be comforted (v. 11; see 40:1). The city, with its stones, foundations, gates, and walls, will be generously beautiful and wealthy (vv. 11-12). Its children, the ones anticipated in vv. 1-3, will be safe, instructed, and prosperous (vv. 13-14). And God will be the great military defender of the city that will no longer be vulnerable (vv. 15-17). To be sure, this is only poetry. But the poetry makes a remarkable claim in its capacity to connect *divine fidelity* to *the real world of risk and danger.*

This chapter offers a remarkable collage of images, all of which together testify to a new divine resolve that issues in a new historical reality. It is evident that hope, in this poetic offer, is grounded in nothing other than the resolve of God. Or in Calvin's words:

> Our hope is in no other save in thee,
> Our faith is built on Thy promise free;
> Lord, give us peace, and make us calm and sure,
> That in Thy strength we ever more endure.[9]

There is no other ground for hope for Israel . . . or for the world. Thus I judge that the teaching task of bishops is to show how the performance of hope runs from *the internal conflictedness of God* to *the project of social restoration.* But unless that internal conflictedness is at the root of our testimony, the dream of restoration is groundless.

Finally, concerning this text, I suggest that we have watched while YHWH *performed hope.* It is a process, according to the poem, whereby God moves

> from savage rejection that matches the dismay of the psalmist,
> to anguished conflictedness that matches
>
> the rhetorical questions of the psalmist,
>
> to a resolve of compassion that matches the psalmist's affirmation
> of transformation.

This divine performance of savage rejection, anguished conflictedness, and resolve of compassion constitute the script for the drama of hope that (a) is performed by the Christian triduum of Friday/Saturday/Sunday that (b) is anticipated in the lament/praise of Israel.

IV

I turn now to Isaiah 40:27-31, another oracle of 2 Isaiah. Whereas the grief and complaint of Israel were at best implied in Isaiah 54, in this poem Israel speaks, or is quoted by YHWH. The structure of the poetic unit as lament (v. 27) and divine response (vv. 28-31) is not unlike the grief of 54:1-6, the divine acknowledgment of vv. 7-8, and the restoration of vv. 9-17.

The complaint of v. 27 that accuses God of not noticing Israel's plight is "from a lament in actual use by the exiles at the time."[10] Although the poet does not use the terms "forget/forsake" (as in 49:14), the issue is the same: divine abandonment, the very abandonment that God has conceded in 54:7-8.

The divine answer in vv. 28-31 opens with a double rhetorical question in v. 28. The questions, not unlike those of the psalmist in Psalm 30, are a reprimand to Israel for not knowing and hearing what is new from God. Beginning in v. 28b, the rest of the oracle is a declaration of divine resolve that will be decisive for the future of Israel. The God who addresses Israel is the everlasting God, the creator, the ultimate source of life in the world. Because this God has energy and power and stamina, God will faithfully engage Israel precisely when Israel has no energy, power, or stamina.

> The LORD God is the everlasting God,
>   the Creator of the ends of the earth.
> He does not faint or grow weary,
>   his understanding is unsearchable.
> He gives power to the faint,
>   and strengthens the powerless.

The poem offers a sharp contrast between the *faint and weary* and the one with *power and stamina.* In that ancient world, the Jews without God are faint and weary and without prospect for the future, fully contained in the limits of Babylon. The promise and offer of YHWH is a precise inversion of this dire situation, so that *weariness* is converted to power and *faintness* is transformed into strength. The exiles without God have no possibility for the future. The exiles, with this faithful God, have energy for homecoming and restoration, a move that requires great resolve and courage. Mutatis mutandis, in our world the hopeless are without energy for newness in the world. Clearly energy comes from reliable fidelity, so that those grounded in the God of all hope have energy for social restoration. Thus the matter is not narrowly "religious" but has immense, even incredible implications for socioeconomic, political transformation. The poem rightly asserts that the bottom line for social energy and courage is not political or economic; it is theological. Futures are open for those who have the courage to defy the totalism of the empire, ancient or contemporary, and move to a new social possibility that is not under the aegis of the empire.

The contrast continues in vv. 30-31. We would expect the people of God to have strength, energy, and courage. But they are the ones faint and exhausted, because despair saps energy. The poet selects the best candidates for energy—youths, the young—and then characterizes them as hopeless, lethargic, conformist, and passive before the empire. The contrast consists in those who are linked to YHWH and so have strength:

> who soar like eagles,
> who run without weariness,
> who walk and do not faint.

The trigger from hopeless to hope-filled is *the wait*. The verb is *qawah*, which means "to watch expectantly, to hope, to anticipate," to watch for the newness about to be given by the God of all newness.

I want to digress here to mention the programmatic essay of Emmanuel Levinas, the great Jewish exegete. His definitive book is entitled *Totality and Infinity*.[11] By "totality" Levinas means a self-contained world-system in which nothing is left out of control and explanation, a system that moves toward totalitarianism. By "infinity" he means an openness to possibility that has not been domesticated by administration or explanation. In the ancient world of Israel, the totality of Babylon contained all possibility and so had silenced Jewish hope. Against that, in prophetic poetry YHWH's oracles kept opening the world beyond Babylonian control. In our world, the totality is the closed system of military consumerism that reduces everything to commodity, that leaves nothing to chance or to possibility, and that thins life to a closed system of despair. Except that it is the testimonial work of the church to point to that which lies outside the reach of the empire and teems with God's impossible freedom. Those who cling to that divine freedom watch for new possibility, whereas those who fully submit to the system are without hope in the world.[12] It is clear, moreover, that much of the theology and practice of the church has unwittingly served a totalism that runs toward totalitarianism. But the church as hoper refuses such submissiveness.

Thus our text pivots on "the wait" of hope. It is the wait for the new to which Jesus summons his disciples in his admonition to "watch" and "keep alert" (Matt 24:42; 25:13). It is the case, is it not, that those who know about the freedom of God who gives new gifts of compassion are the ones who soar because they are not preoccupied with themselves, their security, and their well-being.

This text, addressed to Israel in its exile of despair, is readily seen as:

an authentic *lament* among those who bring their despair to speech;

a *wait* that transfigures;

a *soaring*, a *running*, a *walking* undeterred.

That is the performance of hope that we can see in Psalm 30, that Israel did in exile, and that God's people in a failed society may do yet again.

The sequence of lament-wait-soar is the script for God's people. But I suggest it is also God's script:

It is God who grieves the loss of people and city;

It is God who waits and struggles for a renewed resolve, a renewed sense of goodness;

It is God who leads the procession home so that all flesh can see the glory of God.

I mean then to argue that the performance of hope has its model and its master practice in the God who is able to say, "I abandoned . . . I have compassion." A settled God who has no script to perform yields a people that, in turn, has no script to perform and no new life to live because of no new gift given.

V

These texts—Isaiah 54:7-8; 49:14-18; and 40:27-31—lead me to conclude that the performance of hope is the capacity to engage in *an ongoing, conflicted dialogic transaction* with God who is known in Israel as the God of all compassion who was also known as the God of all abandonment. It is *the drama of abandonment and compassion* that is the truth of our life. And faith is the capacity to move in and through, over and over, this interactive process that eschews settlement and is vigorously under way.[13]

Conversely, the refusal to engage in that performative dialogue inevitably, I believe, ends in despair.

1. There is a match between the abandonment of God and the abandonment of Israel. There is no doubt that YHWH is abandoned by Israel in its disobedience:

> They will *forsake* me, breaking my covenant that I have made with them. (Deut 31:16; see 28:20)
>
> And I will utter my judgments against them, for all their wickedness in *forsaking* me; they have made offerings to other gods, and worshipped the works of their own hands. (Jer 1:16)

And, as we have seen in the psalms, Israel knows itself to be abandoned by YHWH. It belongs to the notion of covenant, that dialogue of fidelity in which abandonment becomes a subject of polemical conversation.

The focus on abandonment as a reality in this dialogic relationship is immediately contemporary for us. It is a sense of abandonment—by God, by the economy, by all sorts of partners pledged to fidelity—that fuels much of the public adrenalin in our society. And when denial about that abandonment can no longer be sustained, the abandonment becomes a crucial venue for truth-telling, a truth-telling in which YHWH and Israel variously engage. They perform that engagement endlessly because the covenant is a relationship in which no secret can be hid.

2. There is a match between the compassion of God and the rescue and well-being of Israel, a genuine coming together and being together. Thus the psalmist, the voice of Israel, can attest to the wonder of life with God:

> Surely goodness and mercy shall follow me
> all the days of my life,
> and I shall dwell in the house of the LORD my whole life long. (Ps 23:6)
>
> I was glad when they said to me,
> "Let us go into the house of the LORD!"
> Our feet are standing
> within your gates, O Jerusalem. (Ps 122:1-2)

Conversely YHWH is an abiding presence in fidelity with Israel:

> How lovely is your dwelling place,
> O LORD of hosts! (Ps 84:1)

Before they call I will answer,
    while they are yet speaking I will hear. (Isa 65:24)

In both cultic practice and in anticipation, Israel can imagine being fully with God in a reconciled relationship of mutual well-being and delight.

3. There is a match between the waiting of YHWH and the waiting of Israel because both wait for the transformation of abandonment into compassion, a wait that cannot be hurried or commandeered. Thus we imagine a waiting as the assurance Isaiah 40:31 has it. Indeed:

my soul waits for the Lord
    more than those who watch for the morning,
    more than those who watch for the morning. (Ps 130:6)

We can also imagine YHWH waiting and watching. Thus I imagine YHWH waiting at the comma between the two lines of Isaiah 54:7 and then again at the comma between the two lines of v. 8. Or I can imagine YHWH waiting in the midst of Jeremiah 31:20 after the rhetorical question: "Is Ephraim my dear son?" The answer to the question is not obvious. The data behind the question is not clear. This is a moment in which the Father waits to see if Ephraim, his dear son, will return to the waiting father.

Thus I suggest a performance of hope that moves from *abandonment* through *waiting* to *newness*. It is the defining process of the covenant, the process in which God and Israel are together engaged, upon which the life of both of them depends.

Thus we may call the roll of those who are engaged with this performance of hope:

1. I have said, and will not repeat, that *the God of the covenant*, waiting for the prodigal son, is engaged in this drama of possibility. YHWH is in a mix of anger and sadness over the fickleness of Israel. Through that performance YHWH runs the gamut of emotion that moves from hope to anger and back to hope, always one more time.

2. I have said, and will not repeat, that *Israel, the people of the covenant*, is engaged in the drama of possibility. In its psalms of lament that turn regularly to hope and praise, and more particularly in the season of exile, Israel suffers divine absence and abandonment. In that abyss of despair, however, the voices that matter most in Israel are voices of poetic possibility, principle among them 2 Isaiah. It is poetry because in its abyss the script of hope mobilizes imagined futures of new covenant and new temple and new city, of new heaven and new earth and new Jerusalem.

3. It is not a surprise then that *Christ participates in this same drama of hope.* In his ministry he is regularly descending into the abyss of brokenness concerning lepers and hunger and poverty and uncleanness and despair. He dwells there with his friends. But characteristically his dwelling in the midst of the brokenness of creation causes a welling up of food, and healing, and forgiveness, and cleansing, all gifts that are possible only because he goes there and dwells there.

And of course, he gets through the three-day process of Friday, Saturday, and Sunday as a performance of hope that moves from the deep grip of death to the dread of Saturday to new Sunday life. Surely it is the case that the drama he performs is a replication of Israel's long performance that is in turn the shadow of God's readiness to practice such a life in the world.

4. After God and after Israel and after Jesus, it is *we who perform the process.* The life of faith is a life that moves from brokenness to healing, always yet again through waiting. We specify this in our regular confession of sin and assurance of pardon. But of course every pastor knows that much of the brokenness is not rooted in guilt but is simply the raw fact of pain. And we have resources, pastoral, liturgical, and theological, for getting through that process.

The season of abandonment is always upon us in personal ways. And now that season is acutely upon us in public and social ways, out of which, in our fearful anxiety, we do foolish and destructive things to each other. The alternative to doing what is foolish and destructive is to hope, to wait, to be tilted in courage and energy and freedom toward gifts that are being given. Thus I can imagine that the church's performance of faith that runs from high liturgy to soup kitchens to youth fellowships to international mission to public witness constitutes a rich collage of performances of hope that are deeply and radically counterimperial. The empire, ancient or contemporary, does not want us to notice the abandonment, does not want us to host an expectation, and does not want us to receive compassion. It does not want any of that because people performing this script in unanxious freedom jeopardize every status quo. We are then, I propose, in a great company under way to newness.

I finish with two observations. First, what I have lined out we say succinctly in the eucharistic mystery of faith:

> Christ has died . . . in abandonment;
> Christ is risen . . . after a Saturday wait.
> Christ will come again . . . as we wait.

Jürgen Moltmann has famously written of that Friday:

> The Fatherlessness of the Son is matched by the Sonlessness of the Father, and if God has constituted himself as the Father of Jesus Christ, then he also suffers the death of his Fatherhood in the death of his Son.[14]

All parties have been *abandoned*; all parties *wait* that long Saturday; all parties *dance* on the third day.

Second, when we see the gospel as the performance of hope through Friday, Saturday, and Sunday, we are free to notice its contemporaneity as it is expressed in the remarkable book of Alan Lewis, *Between Cross & Resurrection: A Theology of Holy Saturday.*[15] Lewis proposes that our time is a long Saturday and finds evidence of that in his pondering of Hiroshima, Auschwitz, and Chernobyl. He identifies the church as the primary practitioner of Saturday on behalf of the world. He writes of that Friday:

> There is one community on earth summoned and able—able, that is, to the limited extent that it obeys its summons—to be a creative critic of our era's Easter Saturday loss of community, a judgment on, but thereby also a redemptive agent within our social brokenness and cultural collapse.[16]

Of the move to Sunday, he writes:

> Of course, this is the body, too, that was raised and glorified; and as Christ's Easter body the church indeed is that community which has itself been brought from bondage to emancipation, from burial to new life (Rom 6:4ff.), from humiliation to exaltation, proleptic promise to all humanity and to the cosmos of its own deliverance and eschatological fulfillment.[17]

Between the burial and the new life, Lewis focuses on the Saturday of wait. Of that Saturday, the great Jewish critic George Steiner has written,

> But ours is the long day's journey of the Saturday. Between suffering, aloneness, unutterable waste on the one hand and the dream of liberation, of rebirth on the other.[18]

At the center of hope is vibrant, expectant waiting. I imagine, if I dare so, that the primary work of a bishop now is to let us fully enter into the

God-givenness of our Saturday. It is the day between Friday and Sunday, between crucifixion and resurrection. It is also a day between an old homogeneous world and a new world of otherness we do not understand. It is the day between manageable certitude and a new neighborliness of shared, limited resources. It is a day at the center of God's life, and of our own. It is a day for all those who, "though they were commended for their faith, did not receive what was promised" (Heb 11:39). At least not yet!

3

MISBEGOTTEN HOPE

The ones deported from Jerusalem to Babylon in the sixth century BCE pined and yearned for Jerusalem:

> By the waters of Babylon,
> there we sat down and there we wept
> when we remembered Zion . . .
> If I forget you, O Jerusalem,
> let my right hand wither!
> Let my tongue cling to the roof of my mouth,
> if I do not remember you,
> if I do not set Jerusalem above my highest joy. (Ps 137:1, 5-6)

They regarded Jerusalem as the epicenter of the world they imagined through liturgical performance. Far from that epicenter, moreover, they experienced their new environment as deeply alienating. More than that, they were abused by their imperial masters, who required them to sing about Jerusalem in order to be mocked for their "illusionary" faith.[1]

> For there our captors
> asked us for songs,
> and our tormenters asked for mirth, saying,
> "Sing us one of the songs of Zion!" (Ps 137:3)

But the deportees knew that "songs of Zion" can properly be sung only in Jerusalem:

> How could we sing the LORD's song
> in a foreign land? (Ps 137:4)

This notorious psalm sets up the central dynamic of our topic, namely, that Zion, liturgically constructed, does not readily accommodate the vagaries of power politics. The transaction reported in the psalm is a typical one between imperial masters and weak or impotent colonialists. That typical transaction is made even more acute by the powerful ideological claims of Jerusalem and its temple. The songs sung there—or the songs sung about being there—are termed "Songs of Zion."[2]

That phrasing from Psalm 137 has been transposed by Hermann Gunkel into a genre or, more precisely, into a subgenre of hymns. Gunkel included in his discussion Psalms 84, 87, and 132, but the discussion turns more precisely on Psalms 46, 48, and 76, which are the primary examples of the genre.[3] Of course it cannot be demonstrated that the phrase in Psalm 137 refers to these psalms, but the connection is a plausible one and we can proceed on that basis. It is, moreover, not quite correct to report that this grouping is a genre or a subgenre because for the most part these psalms are distinguished by content rather than by a distinct and identifiable form; it is the case, however, that Gunkel noted that these psalms tend to lack an introduction or "exhortation to praise." Nonetheless, the recurring subject matter about the theological-liturgical significance of Jerusalem and its temple is no doubt enough for us to proceed.[4] The psalms celebrate the peculiar character of the Holy City and the extraordinary commitment YHWH has made to it; that character and commitment serve to establish a fixed, reliable, unchanging point in a world that is experienced as unstable. Such a fixed assurance made Zion definingly important to its adherents. Thus Zion is taken, with good reason, as a trustworthy contrast to the instability and vulnerability experienced by the Jewish singers in Babylon.

I

These psalms voice a recurring pattern concerning the stability and safety of Jerusalem about which Israel sings.

Psalm 46

This psalm, the best known of the subgenre, begins with a sweeping uncompromising certitude (v. 1) that yields practical assurances for the dwellers and worshipers in Jerusalem (v. 2). "God" is a reliable presence and help; for that reason the inhabitants have no fear or anxiety. The assurance is followed in vv. 2-3 by the churning, stirring waters of chaos that threaten to undo the created order. The four-fold "though" of the NRSV yields more symmetry in the rhetoric than is evident in the Hebrew, but the point is clear enough. The verbs of this description are vivid and forceful, the most important of which is *mwṭ* (v. 2; repeated in vv. 5-6). The term bespeaks a tottering and wavering in which the very structures of creation are destabilized. In vv. 1-3, it is God who makes safe in the face of threat.

In vv. 5-6, however, the psalm moves from "God" to "city." It is the city (unnamed Jerusalem) that is the "city of God," holy habitation of Elyon; now it is the city that will not be "moved" (*mwṭ*). Whereas in vv. 2-3 it is chaotic waters that threaten, in v. 6 it is "the nations" who are in an uproar and it is the nations that "totter" (*mwṭ*) in their opposition to God. The psalm and its liturgical matrix move easily back and forth between cosmic threat (chaotic waters) and historical threat (nations). The threats are of a piece; they both seek to assault the Holy City. They both position themselves as adversaries of the God who dwells in Jerusalem. But they cannot win! They cannot threaten or jeopardize that city because they have no effective power against YHWH. YHWH simply speaks, and the opposition melts away in weakness and impotence. The verb "melt" (*mwg*) would seem to be a counterpoint to "change" (*mwr*) in v. 2; indeed some propose to amend the verb *mwr* in v. 2 to *mwg*, which would make an *inclusio* of the two uses of the term for all of vv. 2-6. The double use of *mwg* would thus contain the three uses of *mwṭ*. However the verb is read in v. 2, the five uses offer a portrayal of seething instability. All of that, however, is voided by divine utterance in v. 6, an utterance that brings calm and safety as the threats are "dissolved." It is no wonder the refrain in v. 7 follows in complete confidence.

In the second stanza of the psalm, the reader is invited to a review of the conflict that is described and resolved in vv. 2-6.[5] The residue of that violent struggle is now evident. YHWH has prevailed (v. 8), and now one can see the destroyed weapons that belonged to the enemy (v. 9). YHWH has brought quiet in the place of seething and is now exalted everywhere (among the nations of the earth). The refrain in v. 11 reiterates the conviction of Jerusalem theology that God is "with us."

The psalm describes an assault on the city (cosmic and/or historical) and the divine rebuttal of that attack. Israel is safe; God is faithful; the city is secure; the assault is frustrated. It is no wonder that Zion can summon the confidence of Israel, no wonder, moreover, that the deported continued to refer to that reliable point for a world guaranteed by the faithful God.

Psalm 48

Like Psalm 46, this psalm celebrates the safety of the city; in addition, it affirms its beauty. The psalm begins with a recognition of "our God" (v. 1), a phrase repeated at the conclusion (v. 14). The aesthetically pleasing city is the residence of the Great King. In a daring parallelism, the citadels of the city function to exhibit YHWH as a high place of safety (v. 3). One can see the shrewd intermingling of *city* and *God* in a way that pertains throughout the psalm.

As in Psalm 46, vv. 4-7 describe an attack on the city by "the kings assembled"; but they are put to flight in a state of humbling weakness and helplessness. The antidote to such an attack against the city is "The Lord of hosts," the very one exalted in the refrain of Psalm 46:7, 11. The enemies of Zion are no match for the God who has now established the city "forever" (v. 8). The city is no longer vulnerable because God has now guaranteed it.

The outcome of the divine guarantee of the city is a celebration of YHWH's covenantal fidelity (*ḥesed*), which is based on victory (*ṣedeq)* and practiced by YHWH's judgment (*mišpaṭ*). These three terms in vv. 9-11 mark Jerusalem as a place of covenantal administration; it is, however, an administration made possible by ferocious military capacity. By v. 12 all the turmoil, threat, and conflict are past and resolved. Now there is peaceable leisure to enjoy the architectural wonder of the city and its temple. The rhetoric of vv. 12-13 sounds like the speech of a tour guide who invites the visitors to relish the detail and marvel of construction, so that its wonder can be transmitted to the children when the trip is reported back home. Verse 14 brings the aesthetic and military accents together with a high theological claim, "Surely this is God." The phrase is followed by "our God," which draws the claim close to Israel and reiterates the phrase of v. 1.

We may, however, linger over the opening phrase of v. 14. The question concerns the antecedent of "this." Common sense would indicate that the phrase looks back behind vv. 12-13 to the affirmation about YHWH in vv. 9-10. This is the way it is likely to be taken:

> There would be no need to tell them that these are Jerusalem's battlements; they can see for themselves. What they need to hear is what the battlements stand for. By going around them, the present generation reminds itself of their meaning. It is not that the battlements

> demonstrate the strength of the city but that the battlements demonstrate the strength of the God who kept them intact.[6]

Nonetheless it is to be noted that the psalm comes very close to the identification of city and temple with God.[7] Indeed city and God are tightly bound together in the ideology of this psalm, so that it is impossible to think of this God apart from this residence; and who would want to! Samuel Terrien judges,

> The poet of Psalm 48 maintained an equilibrium between the architectural wonder and the omnipotence of Yahweh.[8]

While we have had "forever" in v. 8, the final word of the psalm is properly "until death." While the NRSV rendering, "forever," may be legitimate, it claims too much.

This quite remarkable psalm holds together architecture, aesthetics, military success, administration of justice, and geographical reference prior to Jerusalem, alongside the affirmation of YHWH. But of course the claim made here depends exactly upon this convergence whereby God is seen to be a carrier of military, aesthetic, architectural, geographical, and juridical interests. When the deported yearned for Jerusalem, they yearned for the entire package.

Psalm 76

Unlike Psalms 46 and 48, this psalm reflects not so much on Zion, city or temple, but upon the God who dwells there, who fights from there, and who governs from there. On the one hand, this God has "awesome" (fearful) power and resolve (see the repeated usage in vv. 4, 7, 11, 12).[9] On the other hand, in vv. 8-9, the purpose of such divine resolve is exactly for the poor who have been oppressed. This latter note is peculiar and may especially have served the deported, who were reduced to impotence.[10] These two accents (awesome/for the poor) provide a perspective for reading the psalm.

This God is known to dwell in Salem/Zion and from there moves against enemies to disarm them (vv. 1-3). Those adversaries do not stand a chance against such resolved power.

Verses 4-6 begin in doxology. ("Glorious" is yet another rendering of "fearful"). God's enemies were valiant ("stouthearted"), but they were no match for the God of Zion, who leveled the adversary and negated the enemy.

God, awesome in power and anger, dominates the entire scene and silences the restless turmoil of chaotic disturbance (vv. 7-9). The God who is effective militarily is the same one who will give judgments for the poor. These verses introduce a societal note that is absent in Psalms 46 and 48.

The psalm concludes with yet another affirmation of God as "awesome," and summons the adherents of this God to make and perform vows to God and to bring offerings to the one who prevails over all threats (vv. 11-12). Of special note is that only here, in v. 11, is YHWH mentioned by name, an identification that is perhaps congruent with the focus on the poor in v. 9.

The God attended here is like a ferocious lion and a fearless warrior, an indefatigable advocate, and a sure winner. YHWH is thus contrasted with the gods of the stouthearted (v. 5), the princes and kings (v. 12) who dared oppose. The narrative account of the psalm creates a world of assurance for those who are otherwise exposed and vulnerable. Erich Zenger suggests that the psalm is a "counterproject" that offers Jerusalem and the temple as a "counterworld" that makes safe.[11]

II

When taken all together, the primary plot of these psalms is not very difficult to trace. It consists in an acknowledgment of *threats of disorder* that are powerful and concrete, and in a doxological recognition that YHWH, resident in Zion, is more than adequate for the *defeat of those threats*. YHWH thereby makes the world safe. There has been a great deal of scholarly discussion about how to interpret these psalms, both in terms of origin and of subsequent use in Israel. Four considerations are obvious in the scholarly literature:

1. The psalms have *mythological* underpinnings that are not explicitly Israelite but are drawn from a common Near Eastern deposit. This is evident, for example, in the mention of "Mount Zion in the far north" (48:2), a reference to a site much older than Jerusalem. Zenger, moreover, has offered rich evidence both for older practices of the worship of the sun god and in the portrayal of God as an attacking lion.[12] There is no doubt that a very old notion of YHWH as the creator overriding the threats of

primordial chaos (that may take historical form) is operative here.[13] In Psalm 76:5-6, there are echoes of the Song of Moses (Exod 15:5-10), a song that "historicizes" old mythological usage.[14]

2. The presence of generic cultural mythology in the tradition, even though drawn into the historical particularity of Israel, has given credence to a hypothesis of the *liturgical reperformance* of the battle of the gods in regularized festival occasions. The remarkable hypothesis of Sigmund Mowinckel has made it possible to interpret these psalms as part of a liturgical reperformance of the struggle of the god of order with the gods of chaos. That is, the mythological need not be understood simply as an ancient residue in the tradition but as an imaginative claim that is still palpable and operative in the imagination of Israel's liturgy. Mowinckel's hypothesis, recently given a positive review by J. J. M. Roberts, suggests that the ancient memory of combat and victory was imaginatively reperformed in the temple, so that the "counterproject" of Zenger was generative and constructive through dramatic performance of a counterworld.[15]

3. There is no doubt that the mythological-liturgical drama of this narrative is given, in a variety of circumstances, specific *historical particularity* in ancient Israel. Thus the battle with the forces of evil was readily transposed into a battle with an enemy army that could be understood in a liturgical mode as a force of chaos. (This is clearly what happened in the formation of the exodus narrative.) It is in the dramatic force of such mythological-liturgical performance that the material becomes attached to specific historical struggles (as has been evident, yet again, in recent U.S. wars wherein a historical crisis is rendered as a cosmic confrontation of "good and evil"). Such linkage to historical specificity may give aid and comfort to people in crisis, as, for example, the deportees pondered the contest been YHWH and the Babylonian gods (see Isa 46:1-4). The Old Testament, however, is more likely to historicize around the Assyrian crisis, for inhabitants of Jerusalem could remember the wonder of the inexplicable deliverance of that city from the hand of Sennacherib.[16] Such historicization of the psalms is indicated, for example, by the fact that the LXX of Psalm 76 adds "against Assyria," thus linking the poem to the crisis of Sennacherib. Thus in the sixth century, practitioners of the psalms could remember and anticipate that God would act against Babylon as God had acted against the Assyrians. It is not surprising that the Assyrian deliverance, in the repeated telling of Israel, took on mythic proportions of its own.

4. These psalms can also be taken *eschatologically*, so that God's great defeat of the powers of chaos is still to come. Gunkel was a great advocate of an eschatological reading, which, as near as I can determine, has two motivations. First, on any reading of world history (or the history of ancient Israel) it is clear that the powers of chaos have not yet been defeated, so that the ultimate victory of God is still to come in the future. The psalms thus become an act of hope for the way God will triumph in time to come. A second reason for such a view, I suspect, is that many interpreters refuse a mythological-liturgical reading because they resist, in classical Protestant fashion, any notion that worship performance can be generative, constructive, or constitutive of reality.[17] In this reading, the liturgical recital (performance) of a psalm does not *do* anything but only *waits* in eager longing for what has not yet been enacted.

It is clear that with the options of a *mythological, liturgical, historical*, or *eschatological* reading, the stance taken by any particular interpreter is determined not by the nature of the material itself, but by the context, history, and perspective of the interpreter. In practical usage, as in sixth-century Babylon, it was surely the case that practitioners of these psalms did not bother to specify which of these angles was operative. They simply *did* the psalms, and in doing them they were able to participate in all of these dimensions of imagination. If that is so, as surely seems to be the case, this means that performance of these psalms, as suggested by Psalm 137, all at the same time pushed deeply into cultural deposits (mythological), found liturgical performance to be effective in the construction of a "counterworld," understood the imagery with reference to the particular historical crisis of Babylonian hegemony, and found themselves empowered to hope by the enactment of the psalms.

Such participation without excessive critical reflection—participation in all of these available angles of the Zion tradition—did not wait for scholarly niceties of discrimination. It is more likely that the rubric of Karl Mannheim, "ideology and utopia," is useful for coming to terms with the practice of the psalms.[18] The *ideology* of the Zion psalms creates a fixed point that is beyond criticism. The psalms of Zion offer a *utopian possibility* for an alternative to the facts on the ground in Babylon. Thus they experienced the world of the psalms of Zion as future expectation and as present reality in a liturgical milieu that offered YHWH as more faithful, reliable, and powerful than all alternatives. The effect of such performance is, at the same time, cosmic and particular, present and future. The *narrative* of combat and victory and the *character* of YHWH are rendered together in dialectical fashion. There is no doubt that YHWH, as agent, evokes and enacts the reassuring victory that makes the narrative possible. But there is also no doubt that the narrative, recited in many variations, is the appropriate venue for the character of YHWH. In practical ways, the narrative mediates the agency of YHWH.

Thus there is high irony in the requirement of "our captors, our tormenters" who "asked for" these songs (Ps 137:3). They did so for purposes of mocking contempt. In doing so, however, they unwittingly permitted the deported, in their very presence, to perform their alternative world that offered *mythological rootage* beyond the reach of empire, that entertained *new historical possibility*, and that mediated *long-term hope* against the empire. Thus the tormenters created a venue for counterpossibility to their own brutalizing mastery. The performance they required was itself an act of hope that contained dangerous seeds of revolutionary imagination.

III

This is as far as conventional interpretation of these psalms tends to go. My task is, however, to explore "misbegotten hope" in these songs. There is no doubt that the Songs of Zion are formed and situated in the ideological environment of the urban elite in Jerusalem. It is the articulation of these theological-liturgical claims that served that exclusionary population that attracts the term "misbegotten."[19]

To understand the ideological pull of these psalms, it is important to situate them in a broader liturgical frame. The matrix of the Songs of Zion is no doubt the Jerusalem establishment of David and Solomon, either as experienced, remembered, or imagined. The establishment of David and Solomon, moreover, is grounded in the twinned institutions of temple and dynasty. The temple claim is given primal expression in the narrative of 1 Kings 8, which concerns the dedication of Solomon's temple. The liturgical apex of that experienced/imagined event is the anthem of 1 Kings 8:12-13:

> The LORD has said that he would dwell in thick darkness.
> I have built you an exalted house,
> a place for you to dwell in forever.

These lines assure YHWH's permanent residence in the temple and therefore as guarantor and patron of temple and city.

The dynastic claim is rooted in the oracle of 2 Samuel 7, Nathan's declaration to David, in which YHWH promises abiding, unconditional fidelity to David's house:

> Your house and your kingdom shall be made sure forever before me;
> your throne shall be established forever. (2 Sam 7:16)

It may be doubted whether these two traditions are so intimately connected. Indeed Ben Ollenburger is at pains to maintain that the temple tradition is quite distinct from the royal tradition.[20] In the self-justifying Psalm 78, however, the two are closely connected:

> He abandoned his dwelling at Shiloh . . .
> He rejected the tent of Joseph,
>   he did not choose the tribe of Ephraim;
> but he chose the tribe of Judah,
>   *Mount Zion*, which he loves.
> He built his sanctuary like the high heavens,
>   like the earth, which he has founded forever.
> He chose *his servant David*,
>   and took him from the sheepfolds . . .
>   to be the shepherd of his people Jacob,
>   of Israel, his inheritance. (78:60, 67-71)

While the two themes may have somewhat different histories as Ollenburger proposes, in practice they are merged because the Jerusalem temple was indeed the royal chapel designed to serve for the performance of royal liturgies that are shot through with ideological claims.[21] In practice there can hardly be any doubt that the theological claims of liturgy readily shaded over into political claims. As a consequence, the monarchy and temple are treated, according to the "choice" of YHWH, to an "exceptionalism" that exempts the city from the normal demands and requirements of history. The normal ethical conditionalities of history are voided so that the practitioners of power (kings and priests) are given an exemption from normal ethical expectation. It turns out, on grounds of both of historical reality and theological morality, that no concentration of liturgical-ideological power can, in the end, be credited with such an exemption.

It is the task of the prophetic tradition in ancient Israel to expose and call into question such misbegotten hope that is fundamentally an act of ideological self-deception. For that reason it is remarkable that the biblical text itself exposes the misbegotten hope of the Songs of Zion. I will identify three evidences of such exposure.

1. The Deuteronomic conditionality is, as Gerhard von Rad saw, deeply in tension with the royal-temple claims of the Jerusalem establishment.[22] This is evident in what I have called the "Deuteronomic proviso" that is inserted as an "if" into the Solomonic narrative (1 Kgs 3:14; 6:12; 9:4-9).[23] These texts assert the penultimate quality of Jerusalem that is subject to the Torah provisions of the older covenant. No amount of wealth, power, or wisdom will permit establishment ideology to outrun that reality.

2. More specifically, amid the temple dedication narrative of 1 Kings 8, v. 27 disputes the temple claim just made:

> But will God indeed dwell on the earth? Even the heaven and the highest heaven cannot contain you, much less this house that I have built!

In that abrasive verse it is asserted that the extravagance of the Jerusalem liturgy cannot contain the freedom of God, and therefore cannot contain the sovereignty of God that brings with it the bite of judgment. That verse is followed, in the remainder of chapter 8, by a long meditation on covenant curses, the need for repentance, and eventually the deportation that evoked Psalm 137 (vv. 26-53). The hope of the temple, echoed in the long poem of Psalm 89, is a failed hope because it is built upon the premise of exceptionalism whereby theological claim is extended into the spheres of political and military power. It is a misconstrual to imagine that sufficient power makes a regime immune to the requirements of justice that are intrinsic to the creation of the world.[24]

3. In the same tradition as Deuteronomy, Jeremiah, in his famous temple sermon, mocked the self-assurance of the liturgy. Jeremiah is rooted in the old covenant tradition that was connected to the old sanctuary of Shiloh (see Ps 87:60).[25] As a spokesperson out of that tradition, he mocks liturgical pretense in Jerusalem:

Do not trust in these deceptive words:

> "This is the temple of the LORD, the temple of the LORD, the temple of the LORD." (Jer 7:4)

And then, not unlike Deuteronomy, he asserts the conditions of Torah obedience:

> For if you truly amend your ways and your doings, if you truly act justly one with another, if you do not oppress the alien, the orphan, and the widow, or shed innocent blood in this place, and if you do not go after other gods to your own hurt, then I will dwell with you in this place, in the land that I gave of old to your ancestors forever and ever. (Jer 7:5-7)

The appeal here, as in Deuteronomy, is not just to the historical vagaries of empires waxing and waning; it is as well an appeal to an ethical requirement that is preoccupied with social justice that cannot be circumvented.

It is a summary conclusion of the prophetic tradition that the demise of the Jerusalem establishment is due to the disregard of covenantal obligation, a disregard that is legitimated and sustained by the false assumptions of the Songs of Zion that YHWH will protect regardless. The prophetic tradition makes an extraordinary connection between ethical distortion (indictment) and historical assault (sentence) that together constitute the characteristic prophetic speech of judgment:

> Yet the LORD warned Israel and Judah by every prophet and every seer, saying, "Turn from your evil ways and keep my commandments and my statutes, in accordance with all the law that I commanded your ancestors and that I sent to you by my servants the prophets." They would not listen but were stubborn. (2 Kgs 17:13-14)

The royal-temple ideology imagined that there was no such factor of conditionality to which attention must be paid.

IV

It remains to consider how the Songs of Zion might be construed in a postcolonial context, that is, in a context that is realistic about worldly power but with critical courage that has not succumbed to either despair or cynicism.

1. There can hardly be doubt that the Songs of Zion articulate the faith (ideology) of the urban elites who clustered around the David-Solomon establishment. That ideology of the urban elites justified its preeminence in Israel by a theory of exceptionalism that gave the city its unconditional privilege in the historical process. Under the rubric of "chosenness" (chosen king, chosen city, chosen temple) the liturgically performed exceptionalism contradicted the contingency of the historical process and skewed political and economic reality.

2. That sense of chosenness (king, city, and temple) as a theological affirmation inevitably spilled over into sociopolitical-economic matters to become, on a small scale, an imperial ideology. Roberts is clear that the Davidic–Solomonic empire could very quickly develop an ideology that gave theological legitimacy to its practical claims:

> But the whole issue of how long the Davidic-Solomonic empire existed is irrelevant to the question of whether the Davidic court created an imperial ideology. Contrary to [Erhard] Gerstenberger's claim that an empire must endure a long time before it can create an imperial ideology, the examples from the Ancient Near East show that such ideologies were created relatively quickly during the reign of the king who first achieved imperial status.[26]

Close to home, that ideology justified the flow of consumer goods and wealth from the peasant countryside to the surplus value of the urban economy, a flow that is confirmed by Solomon's decorous building projects (see 1 Kgs 7:1-12).[27] On a larger scale and outside Israel, that same ideology of exceptionalism offered an imagined preeminence among the nations and offered a kind of security that, in the end, did not resonate with the facts on the ground. Clearly the deported continued to adhere to that ideology of exceptionalism after the facts on the ground deeply contradicted the claim (Ps 137). It is that contradiction that evokes the pathos voiced in Psalm 89:

> Lord, where is your steadfast love of old,
> which by your faithfulness you swore to David? (v. 49)

3. While there were those who tenaciously held to that imperial theology that delivered political perspectives, it is clear that others did not and could not accept that claim. The twinned work of Jeremiah and Shaphan in the book of Jeremiah suggests that the old covenantal tradition (now voiced as political opposition) plus the political realism represented by the family of Shaphan saw that it was futile to adhere to that ideology.[28] Thus it would be the twinned reasons of the traditional (Jeremiah) and the pragmatic (Shaphan) that led to the conviction that the destruction of Jerusalem (king and temple) was the will of YHWH enacted by "Nebuchadnezzar my servant" (Jer 25:9; 27:6). We may conclude that even among the deportees the matter was highly contested.

4. It is plausible to think that as the Babylonian imperial hegemony gave way to the Persian imperial hegemony, many deported Jews could no longer embrace the claims of the Songs of Zion because everywhere (including in the province of Yehud) turned out to be Persia, the all-encompassing empire. The acknowledgment of Persian hegemony, moreover, is expressed not only by Ezra and Nehemiah, who benefitted from Persian credentialing and finance, but by 2 Isaiah before them, who can imagine that Cyrus is YHWH's messiah (Isa 45:1). Such a move is clearly outside the old imperial ideology of Jerusalem.

5. It turned out that the primary line of Jewish faith under Persian and Hellenistic governance was scribal activity that involved the teaching and interpretation of Torah.[29] Thus Ezra stands as the representative and defining figure for Jewish faith; his preeminence is quite in contrast to the marginal hopes for the Jerusalem ideology of political-liturgical restoration, a hope still voiced by Haggai (Hag 2:23).[30] The practice of Torah interpretation and Torah piety was not only an embrace of the tradition that came to be regarded as normative in emerging Judaism, it was also the embrace and practice of a faith that could take seriously the conditionality of history and the contingency of Jewish reality in the world. The Jerusalem ideology, voiced in the Songs of Zion, offered a flat, one-dimensional certitude that allowed for no dialogic interaction. In contrast to that, Jewish interpreters who worked outside of that illusion could engage with lived reality, an engagement that made vitality of faith possible and permitted negotiation with imperial power for the sake of Jewishness. The hard, flat ideology of the Songs of Zion turned out to be no way forward, and increasing numbers of the faithful could see the unbearable contradiction between that certitude and the reality of colonial status. That unbearable contradiction permitted and empowered some of the faithful to move beyond an illusionary hope to active negotiation with imperial power. The rejection of such misbegotten hope permitted a move beyond immobilized colonial waiting to life in the real world of political power and political possibility.

V

My topic—"Misbegotten Hope" in "the Songs of Zion"—set me in the direction of a hermeneutic of suspicion. The term "misbegotten" suggests that the hope of these psalms is illusionary and self-serving. The so-called genre of "Songs of Zion," moreover, has made it easy (unavoidable?) to link the illusionary faith of these psalms to the cadre of the privileged elite in the Jerusalem establishment. That is the task of this chapter that I have attempted to exposit in a responsible way.

Having pursued that "suspicion," however, I now move beyond "suspicion" to "retrieval."[31] Eventually the confidence of the urban elite in Jerusalem failed, with the demise of the city. Derivatively, it is clear that contemporary "Zionism," especially in its militant forms, has failed in the quest for peaceable security. And even more derivatively, the confident exceptionalism of the church (as the new Zion) or the United States (as the new Zion) has also failed. That is, suspicion about "misbegotten hope" that assumed a guaranteed exemption from historical vagaries has been verified in contemporary as in ancient context.

As Paul Ricoeur has taught us, however, the verification of suspicion is not the end of the interpretive task. After the critical practice of suspicion, there is a chance of a "second naiveté" that is no longer naively innocent but still hope-filled, albeit with critical awareness.[32] This "retrieval" concerns the hope attested in the psalms after the "genre" of the urban elites is abandoned. In turning to retrieval, one may recognize that the modern imposition of "genre" on these psalms introduces an ideological tilt to the psalms themselves and links them to power assumptions that surely were operative. That connection to power assumptions, however, does not exhaust the "surplus" of the psalms themselves or the hope that they articulate.

I am enormously indebted to Mark Braverman, who responded to a draft of this chapter and rightly urged a move beyond the critique of the hope of the elite.[33] He helped me to see that after the ideological dimension that is at the core of my argument, one must say more. One must stay with the psalms beyond such elites, beyond such ideology, beyond such genre, beyond such "misbegotten" hope; beyond all of that, these psalms continue to be a script for authentic covenantal hope:

> Certainly, Jerusalem has assumed huge political significance in our day, but Zionism is not about Jerusalem. Zionism was and is about land, about Palestine, about all that it confers on the people who come into possession of it. Jerusalem, on the other hand, derives its power from what it means on a symbolic level. And I think we should take the psalms this way, thereby liberating them from a Temple-King frame. So also, the chaos set out in these psalms against which Zion provides defense and refuge is not only the raging of the nations in a military sense. Rather, the chaos is the sense of terrifying rootlessness, the

> terror, shapelessness and boundarylessness of a world in which land is gone, rootedness is gone, and there is no "there" (or "here") that is ours, no place where we belong.[34]

After the social, political celebration of Jerusalem, "Zion" takes on a broader, deeper metaphorical power; the "order" it offers against the threat of chaos goes deeper:

> The "order" of Jerusalem is not merely political stability against the raging of the nations, i.e., discord, violence, threat, insecurity, but a deeper spiritual rooting, foundation, anchor. This again is covenant talk. And this right: the covenant is rooted in land—so the psalm takes us to that. And in that we see another aspect of and source of the problem that you are getting to—the claim that is embedded in the faith. A grounding, a comforting, faith, yoking the people to God.[35]

Thus, as Braverman has seen, these psalms permit more than one reading, because they reflect the "two sides of Zionism." These psalms then may not only foster a certitude that leads to violence but are also the key to the way out:

> That way out is the impulse of the people to recover, to grow and to learn, to find the heart of it, to find the true Zion. History shows that this process was left unfinished by the Jews, but was picked up and carried by Christianity. Sadly for the Jews, this return to the geographical Zion has led us to a very violent pass. Sadly for Christians, Christianity institutionally and on an ecumenical level seems to now want to undo that spiritualization of Zion and join with the Jews in this re-sacralization of the Holy Mountain. But really, the job is never finished, and both faiths now face the disorienting crisis served up by modern Zionism.[36]

The attempt of these psalms "to deal with the disorientation of exile and military threat, the loss of safety, security, autonomy" was an important interpretive effort in ancient times.[37] These psalms, beyond the ideological illusion that tempts both Jews and Christians, may be a contemporary invitation to a new orientation. Such a reading is beyond the "misbegotten," self-serving violence of every narrow ideology.

VI

I finish with two notations. First, it is clear that one cannot, from a postcolonial perspective, deal with the Songs of Zion without acknowledging that contemporary Zionism is fed and authorized by that ancient Zionism. Contemporary Zionism, especially in its militant, military form, continues in a stance of exceptionalism that spins off political policy in absolutist ways.[38] The immediate impact of such ideological thinking is to reduce the Palestinian population to a helpless, hopeless colonial status, so that the old ancient Israelite imperial mode of thinking dominates again. But the long-term prospect is that as Palestinians refuse such colonial status, the imperial center is increasingly in jeopardy, precisely because of its absolutist claims, which are at profound variance from the facts on the ground. In the end, the absolute ideology of Zionism, contemporary as ancient, makes impossible the kind of political realism that could permit a negotiation of genuine peace. That ideology has no patience for the reality of justice that is an inescapable precondition of genuine peace; its practitioners are unable to see why justice questions should impinge upon the flat claim of the ideology. This contemporary reliance on the ideology of Zionism yields its own version of misbegotten hope that lacks realism about the interface of ideology and the contingency of history. In the ancient city of Jerusalem, the urban elites stayed with the ideology of Zionism in a blind way and missed the facts on the ground, facts concerning internal injustice and external threat. The contemporary practice of that same ideology runs the same risk. And mutatis mutandis, the same self-deception is true of every such ideology of exceptionalism wherever it is practiced as defining truth and as defining claim. Thus the critique pertains not only to contemporary Zionism but also to every absolutist claim that is translated into political, military policy.

Second, as I reflected on the Songs of Zion, it struck me as astonishing that with almost no exception, scholars have offered commentary on the Songs of Zion (as have I) without any critical edge of interpretive suspicion.[39] That is, that absolutist ideology has been taken at face value, without any awareness of its deeply problematic character. I have wondered, for example, in delineating the genre of "Songs of Zion," why such psalms as 74 and 79 have not been included in the genre. These psalms that portray the failure of the ideology and that report the destruction of the Jerusalem temple are of course "Zion-focused" and may qualify if the genre is otherwise construed:

> Remember *Mount Zion*, where you came to dwell.
> Direct your steps to the perpetual ruins;
>   the enemy has destroyed everything in the sanctuary.
> Your foes have roared within your holy place. (Ps 74:2b-4a)

> O God, the nations have come into your inheritance;
>   they have defiled *your holy temple*;
>   they have laid *Jerusalem* in ruins. (Ps 79:1)

But critical scholars, not unlike ancient ideologues, could not entertain the historical reality that the imperial ideology of the "Songs of Zion" could not prevail. In a more inclusive genre, these songs of failure would have provided important ballast against the ideology, but scholars have seldom made the connection between ideology (arrived at by genre) and the lived reality that defies the ideology. The conclusion of this chapter may be found in the pathos-filled final verses of Lamentations, which make a bold petition to God that depends upon the claim of Zion (5:21) and then end in a lingering, haunting possibility that stares reality in the face (5:22):[40]

> Restore us to yourself, O Lord, that we may be restored;
>   renew our days as of old—
> unless you have utterly rejected us,
>   and are angry with us beyond measure.

When the loss is contained within the ideology, without grief, it may, perforce, end in the kind of violence that is entertained in Psalm 137.

4

POEMS VS. MEMOS

The remarkable book by John O'Banion, *Reorienting Rhetoric*, is a study of the sweep of Western rhetoric.[1] It has the seductive subtitle, *The Dialectic of List and Story*, which is the dialectic I will pursue in this chapter.

I

O'Banion lays out his thesis by seeing "list and story" as "a dialectic of literacy and orality that underlies the dialectic of logic and narrative."[2] He anchors his argument in a remarkable, obscure etymology: (1) On the one hand, the Indo-European root *or* means "to pronounce a ritual formula" and yields such terms as "rhetoric, orator, exorable, perorate," all practices of the oral. (2) On the other hand, the Latin term for a canon of rhetoric, *disposito*, is derived from *apo*, a root that implies opposites and yields "oppose, opposite, dispose, expound, impose, position, exposition, propose, suppose, posture, deposit, composition, preposition."[3] The same root turns up in mathematics as "exponent, exponential," which point in the direction of the "powers" of "logarithms" that eventuate in "proofs."[4]

O'Banion judges that the "demise" from "story" to "list" began with Aristotle, who took the "first step away from 'dramatism.'"[5] He asserts:

> In Aristotle's hands, all thought, including thought about rhetoric, became subservient to the demands of logical systematicity. Under his (and others) influence, rhetoric and philosophy have had difficulty recognizing the dangers of "monopolies of knowledge" . . . let alone seeing the importance of narration, as well as other ways of understanding, except as the object of systematic, philosophical reflection. As a result the disciplines joined in a trek that would, with only a few hesitating

> steps lead to Western culture's eventually becoming secularized and compartmentalized. . . . Aristotle's intense allegiance to logic continues to be shared by most Westerners, including most contemporary rhetorical scholars.[6]

The old poets and playwrights (even through Plato) appealed to the dramatic. It was, consequently, Cicero and Quintilian who worked at the recovery of narrative and the rhetoric of story. While these matters lie well beyond my competence, I am nonetheless instructed by O'Banion's commentary on the crisis as narrative came to be replaced by list.[7] He organizes his discussion around the following theses:

> Rhetoric is denigrated as being merely an art of appearance, failing to express reality.
>
> Rhetoric is accused of unhealthy skepticism.
>
> Rhetoric, rooted in orality, is judged obsolete by literate thinkers.
>
> Rhetoric is attacked for its reliance on traditional modes of knowledge.
>
> Rhetoric is cut off from the heart of its way of thinking.
>
> Rhetoric is considered inappropriate for the Age of Reason.
>
> Rhetoric casts about for ways to survive.
>
> Rhetoric is marked by a glaring void—narration has disappeared as a way of thinking and arguing.
>
> Rhetoric is reclaimed by a few, Kenneth Burke being a pioneer.[8]

O'Banion finishes by citing contemporary advocates of narrative including Hayden White, Northrup Frye, Alasdair MacIntyre, and most especially Kenneth Burke. On the other hand, he takes Descartes as the typical and foremost example of the advocates of list. Descartes judges that "rhetoric" is irrelevant to the articulation of truth. And behind Descartes are Gutenberg and his printing press:

> The mode of thought enamored of list and unconcerned with Story . . . is one that made explicit the implications of the printing press. Descartes achieved for philosophical thought what Gutenberg first did for language—he made it more abstract, more methodical, and more isolative (separating even further rhetor, audience, and discourse) . . .
>
> Descartes preferred to give total attention to the List. Descartes recommended, for all thought and decision-making, the "clarity" and

"intelligibility" inherent to lists, categorization, and especially to mathematics.[9]

O'Banion quotes Donald Phillip Verene,

> Descartes cuts himself off from time; the rational truth that he seeks is eternal, without basis in history. . . . Descartes missed the sense of eloquence wherein language is used to arrive at insight. . . . Rhetoric, in Descartes's view, is something outside rather than inside the process of truth.[10]

Descartes, moreover, is in the company, says O'Banion, of Socrates, Tertullian, Locke, Hume, Kant, and Hegel. In the end, the "storyteller 'knows' through the multiple relationships and nearly endless choices that occur in contexts or 'scenes' . . . not, as with the list-maker, through decontextualization and forced binary choices."[11] This latter path leads eventually, concludes O'Banion, to anomie and anxiety. In his chapter 9, O'Banion dramatically enumerates some of the losses in the pursuit of list: loss of the language of order and disorder, loss of criteria for morality, loss of life as quest, and loss of the significance of actual situations. Everything dissolves into a scenario from Dr. Strangelove.

II

From O'Banion's complex and shrewd review of the history of Western rhetoric concerning the fall and rise of narrative as a mode of knowledge, I wish to comment on the rhetorical practices in the Old Testament, a comment that will culminate in prophetic discourse. I recognize at the outset that I make only heuristic use of O'Banion's thesis, and in such use no doubt twist and skew his intent. I am willing to enact such an anachronism because it occurs to me that the dialectic of *list* and *story* takes on force in the Old Testament itself and continues to be a force among those who continue to interpret the Old Testament. For my purposes I wish to transpose O'Banion's terms from "list" to "memo" and from "story" to "poem." I believe that in doing so, I do not distort the intent of his argument. I prefer the term "memo" because its contemporary use is more available for us, and I prefer the term "poem" because in the Old Testament, before narrative there was poem. But it is the same argument.

I understand "memo" to be a one-dimensional mode of communication that will likely be instructive and directive, admitting no ambiguity, and thus compelling a certain reasoning, a certain action, a certain conclusion. Current scholarship in Old Testament study has focused great (hostile) attention on those identified as the "urban elites," a term that may variously refer to the Davidic royal-priestly establishment in the monarchal period or to the scribal priestly managers who belatedly colluded with the Persian Empire and eventually with the Roman Empire. In the Old Testament, it is this class of "urban elites"—legitimated political leaders and authorized priestly officers—who generated great numbers of memos that have come to us in Scripture. In a reconstructed presentation of ancient Israel (reconstructed and so begging historical questions), I propose that Solomon is the quintessential generator of memos that were designed to advance and sustain royal power and legitimacy.[12] I refer to the texts that preserve the inventories that bespeak planning, administration, and control, all of which required some persuasive force. I submit that Solomon's memos are a clear example of the way in which the powerful consolidate "power as truth" in the interest of control. Thus we have:

1. A roster of bureaucrats that indicates the flow of administrative power:

    > King Solomon was king over all Israel, and these were his high officials: Azariah son of Zadok was the priest; Elihoreph and Ahijah sons of Shisha were secretaries; Jehoshaphat son of Ahilud was recorder; Benaiah son of Jehoiada was in command of the army; Zadok and Abiathar were priests; Azariah son of Nathan was over the officials; Zabud son of Nathan was priest and king's friend; Ahishar was in charge of the palace; and Adoniram son of Abda was in charge of the forced labor.
    >
    > (1 Kgs 4:1-6)

    The list not only shows intentionality but is also saturated with pedigree; everyone has a known, named father!

2. We have a map of tax districts that tell how Solomon's avarice was financed, a list that begins this way:

    > Solomon had twelve officials over all Israel, who provided food for the king and his household; each one had to make provision for one month in the year. These were the names: Ben-hur, in the hill country of Ephraim; Bendeker in Makaz, Shallbim, Bethshemesh, and Elonbethhanan; Benhesed, in Arubboth. (1 Kgs 4:7-10; the list continues through v. 19)

    Nothing left here to happenstance!

3. We have a list of provisions for the daily maintenance of the royal entourage, perhaps reflective of budgetary considerations:

> Solomon's provision for one day was thirty cors of choice flour, and sixty cors of meal, ten fat oxen, and twenty pasture-fed cattle, one hundred sheep, besides deer, gazelles, roebucks, and fatted fowl. (1 Kgs 4:22)

4. We have the blueprint of the temple to be sure that God's holiness is properly maintained and not violated or offended:

> The house that King Solomon built for the LORD was sixty cubits long, twenty cubits wide, and thirty cubits high. The vestibule in front of the nave of the house was twenty cubits wide, across the width of the house. Its depth was ten cubits in front of the house. For the house he made windows from recessed frames. He also built a structure against the wall of the house, running around the walls of the house, both the nave and the inner sanctuary; and he made side chambers all around. The lower story was five cubits wide, the middle one was six cubits wide, and the third was seven cubits wide; for around the outside of the house he made offsets on the wall in order that the supporting beams should not be inserted into the walls of the house. (1 Kgs 6:2-6)

Is that clear?

5. The blueprint for the temple is echoed in a summary report from the committee on ornamentation and decor:

> So Solomon made all the vessels that were in the house of the LORD: the golden altar, the golden table for the bread of the Presence, the lamp-stands of pure gold, five on the south side and five on the north, in front of the inner sanctuary; the flowers, the lamps, and the tongs, of gold; the cups, snuffers, basins, dishes for incense and fire pans, of pure gold; the sockets of the doors of the innermost part of the house, the most holy place, and for the doors of the nave of the temple, of gold. (1 Kgs 7:48-50)

It is splendid! Nothing is spared for this most blessed, most pious king.

6. The propaganda machine cannot refrain from exhibit:

> The weight of gold that came to Solomon in one year was six hundred sixty-six talents of gold, besides that which came from the traders and from the business of the merchants, and from all the kings of Arabia and the governors of the land. King Solomon made two hundred large shields of beaten gold; six hundred shekels of gold went into each large shield. He made three hundred shields of beaten gold; three minas of gold went into each shield; and the king put them in the House of the Forest of Lebanon. The king also made a great ivory throne, and overlaid it with the finest gold. The throne had six steps. The top of the throne was rounded in the back, and on each side of the seat were arm rests and two lions standing beside the arm rests, while twelve lions were standing, one on each end of a step on the six steps. Nothing like it was ever made in any kingdom. All King Solomon's drinking vessels were of gold, and all the vessels of the House of the Forest of Lebanon were of pure gold, none were of silver; it was not considered as anything in the days of Solomon. (1 Kgs 10:14-21)

   If we are not impressed, we have not been listening.

7. The list concludes with a brief reprise:

> Everyone of them brought a present, objects of silver and gold, garments, weaponry, spices, horses, and mules, so much year by year. (1 Kgs 10:25)

Evidently these are not free gifts but assigned quotas of tribute and protection money.

We have no idea what of this, if anything, is historical. But what we are studying is the way in which list (or memo) was taken to be the proper mode of discourse that would match the power and the control that are to be attributed to this grandest of all kings, power and control that were then appropriated by the makers of the texts.

And because Solomon is the champion of the temple as well as the great beneficiary of it, we can move easily from Solomon's memos to the priestly material that is commonly dated to the sixth century, even if it has older antecedents. We may observe among the priests several characteristic concerns and prescriptions:

1. The construction of a holy environment has to be perfect and precise, or it cannot house credible holiness:

> They shall make an ark of acacia wood; it shall be two and a half cubits long, a cubit and a half wide, and a cubit and a half high. You shall overlay it with pure gold, inside and outside you shall overlay it, and you shall make a molding of gold upon it all around. You shall cast four rings of gold for it and put them on its four feet, two rings on the one side of it, and two rings on the other side. You shall make poles of acacia wood, and overlay them with gold and you shall put the poles into the rings on the sides of the ark, by which to carry the ark. The poles shall remain in the rings of the ark; they shall not be taken from it. (Exod 25:10-15)

2. The official must be properly legitimated in order to function in the context of holiness. The provisions for ordination are delineated in detail:

> Now this is what you shall do to them to consecrate them, so that they may serve me as priests. Take one young bull and two rams without blemish, and unleavened bread, unleavened cakes mixed with oil, and unleavened wafers spread with oil. You shall make them of choice wheat flour. You shall put them in one basket and bring them in the basket, and bring the bull and the two rams. You shall bring Aaron and his sons to the entrance of the tent of meeting, and wash them with water. Then you shall take the vestments, and put on Aaron the tunic and the robe of the ephod, and the ephod, and the breastplate, and gird him with the decorated band of the ephod; and you shall set the turban on his head, and put the holy diadem on the turban. You shall take the anointing oil, and put it on his head and anoint him. . . . You shall take the other ram; and Aaron and his sons shall lay their hands on the head of the ram, and you shall slaughter the ram, and take some of its blood and put it on the lobe of Aaron's right ear and on the lobes of the right ears of his sons, and on the thumbs of their right hands, and on the big toes of their right feet, and dash the rest of the blood against all sides of the altar.
>
> (Exod 29:1-6, 19-20)

3. The actions of the holy place are detailed:

> When you present a grain offering baked in the oven, it shall be of choice flour: unleavened cakes mixed with oil or unleavened wafers spread with oil. If your offering is grain prepared on a griddle, it shall be of choice flour mixed with oil, unleavened; break it in pieces, and pour oil on it; it is a grain offering. If your offering is grain prepared in a pan, it shall be made of choice flour in oil. You shall bring to the LORD the grain offering that is prepared in any of these ways. And when it is presented to the priest, he shall take it to the altar. The priest shall remove from the grain offering its token portion and turn this into smoke on the altar, an offering by fire of pleasing odor to the LORD. (Lev 2:4-9)

4. The laity is compelled to the same attentiveness in their daily lives:

> You shall not let your animals breed with a different kind; you shall not sow your field with two kinds of seed; you shall not put on a garment made of two different materials. (Lev 19:19; see Deut 22:9-11)

We can see binary thinking in all of this, as everything is sorted out according to singular punctilious clarity. Eventually the priests are indicted because they have not maintained the clear categories required by binary thinking:

> Its priests have done violence to my teaching and have profaned my holy things; they have made no distinction between the holy and the common, neither have they taught the difference between the unclean and the clean. (Ezek 22:26)

It is not my purpose to mock such close reasoning, nor do I want simply to restate the old popular antithesis between priest and prophet. Rather it is important to see how much of this discourse is in the text, how seriously it was taken, and how it was related to social-political elitism.

O'Banion makes the important point that "lists" are indispensible and we cannot do without them. That is, we depend upon logical scientific knowledge for important aspects of our common life. The argument turns on the question of whether such reductive thought is by itself adequate for life. O'Banion draws the conclusion that such a mode of discourse, reason, and conduct eventually leads to anxiety, "anomie and an inability to perceive life as a significant, unified whole."[13]

In the practice of memo by kings and priests in ancient Israel, we can see that they attempted to maintain a certain kind of order by exhibits of power and management of holiness. And when those exhibitions of power and management of holiness are allied, the outcomes are sure to be problematic.[14] Thus it is clear:

that priestly memos are tilted toward *exclusion* by the terms of impurity, uncleanness, and profanation.

that the temptation to exclusion is in the direction of *monopoly*. The monopoly is dramatized in the ordering of the Solomonic temple with its gradations of holiness from the outer court to the holy place to the holy of holies, so that access is more and more limited until in the end it is only one person who has access.[15] I judge that the graded access of the temple is, in our time, paralleled in the graded access of commercial airplanes.[16] There is no doubt, moreover, that liturgical access is related to social qualification that was linked to economic entitlement and political clout. Thus Solomon's memos made an unmistakable connection between holy place and unholy place, holy people and unholy people, and that divide made a distinction as well between the urban elites and all the poorly paid, overtaxed peasants. It must have been a truism, then as now, that in such binary thinking, the ones with holy access are also the ones who get the best education and the social privileges that come with it, including seeing the doctor first.

It is not at all a surprise that Solomon's entourage was well-off:

> Judah and Israel were as numerous as the sand by the sea; they ate and drank and were happy. (1 Kgs 4:20)
>
> Happy are your wives! Happy are these your servants who continually attend you and hear your wisdom! (1 Kgs 10:8)

While that narcotized well-being was going on, the Lord, we are told, was "raising up" the kind of resistance that would erupt, at Solomon's death, in a tax revolt powered by profound resentment (1 Kgs 11:14-20). The ordering of kingdom, power, goods, and access in a binary way produced illusions of virtue and wisdom, the kind of illusions that continue among the elite who know better and who consequently live better. The memo writers, in the end, lost touch with the poignancy and pathos of social reality.

III

From the outset, ancient Israel was wearied of and resistant to Pharaoh's memos that were preoccupied with brick quotas:

> Go to your labors. (Exod 5:4)
>
> You shall no longer give the people straw to make bricks as before; let them go and gather straw for themselves. (v. 7)
>
> Let heavier work be laid on them; then they will labor at it and pay no attention to deceptive words. (v. 9)
>
> Go and get straw yourselves, wherever you can find it; but your work will not be lessened in the least. (v. 11)
>
> Complete your work, the same daily assignment as when you were given straw. (v. 13)
>
> Why did you not finish the required quantity of bricks yesterday and today, as you did before? (v. 14)
>
> You are lazy, lazy; that is why you say, "Let us go and sacrifice to the Lord." Go now, and work; for no straw shall be given you, but you shall still deliver the same number of bricks. (vv. 17-18)
>
> You shall not lessen your daily number of bricks. (v. 19)

It does not matter whether the quotas concern economic production, or moral expectation, or theological orthodoxy, or social requirement. Memos are intrinsically directive and easily become coercive. The binary thinking concludes that one either meets the production requirement or "you are lazy" (or immoral or heretical or irresponsible or even with a "bad odor" [Exod 5:21]). Nor does it matter if this is ancient Pharaoh in Egypt or if he is a metaphor for Nebuchadnezzar or Antiochus or Herod, for he is a stand-in for all memo-writers.

The weariness and resistance of ancient Israel to Pharaoh's memos evoke stories, as stories always counter memos. They told stories of alternative possibility that arose from the hopefulness of their pained bodies. Indeed Psalm 136 is an inventory of their stories that affirm:

who alone does great wonders . . .
who struck Egypt through their firstborn . . .
and brought Israel out from among them . . .
with a strong hand and an outstretched arm . . .
who divided the Red Sea in two . . .
and gave them their land as a heritage. (Ps 136:4, 10-13, 21)

Each line in the psalm is a long story of alternative; each line, moreover, evoked a litany of gratitude, “for his *ḥesed* endures forever.” The stories are about fidelity that counters the ruthlessness of quota-imposing economics. Biblical faith is endlessly preoccupied with such stories that break the authority of memos. Stories are so potent because they focus on the particular not the universal, as do memos. All kinds of things are possible in stories that memos regard as impossible. Stories introduce characters and agents who act beyond the directives that are usually cast in passive voice.

Behind stories in ancient Israel, moreover, come poems. Before the exodus narrative is the song of Miriam who sang:

Sing to the lord, for he has triumphed gloriously;
horse and rider he has thrown into the sea. (Exod 15:21)

Behind the land seizure in the book of Joshua is the song of Deborah:

Tell of it, you who ride on white donkeys,
    you who sit on rich carpets
    and you who walk by the way.
To the sound of musicians at the watering places,
    there they repeat the triumphs of the LORD,
    the triumphs of his peasantry in Israel. (Judg 5:10-11)

Behind the story of monarchy is the poetry of Hannah:

The LORD kills and brings to life;
    he brings down to Sheol and raises up.
The LORD makes poor and makes rich;
    he brings low, he also exalts.
He raises up the poor from the dust,
    he lifts the needy from the ash heap,
to make them sit with princes . . .

The Lord . . . will give strength to his king,
    and exalt the power of his anointed. (1 Sam 2:7-8, 10)

Behind the story of Jesus is the song of Mary:

He has filled the hungry with good things,
    and sent the rich away empty. (Luke 1:53)

Behind the argument of Paul is the lyric of Philippians:

    he humbled himself
    and became obedient to the point of death . . .
    even death on a cross.
Therefore God has highly exalted him. (Phil 2:8-9b)

Poems, like the stories that reflect the poems, are so wonderful because they are sweeps of freedom in which reality is shifted and repositioned and reshaped by words. Poems (and stories that reflect poems) are capable of disjunction and contradiction and tension and surprise and hyperbole. They voice the saving possibilities of hope as Israel emotes beyond empire. They sound the cries of loss and distress that cut underneath the flaccid confidence of the memos. They take in the full range of emotive possibility that entertains change and hurt and hope and rage and justice.

The outcome of a poem uttered and remembered and uttered again is that the world is made

thick with subversive possibility;

conflicted because there is seething bodily sensibility that can never be fully nullified;

disclosing because they dare to voice reality as high as the sky, as wild as the ocean, and as deep as the earth.

No wonder the poets could say and sing in their prescientific doxology:

You stretch out the heavens like a tent,
    you set the beams of your chambers on the waters,
you make the clouds your chariot,
    you ride on the wings of the wind,
you make the winds your messengers,
    fire and flame your ministers.

> You set the earth on its foundations,
>   so that it shall never be shaken.
> You cover it with the deep as with a garment;
>   the waters stood above the mountains.
> At your rebuke they flee;
>   at the sound of your thunder they take to flight.
> They rose up to the mountains, ran down to the valleys
>   to the place that you appointed for them. (Ps 104:2b-8)

All the while the memo seeks to pull the sky down and tame the waters and order the earth for more production. The disclosure is that the world is not on its own nor is it ours; it is held and valued and watched over. The disclosure is that the covenant people are not abandoned to bondage and brick quotas because there is this one who sees and hears and knows and remembers.

The poem sings a place for human dignity, human worth, human freedom, and human responsibility. The narrative, unflinching in its cadence, declares that the human agent of worth, dignity, freedom, and responsibility is of frail clay and yet "in image." And so the poem breaks out:

> What is man? What is woman? (Ps 8:4)

It sings of dominion. The disclosure is an awareness that the human and the nonhuman creatures are cared for:

> The eyes of all look to you,
>   and you give them their food in due season.
> You open your hand,
>   satisfying the desire of every living thing. (Ps 145:15-16)

The poetry—thick, conflicted, disclosing—is poignantly subversive. It refuses the settled world of the memo. It defies kings and pharaohs and authorizes energy, courage, and freedom. It is no wonder that at Selma they sang as they marched. It is no surprise that the Apartheid regime in South Africa banned Christmas carols because the carols imagined an intrusive counterforce. It is no wonder that totalitarian regimes know that artists, most particularly poets, are a restless presence that exposes power as self-serving ideology that must not be trusted or obeyed.

There is, as a result, a deep tension in ancient Israel. There is the anxious Solomon imitating his anxious pharaonic father-in-law. And there is, right in downtown Jerusalem, the temple, inescapably a venue for artistry. There are the functionaries in the temple—or perhaps in the belated second temple—who collected and wrote and treasured poems and songs and produced the songbook of the psalms. Even while they are on the payroll of the memo-writing powers, they had these poems entrusted to them. So they sang, either remembering or anticipating Hannah:

> He raises the poor from the dust,
>   and lifts them from the ash heap,
> to make them sit with princes,
>   with the princes of his people. (Ps 113:7-8)

They sang of the coming divine king:

> Say among the nations, "The LORD is king!"
>   The world is firmly established; it shall never be moved.
>   He will judge the peoples with equity. (Ps 96:10)

They sang out the real king, the one with equity and righteousness and truth. Some, as always, thought it was lovely and did not notice. But some noticed. They noticed and they saw that the psalms are deeply subversive, for this is a coming real king whose rule will delegitimize all the memo-writing, power-craving kings of the moment.

I imagine that the Old Testament is this tense contest between *memo* and *poem*, between *list* and *story*, the same tension that O'Banion traces subsequently all around Descartes. The poem serve to recruit YHWH, the God of the covenant, who does wonders. The poem imagines that this God is allied with the world in covenantal ways. I take the trouble to engage us, yet again, in this contest, for the force of memo is so strong among us.[17] And the opening for poem is so small. And when we juxtapose *strong memo* and *small poem*, we may come to the failure of possibility, reduced to technical capacity, governed by anxiety that legitimates all kinds of violence for the sake of the status quo.

It was a little poetic mantra that offered a summons to Israel in the midst of the memo writers. The poetic mantra, apparently a popular saying, is twice repeated in the tradition. In 2 Samuel 20, Sheba, a Benjamite who represented the continuing challenge of Saul's company to the rule of David, issues a taunting challenge to David and his retinue. He is soon hunted down and killed. But our interest is in the initial summons he issues to his constituency in the north who tried to secede from David's kingdom. His summons is issued in three lines of poetry:

> "We have no portion in David,
> no share in the son of Jesse!
> Everyone to your tents, O Israel." (2 Sam 20:1)

The call is to reject Davidic power and authority, and Davidic memos, to evaporate into the peasant community symbolized by "tents" that contrast with royal "houses."[18] The summons is in poetry and is accompanied by a trumpet, that is, an emotional call to arms. The summons, suggesting an alternative ordering of public power, required risky public action.

In 1 Kings 12, Solomon's son, Rehoboam, seeks to consolidate his royal power at Solomon's death. He meets with the elders of the North, seeking to negotiate the terms of his governance. The controversy turns on tax policy. The young king rejects wise counsel and raises taxes. By the end of the meeting, the northern leadership has rejected Rehoboam and the Davidic dynasty and its tax-collecting apparatus in Jerusalem. It secedes from the United Monarchy. The answer they gave to Rehoboam is in poetry:

> "What share do we have in David?
>   We have no inheritance in the son of Jesse.
> To your tents, O Israel!
>   Look now to your own house, O David." (1 Kgs 12:16)

This is the same poetic utterance from the earlier Davidic crisis. Now a fourth defiant line has been added. Thus the mantra, in poetry, will have been a standard peasant cry of defiance and secession from a memo-writing, tax-collecting governance. Twice the formula is used, twice the memo-writing apparatus is diminished. Twice the poetry-chanting peasants entertain an alternative.

"To your tents" is a formula of secession. I have wondered what they did when they got to their tents. No doubt they organized a resistance movement in anticipation of a civil war. In the midst of organizing a resistance movement, however, I imagine that they also shared their angry grievances. I imagine that they generated new utterances of hope about alternative possibilities. I imagine that they said, "We will run risks in order that my sons will be better off than am I." They articulated their anger but also their hope, confident that the rescuing God of the peasants was allied with them. And they ran the risk of their poetry.

Or said another way, they hosted poetry. They remembered poetry. They created poetry. They lined out their life in rich imagery and in metaphor that had been prohibited by the prose managers of memes. They hoped and imagined that their hosting, remembering, and creating opened a zone of freedom that would not be reduced to the tax quotas or production quotas of the central power. And because they did poetry, they opened economic-political power to the dimension of the generative spirit of God, the one who blows open, raises up the poor, and sends the rich away empty.

IV

In the big house matters are always thin and clear and without ambiguity. But in the "tents" of the peasants, matters are thick with intrigue, possibility, and alternatives marked by conspiracy and playfulness. The communication of such alternatives requires emancipated practice.[19] They did not have a blueprint; they could not know. But they could imagine; they could dream; they could risk. They stood, in ancient Israel, in the poetic stream of Mother Miriam and Mother Hannah. They reiterated old stories . . . or made them up. They remembered how Joshua had recited poetry in order to borrow more daylight hours for a longer battle:

> "Sun, stand still at Gibeon,
>   and Moon, in the valley of Aijalon."
> And the sun stood still, and the moon stopped,
>   until the nation took vengeance on their enemies. (Josh 10:12b-13)

The remembered how Deborah recited Jael's murder of Sisera with his naive trust in her:

> "Most blessed of women be Jael,
>   the wife of Heber the Kenite,
>   of tent-dwelling woman most blessed.
> He asked water and she gave him milk.
>   she brought him curds in a lordly bowl.
> She put her hand to the tent peg
>   and her right hand to the workmen's mallet;

she struck Sisera a blow,
she crushed his head,
she shattered and pierced his temple." (Judg 5:24-26)

They relished the lines wherein the staggering death of the enemy was prolonged:

"He sank, he fell,
he lay still at her feet;
at her feet he sank, he fell,
where he sank, there he fell, dead. (Judg 5:27)

They had stories to tell of Gideon and of Samson:

> And what more should I say? For time would fail me to tell of Gideon, Barak, Samson, Jephthath, of David and Solomon, and the prophets—who through faith conquered kingdoms, administered justice, obtained promises, shut the mouths of lions, quenched raging fires, escaped the edge of the sword, won strength out of weakness, became mighty in war, put foreign armies to flight. (Heb 11:32-34)

Even as they remembered and created and recited and chanted, no doubt some Cartesian expert wrote to ask them if this were really true and could it be validated. But they did not pause to answer such a memo or even to consider the question because they were fully occupied, generating an alternative world outside the zone of the urban elite. So they danced and refused to submit.[20] And their poetry rang true!

V

Now I tell you this, so that you can imagine with me the appearance of the prophets who embody a counterhistory, counter to the memo-writing force of established power. The prophets are not, as conservatives might have it, predictors. They are not, as liberals might have it, social activists. They are poets. They poetize social reality, letting it disclose what the world is like when YHWH is voiced as an agent and a character at the center of the process. Their poetry offers and permits a presence that has been squeezed out of all the tightly drawn memos. And when this character and agent appears on their poetry-spouting lips, everything is different. The poetry is unrestrained by the thinness of Descartes or by Solomon or Pharaoh or Herod or Caesar. Because it comes from the "tents." So imagine tents that yield alternative texts. I shall propose, in what follows, that there is weighty continuity between the poetry of the prophets and the poetry generated in the tents of those who have withdrawn from the memo-writing regime of David.[21]

I

The prophets—from the neighborhood around the tents—offer *poetry of loss*. Everywhere there was loss, palpable and unavoidable. The prophetic task is to situate that loss in a covenantal context so that it can be understood coherently. They bring the loss to speech. I will cite three representative utterances of loss:

1. There is *profound loss*, and that loss in a society of deep denial. Jeremiah, master of the lament, brings the loss to utterance. The loss may be invasion or drought; either way, the poetry will cover:

> Take up weeping and wailing for the mountains,
>   and a lamentation for the pasture of the wilderness,
> because they are laid waste so that no one passes through,
>   and the lowing of cattle is not heard;
> both the birds of the air and animals
>   have fled and are gone.
> I will make Jerusalem a heap of ruins,
>   a lair of jackals;
> and I will make the towns of Judah a desolation,
>   without inhabitant. (Jer 9:10-11)

The loss requires grieving, so the poet imagines a funeral:

> Consider, and call for the mourning women to come;
>   send for the skilled women to come;
> let them quickly raise a dirge over us,
>   so that our eyes may run down with tears,
>   and our eyelids flow with water.
> For a sound of wailing is heard from Zion:
>   "How we are ruined!
>   We are utterly shamed,
> because we have left the land,
>   because they have cast down our dwellings." (Jer 9:17-19)

Death, a palpable force visible in courageous imagination, is everywhere, in the thick of war, of course, in the city slums, in teenage suicides, among the poor who cannot live, with the birds on the oil-spoiled coast. The poet invites the "casserole brigade," the professional mourners, and all who know how to grieve:

> Hear, O women, the word of the LORD,
> and let your ears receive the word of his mouth;
> teach to our daughters a dirge
> and each to her neighbor a lament. (v. 20)

And here is the dirge to be offered over the land that is dying:

> "Death has come up into our windows,
> it has entered our palaces,
> to cut off the children from the streets
> and the young men from the squares."
> . . . "Human corpses shall fall
> like dung upon the open field,
> like sheaves behind the reaper,
> and no one shall gather them." (vv. 21-22)

The poem sounds like yesterday's newspaper! Except that it is open enough to permit each listener to focus upon the funeral of her choice, death upon death, failure upon failure, loss upon loss, like dung heaped up, and no one to pay attention.

2. The loss compels *moral reflection and entertains culpability.* The big prophetic word is *ergo*, "therefore." The word permits poets to connect what is otherwise beyond connection. The loss is massive, a drought that dissipates all of creation:

> Therefore, the land mourns,
> and all who live in it languish;
> together with the wild animals
> and the birds of the air,
> even the fish of the sea are perishing. (Hos 4:3)

But that outcome is not causeless. There is a cause for the disaster; it is Israel's conduct:

There is no faithfulness or loyalty,
and no knowledge of God in the land.
Swearing, lying, and murder,
and stealing and adultery break out;
bloodshed follows bloodshed. (Hos 4:1b-2)

Israel is a commandment breaker! All ten of them! And between the outcome of deathly drought and the cause of disobedience, the poet places an *ergo*. The poetry connects sideways what cannot be connected rationally. Who would think that disobedience would cause acute drought? Certainly no memo writer. But behind all memos is the poetry that attests to the creator who brings a suit against Israel (Hos 4:1). Now loss takes on culpability; grief is seasoned by guilt. The world remains sensible; but the sense depends on this elemental guarantor who guarantees what Israel can never escape.

3. In the oracle of Hosea there is cause and effect, deed and consequence; but not yet *an active agent*. That agent, however, appears in Jeremiah 4:23-26. The loss to be uttered is loss of world, demise of creation, failure of reliable order. It sounds like this:

I looked on the earth, and lo, it was waste and void;
and to the heavens, and they had no light.
I looked on the mountains, and lo, they were quaking,
and all the hills moved to and fro.
I looked, and lo, there was no one at all,
and all the birds of the air had fled.
I looked, and lo, the fruitful land was a desert,
and all its cities were laid in ruins. (4:23-26)

The poet reads Genesis 1 backward. But Genesis 1 is itself a great poem. And now the remembered poem is unraveled by this newly uttered poem. The poet turns out the lights, banishes the birds, and rocks the mountains into chaos. And then this:

. . . before the LORD, before his fierce anger. (v. 26)

Before . . . before . . . before divine anger. This is a God who will not be mocked. It turns out, in this utterance, that God's self-regard is even greater than God's love of creation. And now it is gone! This is, as we sing, "my father's world." God does indeed have the whole world in

God's hands! And those hands, in the way of this poem, turn into crushing fists.

Thus we have:

an imagined funeral with professional grievers;

the *ergo* that connects to judgment;

a poem rereading an old poem, one that now leaves us in the dark.

It is all poetry. It is not a memo about divine wrath or judgment. It is simply unauthorized poetry; the listener decides what to take of it, perhaps *grief*, perhaps *guilt*, perhaps *divine rage*. The poetry pushes the limits of the thinkable in old denying Jerusalem. Jerusalem counts on divine forbearance. Jerusalem expects a quick return to normalcy. Jerusalem trusted old promises made to David. And now poetry interrupts the narcotic and announces the day they never thought would arrive:

For the LORD of hosts has a day
    against all that is proud and lofty,
    against all that is lifted up and high;
against all the cedars of Lebanon,
    lofty and lifted up;
    and against all the oaks of Bashan;
against all the high mountains,
    and against all the lofty hills;
against every high tower,
    and against every fortified wall;
against all the ships of Tarshish,
    and against all the beautiful craft.
The haughtiness of the people shall be humbled,
    and the pride of everyone shall be brought low;
    and the LORD alone will be exalted on that day. (Isa 2:12-17)

That day will be a day of wrath,
    a day of distress and anguish,
a day of ruin and devastation,
    a day of darkness and gloom,
a day of clouds and thick darkness,
    a day of trumpet blast and battle cry
against the fortified cities
    and against the lofty battlements. (Zeph 1:15-16)

Such poetry could never arise in the big house. Such words are given to those who have fled to the tents.

The wonder of this poetry is that it is transferable. It is to be reuttered and reheard in many contexts, and always with the cadences of *grief, guilt*, and *divine wrath*. Thus the undoing of creation may sound like an oil spill; the grief will crackle like a full, burning school bus. The loss is linked to disobedience, and oddly, to holiness. And the truth is told!

II

The prophets—from the neighborhood around the tents—utter *poetry of possibility*, the future as gift. They are not bound to the facts on the ground . . . the smell of smoldering Jerusalem, or the discomfort of Babylon, or the failed economy, or the endless savagery of war. There is, on these daring lips, a future beyond these intractable facts, a future grounded in divine resolve that sounds, in the poetry, undefeated. It is as though the poetic text explodes with "I have a dream." The dream does not belong to Martin, though he said it well, nor to Isaiah who said it before Martin. The dream belongs to the creator God who intends more than we know, beyond all that we can ask or imagine.

1. There is the poetry of *a new day* beyond this unbearable day. The sun will set on this day; but the sun will rise on a new day as a gift from God:

> I will make for you a covenant *on that day* with the wild animals, the birds of the air, and the creeping things of the ground; I will abolish the bow, the sword, and war from the land; and I will make you lie down in safety . . .
> *On that day*, I will answer, says the LORD,
> I will answer the heavens
> and they shall answer the earth;
> and the earth shall answer the grain, the wine, and the oil.
> (Hos 2:18, 21-22)

> *On that day* it shall be said to Jerusalem,
> Do not fear, O Zion;
> do not let your hands grow weak.
> The LORD, your God, is in your midst,
> a warrior who gives victory. (Zeph 3:16-17)

It will be a day of well-being. It is promised by the God who is the governor of all our times, for "our times are in God's hands."

2. The poets find scores of ways to *utter newness* beyond defeat and despair. Remarkably, the great poems of new possibility were uttered, characteristically, in the abyss. The book of Isaiah opens with a disarmed economy:

> In the days to come . . .
> He shall judge between nations,
> and shall arbitrate for many peoples;
> they shall beat their swords into plowshares,
> and their spears into pruning hooks;
> nation shall not lift up sword against nation,
> neither shall they learn war any more. (Isa 2:2, 4)

That economy will emerge because God's shalom-generating Torah will be known in Jerusalem by the nations.

The book of Isaiah finishes with a transformed world, a new heaven, a new earth, a new Jerusalem . . . and a new Gaza, a new Baghdad, a new Kabul, a new Belfast, a new Newark, even a new Boston. It will be a city where there is no more infant mortality, no more foreclosures, no more hurting or destroying (Isa 65:17-25). Can you imagine such a poem? Can you imagine hearing such a poem? Can you imagine uttering such a poem? Can you imagine the God who generates such poetry?

3. The poets imagine and promise *renovated institutions*. So Ezekiel ponders the old failed temple that is deserted of God's holiness. And then he conjures a new temple where the Glory dwells in perpetuity. More than that, in the new temple to be given there is an altar signifying divine presence. And beneath that altar, there is a spring of water, "coming out of the south side." It is water that is fresh and life-giving. It keeps flowing:

> by Ezek 47:3, it is ankle-deep;
>
> by v. 4a, it is knee-deep;
>
> by v. 4b, it is waist-deep;
>
> by v. 5, it is too deep to cross, unless one swims.

That rising river—coming from the temple that bespeaks God's presence—flows out east from Jerusalem to the Arabah. It runs to "the sea of stagnant water," the Dead Sea, the sea of death and salt from which there is no exit. The fresh water flows in, and the sea will become fresh:

> Wherever the river goes, every living creature that swarms will live, and there will be very many fish, once the waters reach there. It will become fresh; and everything will live where the river goes. People will stand fishing beside the sea from Engedi to Eneglaim; it will be a place for the spreading of nets; its fish will be of a great many kinds, like the fish of the Great Sea. (Ezek 47:9-10)

This is a vision for an arid climate. Imagine waters flowing out! We are meant to recall the four rivers that flow out of Eden to water the earth (Gen 2:10-14). This is new creation; now the life-giving waters come from God's own presence.

It is only a poem. But alas, we have no other way to break the power of memo. The memo says there is not enough water, so we must fight. Georgia, Florida, and Alabama keep fighting over the waters of the Chattahoochee. That war is conducted by memo, with no new thinking, no new possibility, no imagined gift that transforms. And then come poems of gift, no explanations any more than Martin could have "explained" the dream. But covenanted people do not live by status quo memos. They live from gifts that are given in utterance. Always again, like the people clustered around Martin with his dream, such folk find ways to "overcome."

> Thus there are *poems of loss*, construed as divine judgment;
> There are *poems of possibility*, the future construed as divine gift.

The poems process loss in God's presence; the poems evoke future as God's gift. The prophets take on the deep subjects of *loss* and *gift*, the great defining realities of the human spirit. How else to say *loss*, but in poem? How else to say *gift*, but in poem? In the memo there are *no losses*, only management and more quotas. In the memo there are *no gifts*, only commodities. But life without prophetic utterance remains in the safe middle ground, away from the sinking reality of *loss*, away from the soaring lift of *gift*. No wonder it is always again, "To your tents, O Israel," there to make another poem.

VI

I finish by thinking with you about "a poetry-hosting culture." We live in a memo-writing culture. The memos show up:

in the technical reason of corporations, governments, and media that refuse serious human questions;

in the psycho-babble of self-help culture that lacks depth about the intractable;

in the reduction, in market ideology, of persons to commodities;

in didactic moralism that aims at control;

in church "orthodoxy" that reduces creeds to tests;

in the ideologies of the Right that lack self-criticism;

in the ideologies of the Left that assume it is all up to us;

in techno-speech that lacks agency and utilizes the passive voice.

The list (see O'Banion!) may be longer, but that is enough to point to the idolatries by which we organize our common life, as we are inured to idols that have no power to save.

In the midst of that social reality is the church—sometimes allied with the artistic community, sometimes even with the academy—but finally the church. The church lives by stories that we love to tell, the old, old stories that become the new, new songs. And behind the stories are the poems that dive deep and soar high:

Thus, what pastor among us, standing at a graveside, has not recited the lyrical Romans 8?

> For I am convinced that neither death, nor life, nor angels, nor rulers, nor things present, nor things to come, nor powers, nor height, nor depth, nor anything else in all creation will be able to separate us from the love of God in Christ Jesus our Lord? (vv. 38-39)

Paul is "convinced," and we are convinced in his wake. This is not a memo about life after death. It is a poem that resituates our life in the life of God, just when our life short of God has run out, daily and finally.

Thus the church rises to "say what we believe." We say out loud these poetic phrases, "God from God, Light from Light, true God from true God, begotten not made"; we take a deep breath and watch as the rhetoric comes down from heaven to earth where we are, and we say, "and was made man." The chill-bumps of poetry surge over us. We do not know what we have said; but we will not live without saying it out loud regularly in each other's presence.

Thus the church, for the most part, refuses the thin monosyllables of so-called praise hymns and insists upon something thicker to speak the thickness of our life with God. We imagine heaven and earth mobilized in doxology together:

> Ye watchers and ye holy ones,
> Bright seraphs, cherubim, and thrones,
> Raise the glad strain, alleluia!
> Cry out, dominions, princedoms, powers,
> Virtues, archangels, angels' choirs, Alleluia!
> Respond, ye souls in endless rest,
> Ye patriarchs and prophets blest, Alleluia,
> Ye holy twelve, ye martyrs strong,
> All saints triumphant raise the song, Alleluia![22]

We sing about a love beyond our love, and live in hope of a "strong finish" in "wonder, love, and praise":

> Love divine, all loves excelling, joy of heaven to earth come down,
> Fix in us thy humble dwelling, all our faithful mercies crown!
> Jesus, you are all compassion; pure, unbounded love thou art,
> Visit us with your salvation, enter every trembling heart . . .
> Finish, then, thy new creation; pure and spotless let us be;
> Let us see your great salvation perfectly restored in thee;
> Changed from glory into glory, till in heaven we take our place,
> Till we cast our crowns before thee, lost in wonder, love, and praise.[23]

We imagine the ultimate end of our lives and know it to be lost amid the reality of God. We watch for the gift of a new day from the creator:

> Morning has broken like the first morning,
> Blackbird has spoken like the first bird.
> Praise for the singing! Praise for the morning!
> Praise for the springing fresh from the word![24]

> And on and on, beyond us, bringing ourselves, wounded, hope-filled, mixes of denial and despair, but acting toward a truth we can scarcely name.

The church meets; it has cadences that memo writers think are foolish—a little bread, a little wine, a little water, a little oil, and a towel—signs and the realities that these signs represent, and the world pulses with grace. The church, in its poetic cadences, is intrinsically subversive. It reminds us, always again, that our reason, our control, and our power are penultimate; we had best not stake our lives on knowledge, power, or control, or any such false god. The poem places the memo in jeopardy, and we have another chance. Too bad the church regularly fails its own offer of Poetry 101 and settles for memos of piety or doctrine or morality or liturgy or social action. Too bad because the poetry sounds a more excellent way.

So I finish:

> I have not wanted to accent over much, just the play of words or the management of images;
>
> I have not wanted to make a facile contrast between priestly order and prophetic requirement.

I have, rather, been guided by the defining word pair of Emmanuel Levinas, "Totality and Infinity."[25] By "totality" Levinas means totalizing explanations that move toward totalitarianism. By "infinity" Levinas means an openness that is seen especially in the face of the neighbor that is beyond our control or decipherment, an expansiveness always capable of one more surprise for us. I have taken open, imaginative utterance, the kind practiced by the prophets, as a way of speaking of loss and grief . . . and absence . . . gift and miracle and wonder and possibility, all dimensions of the truth that power is from "elsewhere" and not of our conjuring. In the end, Levinas' "Totality and Infinity" is a parallel to the "List and Story" of O'Banion. In our time and place, the capacity of the church to host poetry matters enormously. The ancient kings in Israel tried to silence and banish those poets, to their great demise. Such poetry, now as then, is a surging of life amid a culture of memos that is bent on self-destruction. The news is that "otherwise" is on offer, mediated, broken, blessed, and given among us. More than that, it may be shared with a world where fear competes with possibility.

5

BIBLICAL LANGUAGE

In what follows I consider the vexed and long-standing contestation between the *covenantal-dialogical rhetoric* of the Bible and the alternative of *Cartesian-modernist rhetoric* that is everywhere around us. That contestation, so it seems to me, now has peculiar urgency among us. My current interest in this subject is triggered, most immediately and quite practically, by the bewildered comment of a "progressive" Protestant lay person who said, in innocence, "Since none of us believe all this YHWH stuff, what are we to do with the Bible?" My interest, consequently, is a quite practical one as well because there can hardly be any doubt that the rhetoric we employ yields the world in which we live. Or as Paul Ricoeur has programmatically stated, "Symbol gives rise to thought."[1] Or to paraphrase, the way we imagine (and so utter) is the way we will live. While the problem of what someone who is shaped by Cartesian-modernist rhetoric is to do with covenantal-dialogic rhetoric may be peculiarly and currently acute in progressive (liberal) Protestantism, I submit that it is a deep issue finally for Jewish and Christian faith and more broadly for our society, precisely because the rhetoric we utilize will generate the world that is available and compelling to us.

I will develop my argument in four moves. First, in an extended section I will consider how the language of "Thou" permeates the text of Israel, without which Israel cannot say what it wants to say. Second, I will consider the interruption of that rhetoric by the alternative rhetoric of modern Enlightenment reason. Third, I will consider the ways in which modern reason and rhetoric have bequeathed to us a certain kind of anxiety-ridden world; finally I will reflect on the task of the recovery of "Thou" language and what is at stake in that recovery.

I

There is no doubt that the Bible is deeply and resolutely committed to personal/interpersonal language that Martin Buber has characterized as "I-Thou."[2]

1. Thus YHWH, the creator of heaven and earth and the deliverer of Israel, is addressed as "thou" and is credited with being a lively character who has the undoubted capacity for decisive agency.

On the one hand, YHWH is the "You" of Israel's hymns of praise and songs of thanksgiving. As Claus Westermann has shown, many such songs are "descriptive" of God in the third person and speak of God's actions and attributes.[3] But more visceral are the "declarative" songs that address God directly:

> I love you, O LORD, my strength. (Ps 18:1)

> I will extol you, O LORD, for you have drawn me up,
> and did not let my foes rejoice over me.
> O LORD my God, I cried to you for help,
> and you healed me.
> O LORD, you brought up my soul from Sheol,
> restored me to life from among those who had gone down to the Pit . . .
> You have turned my mourning into dancing;
> you have taken off my sackcloth and clothed me with joy.
> (Ps 30:1-3, 11)

> For you, O God, have tested us;
> you have tried us as silver is tried.
> You have brought us into the net;
> you have laid burdens on our backs;
> you let people ride over our heads;
> we went through fire and through water;
> yet you have brought us out to a spacious place. (Ps 66:10-12)

> But you, O LORD, are enthroned forever;
> your name endures to all generations.
> You will rise up and have compassion for Zion,
> for it is time to favor it.
> the appointed time has come. (Ps 102:12-13)

And even descriptive psalms that speak of YHWH in the third person credit YHWH with decisive agency:

> The LORD upholds all who are falling,
> and raises up all who are bowed down.
> The eyes of all look to you,
> and you give them their food in due season.
> You open your hand,
> satisfying the desire of every living thing.
> The LORD is just in all his ways,
> and kind in all his doings.
> The LORD is near to all who call on him,
> to all who call on him in truth.
> He fulfills the desire of all who fear him;
> he also hears their cry, and saves them.
> The LORD watches over all who love him.
> but all the wicked he will destroy. (Ps 145:14-20; see Ps 146:7-9)

Thanks tends to be more specific than praise, and therefore the intimate address of "you" seems natural and appropriate:

> See, I have not restrained my lips, as you know, O LORD.
> I have not hidden your saving help within my heart,
> I have spoken of your faithfulness and your salvation;
> I have not concealed your steadfast love and your faithfulness
> from the great congregation. (Ps 40:9b-10)

> I give thanks to you, O LORD, with my whole heart;
> before the gods I sing your praise;
> I bow down toward your holy temple
> and give thanks to your name for your steadfast love and your faithfulness,
> for you have exalted your name and your word
> above everything.
> On the day I called, you answered me,
> you increased my strength of soul.
> All the kings of the earth shall praise you, O LORD,
> for they have heard the words of your mouth. (Ps 138:1-4)

The praise and thanks of Israel constitute speech acts whereby Israel gladly cedes itself over to God in wonder (as in praise) and in gratitude (as in thanks). These self-transcending and self-yielding acts are clearly evoked by and aimed toward a remarkable character who has both a narrative past and a promised future with Israel.

On the other hand, the "thou" language of Israel is even more direct and intense in Israel's poetry of lament, complaint, and protest. The second-person pronoun figures large in Israel's accusations against God; for the simple language of prayer does not linger over secondary causes but readily attributes trouble to God as the primary cause. Perhaps most familiar and famous is the "unredeemed" speech of Psalm 88:

> You have put me in the depths of the Pit,
> in the regions dark and deep.
> Your wrath lies heavy upon me,
> and you overwhelm me with all your waves.
> You have caused my companions to shun me;
> you have made me a thing of horror to them.
> I am shut in so that I cannot escape . . .
> O Lord, why do you cast me off?
> Why do you hide your face from me?
> Wretched and close to death from my youth up,
> I suffer your terrors; I am desperate.
> Your wrath has swept over me;
> your dread assaults destroy me.
> They surround me like a flood all day long;
> from all sides they close in on me.
> You have caused friend and neighbor to shun me;
> my companions are in darkness. (88:6-8, 14-18)

And of course the petitionary summons to God that God should respond and intervene are in the imperative of the second person. Israel exhibits stunning courage in addressing God in imperatives, a mode of speech that I characterize as a provisional role reversal in which Israel seeks to command Yhwh, a role reversal that in its urgency is commensurate with the speaker's dire straits:

> Rise up, O Lord! Deliver me, O my God! (Ps 3:7)

> O Lord, do not rebuke me in your anger,
> or discipline me in your wrath.

> Be gracious to me, O LORD, for I am languishing;
> O LORD, heal me, for my bones are shaking with terror.
> My soul also is struck with terror,
> while you, O LORD—how long?
> Turn, O LORD, save my life;
> deliver me for the sake of your steadfast love.
> For in death there is no remembrance of you;
> in Sheol who can give you praise? (Ps 6:1-5)

> O LORD, my God, in you I take refuge;
> save me form all my pursuers, and deliver me . . .
> Rise up, O LORD, in your anger;
> lift yourself up against the fury of my enemies;
> awake, O my God; you have appointed a judgment. (Ps 7:1, 6)

> For you have maintained my just cause;
> you have sat on the throne giving righteous judgment.
> You have rebuked the nations, you have destroyed the wicked;
> you have blotted out their names forever and ever.
> The enemies have vanished in everlasting ruins;
> their cities you have rooted out;
> the very memory of them has perished . . .
> Rise up, O LORD! Do not let mortals prevail;
> let the nations be judged before you. (Ps 9:4-6, 19)

> Rise up, O LORD; O God, lift up your hand;
> do not forget the oppressed. (Ps 10:12)

> Contend, O LORD, with those who contend with me;
> fight against those who fight against me!
> Take hold of shield and buckler,
> and rise up to help me!
> Draw the spear and javelin
> against my pursuers;
> say to my soul,
> "I am your salvation." (Ps 35:1-3)

The examples of this mode of prayer are nearly limitless. They voice an intensity, a connectedness, and a leverage that are possible only in the direct address of dialogic speech. Thus all the way from exuberant praise through aggressive imperative to energetic gratitude, all the way from praise through lament to thanks, Israel addressed God in intensely personal terms and could do so in no other terms.

2. More than that, the "Thou" of God can speak as an "I," a practice of self-announcement, self-resolve, and agency. While such divine articulation is, perforce, mediated through human rendering, the rhetoric itself is recurringly direct and without any footnotes that qualify by acknowledging human mediation. YHWH is a robust defining character in the rhetoric and imagination of Israel.

God is self-affirming and self-celebrating in self-praise. God unembarrassedly offers self-doxology in which YHWH struts before the nations and before the other gods.

> When the poor and needy seek water,
> and there is none,
> and their tongue is parched with thirst,
> I the LORD will answer them,
> I the God of Israel will not forsake them.
> I will open rivers in the bare heights,
> and fountains in the midst of the valleys;
> I will make the wilderness a pool of water
> and the dry land springs of water.
> I will put in the wilderness the cedar,
> the acacia, the myrtle, and the olive;
> I will set in the desert the cypress,
> the plane and the pine together,
> so that all may see and know,
> all may consider and understand,
> that the hand of the LORD has done this,
> the Holy One of Israel has created it. (Isa 41:17-20)

> I, I am the LORD,
> and besides me there is no savior.
> I declared and saved and proclaimed,
> when there was no strange god among you;
> and you are my witnesses, says the LORD.
> I am God, and also henceforth I am He;
> there is no one who can deliver from my hand;
> I work and who can hinder it? (Isa 43:11-13)

I am the LORD, who made all things,
who alone stretched out the heavens,
who by myself spread out the earth . . .
who says of Jerusalem, "It shall be inhabited,"
and of the cities of Judah, "They shall be rebuilt . . . "
(Isa 44:24b-26)

My purpose shall stand
and I will fulfill my intention,
calling a bird of prey from the east,
the man for my purpose from a far country.
I have spoken, and I will bring it to pass;
I have planned it, and I will do it. (Isa 46:10b-11)

This is indeed a Magnificat through which God magnifies God's own self. The "I" utterances are not only world-defining but also world-disrupting. The divine utterance dramatically changes everything for Israel, who hears the doxology.

God's capacity for self-praise has a counterpoint in God's impatience and irritation with all that does not conform to YHWH's self-celebrating governance. Thus the "I" of YHWH resounds in oracles of judgment wherein God resolves to take action to reclaim governance where it has been diminished or disregarded. Thus in the exodus narrative,

> I will gain glory for myself over Pharaoh and his army, and the Egyptians will know that I am the LORD. (Exod 14:4, 17)

The niph'al form of the verb (*kbd*) serves well that the God who self-declares effectively acts. Prophetic utterance exhibits YHWH in direct intervention:

Therefore I will take back
my grain in its time,
and my wine in its season;
and I will take away my wool and my flax,
which were to cover her nakedness.
Now I will cover her shame
in the sight of her lovers,
and none shall rescue her out of my hand.
I will put an end to all her mirth,

her festivals, her new moons, her sabbaths,
and all her appointed festivals.
I will lay waste her vines and her fig trees,
of which she said,
"These are my pay
which my lovers have given me."
I will make a forest,
and the wild animals shall devour them.
I will punish her for the festival days of the Baals. (Hos 2:9-13a)

Or in the catalogue of curses in Amos:

I gave you cleanness of teeth . . .
And I also withheld the rain from you . . .
I struck you with blight and mildew;
I laid waste your gardens and your vineyards . . .
I sent among you a pestilence after the manner of Egypt;
I killed your young men with the sword;
I carried away your horses;
and I made the stench of your camp go up into your nostrils . . .
I overthrew some of you
as when God overthrew Sodom and Gomorrah.
(Amos 4:6-11; see Amos 8:9-10; Jer 5:14-17)

In the cadences of Jeremiah 51:20-23, the "with you" suggests a mediating agency, but the rhetoric is dominated by the divine "I":

. . . with you I smash nations,
with you I destroy kingdoms,
with you I smash the horse and its rider;
with you I smash the chariot and the charioteer;
with you I smash man and woman;
with you I smash the old man and the boy;
with you I smash the young man and the girl;
with you I smash shepherds and their flocks;
with you I smash farmers and their teams;
with you I smash governors and deputies. (51:20-23)

And perhaps the most extreme self-resolve:

> I will stop you from playing the whore, and you shall also make no more payments. So I will satisfy my fury on you, and my jealousy shall turn away from you; I will be calm, and will be angry no longer.
> (Ezek 16:41-42)

Remarkably the divine "I" of self-praise and of judgment is capable of a reversal of field. The "I" pledges itself to a promise-filled future wrought only by the generosity of divine resolve through the processing of divine pathos:

> How can I give you up, Ephraim?
> How can I hand you over, O Israel? . . .
> My heart recoils within me;
> my compassion grows warm and tender.
> I will not execute my fierce anger;
> I will not again destroy Ephraim;
> for I am God and no mortal,
> the Holy One in your midst,
> and I will not come in wrath. (Hos 11:8-9)

> Is Ephraim my dear son?
> Is he the child I delight in?
> As often as I speak against him,
> I still remember him.
> Therefore I am deeply moved for him;
> I will surely have mercy on him, says the LORD. (Jer 31:20)

It is on this basis of a complex interior life that the divine "I" resolves to restore Israel fully and to revivify creation, which has been defeated and lost through divine anger:

> I will seek the lost, and I will bring back the strayed, and I will bind up the injured, and I will strengthen the weak, but the fat and the strong I will destroy. I will feed them with justice. (Ezek 34:16)

> I will save you from all your uncleannesses, and I will summon the grain and make it abundant and lay no famine on you. I will make the fruit of the tree and the produce of the field abundant, so that you may never again suffer the disgrace of famine among the nations.
> (Ezek 36:29)

> I am going to open your graves, O my people; and I will bring you back to the land of Israel. . . . I will place you on your own soil; then you shall know that I the LORD have spoken and will act, says the LORD.
> (Ezek 37:12-14)

In every dimension, the self-declaration of YHWH in a first-person pronoun matches the second person address of Israel who does not doubt the reality of the connection. Thus Israel can discern in its life the making, the unmaking, and the remaking of all reality by the agency of YHWH. Its rhetoric exhibits an awareness that every facet of this drama of death and life is wrought through an agency other than its own. It is, perhaps, not so difficult to acknowledge the limited capacity of human agency, but it is an act of immense chutzpah of the highest order to dare to give name and voice to the character of freedom and fidelity on which everything depends. There are, to be sure as Fretheim observes, many cautions and qualifications in the text to such voicing of divine agency, but the sum of the rhetoric is clear on the point.

The outcome of such sustained rhetoric is that the world is rendered in a dialogic way in which the self-announcement of Israel is matched and overmatched by the self-announcement of God. Faith is the capacity and readiness to participate fully and confidently in that ongoing exchange, an exchange that has become the substance of memory and of hope, and of buoyancy in the present. That ongoing exchange, moreover, is a bilateral practice of fidelity, and of freedom that can take the form of infidelity. Both parties are, in such rhetoric, pledged in fidelity; and amid the vagaries of history both parties become subject to critique for fidelity violated. On the one hand, Israel can, in its nadir of displacement, rally in this way:

> The steadfast love of the LORD never ceases,
> his mercies never come to an end;
> they are new every morning;
> great is your faithfulness. (Lam 3:22-23)

In that same crisis, on the other hand, Israel can in bewilderment wonder:

> Lord, where is your steadfast love of old,
> which by your faithfulness you swore to David? (Ps 89:49)

The "I" of Israel addresses the "Thou" of YHWH and the "I" of YHWH addresses the "Thou" of Israel; that mutual address yields risk and gift and loss and always lively engagement. In the depth of the crisis of fidelity, YHWH can both admit and reassure. The divine admission consists in the first two lines of the double verse:

> For a brief moment I abandoned you . . .
> In overflowing wrath for a moment
> I hid my face from you. (Isa 54:7-8a)

The reassurance comes in the two lines folded in with these:

> but with great compassion I will gather you . . . (v. 7b)
> but with everlasting love I will have compassion on you,
> says the LORD, your Redeemer. (v. 8b)

Even though divine wrath "overflows," the steadfast love outruns it in its everlasting durability. To be a faithful participant in the covenantal-dialogical relationship, each party must be willing to subject the other and to be subject themselves to charges of fidelity and infidelity. A faithfulness that is inherently open to infidelity is necessary not only because each party has the freedom to violate the terms that define fidelity but also because the terms that define fidelity remain open to transformation, either by the vagaries of history or the freedom of each party. When Israel calls on God to show God's faithfulness once again to them in exile, their petition is undoubtedly for a different faithful act than it was when they petitioned God for faithfulness during the monarchic period. This dialogic engagement is the primary speech of Israel and of the God of Israel. It has become, in due course, the primary speech of the church, divine speech that the church says came to be "enfleshed."

II

There is no doubt, moreover, that what is modeled as divine "Thou" language in the psalms and as divine "I" speech in prophetic oracles persists in Israel's narratives and historiography. Consequently YHWH is portrayed in Israel as a lively character and effective agent in the historical process, capable of emancipation and emancipatory action and not subject to the rulers or the rules of the day. In the rhetoric of Israel, this is a God who acts in transformative ways.

I have taken so much time with so many texts in order to underscore the way in which this dialogic rhetoric is characteristic and defining for the imagination of Israel and so for the practice of its life.[4] I have taken so long with so many texts in order to focus on the fact that in the modern Western world, the credibility and effectiveness of this dialogic rhetoric has been seriously interrupted and disrupted. That interruption/disruption has occurred with the rise of modern rationality that was, in some sense perhaps, a response to the sectarian failure of European Christian theology in the seventeenth century with its quest for an alternative rhetoric and an alternative practice of faith and reason.[5] In that axial moment in Western history, the explorations of Descartes and the genius of Newton converged to produce a world that was mathematically exacting, that was universal in its credibility, and that made the world ordered and predictable in a mechanical way.[6] That ordering, which functioned to produce manageable knowledge of the world, served the expansionist propensity of the European powers in the pursuit of economic domination through exploration and colonization.

Another consequence of such rationality was that the dialogic logic of faith, Jewish and/or Christian, was judged to be primitive and prerational, a logic that could yield only a world of superstition.[7] Thus modern rationality produced, instead of such superstition, a generic mode of "religion" in its quest for universal truth and, as James Buckley has shown, out of such generic universal categories Christian faith was to be defended in the early modern period in distinctly non-Christian categories, that is, according to the closest reasoning that conformed to the mathematical requirements of Cartesian, Newtonian reason. From such a perspective the practice of dialogic language seems irrelevant and foolish. Such speech constitutes the rhetoric of (in)fidelity that issues in daring freedom for which modernist categories cannot account since it violates what is presented as a symmetrical, inviolable, "universal order." That perspective has no patience for fidelity or the risk of infidelity, since it allows for everything to be safely reduced to reasonableness that could yield certitude. I deliberately interface and contrast fidelity and certitude. Because of a confusion of categories, the hunger for fidelity is often mistaken for a quest for certitude. That confusion leads to the seeking for a relational reality by reducing it to a cognitive claim, a reduction that misleads and distorts, and fails to satisfy.[8]

The result of this disruption as concerns Scripture study was deep and all-inclusive. It resulted in a history-of-religions approach, so that all faith articulations, including that of dialogic practice, came to be seen as nothing more than human imagination and human projection. Resistance to such *historical relativism* in turn evoked *absolutist propositional language* that eventually became fundamentalist. Such scholastic absolutism was cast in the same rationalistic categories, so that both the relativists and the absolutists confirmed and adhered to the requirements of modern reason. The outcome was and continues to be antagonism between the philosophies of *eighteenth-century absolutists* and *nineteenth-century relativists* that we now label, respectively, as *fundamentalism* and *liberalism*.

That crisis in Scripture study was acknowledged only belatedly, notably in the remarkable, brief article of Langdon Gilkey in 1961 in which he spoke of "The Travail of Biblical Language."[9] Gilkey argued that biblical rhetoric about "the God who acts" struggles mightily to be intelligible. In his attempt to locate language that would adequately express universal and immanent meaning, Gilkey concluded that the language of "God who acts" is unintelligible. It is impossible to overstate the influence of Gilkey's article and his line of reasoning in the wake of the so-called Biblical Theology Movement with particular reference to the work of Gerhard von Rad and G. Ernest Wright.

It was not much noticed that Gilkey's argument, without acknowledgment or self-awareness on his part, simply took for granted that "intelligibility" meant and had to mean conformity to the Enlightenment rationality rooted in Descartes and Newton. That is, such mathematical predictability precluded any thought or speech about divine agency that could violate such order. Consequently the dialogic rhetoric of biblical faith turns out to be nonsense, that is, nonsense from the angle of modernity. Since the demise of the so-called Biblical Theology Movement, interpreters have worked overtime to find other ways of making credible the biblical rhetoric of I-Thou that offers YHWH as agent and character.

I suggest two extrapolations from this wholesale disruption. On the one hand, the "character of God" has been transposed from an active subject to a harmless object that is no more than an image, or an icon, or an idol that is completely without capacity for agency. The disposal of YHWH as agent echoes the cynical verdict reported by Zephaniah:

> The LORD will not do good,
>   nor will he do harm. (Zeph 1:12c)

This articulation of the irrelevance of God as object is echoed in the psalmic characterization of idols who cannot make any impact on their environment:

> Their idols are silver and gold,
>   the work of human hands.
> They have mouths, but do not speak;
>   eyes, but do not see.
> They have ears, but do not hear;
>   noses, but do not smell.
> They have hands, but do not feel;
>   feet, but do not walk;
>   they make no sound in their throats. (Ps 115:4-7)

And then in a shift from a Marxist heaven to a Marxist earth:

> Those who make them are like them;
>   so are all who trust in them. (v. 8)

That is, we become like that which we worship (see Jer 2:4; Hos 9:10). And if we worship flat objects, we become objects and not subjects in our own history. And of course, power "from above," divine or human, prefers us not to be subjects of our own history. The reference to "silver and gold," moreover, suggests the reduction of agency to commodity (Ps 115:5). In the modern world, that reduction that makes God impotent causes God to be banished from public domain and public relevance and consigned to the safety of interpersonal interactions, thus a major abandonment of the claims of biblical faith.

On the other hand, the vacuum left by the loss of dialogic rhetoric and consequently the loss of a "significant Other" has been occupied by the "turn to the subject." As a result the "I" of human agency takes up all the space and energy and yields an unfettered human freedom, unfettered in its exploitation of the environment (now no longer "creation") and the exploitation of human persons (now no longer "neighbor"). Modernist rationality has rendered impossible dialogic articulation and has led to a complete abdication of dialogic capacity, either before the coldness of absolute reality that is unbending, unengaging, and unresponsive, or before a complete conquest of reality by human ingenuity without answerability to anyone for anything. Either cold absoluteness or totalizing subjectivity leaves no possibility of mutual engagement of the kind that belongs to dialogic speech and life.[10]

III

This disruption of dialogic speech and faith has two practical outcomes that we may consider. On the one hand, the outcome of unfettered human freedom has led to an unrestrained and undisciplined human control and exploitation of all visible reality. If knowledge is power, as Bacon averred, then the pursuit of power is advanced by the remarkable capacity for knowledge appropriated in unfettered freedom, a knowledge enacted through limitless scientific imagination that is, in turn, generative of unlimited technological administration. The immediate and visible outcome of the loss of the dialogical is a technological rampage in the interest of control and an effort at self-sufficiency and self-security. Thus the continuing threat of nuclear damage (now from power plants as much as from bombs), the endless thirst for energy that produces such crises as the Gulf oil spill, and the onslaught of global warming that jeopardizes the health of creatureliness are not aberrations but are the playing out of the extremity of the human eagerness for technological control.[11] Zygmunt Bauman, moreover, has been able to argue, credibly, that even the Shoah in Germany, with its amazing technological capacity and organizational finesse, was not an aberration of evil in a civilized world but was in fact a part of the endgame of modernism.[12] Thus the capacity for human brutality, now visible on such a large scale, is a counterpoint to unbridled technology that can mobilize power for control at the cost of all things human. That mobilization, moreover, depends on an economic practice that is void of covenantal, dialogical restraint. The concentration of large wealth can manage the political process and render social, covenantal control over technology null and void.

I should add an important qualifier to this broadside against technological aggression. Clearly this is not to critique much of the current scientific enterprise, especially in the neurosciences and the life sciences that are alert to the plasticity of the natural world and that ponder the ways in which that world is wired and rewired. An important distinction must be made between thin technological positivism that lacks self-criticism and scientific ventures that are open to the surprise and wonder of the natural world in which new gifts emerge beyond our flattened expectations. My impression is that such flat positivism more likely grips those who quest for certitude than those who attend to the complex and generative reality of the world that is in front of us.

On the other hand, the crisis of technological reductionism is matched by a theological obtuseness that has in concrete ways reduced faith to modernist rationality. That reductionism is evident of course in fundamentalist circles that blithely sign on for the technological-capitalist engine of totalism. But more important, in my judgment, is the fact that theological "progressives" shiver in aversion to "an interventionist God" who may speak and act freely to upset the carefully arranged orderliness of a world under safe management. Such "progressives" cannot entertain the thought of a God who is free or faithful or sovereign enough to assert purpose in the real world. It is impossible in such a purview to imagine a dialogical, covenantal exchange in which there really is a voice and an agency on the other side other than our own. The practical outcome of such theological reductionism is to downsize the mystery of God to modernist proportions so that there is no meaningful theological dimension to human discernment or practice. There is then in fact nothing left to say that might critique, restrain, or summon the self-serving system of control that is beyond criticism or alteration. The God "approved" in such context "will not do good or do evil"!

IV

Given such a disruption of dialogic rhetoric and the human crisis that arises with that disruption, the hard work of theological interpretation amid the closed system of modernism leaves us with two tasks: the critical and the constructive.

The critical task, I suggest, is to think clearly about the cost and consequences of the antidialogical legacy that is indispensible for the world of knowing human control. Gilkey was preoccupied with "The Travail of Biblical Language." It may now be time to reverse his proposition to consider "The Travail of Modernist Language." That is, the work is to consider the deficits of such modernist rhetoric and the impossibly hard work such rhetoric has to do in order to carry more than it is able to carry. Specifically the transposition of our rhetoric from dialogue to rational control has meant the loss of the categories of freedom, fidelity, and responsibility, and inevitably the loss of the notion of neighbor or neighborhood, that is, the loss of nothing less than the disappearance of "the common good."[13] The "turn to the subject," that is, the preoccupation with self, or more specifically "the possessive self," as the only agent, has yielded an autonomous agent who is not organically connected to any other.[14] The ultimate loss in such rhetoric of the autonomous self is the loss of the "holy Other" who eagerly engages the world and its creatureliness or, as Israel puts it, "The Holy One in your midst" (Hos 11:9).[15]

The loss and the gap left by the loss are perhaps signaled by Fukuyama's recognition that "trust" is indispensible to the viable working of society.[16] To be sure, Fukuyama, in good Enlightenment fashion, tries to quantify the requirement of "trust," an ironic juxtaposition of the dialogic (trust) and monologic (quantified) modes of reality and an effort that misunderstands trust but is at least an acknowledgment of that requirement.

But the more important work in the emergency is the recovery of dialogic rhetoric that at bottom can generate a very different practice of humanness in the world. The recovery of dialogic reality is the fundamental burden of Karl Barth in his explosive commentary on Romans, in which he saw in the Epistle that the only ultimate and genuine dialogue depends on the presence and participation of the Holy One of Israel.[17] Without that voice from the other side, Barth saw that there can be no dialogue of an ultimate and defining kind. Barth witnessed, after the witness of Paul, to the shape and quality and order of reality that refused and violated all the reductions of monologue. The legacy of Barth has most recently been brought to terse expression by Robert Jenson:

> It is time and past time for the church to say without hedging that modernity has it backward. Few would want to eschew modernity's many material and political blessings, but the way in which modernity related truth and tradition is now manifest as the great error that it was, and indeed, as culturally and even demographically suicidal error. . . . We must summon the audacity to say that modernity's scientific/metaphysical metanarrative . . . is not the encompassing story within which all other accounts of reality must establish their places, or be discredited by failing to find one. It is instead a rather brutal abstraction from reality. . . . As pop scientists urge over and over, the tale told by Scripture and creed finds no comfortable place within modernity's metanarrative. It is time for the church simply to reply: this is certainly the case, and the reason it is the case is that the tale told by Scripture is too comprehensive to find place within so drastically curtailed a version of the facts.[18]

Philosophical underpinnings for this work of recovery have been available to us through important long-standing probes of which I will mention two. Susanne K. Langer, already in 1942 in her book *Philosophy in a New Key*, proposed an alternative to the rationality of modernity.[19] She did so by accenting the way in which language, symbol, art, music, and sacrament make meaning that does not depend upon the mathematical certitude of modern rationality. She builds from the programmatic statement of Edward Sapir, who writes:

> Language is heuristic . . . in that its forms predetermine for us certain modes of observation and interpretation. . . . While it may be looked on as a symbolic system which reports or refers or otherwise substitutes for direct experience, it does not as a matter of actual behavior stand apart from or run parallel to direct experience but completely interpenetrates with it.[20]

Langer comments:

> The fact is that our primary world of reality *is* a verbal one. Without words our imagination cannot retain distinct objects and their relations but out of sight is out of mind. . . . The transformation of experience into concepts, not the elaboration of signals as symbols, is the motive of language. Speech is through and through symbolic; and only sometimes signific.[21]

Second, Michael Polanyi, in his 1958 book *Personal Knowledge*, protests against the reductionism of scientism and argues that serious knowledge is inescapably personal and interpretive.

> Having made a discovery, I shall never see the world again as before. My eyes have become different; I have made myself into a person seeing and thinking differently. I have crossed a gap, the heuristic gap that lies between problem and discovery. Major discoveries change our interpretive framework.[22]

It strikes me as crucial that both Langer (building on Sapir) and Polanyi focus on the *heuristic* function of language. That is, language is generative and forward-leaning, leaning toward possibility that is not available before utterance.[23] While neither Langer nor Polanyi has an explicit interest in theology, clearly their work creates a philosophic environment amenable to resistance to the totalism of modernity.

This alternative to the Enlightenment rationality of modernity is an affirmation that linguistic, rhetorical, artistic, interpretive imagination generates futures. And clearly such work of utterance requires *an utterer* and leads us to dialogic practice with a person and the personal that is outside and beyond us. This accent on the active and the personal as we ponder faith is recently probed by Marilyn McCord Adams as she thinks through the problem of evil:

> My philosophical instinct to make human personality fundamental is matched by a drive . . . to join the mainstream of Christian theological tradition in regarding divine agency as personal—that is, at bottom, agency that acts by thought and will. . . . Once freed from this down-sizing disadvantage, Divine personhood offers systemic advantages where the problem of horrendous evils is concerned. For horror-defeating power is meaning-restoring power, and meaning–making is personal activity par excellence![24]

In a world beset by limitless exploitation of "nature" and unrestrained savagery against neighbor, Adams' phrasing seems particularly pertinent. What is surely required now among us is power that is capable of "horror-defeating," "meaning-restoring," and "meaning-making." Such work is surely personal. And while human agents can address these dreadful issues in modest ways, faith attests a larger, more compelling, more effective personal agency, surely "the holy one in your midst." Of course for the so-called progressives who continue to have confidence in the modern world that "has been so good to us," the horror is not seen to be so deep, and the loss of meaning not so acute when present manageable meanings continue to be available. But such a so-called innocent view of social, worldly reality is possible only among those privileged and protected.

Such innocent claims, moreover, are indispensible when this rationality is given concreteness in the economic claims of capitalism.[25] Such innocent faith, incapable of thinking or imagining outside the promise and possibilities of capitalism, reduces everything to commodity, and more than that, to measurable, manageable commodity that does not allow for the immeasurability of the Holy One who can and does make all things new. Such innocence is a practice of totalism in which the narrative of sufficiency and control screens out and denies the real world of life and death, of estrangement and reconciliation, of enslavement and emancipation, of wealth and poverty, of despair and hope, of denial and truth.[26] These elemental facets of real life that refuse to go away require us to host dialogic rhetoric that inevitably disrupts the disruptions of modernity.

V

In the end the crisis is a practical one and not a theoretical one. The practical issue is to disrupt the totalizing capacity of modernity-cum-capitalism by a rhetoric and by a life of freedom and fidelity. Such a rhetoric and such a life entail regard and respect for the God who engages in dialogic discourse with those who pay attention, who are, like Moses, able to "turn aside" (Exod 3:3). We may not, in the first instant, anticipate that such an alternative life will be visible in the corridors of modernity that are pledged to a different narrative of reality, a narrative that leaves us variously in hubris or in despair, but always in anxiety.

But then, the faith community, Jewish and Christian, is not pledged to that narrative or that rationality. The language and imagination of the faith community is of another kind, pledged to love God and to love neighbor, that is, to acknowledge *Another* who summons and compels us, to regard *the other as neighbor* and not as threat or competitor. That mandate, rooted in Sinai, is a practical one that implies a different construal of social and economic power. But that concrete and practical alternative construal depends upon imagination that is carried and evoked by rhetoric.

For that reason, surely, the faith community cannot afford the so-called innocent rhetoric of progressives who expect or welcome no initiative other than their own. For that matter, it also cannot afford the triumphal rhetoric of conservatives who traffic in absolutes. Neither such innocence nor such triumphalism can produce a viable world. Such a world depends on discourse that concerns freedom and fidelity and responsibility, all the language of dialogue.

Thus the most immediate and practical work of faith communities, I propose, is the recovery of the language of I and Thou and the nerve to trust it. Such rhetoric, deep in the tradition, attests an "I" who can self-announce and a "Thou" who is present in tradition and in contemporary liturgical performance, the Thou who gives and commands and emancipates and summons and promises.

I am moved by the proposal of Terry Eagleton that the ground of faith from which to refute the "new atheists" is not theoretical but practical. It is the deep valuing of "the scum of the earth."[27] The story of faith, Jewish and Christian, concerns the way in which the Holy One engages with "the scum of the earth." In ancient Israel it is "rabble" (*'asapsup*; Num 11:4) or the "mixed multitude" (*'ereb rab*; Exod 12:28; see Neh 13:3), an undifferentiated mishmash of unidentified people. In the early church it is "tax-collectors and sinners," folk who do not belong to or qualify for the successful world of propriety (Luke 5:30; 7:34). It is with these that the Holy One engages. It is to these that the Holy One speaks. It is among these that the Holy One creates a community of those who will pray imperatives of hope and sing doxologies that bespeak the "Thou" of the Holy One. It is in that entourage that the juices of life are unleashed. And where that rhetoric is not practiced and those juices are not released, we are consigned, by our innocence or by our triumphalism, to a world of control and threat and anxiety and loneliness and despair. The news that arises in dialogic exchange is that it need not be so. And because the "Thou" of the Holy One has been found to be reliable, it will not be so.

The several monologues of modernity shrivel the human spirit and human possibility. Israel's dialogic language refuses such shriveling. Thus I return to my beginning point:

Doxology is the glad yielding of self while the modern self never yields:

> I will extol you O LORD. (Ps 30:1)

Thanks is the voice of gratitude for gifts generously given:

> I give thanks to you, O LORD, with my whole heart;
> before the gods I sing your praise;
> I bow down toward your holy temple
> and give thanks to your name
> for your steadfast love and your faithfulness. (Ps 138:1-2)

The modern self has no reason to be grateful or to give thanks or to hope.

Petition is the insistent voice of expectation:

> Rise up, O LORD!
> Do not let mortals prevail. (Ps 9:19)

> Rise up, O LORD;
> O God, lift up your hand. (Ps 10:12)

The modern self does not expect or hope or ask. Faithfulness listens; faith waits; faith hears. The Thou addresses and sometimes speaks a newness that authorizes a new world that can be given only in such utterance.

It is *the speaking Thou* who rejects hubris:

> Therefore I will take back
> my grain in its time,
> and my wine in its season. (Hos 2:9)

It is *the speaking Thou* who undertakes possibility:

> I will open rivers on the bare heights,
> and fountains in the midst of the valleys. (Isa 41:18)

It is *the speaking Thou* who imposes the pain of alienation and then reaches into that pain to embrace:

> How can I give you up, Ephraim,
> how can I hand you over, O Israel? (Hos 11:8)

It is *the speaking Thou* who inhabits and convenes alternative worlds of fidelity and freedom.

The faith communities, Jewish and Christian, even in a world of monologue, are in the Thou business. And that in a culture of conformist capitalism and illusionary freedom that begins with no "Thou" and ends with a feeble "I" that is soon dismissed. When the faith community refuses its proper rhetoric and opts for either innocence or triumph, the world is left in bottomless anxiety, and there is a complete disruption of our humanness. It is in such a world, marked by innocence, triumphalism, and anxiety, that this Thou sometimes surprises, evoking new possibility.[28]

PART II

NARRATIVE COMPLEXITIES THAT CHALLENGE

6

FOOD FIGHT

MONOPOLY: ACCOUNTABILITY FOR THE FOOD FIGHT

In this chapter I will consider the crisis of hunger in our society and in our world. I focus on hunger

because everyone has to eat; "bread" is our most elemental requirement;

because food *production* leads to issues of the environment, for a diminished environment will not and cannot "bring forth" as intended;

because food *consumption* leads to the cluster of issues around "consumerism" and the mad pursuit of more commodities, in the futile hope that they will make us safe and happy;

because food *distribution* raises economic questions between haves and have-nots, about who gets what, on what terms, and by whose decision;

because there is an overlap between "hunger for food" and "spiritual hunger," and the connection and tension between the two is crucial for our common life.[1]

In short "hunger" touches the great practical questions of our contemporary world and drives us back to theological wonderment. Thus the issues are enormously complex. I do not imagine that we will find clear resolution of the food issues in a probe of biblical texts, for the Bible does not function in that way. I have the more modest goal of tracing some texts that may permit us to think afresh and faithfully on these urgent questions.

Given the theme of "hunger," I formulate our reflection as a "food fight." At the outset I had in mind some of the disconcerting scenes of John Belushi in *Animal House* wherein social interaction quickly devolved into a food fight. And of course in any restaurant where young children have been eating, it is possible to imagine, when they leave, that there has been a food fight because the remaining evidence is less than neat and tidy.

I

The more I considered the phrase "food fight," however, the more I found the term apt for our reflection. First it occurred to me that the struggle for food between those who have advantage, resources, markets, and leverage and those who lack those advantages is a long-term fight that is waged in many modes. Given the many modes for the conflict, however, the great struggles are finally about "bread," with the term "bread" standing for all the dimensions of wealth, control, status, and the capacity to be an agent in one's own history.

As I thought more, it occurred to me that the Bible itself is a venue for that long-term food fight, that is, a struggle between competing ways to think about food and hunger. The fight for food is a fight between ideologies about food, or theologies about food, or explanatory narratives about food. The Bible is a map of profound contestation that turned up in public practice and that was given theological rationale and eventually came to be taken as authoritative. That tension in the Bible itself is a counterpoint to the tension we ourselves know about. Thus I suggest that each of us is variously involved in a food fight concerning the legitimacy of our own hungers and the pressure of the hungers of others that impinge upon our cache of food. In the midst of that struggle that is grandly biblical and acutely personal, we carry on an inquiry about what is right and what is true, what is permitted and what is required.

In this article I will trace out these two ideologies (theologies, explanatory narratives) of food to consider how that food fight may matter to any other local congregation. By connecting a sequence of texts, I will want to show that there is continuity and a coherent logic to each of these ideologies and that they are in profound tension with each other.

Here is my thesis for the first of these trajectories that I will line out: One stance in the food fight is a system of food production, distribution, and consumption that is based on the conviction that the world is a closed system of limited resources. The accent is upon scarcity. The supplies are limited. The emotive result is anxiety about not having enough. The practical consequences consist in practices and policies of accumulation that aim at monopoly.

The purpose of a monopoly of food resources and supplies is the offer of a "final solution" to the food crisis. The defining terms of this ideology, then, are *scarcity*, *anxiety*, *accumulation*, and *monopoly*. The enactment of this ideology consists in consumerism (which in health may lead to obesity and in policy may lead to agribusiness that seeks to force all the production possible), protected by a strong military that guarantees the safety and security of the entire system.

II

In the Old Testament Pharaoh is the agent, symbol, and metaphor for a food system that is rooted in anxious scarcity and enacted in accumulation on the way to monopoly. It is plausible that Pharaoh in the book of Exodus is a namable (but unnamed) historical figure; scholarship has used great energy trying to identify him. Beyond that, however, it is clear that in the narrative of the book of Exodus, Pharaoh functions as a metaphor that can be variously reidentified in many contexts of crisis. It is this metaphorical dimension that makes the exodus narrative endlessly contemporary and always transferable to a new context. Whatever he may have been historically, Pharaoh functions as the recurring agent of anxious scarcity. His endless mantra is, "Make more bricks" (Exod 5:4-19). The bricks are in order to construct more storehouse cities (Exod 1:11). And the function of the storehouse cities is to accumulate more food, more grain, until Pharaoh controls all of it. He is presented in the narrative as one who wants with an insatiable appetite for more! Here I will mention a series of texts that tell the story of the great accumulator.

1. At the very beginning of the Israelite story in Genesis 12, in the second paragraph concerning Abraham and Sarah, Pharaoh has already appeared. Indeed, Israel cannot tell its story of covenantal alternative without reference to Pharaoh, who is the indispensible durable counterpoint. In Genesis 12:10, it is reported that a famine caused Abraham to go to Egypt for food. The matter is not explained. It is an assumption of the narrative that when everyone else is out of food, Pharaoh still will have food. Pharaoh of course has food because the Nile River is endlessly productive, and because Pharaoh is a genius at administrative authority and knows how to work the irrigation system and make the trains run on time. But beyond that, he is a monopolizer who has the capacity to defy

even a circumstance of famine. The narrative is terse but nevertheless reports that Pharaoh was attracted to Sarah, beautiful wife of Abraham, and "the woman was taken into Pharaoh's house" (v. 15). The food of the monopolizer never comes cheaply. From the outset women have been a bargaining chip in the food fight among powerful men. The fact that the narrative happily resolves the treatment of Sarah does not detract from the plot line concerning the avarice of Pharaoh who assumed, given his food monopoly, that he was entitled to whatever he could possess.

2. A long time later in the narrative, in Genesis 41, it is reported that Pharaoh had two bad dreams, two nightmares. The first dream concerns seven sleek and fat cows that were devoured by seven cows that were thin and ugly (41:2-4). The second bad dream concerned seven ears of grain that were plump and good. And seven ears of grain that were thin and blighted swallowed up the seven good ears (vv. 4-7). Like every dream, these dreams are vivid and concrete, and we are to notice the contrast:

> Cows: sleek and fat / ugly and thin;
> Ears of grain: plump and full / thin and blighted.

The contrast bespeaks indulgent well-being and parsimonious stress. In the nightmares, moreover, the thin stuff prevails and defeats the good stuff. The verbs are "ate, swallowed," verbs of ingestion of food. So these are food dreams.

Pharaoh was troubled in the morning. He could vividly remember the dreams, but he did not understand them. He consulted with his intelligence community, perhaps even the credentialed therapist of his realm. None could tell him the meaning, though none doubted that the dreams had a meaning. It is remarkable, moreover, that the narrator knows the dream. How could an Israelite narrator know the dreams of Pharaoh? Well, because covenantal folk know about the nightmares that accumulators invariably have. They know that accumulators live, always, on orange alert. The narrator notices, but does not underscore, the irony that the one with the most is the one who has the most acute dreams of loss, likely not a nightmare shared by the peasants.

3. Pharaoh had to reach outside his entourage in order to get an interpretation of the dreams. Perhaps all of his advisors were so narcotized by the monopoly in which they lived that none could penetrate the hidden messages of the dreams that witnessed against the monopoly. It is

like asking the chair of a great bureaucracy to pause over a poem that is likely to be misread as a memo. But Pharaoh finds an interpreter. He finds Joseph, a young Hebrew who was a jailed outsider, regarded as an enemy of the state. He is cleaned up, shaven, given proper clothes, and brought before Pharaoh, the accumulator (41:14). Pharaoh patiently tells him his dreams, using the terms of contrast, "fat and sleek, poor, ugly and thin," "full and good, withered thin, and blighted." The terms are repeated, but with two additions. Now the cows are "poor" and the stalks of grain are "withered." It is as though in the retelling, the extremities of the bad in the dreams are underlined.

Joseph knows immediately because, says he, it is "not I" but God who will interpret. The dreams are about the coming famine that will be "very grievous" (v. 31). The irony is that the one with everything has a nightmare about loss. The peasants who had little likely had no such dream because they had not enough to lose.

4. The nightmare, now interpreted, leads to new policy. The nightmare is grounded in anxiety. Anxiety drives policy! Imagine a great superpower that is anxious about loss in a way that leads to new policy! Pharaoh seeks an administrator to manage the nightmare crisis that is coming. Joseph recommends that Pharaoh find someone who is "wise and discerning" (v. 33). Not surprisingly, it is Joseph himself who is the only candidate for the post. Before he is nominated, Joseph presents a plan to Pharaoh about how to manage the scarcity to come. It is like the worst-case scenario of planning procedure in the war office. Pharaoh is taken with the plan and appoints Joseph over his realm:

> You shall be over my house, and all my people shall order themselves as you command; only with regard to the throne will I be greater than you. (41:40)

The narrator pauses, even in the midst of the crisis, to celebrate the appointment. It is a big deal to manage the scarcity that Pharaoh is now bound to face:

> Removing the signet ring from his hand, Pharaoh put it on Joseph's hand; he arrayed him in garments of fine linen, and put a gold chain around his neck. He had him ride in the chariot of his second-in-command; and they cried out in front of him, "Bow the knee!" Thus he set him over all the land of Egypt. Moreover Pharaoh said to Joseph, "I am

> Pharaoh and without your consent none shall lift up hand or foot in all the land of Egypt. . . . Thus Joseph gained authority over the land of Egypt. (vv. 42-45)

Now we have an Israelite who will take care of the nightmare of food scarcity that has already propelled the great accumulator toward monopoly.

5. The move from nightmare to policy is traced in the narrative report of Genesis 47:13-26. There it is reported that Joseph introduced draconian food policies. The peasants, without food of their own, had successively to bargain away their money and then their land and then their livestock, and finally their bodies. In exchange for food from the great accumulator they became Pharaoh's slaves. That is how we reach the slave narrative of the book of Exodus. Slavery as a given in the book of Exodus is the outcome of the food policies of monopoly in the book of Genesis. The force of monopoly is so acute that by the end of the narrative, the newly recruited slaves, victims of the food policy of Pharaoh, are grateful for their own enslavement:

They say, "You have saved our lives; may it please my lord, we will be slaves to Pharaoh" (47:25). The ideology of Pharaoh is now all-encompassing. Even the slaves echo it back to the big house. And the narrator adds laconically:

> So Joseph bought all the land of Egypt for Pharaoh. . . . The land of the priests alone did not become Pharaoh's. (vv. 20, 26)

The narrator does not call attention to the most ironic dimension of the narrative. The implementation of the food policy of monopoly that eventuated in slavery is accomplished by an Israelite! Leon Kass characterizes the narrative achievement as the full "Egyptianization" of Joseph.[2] Pharaoh's ideology of monopoly is so totalizing that none could resist it, not even an Israelite who might have known better. Everything yields to the force of monopoly!

I should pause to notice how we regularly read the Joseph narrative. Following Gerhard von Rad, we regularly focus on Genesis 45:1-8 wherein Joseph twice says to his brothers:[3]

> God sent me before you to preserve life. . . . God sent me before you to preserve for you a remnant on earth, and to keep alive for you many survivors. (45:5, 7)

These statements give positive theological tone to the policies of Pharaoh implemented by Joseph. But while we read chapter 45 in its theological affirmation, we consistently skip over chapter 47 with its economic realism. And we thereby miss the critical systems analysis that is voiced there. We read innocently about the food fight, perhaps not wanting to see the outcome of the ideology of scarce anxiety to which we ourselves are much inured.

If, however, one takes a critical stance on these policies and practices of monopoly, we may see the downside. Pharaoh in his massive power, supported by an ideology of supreme authority, could imagine himself autonomous and free to do what he wanted. He lived in great arrogance, not imagining that his power to control had any limit. We may simply notice that in the belated criticism of Pharaoh in the Bible, the limit on monopolizing power is voiced in prophetic utterances. In Ezekiel 29:3, Pharaoh is called to account for his imagined autonomy:

> Thus says the LORD GOD:
> I am against you,
> Pharaoh, king of Egypt,
> the great dragon sprawling
> in the mist of its channels,
> saying, "My Nile is my own;
> I made it for myself."

Quite clearly in covenantal perspective, it is the Nile that made Pharaoh, not the other way around. Isaiah can imagine, in prophetic poetry, that the Nile that made Pharaoh's bread basket is at the behest of YHWH, the creator, who will curb Pharaoh's self-indulgence:

> The waters of the Nile will be dried up,
> and the river will be parched and dry;
> its canals will become foul,
> and the branches of Egypt's Nile will diminish and dry up,
> reeds and rushes will rot away.
> There will be bare places by the Nile,
> on the brink of the Nile;
> and all that is sown by the Nile will dry up,
> be driven away, and be no more. (Isa 19:5-7)

But of course such prophetic imagination lies well beyond Pharaoh . . . or Joseph. They are practical men who move from their nightmare of scarcity, and by their immense social force they imagine they can fend off the threats about which they dream in their haunted nights.

III

It was easy enough to establish Pharaoh as the "bad guy" in the Israelite narrative. He was an easy target that evoked no sympathy in Israel. But remarkably, Pharaoh's ideology of scarcity, anxiety, accumulation, and monopoly could not be kept at pharaonic distance. It entered right into the midst of Israel's own life in a way that skewed and distorted Israel's covenantal faith.

1. As the tradition stands, they could see it coming among them. They could anticipate the force of this ideology in their own midst. It may be that such foreboding is "after the fact" when they saw the impact of that ideology on their common life. But even if in fact it is a retrospect, the tradition offers it as a foreboding.

In Deuteronomy 17:14-20, in the only Torah commandment on kingship, Moses warns against the power of accumulation because accumulation aimed at monopoly contradicts covenant:

> [Your coming king] must not acquire many horses for himself, or return the people to Egypt in order to acquire more horses, since the Lord has said to you, "You must never return that way again." And he must not acquire many wives for himself, or else his heart will turn away; also silver and gold he must not acquire in great quantity for himself. (vv. 16-17)

The recurring favorites of all accumulators are "horses, women, silver, and gold." But all of that is only "food" writ large, an effort at self-securing, never to lack.

The alert of the Torah is matched by the speech of Samuel who anticipates the coming of monarchy in Israel:

> These will be the ways of the king who will reign over you: he will take your sons and appoint them to his chariots and to be his horsemen, and to run before his chariots; and he will appoint for himself commanders of thousands and commanders of fifties, and some to plow his ground and reap his harvest, and to make his implements of war and the equipment of his chariots. He will take your daughters to be perfumers and

> cooks and bakers. He will take the best of your fields and vineyards and olive orchards and give them to his courtiers. He will take one-tenth of your grain and of your vineyards and give it to his officers and his courtiers. He will take your male and female slaves, and the best of your cattle and donkeys, and put them to his work. He will take one-tenth of your flocks, and you shall be his slaves. (1 Sam 8:11-17)

The operative word is "take." The subject is taxation and the draft. But the undercurrent is that the king will have an insatiable appetite for self-indulgence . . . perfumers, cooks, bakers. The accumulator will seize your grain and flocks (food) and reduce all to slavery. The horrified anticipation is that organized greed will skew all social relationships in the interest of aggrandizement, and the confiscation will run from food to the military, an undifferentiated package in a world of organized appetites.

2. It turns out, in retrospect, that these anticipations in Deuteronomy 17 and 1 Samuel 8 were in fact responses to the regime of Solomon who radically shifted the society of Israel away from a covenantal economy to an economy of accumulation in which the strong could take from the weak in the service of an uncurbed appetite for more. In the horizon of Israel, Solomon becomes the great embodiment of *scarcity, anxiety, accumulation*, and *monopoly*. Who would have thought it? Who would have thought that Israel's covenantal commitments were so readily vulnerable to the incursion of Pharaoh's ideology? Well, try this: Solomon is Pharaoh's son-in-law. He married the daughter of the big guy (1 Kgs 3:1; 7:8; 9:24; 11:1). It takes no imagination to think that Solomon set out to prove to his in-laws that he was competent in their great game of greedy self-indulgence. And so Solomon is portrayed in 1 Kings 3–11 as the full practitioner of the ideology of accumulation:

> First Kings 4:1-6 reports on the king's bureaucracy, an organization of power that some interpreters believe was appropriated from Egyptian models. Of particular moment is the last named official, Adonirim, son of Abda, who was "in charge of forced labor." He was Secretary of Labor. But here it is "forced labor," coerced labor in the service of the crown. The term, recurring in Solomonic reports, echoes Pharaoh's labor policy. The characterization is of a regime that has reduced free members of society into service to the crown, most especially for the construction of self-aggrandizing monuments to monopoly, the temple (5:13-18), his

fortifications, his palaces, and his storehouses (9:15-23). That latter report ends this way:

> These were the chief officers who were over Solomon's work; five hundred and fifty, who had charge of the people who carried on the work. (9:23)

It must have been a huge workforce to require 550 supervisors, a vast program that claimed the resources and people-power of society, all in the service of royal anxiety.

The project cost lots of money. Thus in 1 Kings 4:7-19 we have an organizational chart of Solomon's tax-collecting apparatus, an organization that is worked out to fine detail. It is clear that there were no exemptions from taxation that transferred wealth from peasants to urban elites. It is noted, moreover, that two of the tax officials, Benabinadad (v. 11) and Ahimaaz (v. 15), were sons-in-law of Solomon, married to his daughters. Thus the report suggests a close network of urban elites who were committed to a common process of accumulation.

3. The payout of forced labor (4:6) and tax arrangements (4:7-19) is the report concerning the royal appetite for food:

> Solomon's provision for one day was thirty cors of choice flour, and sixty cors of meal, ten fat oxen, and twenty pasture-fed cattle, one hundred sheep besides deer, gazelles, roebucks, and fatted fowl.
> (1 Kgs 4:22)

It is remarkable that in the midst of all the grand royal schemes, the narrative pauses over food. The appetite of the regime is broad and deep. Imagine every day that much meat while the peasants had none! To be sure, the economic base for such table was not only taxes and cheap labor but also tribute from foreign lands (protection money) and tariff revenue, all in the interest of accumulation. The outcome is an ostentatious self-exhibit that came to mark every part of the urban confiscation that depended on the produce of the disempowered peasants.

The extravagance of food is a kind of symbol in the script of Solomon for systemic accumulation on every front. Thus:

The exhibition of wealth is replicated in the temple that overflows with extravagant gold (6:19-22; 7:48-51).

The accumulation of songs and proverbs posit Solomon as a patron of the arts with a monopoly on beauty and wisdom (4:29-34).

The trade in arms (horses and chariots) suggests that he had a monopoly on the flow of arms due to his strategic geographic location (10:26-29).

He enjoyed lavish tribute from foreign powers, all offered in deference and submissiveness, to his international enhancement (10:14-25).

Eventually he is condemned for his accumulation of women (700 princesses and 300 concubines), women being one more accoutrement to an over-the-top extravagance, perhaps trophy wives for exhibit.

On exhibit is this imagined superpower in its capacity to turn everything and everyone into a collectable commodity in order to capture the imagination of Israel and of the other powers as well, notably the Queen of Sheba (10:1-10). This presentation of Solomon, I believe, does not witness to personal greed. Rather it attests the power of the ideology of accumulation that entranced Israel. What happens in such an arrangement, inevitably, is that the hunger of the peasants, the real food hunger of the disadvantaged, disappears from the screen of policy and of practice. Outside of this ideological venue, there is no one left to notice. The logic of accumulation is secure:

If there is scarcity, get all you can;

If there is not enough, do not share;

If others want some, they are a threat to be repelled.

It cannot be an accident that one of only two psalms related to Solomon is Psalm 72, the great psalm of royal responsibility. That psalm is entitled "of Solomon." It links royal prosperity and longevity to care for the poor:

Give to the king your justice, O God,
    and your righteousness to a king's son . . .
My he defend the cause of the poor of the people,
    give deliverance to the needy,
    and crush the oppressor . . .

For he delivers the needy when they call,
the poor and those who have no helper.
He has pity on the weak and the needy,
and saves the lives of the needy . . .
Long may he live! (72:1, 4, 12-13, 15a)

The psalm rubs up abrasively against the narrative. Perhaps it is an ironic judgment on the king. Perhaps it is a desperate hope. Either way, it is a recognition that an ideology of accumulation is a sure way to guarantee failure. The psalm lines out the positive option. It resolutely implies much that is profoundly negative.

IV

The deep critique of the ideology of accumulation is voiced by the prophetic tradition that sounds with immense emotive force and rigorous theological authority. The prophetic tradition repeatedly takes aim precisely at the ideology of scarcity and anxiety that produced accumulation aimed at monopoly.

1. A somewhat soft form of critique is the narrative of Elisha who proceeded to solve the food problem of ancient Israel without engagement with or even acknowledgment of the ideology of accumulation.

In the narrative of 2 Kings 4:1-7, Elisha provides the widow mother with enough oil to pay her creditors and save her son. She is, moreover, dependent upon her village neighbors to help her catch the oil that will save her life and the life of her son. While we readily focus on the "miraculous" in the narrative, we mostly miss the framing of the narrative as an instance of the food fight between creditors and debtors. The crisis is that her creditors—surely the urban elites—are about to enslave her son for her debt, a practice as old as Pharaoh and as recent as Solomon. Elisha, without pedigree or credential, enacts abundance that defies the ideology of scarcity. In doing so he negates the credit system of the accumulators. Perhaps what we—as a part of the accumulation community—regard as a "miracle" is in fact the common mystery of "abundance" that is accepted among the peasants.

In the narrative of 2 Kings 4:42-44, Elisha again participates in the ongoing food fight by feeding a hundred people with some food left over. The narrative is terse and without explanation. Elisha clearly performs in a way that is outside of and in contradiction to the accumulation system.

2. When we move from narrative to poetry, the critique of the accumulation system is much more poignant. Many texts might be cited. I will begin with two from the poetry of Amos.

In Amos 6:4-7, Amos pronounces a "woe" on those who are "at ease in Zion," that is, those who are narcotized by self-indulgence who trust their ideology.[4] He begins with an inventory of self-indulgences among those who have too much time on their hands:

> Alas for those who lie on beds of ivory,
> and lounge on their couches,
> and eat lambs from the flock,
> and calves from the stall;
> who sing idle songs to the sound of the harp,
> and like David improvise on instruments of music;
> who drink wine from bowls,
> and anoint themselves with the finest of oils. (vv. 4-6)

The poem turns on the conjunction "but" in v. 6:

> *But* who are not grieved over the ruin of Joseph.

The critique is not of their self-indulgence, but of the resultant indifference to social reality. The social crisis that Amos sees (that they do not see) is that "Joseph" (i.e., Israel) is a failed community. The poet knows, as every prophetic poet knows, that the practitioners of self-indulgence at the expense of others are characteristically the last to notice that what they regard as a blessing is in fact a deep pathology that will in the end destroy what they most value. The self-indulgent are so dulled and incapable of social awareness or social criticism that they do not reckon with reality.

The payout of the oracle is the "therefore" of v. 7:

> *Therefore* they shall be the first to go into exile,
> and the revelry of the loungers shall pass away.

The self-indulgent will be deported. The ones most secure will be the most threatened. And the accumulation of excessive goods will offer no protection from the incursions of history that sound here as divine judgment.

In 8:4-8 Amos addresses those whose wealth is linked to dishonest exploitation of the poor. He does not here mention tax or credit arrangements, only the use of dishonest weights in commerce. But the outcome, says he, is the same. The land will "tremble," likely at the pounding of the invading Assyrian army. It is not incidental that the poetic unit ends with reference to the rise and fall of the Nile River. While the reference is to the reliability of the river, the evocation of Egypt is a reminder in Israel that nobody, not even the land of Egypt, escapes the reality of God's governance. This God is not finally mocked by the monopoly of the market as wealth is transferred from the poor and needy by commercial means.

3. Isaiah 3 offers a long poem about the opposition of YHWH to a culture of accumulation. The governing verb is "take away" (vv. 1, 18), perhaps a counterpoint to the verb "take" we have seen in 1 Samuel 8. The poem anticipates the loss in Jerusalem of all the commodity finery so valued in the city. In the poetry, the God of covenant stands in opposition to the commodity accumulation. To accent the point, moreover, the prophet delights to detail the accumulation of goods that will be lost:

> In that day the Lord will *take away* the finery of the anklets, the headbands, and the crescents; the pendants, the bracelets, and the scarfs; the headdresses, the armlets, the sashes, the perfume boxes, and the amulets; the signet rings and nose rings; the festal robes, the mantles, the cloaks, and the handbags; the garments of gauze, the linen garments, the turbans, and the veils. (3:18)

The inventory alludes to the exhibitionism of the "Easter parade" in Jerusalem:

> Because the daughters of Zion are haughty
> and walk with outstretched necks,
> glancing wantonly with their eyes,
> mincing along as they go,
> tinkling with their feet. (3:16)

All of that will be lost because the God of covenant will undo the accumulation system. The prophet knows, as does the foundational covenantal tradition, that such commodity accumulation depends finally upon social exploitation. The indictment concerns the abuse of the vulnerable poor:

> It is you who have devoured the vineyard;
> the spoil of the poor is in your houses.
> What do you mean by crushing my people,
> by grinding the face of the poor? says the Lord God of hosts.
> (3:14b-15)

The "poor" constitute that segment of the population that is turned, through exploitation, into dispensable commodity. But it cannot stand! That food system, says the poet, has no future.

4. Finally I mention a remarkable text in Ezekiel. In his emotive critique of Jerusalem in its self-indulgent infidelity, Ezekiel likens the Holy City (and its self-indulgent population) to ancient, remembered Sodom. He contrasts Jerusalem to Sodom:

> Your sister Sodom and her daughters have not done as you and your daughters have done. (Ezek 16:48)

The affront of Sodom, says he, was self-indulgence:

> This was the guilt of your sister Sodom: she and her daughters had pride, excess of food and prosperous ease, but did not aid the poor and needy. They were haughty, and did abominable things before me. (v. 49)

For that, Sodom was destroyed; and Jerusalem is worse! What interests us here is that in the horizon of Ezekiel, the defining sin of Sodom, and by inference of Jerusalem, is pride expressed as excess of food that precluded care of the poor and needy. The startling language that links the Holy City to Sodom makes this an especially poignant judgment. But for its poignancy, the argument is the same as elsewhere. Arrogant autonomy, expressed as excessive consumption, generated indifference to the poor and needy. Such indifference, which makes perfect sense in the ideology of accumulation, is unbearable in the world that Yhwh governs. The oracle ends with severity:

> You must bear the penalty of your lewdness and your abominations.
> (v. 58)

It is impossible to appreciate the cumulative effect of prophetic poetry unless we see that it joins issue with an ideology that is, in the judgment of the prophets, in deep contradiction to the true character of Israel and certainly to the true intent of YHWH who presides over Israel and over the food supply of the world.

V

The monopolizers keep supplying the prophets with a multitude of case studies. At the beginning of the narrative of Israel there is Pharaoh who needs more bricks. In Jerusalem there is Solomon who eats too well. And now, at the other end of the Old Testament, is Nebuchadnezzar, the great king of Babylon, who destroyed Jerusalem. Indeed, the prophets say that he did so at the behest of YHWH. Like Pharaoh, Nebuchadnezzar became a metaphor and a cipher for all monopolizers. After Jeremiah can attach Nebuchadnezzar to the purposes of YHWH, the tradition will go on to mount a severe critique of him as yet another embodiment of the food fight.

1. Jeremiah anticipates Nebuchadnezzar's coming army, even though, in the poetry, Jeremiah does not specifically name him. The poet imagines the coming of the army of Nebuchadnezzar that will be strong and strange and huge and powerful, sweeping all before it. The great devourer is sent by YHWH against YHWH's own city:

> I am going to bring upon you
>   a nation from far away, O house of Israel, says the LORD.
> It is an enduring nation,
>   it is an ancient nation,
> a nation whose language you do not know,
>   nor can you understand what they say.
> Their quiver is like an open tomb;
>   all of them are mighty warriors. (Jer 5:15-16)

And then the poet describes what this army, like every invading army, will do to the land:

> They shall eat up your harvest and your food;
>   they shall eat up your sons and your daughters;
> they shall eat up your flocks and your herds;
>   they shall eat up your vines and your fig trees;
> they shall destroy with the sword
>   your fortified cities in which you trust. (v. 17)

The poem interests us because it uses the word "eat" four times. Talk about a food fight! The great superpower will seize all the food sources of the vulnerable city. The inventory of confiscation runs from A to Z:

from harvest to food;

from sons to daughters;

from flocks to herds;

from vines to fig trees.

That is what superpowers do, in their appetite for control, to vulnerable subject states. Even the fortified cities of vulnerable Judah will be devoured by Nebuchadnezzar.

2. It is no wonder that Isaiah chides Babylon for acting as if it were autonomous:

> You said, "I shall be mistress forever" . . .
> [You] say in your heart, "I am and there is no one besides me" . . .
> You said, "No one sees me" . . .
> "I am, and there is no one besides me." (Isa 47:7, 8, 10)

When a superpower imagines that it is autonomous and not accountable, then it can eat all the food, take all the resources, gobble up all the treasures, exhaust all the reserves, and never answer. It belongs to the strong in the food fight, says Jeremiah, to "show no mercy" (Jer 6:23). When food is managed without mercy, abuse, suffering, and slavery are sure to eventuate.

3. I cite one other Babylonian text that is a little quirky but perhaps illuminating. Now the king is Belshazzar, son of Nebuchadnezzar; he is a stand-in for his father, who is a stand-in for Antiochus IV Epiphanes, who is a stand-in for all monopolizers. The narrator reports:

> King Belshazzar made a great festival for a thousand of his lords, and he was drinking wine in the presence of the thousand. (Dan 5:1)

Of course; that is what the strong in the food fight do. They give feasts. They invite all the powerful, in order to exhibit their success. The dinner is ostentatious, not unlike the great government dinners, notably the binge of the late great Shah in celebrating 2,500 years of Persia:

> Under the influence of the wine, Belshazzar commanded that they bring in the vessels of gold and silver that his father Nebuchadnezzar had taken out of the temple in Jerusalem, so that the king and his lords, his wives, and his concubines might drink from them. So they brought in the vessels of gold and silver that had been taken out of the temple, the house of God in Jerusalem, and the king and his lords, his wives, and his concubines drank from them. They drank the wine and praised the gods of gold and silver, bronze, iron, wood, and stone. (5:2-4)

The narrative loves to pile up nouns and modifiers and repeats the formulae in order to mock. More than that, the point of lavish enjoyment from the temple vessels is to scandalize the Jews who watched their holy vessels used for such fluff, made more scandalous by the misinformed praise of the powerful in Babylon. The narrative teems with self-indulgence and the narrative mocks the pretense.

And then in v. 5, finally, it is reported:

> Immediately the fingers of a human hand appeared and began writing on the plaster of the wall of the royal palace, next to the lampstand.

We move from the dinner of lavish food to the finger on the wall "immediately." A human hand, quite unidentified, wrote on the decorated wall of the royal palace. The words are in code and none of the intelligence community of the sated empire could decode them. But the appearance of the writing itself terrified the king:

> Then the king's face turned pale and his thoughts terrified him. His limbs gave way and his knees knocked together. The king cried out . . . then Belshazzar became terrified and his face turned pale, and his lords were perplexed. (vv. 6-7, 9)

I guess the theme is "Guess Who's Coming to Dinner." The queen tried to ease the king's anxiety by summoning Daniel, the Jew, who knew the codes of hidden wisdom. Daniel refuses royal rewards, but he read the wall to the king:

> You have exalted yourself against the Lord of heaven! The vessels of his temple have been brought in before you, and you and your lords, your wives and your concubines have been drinking wine from them. You have praised the gods of silver and gold, of bronze, iron, wood, and stone, which do not see or hear or know; but the God in whose power

> is your very breath, and to whom belong all your ways, you have not honored. (v. 23)

It follows, on the wall, that the kingdom will end. And the narrative concludes tersely, "That very night Belshazzar, the Chaldean king, was killed" (v. 30). The banquet is interrupted. Those who indulge at the expense of the peasants cannot eat in peace. Such indulgence is short-term, because alongside the peasants there is the great God who eventually will not be mocked. Belshazzar must, yet again, learn the lesson of his greedy father, Nebuchadnezzar, of whom the narrator recalls:

> But when his heart was lifted up and his spirit was hardened so that he acted proudly, he was deposed from his kingly throne, and his glory was stripped from him. He was driven from human society, and his mind was made like that of an animal. His dwelling was with the wild asses, he was fed grass like oxen, and his body was bathed with the dew of heaven, until he learned that the Most High God has sovereignty over the kingdom of mortals, and sets over it whomever he will. (vv. 20-21)

The lesson is offered to the perpetrators of the food fight, over and over. Those in the monopoly regularly learn too late.

VI

Eventually our study of food must come to Jesus. It is clear that Jesus violated the rules of the food system by eating with publicans and sinners (Mark 2:16).[5] He violated the rules of eating that are, of course, the rules of power. Thus when Rand Paul, a candidate for the U.S. Senate, can opine that lunch counters are private and should serve whom they want, it is understood as an endorsement of a power arrangement that should be beyond challenge. Jesus violates the rules and thereby presents himself as an enemy of those rules and those power arrangements. I cite three texts from Luke, the most socially revolutionary of the gospels.

1. It is no wonder that in the Magnificat, the song of Mary that is the theme song of Luke, Mary sang of food:

> He has filled the hungry with good things,
> and sent the rich away empty. (Luke 1:53)

Mary anticipates that the narrative to follow in Luke will be witness to a food revolution whereby the old rules of food are overthrown so that all may share.

2. In Luke 14, Jesus teaches his host at dinner:

> When you serve a luncheon or a dinner, do not invite your friends or your brothers or your relatives or rich neighbors, in case they may invite you in return, and you would be repaid. But when you give a banquet, invite the poor, the crippled, the lame, and the blind. And you will be blessed, because they cannot repay you, for you will be repaid at the resurrection of the righteous. (14:12-14)

Jesus redefines the social process of eating in an inclusive way. And then he tells his parable of the great banquet. When the honored guests are too busy to attend, the master of the table wants the household filled with those who are on the "roads and lanes," that is, the street people not usually qualified for such a bountiful table.

3. In Luke 12, Jesus tells a parable about a rich man who prospered in agriculture. He frames the story as a warning about greed. And then we watch as the prosperous man wants to store more and more. But his food production is so abundant that he finally can say:

> "What shall I do, for I have no place to store my crops?" Then he said, "I will do this: I will pull down my barns and build larger ones, and there I will store all my grain and my goods." (12:17-18)

And then he said to himself:

> Soul, you have ample goods laid up for many years; relax, eat, drink, and be merry. (v. 19)

This is a guy who has made it in the food world. He builds bigger barns, bigger silos, bigger granaries, and bigger vaults. It occurs to me that wanting more storehouses for his monopoly of food sounds like Pharaoh who built storage cities as Solomon would later build storage cities (1 Kgs 9:19). They are all of a piece, those who secured a disproportionate share of the world's food supply.

And then in the parable, in the middle of his self-congratulations, "But God said to him" (v. 20). The interruption of such self-congratulations sounds like the word of YHWH to Pharaoh, "Let my people go." It reads like the handwriting on the wall to Belshazzar. And like the story of Belshazzar, this story ends with the guy dead that night. Food monopolizers are, sooner or later, interrupted by this inscrutable master of all food. It happens to every great accumulator.

And if that were not enough, Jesus turns the parable of Luke 12 into an instruction for his disciples. He says to them in the next verse:

> Therefore I tell you, do not worry about your life, what you will eat, or about your body, what you will wear. (v. 22)

Do not participate in the anxiety system that is grounded in a mistaken notion of scarcity. Do not be anxious, because your heavenly father, the Food Manager, knows what you need. Then Jesus, master teacher, observes birds and lilies that are not anxious because they trust the creator who gives them their food supply. And then, after birds and lilies, we get this familiar zinger that is so familiar that we do not notice that it is a zinger:

> Yet I tell you, even *Solomon* in all his glory was not clothed like one of these. (v. 27)

Not even Solomon! Not even the great accumulator! Not even Pharaoh! Not even Nebuchadnezzar! Not even Belshazzar! Not any of the accumulators can get outside the anxiety that is intrinsic to the scarcity system.

So, to review, the crisis of scarcity, anxiety, accumulation, and monopoly:

touches *food production* and asks about the abuse of the land;

touches *food consumption* and asks about commoditization;

touches *food distribution* and the redistribution of food at the creator's behest;

touches the environment that overproduces in order to add to the monopoly.

It makes one wonder if the monopolizers had any capacity for an internal life, what they did about their hunger for meaning, whether they noticed the neighbor when they gathered at the table. It keeps ringing in our ears, "Not even Solomon in all his glory" . . . in all his self-indulgence.

The biblical text traces the career of the monopolizers. But it does more than that. It attests that there is another way to do food. When our granaries and our bodies store surpluses, our bodies and the body politic suffer. It can be otherwise: we can meet at the table in another way. We watch and notice while it is taken, blessed, broken, and given. And there is always more than enough, sometimes twelve baskets, sometimes seven baskets; it is shared and ample. No need to accumulate!

COMMUNITY: ABUNDANT FOOD PRACTICE AS ASTONISHED GRATITUDE

There is amazing news for these who trust too much in the ideology of *scarcity, anxiety, accumulation*, and *monopoly*. Here is the news that matters decisively to the faith and practice of the church. There is an alternative to that ideology, an alternative that is grounded in faith that leads to a different daily life. In my church, St. Timothy, we call that "The Other Way." It is a way that invites a move:

from scarcity to *abundance*;

from anxiety to *trust*;

from accumulation to *sharing*;

from monopoly to *covenantal neighborliness*.

My topic in the second half of the chapter is this "Other Way" of obedient trust that leads to sharing and that culminates in covenantal neighborliness. It is from this news in the Bible and on into the life of the church at its best, concerning food and hunger, that we embrace

a different ideology that refuses anxious scarcity;

a different theology that aims at neighborliness and not monopoly;

a different explanatory narrative that centers in the reality of a God who is not parsimonious.

This theological conviction runs through the Bible. It does not, however, run easily or uninterruptedly through the Bible because the ideology of scarcity and anxiety also occupies the Bible and takes up a lot of text time. Thus it seems plausible to me to say that the Bible itself exhibits the food fight and is congruent with the way the food fight exists among us, and indeed exists, for each of us, in our own persons.[6]

I have, in the previous presentation, exposited the theology of scarcity and anxiety as it pertains to food and hunger. Now in this piece I will consider the alternative that is exhibited in God's generosity that evokes the gratitude of Israel and the church. That alternative permits us, on a daily basis, to be astonished by divine generosity that permits gratitude rather than anxiety.

I

The "Other Way" in the food fight is grounded in *creation faith*, in the conviction that the world is God's creation that is designed to exhibit and enact God's good will for the abundant life. The great creation text in Genesis 1 that frames the Bible is not about "origins." It is about the claim that the world is deeply linked to God's will and purpose. On the one hand, the world for that reason is not a closed system that operates on its own, leaving us with a zero-sum game; it is rather a process open to the continued gifts of the creator. On the other hand, the world is not itself sacred so that it possesses of itself the gift of life. Rather the creation is God's partner, God's object, God's vehicle for wellness in the world that God continues to enact in the continuing work of creation.[7] The Genesis recital tells of the ordered goodness of the world that moves progressively from day to day to day until it arrives at "very good" (v. 31). That ordered goodness, moreover, is sustained and reliable even in the face of the deep threat of chaos. Thus at the conclusion of the flood narrative, after the power of chaos has done its worst, God declares:

> As long as the earth endures,
> seedtime and harvest, cold and heat,
> summer and winter, day and night,
> shall not cease. (Gen 8:22)

The full, regular functioning of the creation is assured by divine decree!

The recital has two features that concern us here. First, the world is blessed by God. God had committed God's own life-giving force into the wonder of the world. Second, the effect of that divine blessing bestowed on the world is that the world is to be fruitful, to keep generating food that will sustain all of life:

> And God blessed them, saying, "Be fruitful and multiply and fill the waters in the seas and let birds multiply on the earth." (1:22)

That life-giving force, moreover, has been entrusted to human care and supervision:

> "See, I have *given you* every plant yielding seed that is on the face of all the earth, and you shall have them for food. And to every beast of the earth, and to every bird of the air, and to everything that creeps on the

> earth, everything that has the breath of life, I have given every *green* plant for food." And it was so. (1:29-30)

Right from the start, the creator has known that *green* is the color of earthly well-being!

The relationship of creator and creatureliness is one of committed trust and responding obedience. The news is that the world is articulated in personal-interpersonal categories, that the proper interaction of God and world, creator and creature, is one of dialogic interaction that features trust, generosity, gratitude, and obedience. Such a way in the world, albeit given in prescientific terms, refuses the flat, reductionist language of commodity and control to which market ideology is always tempted. Thus the Bible can imagine that all creatures—human creatures as well as birds, beasts, and fish—are in conversation with the creator.

Specifically that conversation, as concerns human persons, is in the form of prayer, long ago characterized as "the conversation of the heart addressed to God." The most pertinent prayer for the food fight is the simple, regular table prayer that voices thanks to God for food and that acknowledges that food is a gift from God and not a human product or possession. That prayer, practiced on every occasion of receiving food, is one of gratitude that contradicts the self-sufficiency of the accumulators. In the Old Testament, the two most treasured table prayers are situated in psalms of creation. In Psalm 145, the psalm acknowledges God's "wondrous works" of generosity that outrun human expectation (vv. 4-7). The psalm identifies, in stylized terms, the covenantal fidelity of God as "gracious and merciful" (vv. 8-9) and invites all creatures to give thanks:

> All your works shall give thanks to you, O LORD,
> and all your faithful shall bless you. (Ps 145:10)

Then, in vv. 15-16, comes what has long been a reiterated table prayer:

> The eyes of all look to you,
> and you give them their food in due season.
> You open your hand,
> satisfying the desire of every living thing.

The prayer affirms that God feeds "every living creature"; there is a correlation between "desire" and the timely generosity of God the creator who responds to every hunger. The prayer is a defiant refusal of autonomy and self-sufficiency.

The second such prayer is in Psalm 104, a psalm that moves from the large framing of creation as "heaven, earth, and the waters" (vv. 2-9) to the specificities of daily life:

> You cause the grass to grow for the cattle,
> and plants for people to use,
> to bring forth food from the earth,
> and wine to gladden the human heart,
> oil to make the face shine,
> and bread to strengthen the human heart. (104:14-15)

We may notice two things about this list of daily provisions of *wine*, *oil*, and *bread*. The three derive from grapes (wine), olives (oil), and grain (bread). These are the three great money crops in the ancient world, "grain, wine, and oil" (Deut 7:13; 14:23; Neh 13:5; Isa 36:17; Hos 2:8; Joel 2:19). But these money crops that are raised by peasants (and often exploited by the accumulators) are also the sacramental tokens of the church, thus water for baptism, bread and wine for the Eucharist, and oil for anointing. These sacramental claims of the church take the core stuff of creation's fullness as signs of the goodness and presence of God in the world.

While God is celebrated in large scope and then in regular provision, the psalm comes down to the case of daily food:

> These ["creeping things innumerable" in v. 25] all look to you
> to give their food in due season;
> when you give it to them, they gather it up;
> when you open your hand, they are filled with good things.
> (vv. 27-28)

It is God's open hand that feeds "all" who finally rely upon the creator. The creaturely look to the generous creator is one of astonishment, awe, wonder, and gratitude, that the Genesis creator would mobilize such a food-producing energy for such vulnerable cases as carrots and whales and possums and "us." The prayers affirms, "These all look to you," an expectant, trustful look; the language is paralleled in Psalm 145:15, "The eyes of all look to you." The grateful look is one of glad dependence that God will provide.

Such a "look" is well chronicled by Isak Dinesen in her encounter with Jogona Kanyagga, a nonreading tribesman. She wrote down his narrative account of himself, and read it back to him:

> He turned away from me while I was reading, as if to avoid all distractions. But as I read out his name, "And he sent for Jogona Kanyagga, who was his friend and who lived not far away," he swiftly turned his face to me, and gave me a great fierce flaming glance, so exuberant with laughter that it changed the old man into a boy, into the very symbol of youth. Again as I had finished the document and was reading out his name, where it figured as a verification below his thumbmark, the vital glance was repeated, this time deepened and calmed, with a new dignity. Such a glance did Adam give the Lord when he formed him out of dust, and breathed into his nostrils the breath of life, and man became a living soul. I had created him and shown him himself; Jogona Kanyagga of life everlasting. When I handed him the paper, he took it reverently and greedily, folded it up in a corner of his cloak, and kept his hand upon it. He could not afford to lose it, for his soul was in it, and it was proof of his existence.[8]

Such was the "look of Adam" toward the creator. That was *the look* in the first instance of being formed. But that look is also present in awed gratitude every time there is food. It is the gift of food from the creator that valorizes the creature. Such a look is a look of wonder for food given generously, a verification that our life—all of life—is sustained in well-being and joy. That look is such an antithesis to the blank stare of the accumulator who has only a look of self-congratulations: "Self, eat, drink, and be merry." That look of Adam is one of yielding trust and gratitude. Food is sustenance, valorization, and the meeting of elemental desire.

II

"The Other Way"—other than accumulation—is rooted in the conviction that the creator God presides over an abundant food supply with generosity toward all creatures. This conviction cannot be stated with scientific precision or with closely reasoned logic, and Israel never tried to do so. The reality of divine abundance given in generosity requires a very different mode of discourse, namely, doxology. Doxology is the glad self-abandoning exuberance of the creature who holds nothing back in affirmation of the creator.[9] Doxology is a mode of discourse that matches the lived generosity of the creation. Indeed, Genesis 1 itself has the cadences of doxology, the lining out of awe that can never be taken as scientific discourse. The psalms that I have cited that contain the table prayers are full, extended doxologies that take in the scope of all of creation. Psalm 104 celebrates the framing of creation (vv. 1-9) but pivots on *the gift of water*, and this in an arid climate:

> You make springs gush forth in the valleys;
>   they flow between the hills,
> giving drink to every wild animal;
>   the wild asses quench their thirst.
> By the streams the birds of the air have their habitation;
>   they sing among the branches.
> From your lofty abode you water the mountains;
>   the earth is satisfied with the fruit of your work. (104:10-13)

The water here is the same water that flows in the four rivers of the garden of Eden (Gen 2:10-14); it is clear that water is what makes a life-giving world possible. The psalm notices the sustenance of all creatures from the water-providing God (wild animals, wild asses, birds, cattle, storks, wild goats, coneys, lions). It is no wonder that at v. 24 the psalmist must fall back in exuberance, lacking any other form of adequate speech:

> O LORD, how manifold are your works!
>   In wisdom you have made them all;
>   the earth is full of your creatures. (see also v. 35)

The secret of creation is pronounced in vv. 29-30 by the double reference to God's "spirit/breath" on which the word depends. The world is not a self-starter. It cannot maintain itself automatically, nor can any of the creatures that inhabit it. Israel's doxology knows that it is the gift of the wind of God that creates (see Gen 1:2), that renews the face of the ground (v. 30). It is no surprise at all that the psalmist, singing for all those who gladly trust God's abundance, knows that praise defines human creaturely existence:

> I will sing to the LORD as long as I live;
>   I will sing praise to my God while I have being. (v. 33)

It is no wonder that Psalm 148 issues a summons to all creatures to join in praise of the creator:

> Praise him, sun and moon;
>   praise him, all you shining stars!

> Praise him, you highest heaven,
>   and you waters above the heavens! . . .
> Praise the Lord from the earth,
>   you sea monsters and all deeps,
> fire and hail, snow and frost,
>   stormy wind fulfilling his command!
> Mountains and hills,
>   fruit trees and all cedars!
> Wild animals and all cattle,
>   creeping things and flying birds . . .
> Let them praise the name of the Lord,
>   for his name alone is exalted;
>   his glory is above earth and heaven. (148:3-4, 7-10, 13)

The other psalm I have cited ends with a like doxology:

> My mouth will speak the praise of the Lord,
>   and all flesh will bless his holy name forever and ever. (145:21)

Doxology is the rhetoric of overflowing in which the words of awe and astonishment tumble out. The words are not to be uttered to an abstract principle or to an empty sky. They are words back to the limitless generosity of God who gives seed and bread:

> For as the rain and snow come down from heaven,
>   and do not return there until they have watered the earth,
> making it bring forth and sprout,
>   giving seed to the sower and bread to the eater. (Isa 55:10)

The push of doxology beyond human speech is risked in the poetry of Job in the great creation hymn that situates Job in a vast mystery of God's governance:

> Who determined its measurements—surely you know!
>   Or who stretched the line upon it?
> On what were its bases sunk,
>   or who laid its cornerstone
> when the morning stars sang together
>   and all the heavenly beings shouted for joy? (Job 38:5-7)

The question is put to Job, and he cannot answer. He cannot answer because the wonder of creation is beyond knowing. All around the divine question there is wonder and awe and astonishment. In the instant of their appearing, as the darkness is broken and the dawn cracks, the stars at dawn broke into singing. They sang in joy about their existence. They sang in gratitude for the creator who brought the light. They sang because it is in their nature to sing. They exist in order to sing the world back to God. Such doxology is a match to creation as miracle.

In church practice none has known this more fully than Francis of Assisi who could ponder the doxology of all creation:

> Thou burning sun with golden beam,
> Thou silver moon with softer gleam . . .
> Thou rushing wind that art so strong,
> Ye clouds that sail in heaven along,
> Thou rising morn, in praise rejoice,
> Ye lights of evening, find a voice!
> Thou fruitful earth that day by day
> Unfoldest blessing on our way,
> The flowers and fruits that in thee grow,
> Let them God's glory also show.

The refrain is "Alleluia, alleluia, alleluia, alleluia," a somewhat adjusted form of "Praise Yah." That phrase, an imperative summons, cannot be repeated too often, for what else could a rushing wind or a golden beam or a silver moon do? What else except to praise the creator? It is all thanks for endless generosity!

III

Doxology is about awed gratitude. It is response to gifts given by being in a posture of receptivity. That is why we sing such songs best with our hands outstretched. It is for good reason, then, that the creation liturgy in Genesis 1 culminates in Sabbath rest:

> On the seventh day God finished the work that he had done, and he rested on the seventh day from all the work that he had done. So God rested the seventh day and hallowed it, because on it God rested from all the work that he had done in creation. (Gen 2:2-3)

The world, as given by God is not a restless, seething organism of recalcitrance. The world is "very good" as a fruit-bearing process to the benefit of all creatures. For that reason, at the center of biblical faith—indeed at the center of doxology—is the command to Sabbath rest. One can judge that Sabbath rest is the defining mark of God's grateful creatures who rely on the creator's generosity. Imagine: God rests! God is not anxious about creation working well. God is not a workaholic. More than that, it is testified that Sabbath rest for God allowed God to recover God's *nepeš* (Exod 31:17). The phrase translated there as "was refreshed" is a verbal use of the term *nepeš* ("soul" or "self"), so that God was "*re-nepešed*," given life back after depletion. The wonder is that God, even God, is depleted and fatigued by the work of creation, so that Sabbath is recovery from depletion.

It is remarkable enough to imagine a depleted God who requires Sabbath. It is equally remarkable to ponder human persons who are depleted and who require recovery and restoration. Thus Sabbath breaks the grip of feverish work in the world, feverish accumulation. Big time accumulators never take Sabbath rest. It is hard to imagine Pharaoh taking Sabbath rest. So of course Pharaoh is more and more depleted, and consequently more and more anxious. It is, in like manner, hard to imagine a conventional U.S. consumer taking a Sabbath break from restless efforts at accumulation performed for the sake of the children or the career or the church or whatever. It is hard to imagine the vicious cycle of anxiety being broken, but such is the wondrous reality of Sabbath rest that is in sync with the rhythm of creation.[10] On that day, the pay-off day of creation, human persons join God and the birds and the lilies, and all creatures of our God and king and live in astonished abundance in order to ponder and experience and enjoy the abundance given by God. Sabbath is possible because God is known to guarantee what is needed to satisfy the desire of every living thing. Sabbath is a performance of an alternative to assert among ourselves that we are not pressed by scarcity, we are not consumed by anxiety, we are not driven by greed, and we are not available for anxious accumulation. At Sabbath, the creation takes into account the assured reality that "loaves abound." It turns out that the abundance is not a matter of quantity. It is rather about being receptive rather than on the make, being a glad creature rather than posturing as the creator of our own lives.

IV

The convergence of *creation as fruitful food production*, response in *exuberant doxology* that matches God's abundance, and *restful Sabbath* to savor the abundance generates a venue for food sharing in gratitude and food eating in astonishment. That is the truth of the world that Israel confesses that decisively impacts our food production, food distribution, and food consumption.

In the purview of Israel, Pharaoh, the accumulator, had skewed the entire process:

> Pharaoh, in his monopoly, has imagined that he, and *not the creator*, is the one who provides food (see Ezek 29:3);
>
> Pharaoh, in his scarcity, has *reduced the doxologies* of Israel to pained laments (see Exod 2:23);
>
> Pharaoh, in his insatiable appetite, has gotten rid of all Sabbath rest (see Exod 5:4-19).

The annulment of generous creation, *the silencing* of doxology, and *the termination* of Sabbath rest has resulted in a process of food production, food distribution, and food consumption that is unbearable for Israel and for the world.

For that reason, the exodus narrative that follows immediately after the slave-enticing narrative of Genesis 47 is about the departure of Israel from the food system of Pharaoh. The narrative concerns Israel's coming to consciousness about its unbearable status in the food monopoly. Israel becomes an agent in its own history rather than the recipient of what Pharaoh chooses to dole out. Israel breaks the silence of pain long denied, imagines an alternative existence outside the monopoly of Pharaoh, and dares to go there. The exodus narrative of course features Pharaoh the accumulator, who has skewed creation, and Moses, who is a daring and uncompromising leader. Most of all, it spectacularly features the creator God, YHWH, who is the great adversary of Pharaoh, the accumulator. Indeed, YHWH's enigmatic name in Exodus 3:14 that we translate something like "I will be who I will be" contains in it something of the verb "cause to be," thus "the one who creates."[11] The contest between God and Pharaoh, between Moses (and Aaron) and the imperial magicians, is a food fight, a contest between theories and practices of food.

As the story continues, in Exodus 15 Israel, through the leadership of Moses and at the behest of YHWH, departs the food monopoly of the accumulator. After pausing to sing and dance (15:1-18, 20-21), the Israelites make their way into the wilderness, en route to a new land. In the Bible the "wilderness" is a place without viable life supports or reliable food supplies, and they had to go there on their way. They are filled with singing exuberance about the possibility of the new land in chapter 15 that lies beyond the reach of Pharaoh's food policies.

But their exuberance promptly fades. By the second verse of chapter 16, just two verses into the wilderness, they are vexed and contentious; they wish they had never left the regime of the accumulator:

> The whole congregation of the Israelites complained against Moses and Aaron in the wilderness. The Israelites said to them, "If only we had died by the hand of the LORD in the land of Egypt, when we sat by the fleshpots and ate our fill of bread; you have brought us out into this wilderness to kill this whole assembly with hunger. (Exod 16:2-3)

They thought they were going to die, and so they remembered the "meat pots" in the land of the accumulator that now looked better than the hunger of the wilderness. Indeed, in another reading of the same memory, they could recall in some detail the menu that they had enjoyed in Egypt:

> If only we had meat to eat! We remember the fish we used to eat in Egypt for nothing, the cucumbers, the melons, the leeks, the onions, and the garlic; but now our strength is dried up; and there is nothing at all but this manna to look at. (Num 11:4-6)

They did not at the moment remember the burden of their labor, only that they had food. And now, having trusted Moses and having committed to YHWH as an alternative to the accumulator, they were bereft. There is a reason that this story is preoccupied with the accumulator!

In the narrative that follows, they were surprised—and we are surprised in remembering and reading—that the wilderness turned out to be a place where YHWH could and would give gifts. Thus the creator promises meat in the wilderness:

> At twilight you shall have meat. (Exod 16:12)

And they got quail:

> In the evening quails came up and covered the camp. (v. 13)

Before long they complained about the lack of water, and they got water:

> But the people thirsted there for water; and the people complained against Moses and said, "Why did you bring us out of Egypt, to kill us and our children and livestock with thirst?" . . . The LORD said to Moses, "Go on ahead of the people, and take some of the elders of Israel with you; take in your hand the staff with which you struck the Nile, and go. I will be standing there in front of you on the rock at Horeb. Strike the rock, and water will come out of it, so that the people may drink." Moses did so, in the sight of the elders of Israel. (17:3, 5-6)

And in between the meat and the water, God promised bread:

> In the morning you shall have your fill of bread. (16:12)

When it came in the morning, it was indeed bread, but it was not like any bread they had ever experienced. They were astonished and bewildered. They said in their surprise, "What is it?" In Hebrew they said, *mān hû'*, that is, "manna." The wondered about it and knew it was "wonder bread" sent by God when they did not expect it to be given in the wilderness. They were given bread outside Pharaoh's monopoly. We are told only that it was, "a fine flakey substance, as fine as frost on the ground" (v. 14). Moses clarified:

> It is the bread that the LORD has given you to eat. (v. 15)

So now, in its bereavement, Israel has meat, water, and bread. They have all the essentials. It turned out that the generous food supply God has exhibited, even the wilderness, the place without viable life supports, is a part of the life-sustaining creation over which the creator presides. They saw in that moment that the creator God has the capacity to transform wilderness into creation, to transpose the place of hunger into a venue for abundance.

But the narrative does not move to a big theological claim. It remains with the concreteness of bread for the hungry. Moses, manager of the new bread, authorizes a harvest of the surprising bread:

> Gather as much of it as each of you needs, an omer to a person according to the number of persons, all providing for those in their own tents. (v. 16)

The bread was such a contrast to the bread of scarcity in Egypt, for there was enough. There was no scarcity of bread in the wilderness:

> The Israelites did so; some gathered more, some less. But when they measured it with an omer those who gathered much had nothing over, and those who gathered little had no shortage; they gathered as much as each of them needed. (vv. 17-18)

The generous creator had given all that everyone needed. God had indeed "satisfied the desire of every living thing," so that we may find in the narrative an echo of the doxological thanks of the psalm. There is only one catch. Moses provided,

> Let no one leave any of it over until morning. (v. 19)

They cannot store it up, build a surplus, or hoard it. In this way the bread is so unlike the bread of the accumulator, for the one thing not to be done now is accumulate. But, says the narrator, they did not listen to that one qualification; they tried to save it up. The reason they tried to save it up is that they feared scarcity. And the reason they feared scarcity is that they thought like Pharaoh. They were completely inured to the ideology of scarcity and anxiety, and so were propelled to accumulate.

But they could not do it. This bread would not permit surplus! The gifts of God do not lend themselves to accumulation. And so, we are told,

> the bread got worms;
> the bread began to smell badly;
> the bread melted. (vv. 20-21)

On all counts, there is no way to save it up. No possibility of accumulation. No chance to confuse this bread with the bread of Pharaoh, for the bread of Pharaoh falls into monopoly and exclusion and hoarding, and eventually violence with hunger.

There is, however, a strange footnote in the narrative. In vv. 22-23 Moses makes a Friday exception to the rule of no storage. He authorizes them to gather more bread on Friday, to have bread for Sabbath Saturday when they are not to gather:

> Tomorrow is a day of solemn rest, a holy sabbath to the LORD; bake what you want to bake and boil what you want to boil, and all that is left over put aside to be kept until morning. So they put it aside until morning,

as Moses commanded them; and it did not become foul, and there were no worms in it. Moses said, "Eat it today, for today is a sabbath to the LORD; today you shall not find it in the field. Six days you shall gather it; but on the seventh day, which is a sabbath, there will be none.

(vv. 23-26)

Imagine that! Even in the wilderness where they feared scarcity, they are to prepare for Sabbath rest. They are to cease from their eager effort to secure bread. They are to pause to ponder that even there in the wilderness, creation functions. The creator is alive and well. The bread holds for today, even as it multiplies enough for tomorrow when it is Sabbath.

This is a remarkable story. It is impossible to overstate its importance for Israel's memory and its significance for our perception of the food fight that offers an alternative to Pharaoh's hungry drive for monopoly. In this remarkable narrative, all the juices of the *garden* have been transferred to and activated in the *wilderness*. Wherever the glory of God appears, wilderness is transposed. There is no limit to the transformative power of YHWH that contrasts to the impotence of Pharaoh. For that reason, Israel has doxologies about the transformative power of the creator:

The wilderness and the dry land shall be glad,
    the desert shall rejoice and blossom;
like the crocus it shall blossom abundantly,
    and rejoice with joy and singing.
The glory of Lebanon shall be given to it,
    the majesty of Carmel and Sharon.
They shall see the glory of the LORD,
    the majesty of our God. (Isa 35:1-2)

When the poor and needy seek water
    and there is none,
    and their tongue is parched with thirst,
I the LORD will answer them,
    I the God of Israel will not forsake them,
I will open rivers on the bare heights,
    and fountains in the midst of the valleys;
I will make the wilderness a pool of water,
    and the dry land springs of water.
I will put in the wilderness the cedar,
    the acacia, myrtle, and the olive;

> I will set in the desert the cypress,
> the plane and the pine together,
> so that all may see and know,
> all may consider and understand,
> that the hand of the LORD has done this,
> the Holy One of Israel has created it. (Isa 41:17-20)

Pharaoh assumed that the world was a closed system with no new gifts to be given. Israel's doxologies contradict that notion with the lyrical conviction that God has more gifts to give; those gifts are to be given in places where we think it is not possible to have new life. The manna narrative contradicts the ideology of Pharaoh! And the people of God have lived from the truth of that narrative ever since.

V

The food fight of course is not resolved in the Old Testament. It is, for that reason, not surprising that it continues into the New Testament. Now the challenge is not Pharaoh or Nebuchadnezzar. Now the challenge is the imperial option of Rome, and the way in which some Jews, notably the influential priests, colluded with imperial appetites. They did so by "fencing the table" with rules of holiness that carried with them rules of power and access.

It was the vocation of Jesus to exhibit and perform the abundance of God's rule that constituted a stark contrast to the ideology of parsimony that evoked the imperial rules of power and access. In the horizon of Jesus, there was no ground for scarcity, and so no reason for anxiety, and so no need for accumulation, and so no pressure toward monopoly. Almost everything Jesus did in his teaching and in his action challenged those rules and brought him into conflict with the authorities. He is indeed a "transgressor" of the conventional rules of food, a transgression that is one way in which to join in the food fight. Thus at the beginning of Mark, the issue is joined:

> And as he sat at dinner in Levi's house, many tax collectors and sinners were also sitting with Jesus and his disciples—for there were many who followed him. When the scribes of the Pharisees saw that he was eating with sinners and tax collectors, they said to his disciples, "Why does he eat with tax collectors and sinners?" When Jesus heard this, he said to

> them, "Those who are well have no need of a physician, but those who are sick; I have come to call not the righteous but sinners."
>
> (Mark 2:15-17)

Already in Mark 2:1-12, he runs into opposition, for his willingness to heal and his capacity to forgive are acts of unseemly generosity in a theological world that is governed by parsimony. By his readiness to eat with the "disqualified," he makes clear that the food supply of the creator is not limited to those who keep the rules of holiness and power; in fact the food supply is sufficient to be distributed "indiscriminately." Indeed, his initial entry into the synagogue to begin his public life features a declaration of Jubilee by quoting from Isaiah 61:1 (Luke 4:18-19). The Jubilee of course is the most subversive and dangerous teaching in the Bible, for it enacts a different kind of entitlement that pays no heed to conventional rules of distribution and property.[12]

In Luke 14, Jesus is challenged about rules for Sabbath keeping (Luke 14:1-6). This is followed by a narrative about "places of honor" at a dinner. This notice on his part opens the way for his parable about dinner, for he understood immediately that rules for dining reflect power arrangements in society. He reflects on who gets to eat and who decides who gets to eat. His dictum is about inclusive sharing:

> But when you give a banquet, invite the poor, the crippled, the lame, and the blind. And you will be blessed, because they cannot repay you, for you will be repaid at the resurrection of the righteous. (Luke 14:13-14)

That dictum, moreover, is an introduction to his parable of the great banquet about food for street people:

> Go out at once into the streets and lanes of the town and bring in the poor, the crippled, the blind, and the lame. . . . Go out into the roads and lanes, and compel people to come in, so that my house may be filled.
>
> (vv. 21, 23)

His story envisions a great offer of food with proper honor and concern for all the members of the community, without reference to qualification.

Alongside his words, it is Jesus' actions that push the food fight to greater extremity. Jesus twice performs a "feeding miracle." That is, he offers and exhibits food in wild abundance and distributes it to the hungry crowd without attention to qualification. In Mark 6:30-44 he is in a "deserted place," that is, a "wilderness." He observes the hungry crowd and has "compassion for them." He takes what little food is available in the crowd and performs and makes available the abundance of God's new creation. In Jesus, the new creation of God's abundance has begun and is now visible in the wilderness. The convergence of "wilderness" and "compassion" makes clear that Jesus is reiterating the manna narrative of Exodus 16. He brings food where there is none. His actions consists in

> taking the five loaves,
>
> blessing the loaves,
>
> breaking the loaves,
>
> giving the loaves for distribution.

The narrative does not explain or exhibit any curiosity about how this could happen. It does not invite or require or even permit explanation. It is enough that Jesus transforms that "deserted place" into a place of well-being. The hungry crowd consists in "5,000 men." I suppose we are permitted to add the accompanying women and children. There was enough, more than enough, left over for twelve baskets of bread.

In Mark 8:1-10, he is again in the "desert." He again comes to a great crowd without anything to eat. He again has compassion. He again enacts the abundance of the new creation:

> He took the loaves;
>
> He gave thanks for what bread he had;
>
> He breaks the loaves;
>
> He gives them to his disciples for distribution.

There was, again, more than enough. The crowd numbered four thousand, and seven baskets of bread were surplus this time.

This twice-told story about this twice-performed wonder lies outside the grip of anxious monopoly. Jesus is no accumulator. He relies on the bread that is at hand. He passed it all out. He does so because it is needed for the hungry crowd; he knew and trusted that there would be more as it was needed. It is clear that when Jesus comes as the agent of the new creation of God, there is no scarcity and so no anxiety, and so no accumulation. The narrative shows the way in which the food fight is to be resolved, by the embrace of the new creation of abundance that refuses frantic production, that eschews parsimonious distribution, and that allows for consumption that fills but that does not overwhelm. Indeed, it is impossible to imagine anyone in either crowd overeating on that day!

These two episodes in the food fight are the epitome of the message and ministry of Jesus and the sum of the "good news" that the force of God's abundance has broken the power of fearful parsimony.

It is no wonder that in the narrative of Mark, the second episode is followed by a session of critical reflection. Jesus briefly refutes another challenge of the Pharisees (vv. 11-13). But his focus is on his disciples, because something of immense importance has happened among them. His own disciples, however, do not any more discern what he has done than do the Pharisees. His disciples are in a boat without bread. Well, there is "one loaf," a notation that some think refers to Jesus himself in the boat as the bread of life. Jesus warns his disciples about the junk food of those who make the rules of access:

> Watch out—beware of the yeast of the Pharisees and the yeast of Herod.
> (Mark 8:15)

Then he asks them to reflect on what he has done in supplying abundant food. He asks them for discernment, of which they are in fact not capable:

> Do you still not perceive or understand? Are your hearts hardened? Do you have eyes, and fail to see? Do you have ears, and fail to hear? And do you not remember? (vv. 17-18)

They do not get it; they do not respond to his questions, and they likely avoided eye contact with him. They do not understand that the terrain of the food fight has, by his presence and his action, decisively shifted. They do not in fact perceive or understand or see or hear or remember. They are completely oblivious.

Like any good teacher, Jesus retreats from such large and challenging questions back to a concrete operational question:

> When I broke the five loaves for the five thousand, how many baskets of broken pieces did you collect? (v. 19)

The answer confidently: "Twelve."

> And the seven for the four thousand, how many baskets full of broken pieces did you collect? (v. 20)

The answer promptly: "Seven." There is a long pause. The disciples are relieved that they have survived the quiz. But Jesus sees what he has on his hands. He has eager disciples who are good at concrete operational data. They know the statistics. But they have no idea what they have witnessed. They completely miss the point that a new reality about food and hunger is now before their very eyes. And so, upon reflection, he says to his disciples:

> Do you not yet understand? (v. 21)

He says it, perhaps whimsically, surely with disappointment, maybe a tone of rebuke. But this is how it is among us characteristically, as followers of Jesus. The new disclosure is too radical and revolutionary, and we cannot take it in. Because what is exhibited is the fact that the old categories of the food fight are now irrelevant. The old patterns of Pharaoh are obsolete because that old pattern cannot engage in generous sharing. The new creation is a gift that keeps on giving, and there is no excuse now for parsimony toward the neighbor.

Mark offers only a hint of the reason for the obtuseness of the disciples, a hint that explains everything:

> They did not understand about the bread, because their hearts were hardened. (6:52)

Clearly the disciples do not understand about the bread. They did not understand that the creation is now under new rules of generosity. But Mark also hints at why the new reality is greeted with obtuseness. They did not understand because their hearts were hardened. Anyone can recognize that the phrase "hearts were hardened" is an allusion to the exodus narrative and the condition of Pharaoh (see Exod 7:22; 8:19; 9:35). In that ancient narrative, Pharaoh refused to let the slaves go because he had a hard heart. His hard heart made him anxious. Consequently he needed more granaries for more accumulation that in turn required slave labor. His hard heart caused him to misunderstand the emancipatory reality of God in the narrative.

And now the disciples are like Pharaoh. Indeed, they think like Pharaoh and are, like him, enthralled by notions of scarcity. What an amazing summary of our problem! The disciples missed the reality of God's abundant bread enacted by Jesus because they perceived reality in the categories of Pharaoh. Well, so say we all! All of us, give or take a little, are propelled by nightmares of scarcity that are blind and resistant to the truth of divine generosity that pervades creation. In fact the food fight is over. That is the news of the evangelists. But we keep reenacting and reiterating our ancient and abiding loyalty to the mistaken categories of Pharaoh. We order our lives and our communities and we build our policies of food and money and credit and war and supplies on the basis of scarcity. And we do so, even when we have seen otherwise!

VI

To this breathtaking new world of Jesus, I add only one note from Paul. In his great ethical inventory for the new life in Christ, he writes:

> Contribute to the needs of the saints; extend hospitality to strangers. (Rom 12:13)

He underscores the two virtues of abundance: generosity and hospitality (see v. 8). But it is in his great chapter in 2 Corinthians 8 that he brings his conviction about generosity to concrete practice. In that chapter he makes a strong appeal for the church in Corinth to contribute generously to the fund to support the church in Jerusalem. It is a bid for generosity. The ground for that generosity is christological. Do as Jesus did:

> For you know the generous act of our Lord Jesus Christ, that though he was rich, yet for your sakes he became poor, so that by his poverty you might become rich. (2 Cor 8:9)

Paul goes to great lengths not to command but only to persuade by being reasonable:

> I do not mean that there should be relief for others and pressure on you, but it is a question of a fair balance between your present abundance and their need, so that their abundance may be for your need, in order that there may be a fair balance. (vv. 13-14)

And then, most astonishingly, in the interest of the "fair balance" between "your present abundance and their need," he appeals to the manna story by quoting Exodus 16:18:

> The one who had much did not have too much,
> And the one who had little did not have too little. (v. 15)

This is a quite remarkable allusion to the manna narrative. It is used to urge sharing with others grounded in the conviction that there is more than enough for everyone. It is all about generosity that is funded by the prior generosity of God who supplies every need and satisfies the desire of every living thing.

VII

The news of an alternative gives us a new way to participate in the food fight. The news is of a new creation, jump-started by Jesus, that keeps on giving in ways that make parsimony obsolete. The church's dramatic enactment of and testimony to that new settlement of the food fight is the Eucharist in which we reiterate the four great verbs of Jesus in the wilderness, "Take, bless, break, give." Imagine having a regular ritual called "*Thanks*"! This *thank-meal* is an act of defiance, a refusal of Pharaoh's system of accumulation, a resolve to live,

> from *abundance* and not scarcity,
>
> in *trust* and not anxiety,
>
> by *sharing* and not accumulating,
>
> for *neighborly covenant* and not monopoly.

We are left with the question of whether, in a world of fearful parsimony and violent struggle to corner the market on food, the abundance is true and reliable. Well, we have already signed on for it. The truth of abundance follows from Easter in which the power of death has been exposed as a fraud. Our task is to connect the dots between our big affirmation, "Christ is risen; he is risen indeed," to policies and practices of food production, food distribution, and food consumption.

The claim has immediate implications for how we eat, how much we eat, with whom we eat, and how much we eat with whom we eat. It has long-term implications for policy because a bloated military budget is based on a fetish of accumulation. The people who are grounded in the generous abundance of God's new creation are the ones who will, perhaps in time, dismantle the entire system of greed that feeds hostility and requires us to live on orange alert. Were we not the great accumulators, we likely would not attract the envy and hostility of others in the food fight. It is our conviction that the new creation is reliable and will feed us until we want no more. Jesus broke down abundance to its most elemental components:

> I was hungry and you gave me food, I was thirsty and you gave me something to drink. . . . I was hungry and you gave me no food, I was thirsty and you gave me nothing to drink. (Matt 25:35, 42)

The great news is that we no longer need to be on the hopeless, losing side in the food fight!

7

DEPARTURE WITHOUT ARRIVAL

Scriptural Reasoning, as proposed and practiced by Peter Ochs, is a daring initiative and a shocking challenge to those accustomed to conventional critical exegesis. Without being able to penetrate all the subtleties of Peircian pragmatism, this exegete can discern enough to understand that texts can and must be read informed by modern critical tradition, but finally away from such thinness and back toward a communal practice that intends the hard work of reparations. From the essays offered in appreciation for and in response to Ochs' work, I place the accent on the *specificity of the text*, the *communal context* of reading that moves between ancient memory and contemporary appropriation, that *summons to reparations*, sustained *liturgical performance*, and resultant *habits of practice* that push beyond the Abrahamic to the Adamic. An exegete must very soon move to a specific text in order to have much to say. Thus I turn to Exodus 15:22-26 in order to consider a rereading in what I hope is a mode of "Scriptural Reasoning."

I have selected this text because it is a text that is "on the way," as Scriptural Reasoning must always be. There has been a departure from the lethal system of Pharaoh (14:1–15:18). But of course there is no arrival yet in the land of milk and honey. Indeed, there will not be an arrival for a very long time; and even when there finally is an arrival, it will be a contested, disputatious, even violent arrival that waits for peaceableness . . . and is even waiting still.

We are, in this text, well between a remembered departure and an awaited arrival, in the wilderness of Shur. The presenting problem, shortly after the walls of water that drowned Pharaoh, is that there is "no water" (15:22). There is a cry to YHWH (v. 25). There is an immediate response from YHWH, divine action before the divine speech. YHWH exhibits a piece of wood and throws the wood into the bitter water. It is made sweet! We do not know how it is made sweet. We are not told, and the text displays no curiosity about the transformation of the water. The God who can emancipate is fully able to transform water. The sweet water is an act of rescue and preservation and a sign that this community is on the way from the bitter life of bondage to the sweet life of shalom.

The departure and the awaited arrival concern the materiality of life-labor and bondage and food and oppression—circumstances that produce a cry of pain and distress. It is not known yet, but the erstwhile slaves are on their way to a new obedience, even in the desert. They will need to react to the demands of Pharaoh no longer, for Pharaoh is now only at the back edge of the narrative, a remembered source of alienation and oppression that made life sterile and absent of joy. Israel must remember back through the dancing of Miriam to recall Pharaoh, but the pain remains present enough in their bodies that they can recall very well.

When we read that transformative moment of "cry-answer" today, especially when we read it as privileged people who have not felt the bodily scars of the brickyard, we readily transpose that ordered, hollow regime of Pharaoh to the ordered, hollow regime of vacuous reason. The God of the exodus has come to the slave camp and has gathered nameless sufferers into a community ordered around miracle that has no explanation but that has futures of sweetness. If we ask about the departure from Pharaoh's land, surely Scriptural Reasoning intends departure from a system of reason that can bring order and even security but that cannot bring life. Scriptural Reasoning, with texts like this one, is itself a practice of departure.

Having taken that first step of departure, dazzled by the first sip of sweet water, the Lord of bitter water and sweet water now speaks in the text. YHWH has waited to speak until there has been "showing" and "throwing" and eager drinking. Perhaps that first sip of sweet water generates a moment of readiness for listening.

The speech of the one who meets Israel in sweet water is framed in anticipation of Sinai.

First there is narrative report:

> There the LORD made for them a statute and an ordinance and there he put them to the test. (Exod 15:25b)

The "test" follows the water. The "statute and ordinance" are Sinai read back, for the one who saves is the one who will command. And now the same one speaks. The first word is "if" that anticipates the first utterance at Sinai in 19:5.[1] It is a condition, that is, the *truth* of YHWH's offer depends upon the *practice* of Israel. *Truth* comes in and with and under *practice*. The requirement is to "listen carefully," an absolute infinitive that anticipates the same in 19:5. Listening is a price of the rule of YHWH. There had been no listening in Pharaoh's Egypt because there had been no compelling voice and no frame of relationship. Pharaoh had in mind only senseless productivity and did not care about the possibility of hearing. But departure from Pharaoh's rule makes dialogic engagement possible, and for the first time. Israel, in this summons, is empowered to make a difference by its practice. The words tumble out to make the accent clear: "Listen carefully . . . do what is right . . . give heed . . . keep." The conversation is about commandments, the ones to be given at Sinai that will supersede the commands of death in the regime of Pharaoh. The slaves who mindlessly produced have, through the sweet, saving water, become a community of responsive engagement that has a chance to shape a different future by their obedience.

From that chance it follows: "I will not bring" (15:26). There is no grammatical connection, no explicit linking of the command (with the urgent absolute infinitive) to the promise. Except that it follows because YHWH is willing to respond to Israel's obedience. The promise arises from command in a way unlike that of Pharaoh's Egypt wherein there was no promise that followed the commands of Pharaoh:

> I will not bring upon you any of the diseases that I brought upon the Egyptians. (v. 26b)

The diseases are not identified. Scholars, moreover, have used too much energy pretending medical competence. But the intent is self-evident in the utterance itself. The diseases that smite Egypt are alienation, oppression, death to human possibility, nullification of communal opportunity, and finally despair. Nicholas Adams can write of the image of the medical:

> The leading metaphor that runs throughout the model of reparative reasoning is that of medicine, although there are others; I will simplify it somewhat. The reader is invited to consider how a physician treats a patient who offers an account of her suffering.[2]

The divine speech alludes to the lethal pathologies of Egypt. We know, moreover, about the modes of pathology produced by a Cartesian anxiety that of itself precludes community. The promise that follows obedience is an alternative to Egypt. The "logic of repair" is that obedience to the alternative commands of Sinai makes new life possible. Failure to obey Sinai portends the killing fields of Pharaoh every time. And then, as though to seal the deal, the maker of sweet water offers self-identification. "I am YHWH!" What follows is stunning self-acknowledgment. "I am YHWH who heals you." It is crucial that the sentence ends in "you": "heals *you*." More than that, this participle readily converts into a noun: I am YHWH, *your* doctor," not "the doctor." The one for you! YHWH is a doctor for *you*, as though the healing of this company of slaves is the single agenda of the Lord, now the Lord with the supply of sweet water. But not "a doctor." Not "the doctor." "Your doctor," the one fully committed to repair: to repair the torn bodies scarred by Pharaoh, to repair the wounded community staggered by Pharaoh's anticommunity requirements, to enact a logic of repair of the kind Ezra will later enact on the text. There is unleashed in the world of the text a healing agent, one who is able to counter "the diseases of Egypt."[3]

There is no doubt that this text is the pivot of the tradition, anticipating the alternative existence given at Sinai. It is an odd text that disrupts narrative continuity in order to permit the Lord of Sinai to speak in anticipation and to summon to an obedience the shape of which is not yet disclosed.

My reading of this text resonates with what I take to be the accents of Scriptural Reasoning.

1. There is textual specificity. Finally we must move beyond philosophical speculation to see how Scripture itself opens reality. It is a text of only five verses, but it creates an enormous caesura in the traffic from Pharaoh to Sinai. It is a self-announcement that alters the world.

2. The text is situated in a quite specific context. In the final form of the text, the context is the wilderness where a miracle is required whereby the waters are transformed and made life-giving. In our contemporary context, the text meets us with questions about morality and the way in which the logic of repair can carry us beyond Cartesian diseases. More than that, I write this the day after Obama's inauguration in 2009. I do not think the new president has messianic proportions. But I do think this is a new text for the moment, for all parts of the world. Folk are watching and hoping for a new possibility beyond ancient decisions

that have precluded healing hope. We read this text, anciently as best we can; inescapably we read it with contemporary alertness and ponder the command and the promise.

3. The text is clearly an act of reparation. There is an utterance here that aims to repair the defeat of Israel's hope by Pharaoh's brick quota. The reason Miriam and the women could sing and dance is because they knew, through their poetry, that they were not fated to bondage, that healing juices were renovating history and making new life possible. The great repair is surfaced in the ancient declaration that YHWH will "reign forever" (Exod 15:18).

4. The narrative and the divine declaration are available for us in many liturgical performances as is required in many circumstances. There is no doubt that Pharaoh's enlightened productivity is enormously seductive. By Exodus 16:3, the slaves wanted to go back to slavery. This people, like every people, is always again pulled back into the regime of despair with its ready offer of sustenance and order and security. And as often as seduced back, so often is liturgical reperformance of emancipation and repair necessary. Thus the Passover, together with all the narrative accompaniment, must be done again and again, as rehearsal for real departure and real resolve in obedience. The sons and daughters must be told again why this night of passage is different. The daughters and the sons must be schooled in the logic of repair with the enacted news that Pharaoh is not a defining agent or force any longer; the new administration from Sinai is already in effect here. Thus we may imagine that these five brief verses were (and are) the script for reperformance, always again from bitter to sweet, always again from disease to healing, always again from coercion to dialogical obedience . . . always again.

5. And because it is "always again," we may anticipate that the performance will issue in new habits for the freshly healed community. If, as seems likely, the rhetoric of v. 26 is of Deuteronomy, then the new habits are lined out in Deuteronomy, habits concerning widows and orphans and immigrants and the poor (Deut 14:29; 16:14; 24:17-22). The new habits are not sectarian ritual disciplines (though those may be required); rather they constitute a passion whereby the God-given resources of creation are deployed for the sake of all, just like the "sky bread" of Exodus 16 will be when "they gathered as much as each of them needed" (16:18). The tradition of Deuteronomy knows well that obedience does not "produce" healing. But it also knows, in a recovered dialogical wisdom, that without obedience there is no healing. And so this community, from

the lips of Miriam, resolved to the new habits that will form the world afresh:

> Everything that the LORD has spoken we will do. (Exod 19:8)
>
> All that the LORD has spoken we will do, and we will be obedient. (Exod 24:7)

The narrative is of course very Jewish. It is Israel who thirsts and who is addressed. This is an Abrahamic enterprise, albeit featuring Moses and not Abraham. It is the God of Abraham who hears Israel (Exod 2:24) and who addresses Moses (Exod 3:6). But Scriptural Reasoning summons us through and beyond the Jewish reading to ask how the text may be read amid other children of Abraham, and beyond to the community of Adam. How can we let such a particular text perform a larger healing? And of course the answer is with the same components of practice. These components are a gift of Jews, but a gift well given to all the Adamic kinfolk. For what is exclusively Jewish about the transactions of this text is in any case overheard elsewhere by those who know they may be addressed:

The text in its specificity can be reread by many text-heeding peoples. The text is insistent in its particular way but not upon an exclusionary readership.

The context is quite specific concerning this people being on a trek without water. But the context is at the edge of slavery and the boundary of the desert with the mountain in purview. That sequence of "slavery-wilderness-mountain" is not geographically situated. It is a geography of interpretation and imagination. All the children of Adam know about departures and not arriving, about being addressed with command and with promise, and every child of Adam hopes for an initiative of repair, all of these in a community of hope. The context is human geography, a map whereby all may move on from their oases of sweetness.

The repair is on offer. It is a gift of God. It is a gift given through the Jews and their text. It is not administered even by those who preserve the narrative, it being a holy offer of healing.

The text is open to many reperformances wherein a community of exslaves may sense holy possibility. With this utterance of promise, this text becomes a hearable script. And that wonder of redress is everywhere urgent among us.

The text is everywhere visible and embraced and reperformed, so that here and there new habits of care appear. As Randi Rashkover judges, there is care for those who suffer, and no particular community has a monopoly on such a possibility.[4]

The text is to be read particularly, of course. We may imagine, nonetheless, that gathered around the text in overhearing are many other brothers and sisters, not members of the particular community of reading and hearing. They also are eager for repair, capable of performance, prepared for alternative habits. This eagerness, capability, and preparedness are not fruits of pharaonic reason. They are not on the horizon in our many pharaonic venues. No; rather they are evoked and valorized precisely by the text, the particular text that reasons subversively. And where the text is uttered and read, Pharaoh is yet again placed in acute jeopardy.

Steven Kepnes exquisitely concludes:

> Here, Ochs suggests that the best representation of God is the plural voices of the children of God—of Jews, of Christians, of Muslims—joined in a kind of liturgical practice of studying his word, the words of his scriptures, the Torah, the Bible, the Qur'an. The best representation of God today, then, is the sitting of Jews and Christians and Muslims together as brothers and sisters arguing, laughing, and thinking about God, about each other and about the world and how to heal it, to redeem it, and to save it.[5]

The people given us in this text, erstwhile slaves, did just that sort of thing:

They argued. They disputed with Pharaoh. And then they disputed with Moses and Aaron, and with God. They are first-class disputers. (See 15:24)

They laughed. They laughed with Miriam and her sisters, laughed bodily and boldly at the freedom they never thought they would live to see.

They told stories of oracles, miracles, and bushes. They thought about God and wondered:

> Is the LORD among us or not? (Exod 17:7b)

They considered God in God's enigmatic self-disclosure (Exod 3:14), but always with the remarkable residue of YHWH's powerful "preferential option for the poor":

> God looked down upon the Israelites, and God took notice of them. (Exod 2:25)
>
> I have heard their cry on account of their taskmasters. Indeed, I know their sufferings. (Exod 3:7b)

They thought about each other, about being on the way together, about trusting, rebelling, hoping, and doubting. The constituted, from early on, a "culture of interpretation" that moved boldly between old texts of promise and present circumstances of risk.

They thought about the world, that Pharaoh's enterprise was a fake, and that YHWH would reign forever.

They waited and factored out healing; they experimented with redeeming, negotiating about triage with what they valued most (Exod 13:15). They stood still (Exod 14:14); they hosted the text generation after generation, and they marveled at the well-being given them.

I am not sure I get all that is implied in Scriptural Reasoning, as I am sure I do not get most of Peirce. Nonetheless Ochs' wise introduction matters because I read the text in ways available only through his work.[6] In my own particular community of memory and hope, imagination is being converted by this remarkable movement of interpretation. Clearly Pharaoh will not finally stop it!

8

THE NIGHTMARE OF AMNESIA

It is undoubtedly the case that biblical memory, figure, and imagination have played a major role in shaping the political imagination and history of the West, not least the United States. Bruce Feiler, moreover, has told me, out of his current research, that in U.S. history Moses and the imagery of the Hebrew Bible/Old Testament have been much more decisive for U.S. political imagination than has been Jesus or other facets of the New Testament. In U.S. usage, the Hebrew Bible/Old Testament has invited focus variously on God's *providential governance* of history, the conviction of *a chosen people*, and the conquest of *the new land of promise* that has powered continued colonial expansionism.[1] Because that textual tradition has shaped the past, it is legitimate and important to reflect yet again on this textual tradition, as it may fund, correct, discipline, and nurture political imagination in our current socioeconomic crisis.

Thus I will probe major reference points in that memory in order to see the analogues of assurance and requirement that continue to reverberate in the political imagination of our society. I will do so in three obvious moves that will end in a focus on our contemporary context because the text itself characteristically has propulsion toward the contemporary.

I

First it is important to linger at some length over the founding narratives of Moses and Joshua to which later communities of interpretation have always returned. We may line out that founding narrative in three dramatic acts that continue to be definitional.

First, there is no doubt that the exodus memory—whatever may have been its historicity—is defining for the entire textual tradition that follows. The exodus narrative attests to YHWH as the propelling agent for emancipation who exhibits both the capacity and the will to challenge Pharaoh's sovereignty and eventually to overthrow it. Indeed, the culminating Song of Moses in Exodus 15:1-18, which anticipates the entire history of Israel, concludes in exultation over the sovereignty of YHWH:

> The LORD will reign forever and ever. (v. 18)

That conclusion by Moses, moreover, echoes the more primitive celebration of Miriam:

> "Sing to the LORD for he has triumphed gloriously;
> horse and rider he has thrown into the sea." (v. 21)

Israel deduced from this narrative and its liturgical replication that the saving God of Israel is the Lord of the universe who is set against all exploitative order, and who wills and enacts emancipation from every oppressive system.[2] Ancient Israel found it easy to transpose its singing from one circumstance of exploitation to another, from one empire to another because, judged by the will of YHWH, they are all the same, all sure to be judged and overthrown. It is for good reason that Michael Walzer has proposed that the exodus narrative is the founding document for all social revolutions in the modern world.[3] He attests that such a seedbed of social revolution of course summons to bold action; but at the same time, it cannot be understood apart from reference to that inscrutable will and force behind human agency.

Second in the founding memory, Israel arrived at Sinai. The meeting at Sinai is shrouded in mystery, and there is no doubt that the textual tradition is stylized for liturgical reenactment in some sort of covenant renewal replication. At Sinai God spoke; at Sinai God spoke ten times; at Sinai God spoke only ten times. And in those ten terse utterances the God of the exodus laid down an alternative path of communal practice and political power.[4] According to some critical judgment, the Decalogue comes late, and according to some it is only a device to preserve patriarchal control for the benefit of the male elites.[5] But that of course is not how the text has functioned in the interpreting community.

We are given a clue to its function by the awareness that already in Exodus 19:8, well before the ten utterances in chapter 20, Israel assented to the commandments because Israel knew well ahead of time that any requirements by the Lord of the exodus would be preferable to the commands of Pharaoh. Pharaoh's commands are always oppressive requirements for endless productivity and the inescapable commoditization of the human enterprise. Israel readily assented to the alternative countercommandments and pledged its oath of allegiance to this alternative sovereign (Exod 24:3, 7).

In that moment of pledging, Israel becomes what it had not been:

> This very day the LORD our God is commanding you to observe these statutes and ordinances; so observe them diligently with all your heart and with all your soul. Today you have obtained the LORD's agreement: to be your God; and for you to walk in his commandments, and his ways, to keep his statutes, his commandments, and his ordinances, and to obey him. Today the LORD has obtained your agreement: to be his treasured people, as he promised you, and to keep his commandments; for him to set you high above all nations that he has made, in praise and in fame, and in honor; and for you to be a people holy to the LORD your God, as he promised. (Deut 26:16-19)

In that moment of mutual pledging, something happened in the public history of the world that is irreversible, namely, the acknowledgment that the holy creator of heaven and earth is committed to and implicated in the public process of political power. And that process can never again be regarded as an autonomous or indifferent one.

Israel is pledged to two awarenesses. On the one hand, the first three commandments establish the primacy of the holy God and thereby render all political reality penultimate and without claim to absoluteness or ultimacy. These commands preclude the reifying of any form of political-economic power as an ultimate; from that moment Israel has been aware of the seduction of idolatry, seduction that becomes most visible and repellant in the massive statue of Nebuchadnezzar in Daniel 3. From this moment of Sinai utterance, Israel knows that it must resist every such political exaggeration. On the other hand, the last six commandments are designed to protect, honor, and lend dignity to the political processes of the human community. In the rule of YHWH, human persons are granted primacy that cannot be overridden by any acquisitiveness.

The *ultimacy of YHWH's rule* and the *proximate ultimacy of human persons* come together, even though the community of this text has been slow to see that linkage in terms of every social differentiation of class, race, or gender (see 1 John 4:20). This interface of what is ultimate and what is proximately ultimate issues in the belated awareness that the *love of God* takes the form of the *love of neighbor*. This convergence is manifest in the fourth commandment on Sabbath whereby both *creator* and *creatures* are at rest. This vision of Sabbath rest on earth and in heaven is a complete contrast to the restless, seething productivity of Pharaoh's regime of commoditization. Israel departed Sinai now pledged to the ultimacy that keeps political economic power under surveillance and to a proximate ultimacy that refuses indignity or brutality whereby power can override the vulnerable treasure of human well-being.

Israel departs Sinai under oath. The oath pertains to the commandments from the mountain. But the commandments have behind them the emancipatory wonder of the exodus, so that the first and decisive commandment of YHWH's rules is narratively situated:

> The LORD your God who brought you out of the land of Egypt, out of the house of slavery . . . (Exod 20:2)

The commanding God of Sinai is none other than the liberating God of the exodus. And for the rest of the textual tradition of interpretation, both Jewish and Christian, the twinned themes of *emancipation* and *obligation* are decisive and definitional.

Third in the founding narrative, the primal commitment to emancipation and obligation was not an easy vision to sustain in practice, as attested by the wilderness quarrels. The defining memory, moreover, came sideways in the work of Joshua and the seizure of the land of Canaan. They did, nevertheless, mange to incorporate land seizure that is portrayed in the book of Joshua as a part of the story of emancipation.[6] Thus the crossing of the Jordan River is remembered—and perhaps liturgically reiterated—as a replication of the crossing of the waters from Egypt:

> You shall let your children know, "Israel crossed over the Jordan here on dry ground." For the LORD your God dried up the waters of the Jordan for us until you crossed over, *as* the LORD your God did to the Red Sea, which he dried up for us until we crossed over. (Josh 4:22-23)

The answer to the children's question is stylized and so taken as narrative. The statement turns on what Garrett Green terms the "copula of imagination," on "as," as in "as the Lord God did to the Red Sea." Land seizure is now emancipation.[7]

The founding narrative did not linger, as has subsequent interpretation, over the brutality against the indigenous population. It managed to accept such brutality through the subterfuge—a recurring subterfuge—that the Sinai vision of human worth and dignity did not extend to the Canaanites, that is, did not extend to those unlike us outside our covenantal agreement. Of course! That is how the historical is always managed when self-interest overrides visionary passion. And so we are able to say that a core of violence—authorized by divine utterance—belongs to the taproot of the normative tradition.[8] The God who authorizes land conquest is involved in the practice of violence and is not easily extracted from it. Thus the founding memory concerns emancipation and obligation, but emancipation and obligation that are shot through with deep measures of "justified" violence.[9]

I take this long with these founding memories in order to suggest that this narrative account is deeply entrenched in Western political thought and in U.S. history. I am, without any expertise, aware that the founding figures of the United States were not passionate about the Bible and functioned from a deist perspective without the particular passion that belongs to the biblical tradition. But of course there was, always and everywhere, alongside what Robert Bellah has called "the republican tradition," an evangelical passion as well that focused on the imagery of exceptionalism, that had no trouble transposing from ancient Israel providential chosenness that issued in manifest destiny. During the recent election, with deep hopes for Obama's theological sophistication, I was caught up short by the observation no one, not even Obama, could be elected president without a conviction of U.S. exceptionalism. Of course! That affirmation of exceptionalism, over the centuries, has continued to feature emancipation ("leader of the free world") and obligation ("imperial burden") and violent expansionism ("the land of promise") as the engine for self-understanding and self-justification. These founding traditions have continued to be palpable and immediate in the rhetoric and imagination of our society.

II

Such founding traditions of emancipation and obligation are difficult to sustain and are readily seen to be inadequate. At least that is how it turned out in ancient Israel. Thus my second point is to exposit Israel's season of amnesia whereby it used its energy to elude the unsettling of an emancipatory God, and whereby it substituted more palatable mandates for the commands of Sinai. It turned out that the other peoples and other cultures were not as inimical to Israel as the rhetoric of the book of Joshua had proposed. It turned out that the other peoples had alternative features in their life from which Israel borrowed and that Israel wanted to imitate. And of course the urge to imitate and replicate caused a cooling of exceptionalism, for the exceptionalism of Sinai turned out to be excessively demanding. By the time of Samuel, Israel wanted to be "like the other nations," not so rigorously distinguished by obligation (1 Sam 8:5, 20). Very soon they wanted a standing army (for an occasional militia was not enough) and a durable bank, a place in which to store and invest surplus value.

We may, in paradigmatic fashion, trace Israel's accommodation and amnesia in two steps. First, David is portrayed as a master politician who could regularly have it both ways, being larger than life and too agile to be stalled anywhere. David could manage at the same time to be YHWH's anointed and yet be a Canaanite king of a city-state who violated covenant in his self-aggrandizement (see 2 Sam 11–12). That royal agility is dramatized in the fact that he installed two "high priests" who shared leadership, power, and prestige (see 2 Sam 8:17). On the one hand, there was Abiathar, who early sided with David amid the rough and tumble battle for control (1 Sam 22:20-23). On the other hand, there was Zadok, who had no narrative introduction but who simply appears among David's bureaucrats (2 Sam 8:17). While Abiathar is clearly rooted in old tribal, covenantal traditions, scholars suggest that Zadok may have been from among the Canaanite priests in the old city kingdom of Jerusalem (Jebus). In any case the important thing is that he came from nowhere. These priests together evidence David's immense juggling act of *ancient tradition* and *contemporary opportunism*.

But second, David's son Solomon advanced the case of amnesia that loosened Israel's connection to the old narrative of emancipation and obligation. I will identify three facets of Solomon's narrative that show the huge departure from the old tradition that he enacted.[10]

First, it is reported no less than four times that he married Pharaoh's daughter (1 Kgs 3:1; 7:8; 9:24; 11:1). He is the son-in-law of the Pharaoh of Egypt who is remembered as the one from whom Israel had been delivered. There are all kinds of evidence that Solomon's regime borrowed a great deal from Pharaoh's governmental practices, the outcome of which is clearly the relaxation of the intensity of exodus and Sinai.

Second, Solomon could not tolerate the dual priest system of David. When his father, David, had died, there had been a vigorous context for succession to the throne. Alongside Solomon his brother Adonijah was a candidate for the throne. As in all such contests, the leadership chose up sides. It is reported that among the supporters of Solomon was Zadok the high priest, the one who is a priest without covenantal rootage (1 Kgs 1:8). And Abiathar, along with Joab, supported Adonijah (1 Kgs 1:7). And of course they were the losers, as Solomon prevailed in the contest. We are told, moreover, that Solomon promptly executed Joab (1 Kgs 2:28-35) and Adonijah (1 Kgs 2:13-25). We might expect that he would also kill Abiathar, a leader of the opposition; but it is, however, unwise to kill a priest unless absolutely necessary. And so Solomon banished Abiathar to his home village of Anathoth:

> Go to Anathoth, your estate; for you deserve death. But I will not at this time put you to death, because you carried the ark of the LORD GOD before my father David, and because you shared in all the hardships my father endured. (1 Kgs 2:26)

Solomon disposed of the priest who was rooted in the old covenantal tradition. Abiathar must have been a reminder of that deep rootage; and now Solomon could forget.

Third, with the attraction of Pharaoh and the dismissal of Abiathar, it does not surprise us that Solomon went in a very different direction. It may have been a direction in which his father, David, would like to have gone, but he was still restrained. But once Solomon embraced Pharaoh and scuttled Abiathar, he had no more restraint. The narrative of Solomon makes clear that such carefully arranged amnesia leads to unfettered accumulation. Solomon becomes the great acquirer. Now like Midas, everything he touched turned to a commodity. He seemed to have an incessant urge to acquire, collect, and accumulate. In this he is reminiscent of Pharaoh who could never have enough bricks. Solomon, moreover, is an anticipation of the man who built bigger barns and who, by the end of his story, is called a "fool" (Luke 12:20). With his reputation for wisdom, Solomon is given us as a foolish wise one, the one who is thought wise but who is seen, in the end, to have preferred his own self-destruction.

Thus Solomon accumulated goods commensurate with the limitless appetite of his entourage:

> Solomon's provision for one day was thirty cors of choice flour, and sixty cors of meal, ten fat oxen, and twenty pasture-fed cattle, one hundred sheep, besides deer, gazelles, roebucks, and fatted fowl. (1 Kgs 4:22-23)

Solomon accumulated proverbs, enough to exhibit his preeminence in learning:

> He composed three thousand proverbs and his songs numbered a thousand and five. (4:32)

Solomon accumulated enough gold to make his temple a stunning tourist attraction:

> The interior of the inner sanctuary was twenty cubits long, twenty cubits wide, and twenty cubits high; he overlaid it with pure gold. He also overlaid the altar with cedar. Solomon overlaid the inside of the house with pure gold, then he drew chains of gold across, in front of the inner sanctuary, and overlaid it with gold. Next he overlaid the whole house with gold, in order that the whole house might be perfect; even the whole altar that belonged to the inner sanctuary he overlaid with gold. (6:20-22)
>
> So Solomon made all the vessels that were in the house of the LORD: the golden altar, the golden table for the bread of the presence, the lamp stands of pure gold, five on the south side and five on the north, in front of the inner sanctuary; the flowers, the lamps and the tongs, of gold; the cups, snuffers, basins, dishes for incense, and fire pans of pure gold; the sockets for the doors of the innermost part of the house, the most holy place, and for the doors of the nave of the temple, of gold. (7:48-50)

Solomon accumulated fortresses and weaponry:

> Solomon conscripted to build the house of the LORD and his own house, the Millo and the wall of Jerusalem, Hazor, Megiddo, Gezer . . ., Lower Bethhoron, Baalath, Tamar in the wilderness, within the land, as well as all of Solomon's storage cities, the cities for his chariots, and the cities for his cavalry, and whatever Solomon desired to build. (9:15-19)
>
> Solomon gathered together chariots and horses; he had fourteen hundred chariots and twelve thousand horses, which he stationed in the chariot cities and with the king in Jerusalem. (10:26)

Solomon made Jerusalem to be the depository of global wealth:

> Once every three years the fleet of ships of Tarshish used to come bringing gold, silver, ivory, apes, and peacocks. Thus King Solomon excelled all the kings of the earth in riches and in wisdom. . . . Each of them brought a present, objects of silver and gold, garments, weaponry, spices, horses, and mules, so much year by year. (10:22-25)

And as though to cap it all off, Solomon collected women, no doubt designed to create a web of political alliances:

> Among his wives were seven hundred princesses and three hundred concubines, and his wives turned his heart away. (11:3)

It is clear that Solomon dramatically and decisively shifted the foundations and assumptions of society. Whereas Sinai had imagined *a covenantal community of neighbors*, Solomon transposes it into *an aggressive economy of commodities*. We cannot tell about this convergence of amnesia and commodity, whether amnesia permitted commoditization or whether the pursuit of commodity generated amnesia. No doubt they came together and relentlessly reinforced each other.

Solomon did all of this, moreover, under the banner of YHWH. Thus the centerpiece of his narrative is the temple dedicated to YHWH, the God of the regime (1 Kgs 8). The temple is now the place where YHWH would dwell:

> I have built you an exalted house,
> a place for you to dwell in forever. (8:13)

YHWH is there as patron and as guarantor. The temple is the place for reciting the narrative of legitimacy:

> He said, "Blessed be the LORD, the God of Israel, who with his hand has fulfilled what he promised with his mouth to my father David saying, 'Since the day that I brought my people Israel out of Egypt, I have not chosen a city from any of the tribes of Israel . . . but I chose David to be over my people.'" (vv. 15-16)

The temple is a place for sure blessing:

> Blessed be the LORD, who has given rest to his people Israel according to all that he promised: not one word has failed of all his good promises,

> which he spoke through his servant Moses. The LORD our God be with us, as he was with our ancestors. (8:56-57)

All the words and phrases and gestures are right. Except that now we have a truncated, diminished YHWH who fits completely into the state apparatus of amnesia. YHWH has been toned down and has lost edge; YHWH has no freedom and no capacity for truth-telling confrontation.

We are now able to see, in the remarkable Solomonic achievement, that the remembered tradition of exodus-Sinai could be readily and completely accommodated to an aggressive acquisitiveness that was committed to systemic coveting. How odd that the God whose tenth word was "Thou shalt not covet" now becomes the sponsor of a system that covets. The important point is that there was no noticed contradiction between the old covenant and the new passion for commodity. It all seemed to fit in an ideology of self-aggrandizement.

And so it always is with the generation that cannot remember. So it was in Germany with the rise of National Socialism. The church was to a great extent swept along in the new folk ideology of blood and soil. There were, to be sure, important exceptions of dissent. But the accommodators produced the hyphen in "Deutsche-Kristi," German Christians. The famous phrase of Bonhoeffer, "cheap grace," is not a generic phrase among us; rather it points exactly to the crisis of accommodation in which the claim of the gospel is shabbily preempted for ideology, and all without notice.

When we consider covenant-become-acquisitiveness under Solomon and the German Christians under Hitler, it is an easy move to see how the claim of the gospel has been taken up among us in the service of imperial commoditization. For the most part, gospel and American dream feel like synonyms to us. The exceptionalism of the United States has been a sustained theme as the newly chosen that may be traced in a tale of expansionism through the Mexican War of Polk to the Spanish-American war of Teddy Roosevelt and eventually to Iraq. Whatever else we may say, it is characteristically a quest for territory, for resources, for markets, for oil, all of which bear the mark of entitlement. The role of much of the church, moreover, has been to bless and not to notice, to benefit and to forget, so that the ultimacy of God and the proximate ultimacy of the neighbor are lost in an ocean of commodities, and we cannot imagine life without them. As Solomon had to expel Abiathar and as Hitler had to dispatch Bonhoeffer, so U.S. amnesia has had to forgo Niebuhr and King and pretend that we had not yet been told of our immense capacity for self-deception.

The regime of Solomon came to a sorry end. In terms of the facts on the ground, it took four hundred years to complete the demolition job at the hands of the Babylonians. But the theological truth of the matter is enacted much more promptly. The text places an extended prophetic speech of judgment in 1 Kings 11. The indictment against Solomon is that he turned away from the first commandment concerning the ultimacy of YHWH:

> Then the LORD was angry with Solomon, because his heart had turned away from the LORD, the God of Israel, who had appeared to him twice, and had commanded concerning this matter, that he should not follow other gods; but he did not observe what the LORD commanded. Therefore the LORD to Solomon, "Since this has been on your mind and you have not kept my covenant and my statutes that I have commanded you, I will surely tear the kingdom from you and give it to your servant." (11:9-11)

What is ordained against Solomon, says the tradition, is loss: loss of power, loss of territory, loss of prestige, forfeiture of mandate from YHWH. The process of loss is slow. But the tradition asserts that it grinds on because the key claims of Sinai are, in the end, not negotiable.

III

According to the books of Kings, the story of royal Jerusalem, royal David's city, grinds on in its amnesia, missing all the signs and gestures of divine judgment. The amnesia would seem to have been complete—never was heard a discouraging word.

In retrospect, however, we are able to identify a succession of rememberers who lived and worked below dynastic radar. They live a long way from Moses, but there are hints that there was a Levitic priesthood that held on tenaciously to the tradition of Moses, priests who did not succumb to the regnant amnesia.[11] In the eighth century, it appears that movements surfaced with some vitality. It could be that the pivot person in this reassertion was Hosea, who had connections to that ancient tradition. Hosea, commonly located about 740 BCE, could remember enough to see that Israel had forgotten everything important about its life with YHWH:

I will punish her for the festival days of the Baals,
    when she offered incense to them
and decked herself with her ring and jewelry,
    and went after her lovers, and *forgot* me, says the LORD. (Hos 2:13)

My people are destroyed for lack of knowledge;
    because you have rejected knowledge,
    I reject you from being a priest to me.
And since you have *forgotten* the law of your God,
    I also will forget your children. (Hos 4:6)

Israel has *forgotten* his Maker,
    and built palaces;
and Judah has multiplied fortified cities;
    but I will send a fire upon his cities,
    and it shall devour his strongholds. (Hos 8:14)

When I fed them, they were satisfied;
    they were satisfied, and their heart was proud;
    therefore they *forgot* me. (Hos 13:6)

The sum of these indictments is that Israel has practiced indulgent self-sufficiency and can no longer remember the source of its life or the purpose for which it is accountable. The inevitable outcome of such amnesia, says the prophetic poetry, is being punished so that good land is reduced to a forest (2:13), being rejected and forgotten by God (4:6), having fire sent on its citadels (8:14), and having God come against it like a lion, a leopard, a bear who will tear and destroy (13:6-8). Thus amnesia consists in breaking Israel's connection to God's holy, protective, nurturing power and in being left exposed to the forces of death.

We do not know all the factors that led to the generative theological recovery of the Sinai tradition in the eighth century, nor do we know of the historical connection between the memory of Moses and the poetic recovery that clustered around the work of Hosea. What we do know is that after Hosea, in the eighth century and on into the seventh century, this theological-political recovery took on generative force and authority and culminated in the Deuteronomic movement that came to full voice in the late seventh century.

The pivot point of this recovery is the book of Deuteronomy, almost universally taken as the scroll found in the temple in Jerusalem in 621 BCE. (2 Kgs 22). There is it reported that the reading of the scroll evoked a powerful response from King Josiah who, on the basis of the scroll, instituted a great socioeconomic-liturgical reform of the realm. We do not know what so startled the king, but we may imagine that it was the long list of covenantal curses in Deuteronomy 28 that culminates with the most unbearable of all threats, a return to the bondage of Egypt:

> The LORD will bring you back in ships to Egypt, by a route that I promised you would never see again; and there you shall offer yourselves for sale to your enemies as male and female slaves, but there will be no buyer. (Deut 28:68)

The covenantal tradition, at its extreme edge, can entertain the possibility that with enough willful forgetting, the entire tradition of emancipation and obligation can be undone; the community can lose its identity and return to a despairing condition of slavery. It would be as though the entire *providential action* of YHWH were nullified, the *exceptionalism* of Israel were voided, and *the land of promise* were forfeited. Amnesia can lead to a loss and reversal of history!

The most timely tradition of the Bible for us in the United States just now, I propose, is the book of Deuteronomy, which is offered as an antidote to amnesia that inevitably comes along with the mad commitment to accumulation. We may focus in particular on two facets of Deuteronomy about which it is said concerning King Josiah:

> When the king heard the words of the book of the law, he tore his clothes. (2 Kgs 22:11)

First, the book of Deuteronomy voices a vigorous warning against amnesia:

> When the LORD our God has brought you into the land that he swore to your ancestors, to Abraham, to Isaac, and to Jacob, to give you—a land with fine, large cities that you did not build, houses filled with all sorts of goods that you did not fill, hewn cisterns that you did not hew, vineyards and olive groves that you did not plant—and when you have eaten your fill, take care that you do not *forget* the LORD, who brought you out of the land of Egypt, out of the house of slavery. The LORD your God you shall fear; him you shall serve, and by his name alone you shall swear. Do not follow other gods, any of the gods of the people who are all around you, because the LORD your God, who is present with you, is

> a jealous God. The anger of the LORD your God would be kindled against you and he would destroy you from the face of the earth. (Deut 6:10-15)

Prosperity will talk Israel out of its passion for God and cause Israel to abandon the non-negotiable first commandment. Affluence will cause Israel to lose its identity in relationship to YHWH:

> For the LORD your God is bringing you into a good land, a land with flowing streams, with springs and underground waters welling up in valleys and hills, a land of wheat and barley, of vines and fig trees and pomegranates, a land of olive trees and honey, a land where you may eat bread without scarcity, where you will lack nothing, a land whose stones are iron and from whose hills you may mine cooper. You shall eat your fill and bless the LORD your God for the good land that he has given you.
>
> Take care that you do not *forget* the LORD your God, by failing to keep his commandments, his ordinances, and his statutes, which I am commanding you today. When you have eaten your fill and have built fine houses and live in them, and when your herds and flocks have multiplied, and your silver and gold is multiplied, and all that you have is multiplied, then do not exalt yourself, forgetting the LORD your God, who brought you out of the land of Egypt, out of the house of slavery, who led you through the great and terrible wilderness, an arid wasteland with poisonous snakes and scorpions. He made water flow for you from flint rock, and fed you in the wilderness with manna that your ancestors did not know, to humble you and to test you, and in the end to do you good. Do not say to yourself, "My power and the might of my own hand have gotten me this wealth." But remember the LORD your God, for it is he who gives you power to get wealth, so that he may confirm his covenant that he swore to your ancestors as he is doing today.
>
> (Deut 8:7-17)

Forgetting is a recipe for perishing:

> If you do *forget* the LORD your God and follow other gods to serve and worship them, I solemnly warn you today that you shall surely perish. Like the nations that the LORD is destroying before you, so shall you perish, because you would not obey the voice of the LORD your God.
>
> (Deut 8:20)

This document of recovery poses for jeopardized Israel a sharp either/or.

Second, we may become more specific about the remembering that will correct the jeopardy of amnesia. The remembering is not primarily cognitive. It is practical, concrete, and performative. In the commandments of Deuteronomy, the commandments linked to Sinai that go beyond Sinai, the economy is the venue for intentional, countercultural, neighborly activity. There are at least four commandments explicitly motivated by exodus memory, each of which concerns redress of the economic depletion of the vulnerable. The allusion to exodus is not incidental; rather the remembered oppressive situation in Egypt was exactly one in which the vulnerable were exploited and then rescued by YHWH. Now Israel is to recall the exploitation of remembered Egypt and the wondrous emancipation from that exploitation in order to reorganize economic practices according to the neighborly covenant of Sinai.

In Deuteronomy 15:15, the commandment for the year of release concerns the cancellation of debts on poor people, so that there will be no permanent underclass in Israel. Moses provides that the emancipated debt slave will be given wherewithal to reenter the economy:

> And when you send a male slave out from you a free person, you shall not send him out empty-handed. Provide liberally out of your flock, your threshing floor, and your wine press, thus giving to him some of the bounty with which the LORD your God has blessed you. *Remember* that you were a slave in the land of Egypt; and the LORD your God redeemed you; for this reason I lay this commandment upon you. (15:13-15)

In Deuteronomy 16:12, the Festival of Weeks is to be a liturgical recognition of the promise of dignity for the economically vulnerable:

> Rejoice before the LORD your God—you and your sons and your daughters, and your male and female slaves, the Levites resident in your towns, as well as the strangers, the orphans, and the widows who are among you—at the place that the LORD your God will choose as a dwelling for his name. *Remember* that you were a slave in Egypt, and diligently observe these statutes. (16:11-12)

In Deuteronomy 24:17, Moses warns against requiring collateral for a loan for the vulnerable, for such a requirement amounts to injustice:

> You shall not deprive a resident alien or an orphan of justice; you shall not take a widow's garment in pledge. *Remember* that you were a slave

> in Egypt and the LORD your God redeemed you from there; therefore I command you to do this. (24:17-18)

Now we might think this is a subprime loan. But such a loan is a risky one only if the lender proposes to foreclose on the loan; Moses clearly intends no foreclosure against the vulnerable.

In Deuteronomy 24:22 Moses provides what Frank Crüsemann calls the first economic safety net in history by forbidding the stripping of fields and vineyards clear of olives, grapes, or grain.[12] The residue of these money crops is to be left for the foraging of the poor, a strategy for sharing the wealth:

> When you reap your harvest in your fields and forget a sheaf in the field, you shall not go back to get it; it shall be left for the alien, the orphan, and the widow, so that the LORD your God may bless you in all your undertakings. When you beat your olive trees, do not strip what is left; it shall be for the alien, the orphan, and the widow. And when you gather the grapes of your vineyard, do not glean what is left; it shall be for the alien, the orphan, and the widow. *Remember* that you were a slave in the land of Egypt; therefore I am commanding you to do this. (24:19-22)

This commandment pertains to the most important money crops in Israel, so that to some extent the money crops are to be diverted to sustain the vulnerable.

If we take all four of these commandments together—the year of release, the Festival of Weeks, the limit on collateral, and the residue of crops for the poor—it is clear that Moses intends to redirect the economy toward the neighbor. Moses is aware, in Deuteronomy 15:7, that one may be tempted to be "hard hearted" or "tight fisted" toward the poor. Such a posture, however, is overcome by a vigorous act in the economy, by a passionate remembering of one's own status as an exploited worker, by remembering the God who revamped the economy, and by a recall of Sinai where solemn oaths for an alternative economy were enacted. Everything depends upon remembering; everything is at risk in forgetting. Moses recognizes that amnesia is a huge threat to a covenantal ethic but believes that the amnesia-producing power of affluence can be resisted and overcome. Such resistance, however, requires regular assembling in the midst of surplus, regular reiteration of the requirements that remain contemporary, and regular reengagement with the old oaths. Where that action is not sustained, amnesia will win by default.

Deuteronomy is the primary antidote to the strategy of accumulation so well exemplified by Solomon. Indeed, the single commandment concerning kingship in Israel reads, as is often noticed, exactly as though it were intended to be anti-Solomon, antiaccumulation. Moses reluctantly allows a monarch in Israel. But he strongly limits the power of a centralized economy:

> Even so, he must not acquire many horses for himself, or return the people to Egypt in order to acquire more horses, since the Lord has said to you, "You must never return that way again." And he must not acquire many wives for himself, or else his heart will turn away; also silver and gold he must not acquire in great quantity for himself.
> (Deut 17:16-17)

The king is not to be an accumulator of horses, wives, silver, or gold, the big three of arms, allies, or wealth. The prohibition included the curious phrase, "not return the people to Egypt in order to acquire more horses." That is, the king is not to barter away the covenantal freedom of the community for the sake of weapons, for such barter will always end in exploitation.

Alongside Deuteronomy at the end of the seventh century—and close to the destruction of Jerusalem—we may notice one other important voice of covenantal alternative that was rooted in Sinai and situated in the tradition of Deuteronomy, namely, the book of Jeremiah. Jeremiah, like Deuteronomy, is compellingly committed to an exodus vision of social power:

> For I solemnly warned your ancestors when I brought them up out of the land of Egypt, warning them persistently, even to this day, saying, "Obey my voice." (Jer 11:7)

> You brought your people Israel out of the land of Egypt with signs and wonders, with a strong hand and outstretched arm, and with great terror; and you gave them this land, which you swore to their ancestors to give them, a land flowing with milk and honey; and they entered and took possession of it. But they did not obey your voice or follow your law; of all you commanded to them to do, they did nothing. Therefore you have made all these disasters come upon them. (Jer 32:21-23)

Jeremiah develops the tradition of covenant to show that the memory of emancipation and obligation has been completely disregarded in Jerusalem, and so the disaster is sure to come.

We may pay attention to a notation in Jeremiah that completes the loop of our reflection. The very first verse of the book of Jeremiah identifies the prophet:

> The words of Jeremiah son of Hilkiah, of the priests who were in Anathoth in the land of Benjamin. (Jer 1:1)

Jeremiah is rooted in the old village of Anathoth; when we hear "Anathoth," we remember immediately old Abiathar, a priest of David who was banished by Solomon back to his home village: Anathoth. Jeremiah is a descendant of Abiathar; banished Abiathar is his ancestor and progenitor. The crucial theme of *forgetting and remembering* is carried in the Old Testament in a long line from Abiathar in the time of David to Jeremiah in the time of Josiah. The Abiathar-Jeremiah tradition stands as a contrary to the royally sponsored amnesia of the Davidic house and the Jerusalem temple. This tradition constitutes a subversion of reality that subverts the amnesia and summons Israel to remember.

So we come to a three-fold analogue in our own contemporary history:

> There is an initial tradition of providence, exceptionalism, and land promise:
>
> *Moses, Joshua*, and our Founding Fathers;
>
> There is a counterpractice of amnesia wrought through excessive prosperity:
>
> *Solomon*, and the current imperial seduction that has issued in mindless consumerism;
>
> There is a summons to recover memory in the face of amnesia:
>
> *Hosea, Deuteronomy*, and *Jeremiah*; it remains for us to ponder what the analogous point is for us in the recovery from amnesia.

Well, obviously in this conference we take the Bible to be a crucial resource for recovery; here we imagine that the religious community, specifically the church, has a role to play in recovery from the mindless, brutalizing amnesia that has powered our economy of self-destructiveness.[13]

Ours is a time for the recovery of a defining memory that contradicts amnesia. It is a demanding piece of work with great ideological forces bound to resist. We can point, here and there, to voices of recall: Jim Wallis, Daniel Berrigan, Naim Ateek, Michael Lerner, Martin Luther King—and you can continue the list. It is all very uphill, but it is urgent. Here is a piece of encouragement. For perhaps the only time in ancient Israel in its four-hundred-year run of Davidic kings, in the reign of Josiah, the subversive tradition of covenantal remembering did impact public policy. In the astonishing figure of King Josiah, the teaching of Deuteronomy (and perhaps Jeremiah) reached the king. Jeremiah says of this king, in contrast to his own son Jehoiachim:

> Did not your father eat and drink
>   and do justice and righteousness?
>   Then it was well with him.
> He judged the cause of the poor and needy;
>   then it was well.
> Is not this to know me?
>   says the LORD. (Jer 22:15b-16)

"Your father," Josiah, did righteousness and justice. He intervened for the poor and the needy, and he prospered! In that process, moreover, he came to know YHWH, the God of exodus, the Lord of Sinai, the giver of life. Such a king! Such a possibility! The king was possible only because of the tough resilient testimony of the remembering tradition. It is Deuteronomy that created an environment that made an alternative policy possible.

So consider the sequence:

Initial passion and obligation;

Amnesia and accumulation;

Remembering and reconstitution.

We are well along, in our society, in amnesia and accumulation, practices that have brought us to our current crisis. And now we ponder recovery.

I finish with two observations. First, it is useful to think of the work of active recovery. Recovery from any addiction requires intentionality, and certainly Solomon was addicted. But recovery is also a process that requires, along with intentionality, a lot of patience for advance and relapse. Recovery is no quick thing. But it does happen! It would matter among us if the moral teachers of our society were to be understood as intentional agents of recovery from the disease and addiction of amnesia. Good teaching will matter in the face of seduction, the teaching of another way, a more excellent way. What a way to think about local churches as centers for recovery from our societal disease!

Second, I have taken as my assignment the exposition of the biblical tradition, even though our context is global and pluralistic. This is not to impose that theological tradition amid the pluralism of the global public. It is rather to take the Bible as paradigmatic in a way that permits other traditions to have their say about the same ailment. Every culture and every religious tradition has tales to tell of oppression and emancipation, of autonomy and covenantal righteousness, of wounds and hopes. The Bible is an invitation to identify those same deep human transactions everywhere and to imagine the resilient power of holiness that is at work in every narrative of wound and hope.

Our social scene is indeed a nightmare that alarms. It is a nightmare of being lost and displaced and not having a reliable identity with staying power. It is a nightmare that produces waves of anxiety and acres of malfunction. Nightmares may be evoked by a guilty conscience. Or perhaps by an overconsumption of rich food. Perhaps both apply to us in this nightmare, guilt over the neighborhood and excessive consumption of rich food. When President Ford pardoned Richard Nixon he wisely declared, "the long nightmare is over." Well, the long nightmare of amnesia and accumulation is not over and not so finally and easily ended. But it can be addressed and come to an end. The address is to remember, in performative ways, to reengage our humanness that is rooted in God's own holiness and is not reached by the ersatz offers of an imperial consumerism. It turned out—it always turns out—that Pharaoh's prosperity was a death trap. There is no future in an endless round of production and consumption. Sinai is a Sabbath from the rat race of accumulation. The narrative of restful neighborliness looms at the horizon and waits our engagement.

9

THE ANTIDOTE TO AMNESIA

My thesis is a simple one: Grandparents—grandmas and grandpas—have as their primal function to help the grandchildren remember. Grandparents are an active, intentional antidote to amnesia that grandchildren too readily practice. Weary pastors need to be grandparents; they also need to find some grandparents for themselves.

I

One can take that claim generally about grandparents:

> Grandparents remember and recite family lore, the wonders, the coincidences, the peculiarities, the embarrassments, all of which help give identity;
>
> Grandparents trace out the connectedness of uncles and aunts and cousins, so that the grandchildren know that they are situated in a network and are connected to an elaborate system of interaction, so that they are never alone, forgotten, or misplaced;
>
> Grandparents trace out—at best in nonauthoritarian ways—the moral code and moral expectations of the family. The purpose is that grandchildren inherit and inhale a demanding set of expectations concerning what it means to be a member of this family.

All of this—lore, connections, moral expectations—are tributaries in a river of belonging. That role for grandparents is voiced by Paul in his expression of gratitude for Timothy:

> I am grateful to God—whom I worship with a clear conscience, as my ancestors did—when I remember you constantly in my prayers night and day. Recalling your tears, I long to see you so that I may be filled with joy. (2 Tim 1:3-4)

Paul has confidence in Timothy because he trusts that he is well grounded in faith, precisely because of his grandmother and mother:

> I am reminded of your sincere faith, a faith that lived first in your grandmother Lois and your mother Eunice and now, I am sure, lives in you. For this reason I remind you to rekindle the gift of God that is within you through the laying on of my hands; for God did not give us a spirit of cowardice, but rather a spirit of power and of love and of self-discipline. (2 Tim 1:5-7)

Paul writes the son of Eunice and the grandson of Lois. And you know about Lois and Eunice, these women who put their energy into this grandson who would thereby have a spirit of power, love, and self-discipline. It takes a village and it takes a bunch of grandparents to produce such a child of faith.

It was part of the work of Timothy, according to Paul, to tell gospel truth, to give testimony in an imperial environment that was busy investigating those who voiced the resurrection:

> Do not be ashamed, then, of the testimony about our Lord or of me his prisoner, but join with me in suffering in the gospel, relying on the power of God, who saved us and called us with a holy calling, not according to our works but according to his own purpose and grace. This grace was given to us in Christ Jesus before the ages began.
>
> (2 Tim 1:8-9)

Imagine Timothy, bold and free, clear on his identity, and giving thanks for his grandmother Lois!

Now this is a roundabout way to get to the exodus narrative. I do so by beginning with Exodus 10:1-2 where YHWH instructs Moses that the drama of the exodus plagues is continued as a contest for as long as it is, in order that the grandparents will have something to say to the grandchildren:

> Then the LORD said to Moses, "Go to Pharaoh; for I have hardened his heart and the heart of his officials, *in order that* I may show these signs

> of mine among them, and *in order that* you may tell your children and grandchildren how I have made fools of the Egyptians and what signs I have done among them—*in order that* you may know that I am the LORD." (Exod 10:1-2)

This affirmation places the entire exodus narrative in a very different light. The traditionists readily concede, in these verses, that the exodus narrative is not just history. It is, rather, an intentional dramatic construction of a *family curriculum* whereby the grandchildren are recruited into this paradigmatic narrative construal of reality.[1] Imagine that . . . that the entire drama of competition between YHWH and Pharaoh is for purposes of nurture. The text has twice the particle *lema'an* ("in order that"):

> *in order that* I may show these signs,
>
> *in order that* you may tell your grandchildren.

The grandchildren need to know that YHWH "made fools" of the Egyptians, made a toy of and dealt severely with them. At the end of these verses is a third "in order that," this time with a simple preposition, "*in order that* you may know that I am YHWH." So here it is: the exodus narrative is in order that the grandchildren may know—by family instruction—that the entire truth of their life is YHWH versus Pharaoh in which YHWH prevails and Pharaoh is humiliated. You must know that if you want to live knowingly in the world.

II

It turns out, not surprisingly, that the grandparents have good reason to fear that the grandchildren will fall into amnesia. For young people, everything is fast and new and promising; kids sense their own Promethean capacity that has no debt to the past. The past is all overture for this moment of soaring power and success. Kids move into the new and eventually regard the grandparents' stuff as obsolete and uninteresting. Michael Fishbane, in his study of Deuteronomy 6:20-25, suggests a tension "between two generations' memories, sets of experiences, and commitments":

> Deuteronomy 6:20-25 discloses a tension between two generations' memories, sets of experiences, and commitments. It questions the ability of fathers to transmit their laws and faith to their sons, who

> see these as alien and do not feel the same responsibility concerning them. . . . The teaching of the fathers in Deuteronomy 6:20-25 is an attempt to involve their sons in the covenant community of the future, and undoubtedly reflects the sociological reality of the settlement in Canaan. The attempt by fathers to transform their uninvolved sons from "*dis*temporaries" to *con*temporaries, i.e., time-life sharers, is an issue of supreme and recurrent significance in the Bible. . . . As Moses teaches the covenant to the people, so each father is to teach its obligations to his own sons. In Deuteronomy 6:20-25, Moses forewarns future generations that everything would depend on the continuity of spiritual history. The response of the sons is not preserved.[2]

Beyond that generic propensity, however, the grandchildren face pressures toward amnesia that are both seductive and coercive. We have it from the story of the Maccabees that young, Jewish boys, just before the New Testament period, were mesmerized by Hellenistic culture and were embarrassed by their Jewish circumcision.[3] And young Timothy, not so long after the Maccabees, as attested in the book of Acts, faced an anxious imperial government that was ready to imprison anyone who made an Easter claim that subverted the empire. Surely better for Timothy's generation to forget those old miracles and live present tense in stoic compliance. The empire has a vested interest in amnesia that will overcome all peculiar identities that make people odd and difficult to administer.

It is not different in our time in which the global economy, powered by the U.S. military, wants to override all local traditions and impose a common "liberal democracy" on all human communities. In such a pressured, seductive circumstance, it is clear that our newest technologies are not particularistic and local, but generic. And our branded consumerism invites all manner of people to buy and trade and consume and need, and keep all particularities private and hidden. The delete button on the computer is an icon of amnesia—just delete! Delete old memories. Delete old belongings. Delete old embarrassing grandfatherly miracles and grandmotherly narratives. Delete the past and live in the present, world without end, from strength to strength, from stratagem to stratagem, from show to show, from game to game.

It was not different in ancient Israel. You can imagine the kids, by the time they got to be eleven, restless at the old recital about a "wandering Aramean" (Deut 26:5): "I am not an Aramean and I am not wandering.

I have never been in Egypt, and we do not even know the name of Pharaoh. I do not need to be instructed, so do not tell me about the slave liberation. Do not recite the name of the old God who is irrelevant to contemporary society. It's all such awkwardness now."

There was pressure in the land of Canaan, as we are told in the book of Deuteronomy. There Moses says repeatedly, "When you come into the land of prosperity . . . do not forget!"

> When the LORD your God has brought you into the land that he swore to your ancestors, to Abraham, to Isaac, and to Jacob, to give you—a land with fine, large cities that you did not build, houses filled with all sorts of goods that you did not fill, hewn cisterns that you did not hew, vineyards and olive groves that you did not plant—and when you have eaten your fill, take care that you do not forget the LORD, who brought you out of the land of Egypt, out of the house of slavery. . . . For the LORD your God is bringing you into a good land, a land with flowing streams, with springs and underground waters welling up in valleys and hills, a land of wheat and barley, of vines and fig trees and pomegranates, a land of olive trees and honey, a land where you may eat bread without scarcity, where you will lack nothing, a land whose stones are iron and from whose hills you may mine copper. You shall eat your fill and bless the LORD your God for the good land that he has given you. Take care that you do not forget the LORD your God, by failing to keep his commandments, his ordinances, and his statutes, which I am commanding you today. When you have eaten your fill and have built fine houses and live in them, and when your herds and flocks have multiplied, and your silver and gold is multiplied, and all that you have is multiplied, then do not exalt yourself, forgetting the LORD your God, who brought you out of the land of Egypt, out of the house of slavery, who led you through the great and terrible wilderness, an arid wasteland with poisonous snakes and scorpions. He made water flow for you from flint rock, and fed you in the wilderness with manna that your ancestors did not know, to humble you and to test you, and in the end to do you good. Do not say to yourself, "My power and the might of my own hand have gotten me this wealth." (Deut 6:10-12; 8:7-17)

It was more of the same under Solomon's grand regime. The mountain memory was an embarrassment to Solomon because in his Jerusalem everything was new and fresh and brilliant and dazzling. If you could get to Jerusalem you could forget the hill country narrative and get rich and powerful and wise—world without end.

It was the same later on for the Jews deported to Babylon in which the old songs of Zion were marked as empty nonsense. And with the Persians, it was easy to see that the Persians were the wave of the future and offered an easy forgetfulness that did not intimidate Daniel; you could eat imperial food and join the civil service (see Dan 1:8-21). It was an easy step to a kind of generic Hellenism to join the culture of Alexander and forget that old stuff. Those who remembered and cherished the songs and honored the disciplines of holiness were a minority; for the rest it was easier to "move on."

Amnesia threatens indirectly both persons and communities. There are pressures to help us forget awkward particularity and join the modern, generic pursuit of well-being, even with a dose of generic spirituality: "I am spiritual but not religious." This is a coded formula for jettisoning particular memories that are too demanding. The pressure is always there, to lose oneself in a bigger picture that seems benign but that eventually causes the loss of the vitality of belonging.

III

There is a generic remembering that is available and worth doing. It may be that every serious community that lasts over time does generic remembering, teaching the recurring human realities but without too much concrete specificity that might be embarrassing or divisive. In ancient Israel that generic memory is reenacted in the Jerusalem temple under the sponsorship of Solomon. Solomon and his priestly agents know enough to stay rooted in Israelite memory, but they also know that a great kingdom must not be too specific about local tradition.[4] Thus it is not a surprise that the Jerusalem liturgy characteristically lacks the specificity of historical narrative and instead focuses upon great poetic images of creation. Such hymnic images function to construct and legitimate a reliable orderliness that concerns creation and as a byproduct orders political and economic power as well. This practice, moreover, helps to situate the Davidic monarchy as a function and agent of cosmic order, so that political rule is "implied" in liturgical affirmation. Thus the Psalter may pivot around the great hymns of enthronement that do not even mention the Davidic king, and it is now often noticed that the Davidic king, in the canonical sequence of the psalms, gives way to the kingship of YHWH. The outcome of such liturgical memory roots present historical reality in large, deep "prehistorical" claims that attest to the truth of an ordered creation.

In contemporary practice, I suggest that "praise hymns" have the same generic function as every such large liturgy. Such prose hymns, not unlike the broadest claims of royal liturgy, remember nothing in particular, ask nothing in response, and offer no narrative construal of reality. Such singing deals only in "absolute time" without the vagaries, gifts, or anguishes of lived reality. One may depart such wondrous singing with amnesia uninterrupted, vaguely content in an order that has no bite of specificity to it.

While such generic remembering is worth doing, it can eventuate in very little that touches human reality. It is certain that such generic remembering—the kind preferred among the well off and the kind entertained by those situated in authoritarian modes of life—will never produce an intentional community of either deep gladness or of purposeful obedience. It remains after such liturgical recital to go further and deeper and more riskily into specificity. It is that further, deeper, more risky move that is particularly entrusted, by Moses, to the grandparents.

IV

Grandparents can sit through generic praise, but just barely. They move characteristically beyond the generic to the specific. It is the work of grandparents to transform the remembered past into present tense, in order that memory can be available and informative, authoritative, empowering, and summoning. It is my purpose, in this context, to suggest that the exodus narrative is indeed paradigmatic for the grandparental antidote to amnesia among the grandchildren. It is paradigmatic because it provides a complete inventory of the recurring narrative incidents that are pieced together as a life of gladness lived from and toward and in the presence of the Holy One who confounds Pharaoh and offers an alternative that the grandchildren may imagine for themselves. So here is a walk through the grandparental paradigm that refuses amnesia:

Remember the midwives (Exod 1:15-22)

We recall the names of the midwives and list them with prophets and apostles, prophets and martyrs: Shiphrah and Puah. Imagine that, that we know their names. We have long since forgotten Pharaoh's name because if you have ever seen one Pharaoh, you have seen them all. Not so with midwives. Every midwife is different, known and named and remembered for a combination of toughness and gentleness, toughness that refused the command of Pharaoh, gentleness because the women giving birth are the daughters of Sarah and the babies being birthed are the children of Abraham. They refused imperial fear and honored "the force" of creative life that would not be deterred by imperial edict. We remember and recite their names because after all the truth of God's goodness, the future comes down to mothers who give their life over to the children. These are the women who sing with Hannah about impossibility (1 Sam 2:1-10) and with Elizabeth in old age (Luke 1:42-45) and with Mary in scandalous reassurance (Luke 1:46-55). These are the women who time the contractions and bring the hot water and who soothe with talk and do not flinch. We choose mostly not to remember these bodily ministries and, more often than not, find mothers to be nagging and cranky and moralistic, all functions of protectiveness. These are the mothers in Israel who pay attention to small beauties and who bring casseroles at death. These are the mothers who stand silent in Argentina marking their absent, disappeared sons, fearless before the tanks of coercion. These are the mothers—Catholic and Protestant—who march together in Belfast against hate. These are the mothers who finally band together and who say, "Enough, enough already, enough abuse, enough shame."

We are told that they "feared God" (Exod 1:21). They feared God and as old ladies could tell the children how they "made fools" of Pharaoh and the Egyptians. They did not know much theology and they did not have time for texts; but they knew about life and birth and miracles and beginnings, and they guarded the young. In that long inventory of faithful men in Hebrews 11, only a few mothers are mentioned:

> Sarah herself was barren . . . descendants were born, "as many as the stars of heaven." (11:11-12)
>
> By faith Rahab the prostitute did not perish with those who were disobedient. (11:31)
>
> Women received their dead by resurrection. (11:35)

Remember the terrorist activity of Moses (Exod 2:11-12)

> One day, after Moses had grown up, he went out to his people and saw their forced labor. He saw an Egyptian beating a Hebrew, one of his kinsfolk. He looked this way and that, and seeing no one he killed the Egyptian and hid him in the sand.

The past is not all sweetness and light. Someone had to act. You might call him a "terrorist," for he killed a government agent. Or you might call him a "freedom fighter." Call him what you will. The kids need to know that life beyond Pharaoh does not come by innocence. It comes by risky engagement with public power. The story of this killing is a rich didactic moment that sets the community of faith over against the force of empire. The ones who know this story recognize that forced labor—cheap labor, the draft—is always a necessary tool of economic monopoly. The narrative asserts that there is something in our past that stands boldly over against such coercive exploitation. We may be glad that Jesus' facedown of Pilate happened nonviolently, and let that narrative override the old one of violence (John 18:28–19:16).[5] But life in the presence of forced labor and all of its exploitation under any kind of regime is no moment for timidity. So the grandparents can recall the strikes in Detroit with Walter and Victor Reuther and the forcefulness of John L. Lewis, and Lech Walesa in Warsaw and Gandhi's spinning wheel and the refusal of imperial goods and imperial policies, and finally, bodies were put at risk to expose the unbearableness of injustice made into a legitimate system of haves and have-nots, an exploitative labor system that thrives on amnesia; and the kids are so entitled and so privileged that they do not know how we got to this time and place. They do not and will not know unless the grandparents continue to retell their past for them.

Remember the burning bush (Exod 3:1-6)

The proper word is "theophany," the eruption of holiness in the midst of life. The incident itself is beyond explanation. The narrative does not dwell on the visual phenomenon. That is over in three verses. Out of that moment of vision, however, comes a voice. That voice interrupted the life of Moses the fugitive, and the grandparents intend that the kids should be haunted by all such voices, voices of holiness that are hidden but always again keeping things stirred open.

The voice from the bush is one not known by Moses but quickly identified. It turns out to be the voice of the God already known in the tradition of Genesis, the God of Abraham and new beginnings, the God of Isaac and the God of Jacob, the one who has blessed and summoned and wounded. The moment before the bush is so overwhelming that shoes must be removed for the truth of holiness. This is life reduced to fearful awe and magnificent interruption. That voice, now identified as the one who walked this family through barrenness and down into Egypt, is a voice that lines out a future beyond pharaonic exploitation. Nobody can explain this voice because it disrupts without antecedent, and the word to the kids is, "Expect to be interrupted."

What an interruption!

> I have observed your misery . . .
>
> - *A slave camp in Egypt now noticed in heaven;*
>
> I have heard this cry on account of the taskmasters. . . .
>
> - *This is heaven with ears.*
>
> I know the suffering. . . .
>
> - *There is a God filled with attentiveness to the frail, fractured quality of human life.*

Imagine a God who sees and hears and knows! This is not the God of generic memory from the Jerusalem liturgy. This God is the one of specificity that the grandparents find compelling and non-negotiable:

> I have come down . . .
>
> - *down into Egypt, down into exploitative politics, down into the slave camp, down to the bottom of human misery;*
>
> I will bring you out . . .
>
> - *we did not know we would ever exit slavery. But the grandparents remember. God knows . . . and the memory continues to be known because the grandparents have not forgotten.*

Finally the voice in the bush adds one other sentence. After all the self-announcement of divine resolve, v. 10 goes like this:

> So come, I will send you to Pharaoh to bring my people, the Israelites, out of Egypt. (Exod 3:10)

You! The burning bush is not a "phenomenon." It is not a vision; it is, rather, a summons. The grandparents retell the summons into the next generation. The family that revolves around the bush is a summoned family, invited to depart the kingdom of amnesia, the kingdom of exploitation, and the mindless submission of amnesia.

Remember the fearful resistance (Exod 3:13–4:17)

The burning bush is not problematic because it is a religious phenomenon. It is problematic because it creates a clash with Pharaoh, and Pharaoh had seemed beyond challenge. Nobody minds a little glimpse of holiness, but a summons! So they all began to make excuses (see Luke 14:18).

Some said, "Me? . . . to Pharaoh?" (3:11-12). But the grandparents rendered the divine answer, "I will be with you."

Some said, "I do not know your name" (3:13-22). But the grandparents remembered the playful, imaginative answer. The name is "It is what it is." Or if pressed, "I am the God from the Book of Genesis." And then the God with the legitimate name reiterates the promise of newness and that promise will trump by a "wonder," a miracle, an act out beyond explanation or understanding. God's name drives the listener out beyond all that is conventional and familiar, and the grandparents want the kids to know that life is haunted beyond our usual capacity, that it is all about newness and water and wine and bread and oil and hiddenness that will give life.

Some said, "They will not believe this" (4:1-9). Well, what would it take to believe that holy power would interrupt coercive economics? What have holy power and coercive economics to do with each other? Or can they ignore each other, in separate spheres? The divine response is a sign, well, two signs: Try a snake become a staff, try a hand become leprous and then made whole again. Try minor miracles that you can see and touch and measure. But do not linger over minor miracles. Watch for the big public miracle of the renovation of the economy, the ultimate miracle. And if that will not persuade, watch water turn to blood or watch water turn to wine or watch death turn to life. People with amnesia are no good at signs; but the grandparents trust that beyond what is known and controlled there is a restless alternative that breaks our grasp on assumed reality. The signs point to an openness that we had not expected.

Some said, "I can't talk right" (4:10-12). The answer to that one is easy. Do not imagine that you are a self-starter. The feebleness of "you" is overwhelmed by the power of "I": "Who gives speech to mortals? Who makes them mute or deaf, seeing or blind? Is it not I, YHWH?" The self-praise of YHWH anticipates the message belatedly sent to John the Baptist: the blind see, the deaf hear, the lame walk, the lepers are cleansed, the dead are raised, the poor rejoice (Luke 7:22). The initiative belongs to the God who ends that paragraph to Moses by saying: "Now go!" That is all; no excuse will serve.

Some said, "Please send someone else" (4:13-17). Do not make me go. The refutation of that moan of self-pity is this. You are not alone; there is your brother Aaron. He will go with you, and you will make a good pair.

The grandparents know that there are endless excuses that serve to resist the divine summons. The divine summons to liberty and justice places one in contradiction to established authority. That placement in contradiction is elemental in biblical faith. But people with amnesia do not notice because we are not schooled in that long history of contradiction. We imagine only status quo pleasantness; this paradigmatic testimony, however, is about an alternative that makes life possible.

Remember the brick quotas

In the recital of chapter 5, YHWH is a minor player. The key players are the Egyptian Pharaoh, the Egyptian foremen, the Egyptian taskmasters, and the brick-producing Hebrews. There is only one theme: produce! Produce the daily quota without straw being provided. Work a little more. Let your work define your life. That is how it is here in the brickyard.

If you dress up coercive productivity into a good economic theory, it does not seem so coercive. But the grandparents remember: it is all about coercion in the realm of Pharaoh:

It is all about coercion for work to meet a bigger and bigger point spread;

It is all about coercion for the sales rep to meet a quota;

It is all about coercion for second graders to get ready for SATs in order to qualify for the Ivy League;

It is all about coercion with the dress code and Botox and sexual exploitation;

It is all about coercion for the pastor to grow the church and the president to grow the endowment;

It is all about coercion to please mother, to be the best child and the best athlete and the best scholar;

It is all about production and acquiring and exhibiting and coercing and being ahead of the pack . . . world without end.

The grandparents name the coercion and, at their best, provide an oasis for the grandchildren away from productivity. But if you are not a grandchild—but a pastor or a CEO or an athlete or a parent—there are no oases for restlessness, unless you depart.

Remember the contest

The core of the exodus narrative is a contest between YHWH and the gods of Egypt, between Moses and the Egyptian "magicians," that is, the "intelligence community" of the empire (see 12:12). The drama runs from blood through boils and locust. It is a contest of power. It is a trial of strength between the arrogant, visible power of Egypt and the hidden work of this unknown agent of holiness who has pledged emancipation. YHWH had promised, so the grandparents assert, that YHWH will "get glory" over the superpower.

The narrative is a sequence of miracles that, step-by-step, makes fools of Pharaoh and his company. There is cunning bartering and blatant defiance. Mostly, however, the drama concerns the action of YHWH. That, of course, will not be believed by the grandchildren who know and control so much in their own lives. But the narrative does not care, and does not seek to persuade the children. The narrative only testifies to what has been "seen and heard," and the grandparents in turn add their own attestation.

Who would have thought that world history was a contest? Who would have known ahead of time that the superpower is only one contestant, and if only one, a candidate for defeat? Who could possibly have anticipated that the superpower would be humiliated by this hidden holiness? Certainly the grandchildren, in their knowing, would not have thought or have known ahead of time or anticipated such a turn of events. The grandchildren, in their amnesia, had inevitably absolutized present power arrangements, either in buoyancy or in despair. But the grandparents treat present power arrangements loosely and narrate a scenario of otherwise. The grandchildren become aware, through the narrative, that history is a contest, a bid for brutality and defiance and control. It is the same contest that many kings and prophets enact together in the Old Testament, the same contest of Pilate before Jesus, the same contest wherever hope-filled possibility calls into question acquisitive power.

Remember the final dismay

The contest culminates in Exodus 12:29-30:

> At midnight the LORD struck down all the firstborn in the land of Egypt, from the firstborn of Pharaoh who sat on his throne to the firstborn of the prisoner who was in the dungeon, and all the firstborn of the livestock. Pharaoh arose in the night, he and all his officials and all the Egyptians; and there was a loud cry in Egypt, for there was not a house without someone dead. (12:29-30)

The firstborn are privileged, among sons, among cattle, even among prisoners. Rank has its privilege. In this telling, however, YHWH is no respecter of persons, pays no attention to tenure or privilege because the entire catalog of victims is tainted by empire. The scene is brutal, but it is like that when pain surges against acquisitive power. Sometimes, as in Romania and in Watts, it is violent. Sometimes it is the violence of theatre as when the mobs get into the closet of Imelda Marcos. Sometimes it is more reasoned as in Prague or in Pretoria.

But every time there is a cry—a cry of loss, a cry of fear, a cry of powerlessness and impotence. It happens to every arrogant power as the grandparents can attest. Pharaoh is so humiliated that he comes, crown in hand, to Moses to bid at long last for a blessing:

> Take your flocks and your herds, as you said, and be gone. And bring a blessing on me too! (Exod 12:32)

Pharaoh, along with the narrators, now notices that the blessing is not lodged with the powerful. This dramatic moment anticipates the recognition by the Roman soldier at the foot of the cross who belatedly asserts, "Truly this man was God's son!" (Mark 15:39).

What a strange moment for a blessing! We are not told that Moses responds with a blessing for Pharaoh. But blessing is now in the air. The grandparents raise the issue. Where would you look for a blessing? The blessing surfaces just at the moment of a violent end. What a mix:

violence and blessing, blessing and violence, all mingled in the world where truth and pain come against power. And we are left with a cry. What a strange contrast to the world of symmetrical control and management. We are offered, in the narrative, a glimpse into the rawness where dwells transformative holiness.

Remember the departing and the journey

The grandparents line it out in prose narrative:

> Then Moses stretched out his hand over the sea. The LORD drove the sea back by a strong east wind all night, and turned the sea into dry land; and the waters were divided. The Israelites went into the sea on dry ground, the waters forming a wall for them on their right and on their left. (Exod 14:21-22)

The departing slaves were profoundly anxious, but Moses assured them:

> Do not be afraid, stand firm, and see the deliverance that the LORD will accomplish for you today; for the Egyptians whom you see today you shall never see again. The LORD will fight for you, and you have only to keep still. (Exod 14:13-14)

And his assurance turned out to be true.

Before the narrator, Moses, and Miriam—and the women with tambourines—sing the journey, watch Pharaoh drown, and watch the ancestors begin the long trek to the land of promise. They had to go. What courage and nerve it required, to imagine life outside the reach of Pharaoh! The story is told and the poem is recited,

> in order that Jesus could summon to life beyond Rome,
>
> in order that Martin Luther I [the Reformer] could articulate faith beyond the indulgences of sacramentalism,
>
> in order that Wellhausen and his ilk could break the grip of closed dogmatic teaching,
>
> in order that Barth could break Romans again from the weary church,
>
> in order that Martin Luther II [King Jr.] could walk and march and sing the dream,

in order that freedom and justice out beyond coercive politics and acquisitive economics could be available.

The story will not quit. The poem echoes, exhibiting people on the march to a destiny outside the grip of imperial requirement.

Remember the final hallelujah

When Moses sang his song, he ended it dreaming of Jerusalem and he sang:

> The LORD will reign forever and ever. (Exod 15:18)

It is an odd enthronement formula. The grandparents sing of the rule of YHWH. In doing so they anticipate the declaration of Jesus that the good news kingdom has come (Mark 1:14-15). If we listen well, moreover, we can hear inchoately the cadences of Handel, "Forever and ever, forever and ever . . . Hallelujah." The text sings of regime change and new governance, a dramatic liturgical possibility that the world can be reordered.

All of that is on offer in this paradigm. All that is needed is grandparents with freedom, courage, and imagination. The ones with such freedom and such imagination surely refuse any reductive amnesia. They remember; they do so because these stunning occasions of the disclosure of holiness in the midst of the life of the world keeps recurring. It is no wonder that Michael Walzer, the great Jewish political philosopher, could conclude:

> So pharaonic oppression, deliverance, Sinai, and Canaan are still with us, powerful memories shaping our perceptions of the political world. The "door of hope" is still open; things are not what they might be—even when what they might be isn't totally different from what they are. This is a central theme in Western thought, always present though elaborated in many different ways. We still believe, or many of us do, what the exodus first taught, or what it has commonly been taken to teach, about the meaning and possibility of politics and about its proper form:
>
>> first, that wherever you live, it is probably Egypt;
>>
>> second, that there is a better place, a world more attractive, a promised land; and

> third, that "the way to the land is through the wilderness." There is no way to get from here to there except by joining together and marching.[6]

We are always on the way from here to there, by journeying together and singing and dancing, by departing and marching.

It is, moreover, no great stretch from these ancient grandparents of Passover narrative to the Thursday scene, "Do this in remembrance of me." Grandparents are for evoking sacramental dimensions of ordinary life. More concretely, William Cavanaugh has exhibited the way in which this sacramental imagination makes a worldly alternative possible, an act of remembering that enacts holiness and subverts absolutism, offering instead a future poured out, a community broken but not forgetful.[7]

V

Imagine the paradigm entrusted to us, at work in revolutionary ferment. And then imagine a flattened, denying, despairing world in which the exodus grandparents have been silenced. Imagine a world without this text, as much of the world craves to be. Do some forgetting. Reduce the power of this paradigm and think what we have then.

Forget and you will have a closed absolutism with no bold midwives who defy Pharaoh, but only clerks who obey everyone.

Forget and you will have a world of no burning bush, no holy intrusion, no summons to freedom, no resolve from heaven to work newness on the earth.

Forget and you will have conformist docility, without the righteous indignation of freedom fighters who refuse the exploitative violence of the slave masters.

Forget and you will have a narcotized anxiety not capable of doubting or wondering or challenging, not bold enough to ask God's name in order to evoke miracles, but simply a robotic security that goes along with idols who give nothing and who effect nothing and who preclude all challenges of dialogic exchange.

Forget and you will get a society that regards impossible brick quotas as normal and not problematic, glad to be enslaved, fixed on production without meaning or possibility, getting ahead in the brickyard on the way to no joy, living for that which does not satisfy.

Forget and you will have a settled community incapable of conflict, unready for contest, unaware of the alternative, unwilling to risk going against Pharaoh, reducing dangerous holiness to consumerism, shelving the holy God into the woodwork of imperial arrangements, with no Passover in sight, no offer of blessing, only satiation.

Forget and you will be unable to imagine the discomfort of the empire, incapable of laughing at power, unwilling to voice mocking derision of a failed world that has all the trappings of legitimacy, but in fact one that weeps in the night over lost sons and lost cattle and lost futures, unable to imagine the empire on its sad knees.

Forget and the notion of "departure" fades, and we embrace a "realized eschatology" that imagines that this is as good as it will get:

no departure to justice,

no departure to freedom,

no departure to neighborliness,

no departure to Sabbath.

Only complicity in a world without vitality.

Forget and there will never cross our lips any real singing, any vigorous hallelujah, any assertion of new rule. Our recipe for the future becomes a mute despair with no promises that could possibly be kept.

Forget and we end conformist, lost, dominated . . . eventually numbed and dead. There are many ways to forget:

new age spirituality with no demanding energy;

historical criticism with everything adjusted to reasonableness;

dogmatism with all the answers known ahead of time;

privatism that has no energy for the common good;

nostalgia for some imagined past without contemporary realism.

The news from the grandparents is that it need not be so. This exodus text, in sum, proposes an alternative world. It is the alternative work of holy purpose dispatched into public reality in transformative ways. I am aware, as are you, that all I have done is walk with you through the text.

What else?! What else except imaginative revelation, revelation that points at the truth of our life in the world? I have lined it out as a positive revolutionary possibility. I have lined it out briefly as must be done when the grandparents are silenced. The narrative is paradigmatic because the deep themes of faith are all voiced here with a summoning edge.[8]

VI

But notice as Gerhard von Rad noticed: in Isaiah 43, when the great poet addresses his contemporaries in the categories of exodus faith, he urged:

> Do not remember the former things,
> or consider the things of old. (Isa 43:18)

Do not be preoccupied with that ancient narrative. Rather:

> I am about to do a new thing,
> now it springs forth, do you not perceive it?
> I will make a way in the wilderness
> and rivers in the desert. (Isa 43:19)[9]

The new thing God is about to do—is always about to do—is a new exodus.[10] God has done many exoduses and will do more. Amos celebrated Israel's exodus, but he went on to insist that YHWH has done exoduses even among Israel's enemies, for the Philistines and for the Syrians:

> Are you not like the Ethiopians to me,
> O people of Israel? says the LORD.
> Did I not bring Israel up from the land of Egypt,
> and the Philistines from Caphtor and the Arameans from Kir?
> (Amos 9:7)[11]

The world is the drama of exodus writ large because YHWH's holy power is on the loose, holy power that generates new community that breaks all of our weary arrangements. The paradigm always again breaks out with contemporary concreteness. As that happens, it is done so that you may know that "I am YHWH." More than that, it is done so that "the Egyptians will know that I am YHWH when I have gotten glory for myself over Pharaoh and all his army, his chariots and his chariots' drivers" (Exod 14:17). All shall know and the world will be drawn to newness.

A focus on the grand parental text of Exodus 10:1-2 suggests to me an important reread of our situation. The church in the midst of postindustrial belated capitalism may be a community gathered in amnesia, ready to submit to the dominant ideology of American preeminence. In the midst of that pervasive amnesia, the pastor and the teacher and the liturgist say, "Do this in remembrance." Do this narrative. Do this Passover. Do this Eucharist. Enter the narrative and live the world differently. Imagine the grandparental task, a summons, an invitation, an act of defiance. It is possible that folk will depart the meeting marked by new identity, a part of the intergenerational body of those who know YHWH and the way in which Pharaoh has been made to look silly. It was a child of this text who watched Pharaoh sink into the water, did a double-take about the recurring deathliness of Pharaoh, and said:

> "Death has been swallowed up in victory."
> "Where, O death, is your victory?
> Where, O death, is your sting?" (1 Cor 15:54b-55)

I imagine that Eunice and Lois watched and danced and laughed, along with Miriam at the water.

10

DOUBLE AGENCY

The recharacterization of "exile" as "forced migration" is now a centerpiece in recent scholarly work. That recharacterization invites the question, "Forced by whom?" The new formulation of the topic invites the question of agency, to which the biblical narrative characteristically responds with "double agency," thus twinning divine agency and human agency. The notion of double agency—divine and human—is integral to a covenantal–Deuteronomic–prophetic articulation of history. It is voiced, perhaps, already in the Song of Deborah wherein victory is celebrated and credited to "both agents":

> To the sound of musicians at the watering places,
> there they repeat the triumphs of *the* L*ORD*,
> the triumphs of *his peasantry* in Israel. (Judg 5:11)

The same doubleness is likely reflected in the narrative of Gideon, though agency is not made explicit, in the rhetoric of the army:

> "For the LORD and for Gideon." (Judg 7:18)

The doubleness is reflected in the divine verbal assurance to Gideon:

> "But *I* will be with you, and *you* shall strike down the Midianites, every one of them." (Judg 6:16)

That assurance, moreover, is reminiscent of the initial divine confrontation with Moses wherein YHWH makes a series of first-person assurances to Moses about direct engagement but then decisively turns the task to Moses:

> So come, *I* will send *you* to Pharaoh to bring my people, the Israelites, out of Egypt. (Exod 3:10)

The assurance to Gideon in Judges 6:16 is answered with the narrative report of the way in which divine agency ("spirit of God") empowered human agency:

> The spirit of the Lord took possession of Gideon; and he sounded the trumpet, and the Abiezrites were called out to follow him. (Judg 6:34)

I cite these cases, likely earlier than the text on which this chapter focuses (2 Kgs 24–25), to indicate that double agency constitutes no problem in the narrative form of Israel's historiography, even when we recognize that from a critical modernist perspective "forced migration" requires only an explicit human agent. In what follows I will consider the problematic of double agency, not in order to resolve it but to see how these traditions articulate the theological claims that Klaus Koch identifies as "metahistory."[1] It is clear that without this doubleness (that our rationality might regard as problematic), there could be no articulation of what passes for biblical historiography.

I

Second Kings 24–25 is readily divided into seven distinct rhetorical units, two of which are explicit about divine agency, that is, Yhwh as agent of "forced migration."

1. *24:1-7* This text summarizes the final days of Jehoiakim and concerns his rebellion against Nebuchadnezzar that led to the first Babylonian incursion into Judah in 598 BCE. Verses 2-4, sandwiched by the chronicle of vv. 1, 5-7, voice a "metahistory" that is patterned after prophetic speech of judgment. The indictment is twofold concerning the "sins of Manasseh" and "the innocent blood that he shed." The divine judgment is the command of Yhwh to "remove" Judah and not to pardon. The pivotal term is "remove" (*swr*) that is reinforced by a verdict, "not willing to pardon" (*slḥ*). The verb *swr* is already twice used with reference to the Northern Kingdom:

> Therefore the Lord was very angry with Israel and *removed* them out of his sight. (2 Kgs 17:18)

> . . . until the Lord *removed* Israel out of his sight, as he had foretold through all his servants the prophets. (17:23)

In 23:27, moreover, YHWH pledged to remove Judah from the land, a pledge now enacted in our verses:

> The LORD said, "I will *remove* Judah also out of my sight, as I have *removed* Israel; and I will reject this city that I have chosen, Jerusalem, and the house of which I said, 'My name shall be there.'"

In each case, YHWH is unmistakably the agent.[2] The sequence in 24:1-7 is characteristically Deuteronomic: sanction follows conduct; curse follows disobedience. In the curse recital of Deuteronomy 28:64-65, displacement from the land is the ultimate threat for disobedience:

> The LORD will scatter you among all the peoples, from one end of the earth to the other; and there you shall serve other gods, of wood and stone, which neither you nor your ancestors have known. Among those nations you shall find no ease, no resting place for the sole of your foot. There the LORD will give you a trembling heart, failing eyes, and a languishing spirit. (28:64-65)

Thus the threat voiced against Jehoiakim fits squarely as an instance of covenantal history. This will all come "at the command of YHWH" (2 Kgs 24:3). In v. 1 it is "Nebuchadnezzar . . . came," followed in v. 2 by "YHWH sent." Although the object of YHWH's verb is not explicitly Nebuchadnezzar; the point in any case is clear. Thus "come," "sent," and "commanded" evidence the delicate way in which the two agents are rhetorically intertwined, though there is no ambiguity about ultimate causation.

2. *24:8-12* reports on the forced removal of Jehoiachin in the wake of his father's rebellion. In v. 9, it is noted in a formulaic way that he "did evil in the sight of YHWH," but that is all. The actual removal is by the hand of Nebuchadnezzar, so that YHWH is not explicitly implicated in the forced migration. Divine agency here is minimal but surely implied.

3. *24:13-16* offers a report on the Babylonian plundering of the temple and the population. Strikingly it is all Nebuchadnezzar. In vv. 13-15 the agent is only "he," but the "king of Babylon" is twice named in vv. 16-17. There is no explicit theological reference in these verses. The verb *glh* is used three times, so that Nebuchadnezzar is clearly the one who forces the migration.

4. *24:17–25:7* reports on the final disposition of Zedekiah as the last king. The rhetoric of these verses suggests an intentional juxtaposition of the two agents. In 25:1-7, with considerable detail, the actor is

Nebuchadnezzar who breaches the city, pursues the fleeing king, and eventually brings him to Riblah for a final abuse. In these verses, YHWH is absent. In 24:18-20, however, it is all YHWH according to the rubrics of a prophetic speech of judgment:

In v. 19 there is a generic indictment, echoing v. 9 on Jehoiachin:

> He did evil in the sight of YHWH.[3]

In v. 20:

> Judah so angered YHWH that he expelled them from his presence.

It is important in this usage, as with *swr* in 24:4, that it is not exclusion from the land but "from his presence" (lit., "his face"). The judgment of 24:30 is noteworthy:

> He expelled them from his presence. . . . Zedekiah rebelled against the king of Babylon.

The narrative suggests no particular connection between the two, though the sequence would seem to suggest that rebellion follows expulsion from the presence, an acting out of a divine mandate that had not yet been implemented.

5. *25:8-21* provides a long inventory of the way in which Nebuzaradan, on behalf of Nebuchadnezzar, plundered the temple and "every great house." In addition he brought leading Jerusalem officials to Riblah where the king put them to death (v. 21). This long note may be of interest for us for two reasons. First, YHWH is nowhere mentioned. This is completely a Babylonian accomplishment. Second, the inventory is bracketed by the term *glh* in vv. 11 and 25. Forced migration is a costly business for property and a risky business for life.

6. *25:22-26* summarizes the post-state condition of Judah as Babylonian colony under the governorship of Gedaliah. We need linger over Gedaliah only long enough to remember that he is a scion of the family of Shaphan, a great supporter of Jeremiah and an advocate of ready surrender to Babylon. Thus the forced migration opened the way for accommodation of local officials to the claims of empire. The paragraph is dominated by Gedaliah's assurance, "Do not fear" (v. 24). The assurance by a local accommodator assures that cooperation with empire will lead to shalom. The rhetoric of Gedaliah closely parallels the divine assurance

on the lips of Jeremiah in Jeremiah 42:9-12, suggesting the formulation is a standard line of the accommodators who assure that the forcing regime will be benign.

The report on Gedaliah reflects the deep conflict in Judean society between pro-Babylonian and anti-Babylonian factions, the latter led by Ishmael "of the royal family," a conflict that ends with the assassination of the accommodator and the laconic conclusion, "They were afraid of the Chaldeans" (v. 26). While the party of Gedaliah had confidence in Babylon (and should have, given its privilege granted by the empire), this confidence was not shared by others, notably those identified with the royal family. Given the internecine conflict, the people "high and low" ("young and old") fled to Egypt in fear of Babylon (v. 26). Here there is no explicit agent of displacement, but the "forcer" is undoubtedly Babylon. While this narrative lacks one of the signature verbs of expulsion, it may nonetheless be included with the uses of "remove," "expel," and "exile" as ways of speaking of forced migration.

7. *25:27-30* This paragraph on the survival and continued recognition of Jehoiachin as king in displacement completes our text. Elsewhere I have suggested that this paragraph, of itself, has been made to carry more interpretive freight than it is able to carry.[4] Against the promissory accent of Gerhard von Rad, I have suggested that the paragraph is deliberately indeterminate; the narrator does not know what comes next. The paragraph is designed to leave everything open, even against our interpretive propensities. In any case, it does not relieve at all the condition of forced relocation.

In sum then:

I. *Nebuchadnezzar* is all through this passage as agent:

He is the one who came against Jehoiakim (24:1);

He is the one who laid siege and took Jehoiachin as prisoner (24:10-12);

He is the one who plundered temple and city (24:13-17);

He is the one who pursued Zedekiah and executed him (25:1-7);

He is the one who—through his captain—plundered the great houses and executed the leading citizens of the city;

He is the one who appointed Gedaliah as governor;

It is his successor, Evil-Merodach, who released Jehoiachin from prison.

The narrative is straightforward and offers an account of a fierce, demanding imperial force vis-à-vis a restless, vulnerable colony.

II. But of course this narrative is of interest and is unlike other narratives because it cannot leave matters as clear as that. The narrative relentlessly attests *a second agent, YHWH*, who "removes," "expels," and—if we reason from the explicit assertions of chapter 17—"exiles" or forces the displacement of this people that knew itself to be chosen.

It is clear that the narrative has no trouble at all with double agency and could not, I suppose, construe the history of Jerusalem in any other way. It has no trouble, moreover, in representing this first agent as bent on a relentlessly destructive course of action toward Jerusalem. It is, given the starchy premises of the tradition of Deuteronomy, not a problem to have two agents nor that the senior agent could readily mobilize a junior agent against the chosen people, chosen land, chosen city, chosen dynasty, and chosen temple.

II

The parallel version of "forced migration" in the tradition of Jeremiah is equally committed to double agency. Thus in Jeremiah 25:9 and 27:6, Nebuchadnezzar is well credentialed as "my servant." Nonetheless it is remarkable that in 39:1-10, which reports the actual taking of the city, and the narrative account of 52:1-27 (that parallels our narrative in 2 Kings), any mention of YHWH is absent. This is public history of an "ordinary" kind. Here there is nothing of divine anger, divine mandate, or divine action. It is now all Nebuchadnezzar, all Babylon, all empire. Only the last sentence, as an editorial conclusion, uses the term *glh*: "So Judah went into exile" (52:27). To be sure, there is a series of forceful verbs necessary to report imperial action: captured, killed, burned, broke down, carried, broke, carried, took away, took, struck down, put to death. All of these terms, however, serve as nothing more than description of the aggression of empire.

In 52:28-30, a text without parallel in Kings, Nebuchadnezzar is the agent of the threefold displacement with the threefold use of *glh*. Clearly the Jeremiah tradition cannot do without double agency, for it has no interest in the actions of Nebuchadnezzar as such. The case for double agency has already been clearly established elsewhere in the Jeremiah tradition. It need not be explicit here in the actual reportage on displacement.

The matter is not fundamentally different in the Chronicler's account of the demise of Jerusalem in 2 Chronicles 36; we may nonetheless note important variations. In vv. 1-14, the text disposes tersely of four kings in succession, Jehoahaz (vv. 1-4), Jehoiakim (vv. 5-8), Jehoiachin (vv. 9-10), and Zedekiah (vv. 11-14). In each case the "empire of force" is effectively at work:[5]

> Neko, king of Egypt, dispatches Jehoahaz;
>
> Nebuchadnezzar takes Jehoiakim to Babylon in fetters;[6]
>
> Nebuchadnezzar brought Jehoiachin to Babylon;
>
> Nebuchadnezzar made Zedekiah "swear by God," an odd variation indeed.

In the first three cases, YHWH's agency is at best formulaic:

> concerning Jehoahaz, we have only Realpolitik; the reference to "evil in the sight of the Lord" from 2 Kings 23:32 has been omitted. This may be not more than a scribal error; but in any case the result is a one-dimensional statement about the agency of the king of Egypt;
>
> concerning Jehoiakim, he "did what was evil in the sight of the Lord his God";
>
> concerning Jehoiachin, "he did what was evil in the sight of the Lord."

It is the fourth case of Zedekiah wherein theological interests are much more central. We have the same formula, "did what was evil in the sight of the Lord," but then, this royal evil is specified:

> He "did not humble himself before the prophet Jeremiah";[7]
>
> He "stiffened his neck and hardened his heart against turning to the Lord, the God of Israel";
>
> Priests and people are indicted for being "exceedingly unfaithful, following all the abominations of the nations" and for "pollut[ing] the house of the Lord that he had consecrated in Jerusalem."

The final judgment against the city is no longer grounded in "the sins of Manasseh." Now the cause is much more immediate and contemporary (with Zedekiah) and not deferred from Manasseh. The most intense terms of infidelity cluster in this climactic statement. It is of note that in vv. 12-13, the royal rebellion against Nebuchadnezzar is sandwiched between (a) not humbling himself before the prophet and (b) stiffening his neck and hardening his heart against YHWH, as though all three elements (including rebellion against Nebuchadnezzar) are taken with equal theological seriousness. It is astonishing, for all of that, that the narrative does not report on the flight, arrest, or execution of Zedekiah that we have in the report in Kings. In all but the first of these royal reports, the double agency is intrinsically linked to the destruction of the city.

In vv. 15-16 the text appropriates from 2 Kings 17:13-14 concerning the sustained warnings of the prophets that are consistently disregarded by royal Judah; the tradition simply transfers them to the south. Again the terms cluster: "mock, despise, scoff" occur in a sentence that attests to intense willfulness against YHWH. In vv. 10-17, double agency is again explicit: "He (YHWH) brought up against them the king of the Chaldeans." The follow up consists in brutalizing imperial action, culminating in "exile" that lasted "until the establishment of the kingdom of Persia" (v. 20).

It is evident that in the episode with Zedekiah (vv. 11-14) and the prophets (vv. 15-16), the theological dimension of the destruction is acute. The Chronicler has intensified the centrality of divine agency in the retelling of the end. This accent, moreover, is articulated by the double reference to Jeremiah; in the end, it is the disregard of the prophetic warnings that is decisive for the dynasty (vv. 12, 21). Thus the Chronicler handles double agency by references to Jeremiah, who serves the agency of YHWH, perhaps an appeal to *a second human agent* in the interest of YHWH's transcendence.

In the final paragraph of the chapter, the report on Jehoiachin in 2 Kings 25:27-30 and Jeremiah 52:31-34 is displaced by yet a third appeal to Jeremiah, this time apparently with reference to the prophetic oracle of Jeremiah 50:9 with the "stir up" of *yet another human agent*, Cyrus (2 Chr 36:22-23). This verb, "stir up," is of interest because it is an attempt to articulate the linkage of the two agents beyond the usual "command, send," now a usage that allows for maneuverability in interpretation.

Given these distinct nuances of chapter 36, it is nonetheless the case that this third report, after Kings and Jeremiah, does not vary in its primary claim from the first two reports. The intent in all three reports is to connect divine will and Realpolitik, indeed to subordinate Realpolitik to the sovereignty of YHWH to whom the king in Jerusalem, like all kings, is subject.

III

Our task here is to consider the "theological problematic" of this text, and I will do so under five topics.

1. At the outset we must keep available a wonderment as to whether "problematic" is the right word or if so, "problematic" to whom? It is clear that the claim of such double agency is problematic to Enlightenment rationality, even though we have chosen to mumble about that until exposed by the likes of Langdon Gilkey.[8] But long before that modern problematic, it is surely the case that the commitments to the Deuteronomic-prophetic categories expressed in our text were persuasive for only a segment (a small segment) of the Jerusalem population; no doubt much of the population and certainly many of the opinion makers of that population must have found these claims problematic as well, though not likely for reasons of Enlightenment rationality. Rather the ground for the problematic was more likely the deeply grounded exceptionalism upon which the Jerusalem claims were based. That *exceptionalism* may logically be the very antithesis of *Enlightenment rationality*, but the two may also go together in resisting this rendering of the displacement and the forced migration. We may continue to ponder what the affront of the text may, in the end, be for our reading, for the interface of *exceptionalism* and *Enlightenment rationality* continues to hold powerful sway among us.

2. It is of course recognized that the recurring formulation of double agency is employed in order to enact the covenantal-Deuteronomic assumption of "deed-consequence," of commandment and sanction.[9] With variations, the formula of "the ways of life and death" is ironclad and non-negotiable (Deut 30:15-20). And because, in this purview, knowing disobedience was systemic and intense, the whole matter could be readily reduced to a formula. The ironclad formula served to give a reason for the forced migration, served to protect the legitimacy of YHWH, and provided a warrant for the imperial intrusion of Nebuchadnezzar in Judah.

There are, however, signs that the ironclad formulation was recognized as difficult; there are signs of restlessness with the claim. Bernard Levinson has written recently of the ways in which the ongoing interpretive tradition moved against this simplistic formulation of intergenerational punishment; his exposition is important for our theme of forced migration. In Lamentations 5:7,

> the new generation of the deportees complains that it must bear the iniquities of the fathers:
>
> Our ancestors sinned; they were no more.
>
> And we bear their iniquities.

Levinson comments:

> The injustice of the doctrine raises important practical difficulties as well. It inevitably creates an overwhelming sense of the futility of historical action altogether, inasmuch as the progeny cannot free themselves from the consequences of the past. In the grim circumstance of Israel after the catastrophe of destruction and exile, the future would have seemed radically foreclosed, the direct result not of one's own but of a previous generation's action.[10]

In his reading of the proverb of Ezekiel 18:1-4, Levinson suggests that by appeal to Deuteronomy 24:16, Ezekiel reduces the claim of the doctrine of intergenerational punishment to a folk saying and thereby subverts it. By that reduction, a case can be made that the claim is "morally repugnant."[11] It should be noted that Levinson shows the way in which Ezekiel anticipates the moral breakthrough of Immanuel Kant concerning "moral freedom as independence from the burden of the past."[12]

In Deuteronomy 7:9-10, the new generation is exempted from the punishment that is guaranteed by the Decalogue. Thus the interpretation that claims to exposit in fact subverts the original claim of intergenerational punishment. YHWH

> repays in their own person those who reject him. He does not delay but repays in their own person those who reject him.[13]

To Levinson's inventory of Deuteronomy 24:16 and 7:9-10, I may add two more. In Lamentations 3, the appeal to "return" is grounded in a confession of sin, exactly according to the formula of punishment:

> Let us test and examine our ways,
> and return to the LORD.
> Let us lift up our hearts as well as our hands
> to God in heaven.
> We have transgressed and rebelled,
> and you have not forgiven. (Lam 3:40-42)

That much is conventional. But remarkably, only a few verses later, the poet can say:

> Those who were my enemies *without cause*
> have hunted me like a bird;
> they flung me alive into a pit
> and hurled stones on me;
> water closed over my head;
> I said, "I am lost." (3:52-54)

The astonishing term is "without cause" (*ḥinnam*), suggesting that the punishment and suffering are gratuitous.[14] What follows in vv. 56-61 is an assurance that YHWH has heard and has broken the cycle of punishment.

In Isaiah 47:6, in what I regard as a full articulation of a prophetic sense of historical dynamics, the poet concedes that Nebuchadnezzar had a mandate from YHWH but indicts the Babylonian king who had ferociously overstepped that divine mandate:

> I was angry with my people,
> I profaned my heritage;
> I gave them into your hand,
> you showed them no mercy;
> on the aged you made your yoke
> exceedingly heavy. (Isa 47:6)

The general indictment of the empire is premised on the claim that Nebuchadnezzar had gone beyond YHWH's intent in forced migration, for, in the end, YHWH intended mercy for Jerusalem. Such a remarkable claim is surely a surprise to the circles of Deuteronomy, both concerning the symmetrical formulation of deeds and consequences and the poetry of Jeremiah that celebrated Babylon as one dispatched by YHWH who was sent to "have no mercy" (Jer 6:23).

It is clear that the main line of the tradition continues to hold to a symmetrical calculus. It is equally clear that, all around the edges, that symmetrical calculus is resisted and evokes protest. In the end, that tradition refuses a simplistic explanation of its experience of displacement, a refusal that must have been increasingly important to subsequent generations of the migrants who had been forced away. Given such a refusal, we are left either with a God who cannot be trusted or a human agent acting autonomously and without divine mandate.

3. From outside the Deuteronomic calculus, among other factions in the Jerusalem population, it is clear that this hard-nosed divine resolve amounted to a drastic reneging on Jerusalem promises to king and to temple, that is, to the foundation of exceptionalism. The pathos about this divine renege is voiced in Psalm 89 where, after elaborate affirmation of David, the psalm arrives at its unanswerable question:

> Lord, where is your steadfast love of old,
> which by your faithfulness you swore to David? (Ps 89:49)

In the ongoing tradition beyond Deuteronomic closure, it is equally clear that the divine promises could not be so lightly dismissed. In a conviction perhaps held by Ishmael "of the royal family" (2 Kgs 25:25), the royal promises reemerge concerning the migrants, remarkably even in the tradition of Jeremiah that was so deeply against the Jerusalem entitlement:

> Then I myself will gather the remnant of my flock out of all the lands where I have driven them, and I will bring them back to their fold, and they shall be fruitful and multiply. I will raise up shepherds over them who will shepherd them, and they shall not fear any longer, or be dismayed, nor shall any be missing, says the LORD. (Jer 23:3-4)

> The days are surely coming, says the LORD, when I will raise up for David a righteous Branch, and he shall reign as king and deal wisely, and shall execute justice and righteousness in the land. In his days Judah will be saved and Israel will live in safety. And this is the name by which he will be called, "The LORD is our righteousness." (Jer 23:5-6; see 33:14-17)

The reassertion of the royal promise indicates that the migrant community, upon further reflection, found Deuteronomic closure if not unacceptable, then at least penultimate and not the final word. And of course the Jehoiachin report attests, perhaps, to this wistful conviction as well (2 Kgs 25:27-30; Jer 52:31-34).

4. One cannot fail to observe the silence and absence of YHWH in the detailed inventory of the sacking of the temple (2 Kgs 25:9-17; Jer 52:17-23). The silence of YHWH in great stretches of the report of the forcing of the migration leaves the field to the empire. There is no doubt that forced migration was imperial policy, but from a theological perspective, one must wonder about the silence of YHWH in the midst of the dismantling. Perhaps the silence is nothing more than an invitation to imperial rapaciousness over which YHWH exercises no oversight. Or perhaps YHWH is fully implicated in the action. If YHWH is implicated in the action, then the migrants might have wondered about this God who cares not at all for God's own majesty, leave alone the people to whom promises have been made.

The issue is even more acute because it is the temple of YHWH (about which YHWH has made promises) that is being sacked. Perhaps the migrants could not conceive of YHWH acting against YHWH's own interest in such a blatant way, so that they permitted YHWH to "take a walk" during that dismantling act.[15] Or perhaps we are to imagine YHWH watching the imperial plunder—noticing and pondering and weeping—and then blaming Nebuchadnezzar, as in Isaiah 47:6. Or perhaps the absence and the silence are in the service of a transcendence that refuses such blasphemy. In any case, in these passages, the narrative falls short of double agency. Perhaps the tradition simply could not implicate YHWH directly in such destruction, which might suggest that there are limits, even for YHWH, in the stringent calculus. Surely they must have wondered: if YHWH will trash YHWH's own house in this way, why not YHWH's own people as well? And they have departed with grief and longing as they refused to forget the city and its temple.[16]

5. The singular appeal to the "sins of Manasseh" in 2 Kings 24:3-4 led to the conclusion that YHWH "was not willing to forgive" (*slḥ*). That verdict surely anticipates what follows in these chapters, and is echoed in Lamentations 3:42 cited above:

> We have transgressed and rebelled,
> and you have not forgiven. (3:42)

The point is paralleled in Deuteronomy 29:20, which leads to a rigorous defense of YHWH's harsh action:[17]

> The LORD will be unwilling to pardon them, for the LORD's anger and passion will smoke against them. (29:20)

It is clear in the tradition, nonetheless, that "unwillingness to forgive," the decisive claim of our chapters, is not the final word. The term *slḥ* reappears in continued reflection, because it will not do finally, among this people, to attest to such an intransigent and unresponsive God. The migrants who kept at the tradition could not and would not let that be their permanent fate from YHWH. For that reason, we get the term again, first as petition among the migrants (1 Kgs 8:34, 36), and then as assurance:[18]

> I will *forgive* their iniquity, and remember their sin no more. (Jer 31:34)

> I will cleanse them from all the guilt of their sin against me, and I will *forgive* all the guilt of their sin and rebellion against me. (Jer 33:8)

> Let them return to the LORD, that he may have mercy on them,
> and to our God, for he will *abundantly pardon*. (Isa 55:7b)

The developing interpretive conviction among the migrants moved beyond what seemed a settled verdict in the normative calculus.

All of these points, taken together, attest to the restlessness of the tradition and to the inchoate recognition that no explanatory formula, not even from the magisterial voice of Deuteronomy, can adequately corral history.[19] After the tight calculus of sin and punishment, there is more that must be said. Some of it cannot be said yet. Some of it awaits more pondering. Some of it anticipates the daring imagination of the next generation. Some of it, perhaps, attests to YHWH's own restlessness and YHWH's refusal of any so-called final solution, even concerning the unbearable recalcitrance of Jerusalem. The outcome is a dynamic interpretive tradition that can be understood as generative literary energy, as historical requirement in new circumstance, but also as theological buoyancy of an agent who refuses closure.[20] I judge that for the ongoing community of the migrants, the verdict rendered in chapters 24–25 is a credible one that asserts moral sensibility, as long as it is not taken as the final word. The community of migrants, so permeated with song and oracle, had both a historical yearning and a theological conviction that led not only to a "returning" (1 Kgs 8; Deut 30:1-10) but also to an amazing gift received without any returning.[21]

IV

I draw two conclusions that are reflective of my thesis concerning double agency: First, the text may be taken as an effort at Realpolitik in which the defining terms are "empire and colony," or imperial system and vulnerable migrant community, for I take the *colony* and the *displaced migrants* together as a contrast to the *imperial system*. What strikes one as one ponders the royal folk and the party of Shaphan (that included his grandson Gedaliah) is that there are *accommodators* and *resisters* side by side. Indeed, without the accommodators, that is, without Shaphan and Jeremiah and Baruch, Jerusalem would not have been so readily taken. While the memory and action of Ishmael are not seen in a kindly light in the text, he is an agent of resistance to the empire. It would be no easy thing, in biblical teaching, to make a systemic case for resistance or for accommodation because resisters and accommodators dwell together in empire; in both cases they seek to sustain a distinct identity that is partly sociopolitical and partly theological. When seen as Realpolitik, the theological dimension of the attestation may be seen as a function of a very real life-or-death dispute about response to empire, a dilemma that recurs endlessly in a world of empires that characteristically transgress moral coherence.

Second, the God of the Deuteronomic calculus is not exactly winsome. YHWH is portrayed variously as patriarchal and violent and not a happy camper in downtown Jerusalem. In much contemporary interpretation this God is mostly dismissed as an ideological construct as the voice of the "urban elite" who lust for power, even as we who say these slogans to each other are urban elites with tenure. It is not for me to defend the Deuteronomic syllogism in either its cold form or with its more accommodating nuance. We are, however, obligated to ponder what that formulation intended. Surely its intention was to insist that the coming and going of historical vagaries—dynastic, sacerdotal, and imperial—are all penultimate, and that behind them (or in, with, and under them) is a resolved moral intentionality that will not yield. It is convenient among us, in a common interpretive move, to dismiss such hard-nosed conviction as a "paper god" constructed for ideological purposes. Of course! But not more so than other paper gods we may prefer at the moment, for in the end we traffic in paper gods. Thus one obligation in interpretation is to entertain the claim of this voice, problematic as we may regard it.

Because my comments constitute a theological venture, I dare to move from that ancient world of abrasion to the one that we inhabit when we interpret. Such a move toward contemporaneity is, in my judgment, required in fruitful theological work, even if it is every time risky and inescapably subjective. That is, it is an act of theological imagination that seeks to move from and remain faithful to the act of imagination that constitutes the text itself. In my attempt, I arrive at this:

First, amid the dominant superpower in the world today, we as residents of that superpower may consider the colonial contours of faith. In that contemporary mode, the issue remains, as it did in ancient Judah, a mix of accommodation and resistance. These old interpreters understood with great clarity that displaced people must accommodate or perish. They also understood that uncritical accommodation without resistance will inevitably result in the loss of historical identity. It is exactly the work of vigorous interpretation to continue to parse the dilemma of accommodation and resistance.

Second, the Deuteronomic syllogism is, in the end, an effort to articulate an underlying, unaccommodating moral order that pertains amid the rawness of Realpolitik. That unaccommodating moral order is not user-friendly. Every concentration of power that imagines autonomy will, in the end, pay dearly. It is a lesson every such power learns, always too late. Before learning, such powers, with theological appeal, can always imagine with Babylon:

> I shall be mistress forever . . .
> I am, and there is no one besides me;
> I shall not sit as a widow or know the loss of children . . .
> No one sees me . . .
> I am, and there is no one besides me. (Isa 47:7, 8, 10)

Sometimes the tradition teaches us otherwise; sometimes it is the raw reality of history that is a substitute teacher. Either way, the lesson is very hard and requires, like every hard lesson, repetitive learning.

PART III

LEGAL COVENANTS THAT COALESCE

11

FROM NARRATIVE TO POLICY

In the Bible Israel always has the hard work of transposing its treasured narrative memory into contemporary practice. It keeps *treasured narrative memory* and *contemporary practice* together by sustained acts of *liturgical imagination*. That liturgical imagination, regularly performed, is designed to raise the question from mesmerized children, "What is this about?"

> And when your children ask you, "What do you mean by this observance?" (Exod 12:26)
>
> You shall tell your children that day. (Exod 13:8)
>
> When in the future your child asks you, "What does this mean?" (Exod 13:14)

The answer to the child's questions is to perform the liturgy and to have adults capable of contemporary interpretation:

> You shall say, "It is the Passover sacrifice to the LORD, for he passed over the houses of the Israelites in Egypt, when he struck down the Egyptians but spared our houses." (Exod 12:27)
>
> You shall tell your children that day, "It is because of what the LORD did for me when I came out of Egypt." (Exod 13:8)
>
> You shall answer, "By strength of hand the LORD brought us out of Egypt from the house of slavery. When Pharaoh stubbornly refused to let us go, the LORD killed all the firstborn in the land of Egypt, from human firstborn to the first born of animals." (Exod 13:14)

The exchange of child and parent is designed, via Passover, to make a compelling encounter between *what is remembered* and *what is performed.*

I

The treasured narrative memory of Israel is so familiar that we scarcely notice that it is not really a "religious" memory. It is a political-economic memory about the time when we were slaves in Pharaoh's Egypt. Israel can remember the oppressive circumstance when we were nothing more than instruments for the acquisitive economics of Pharaoh (Exod 5:4-19). We were busy making bricks in order to build pyramids that would bestow grand immortality, and busy building granaries where Pharaoh could store and exhibit his economic monopoly as he controlled the world's food supply. We remember the pain and the sweat and the resentment and the anger and the foul smell of the huts in which we had to live.

We are able to remember that there was a dramatic contest between the intelligence community of Pharaoh (now called "magicians") and the daring challenge of Moses who had no credentials. We had heard about the contest that played to a draw as they both turned water to blood, and as they had an even score in frog production. We heard, in the third contest, that Moses bested the magicians because they could not produce gnats (Exod 8:18). They had reached the limit of their productive capacity. After that, the alternative of Moses opened up. Some of us trusted Moses, many doubted him, and some simply refused. The ones who trusted followed him that dark night of death, reached the waters, and crossed. The memory was sealed as Miriam and the other women danced the dance of YHWH, the God of economic emancipation:

> The LORD will reign forever and ever. (Exod 15:18)

We headed out to a new world and departed Pharaoh.

The memory, so vivid to us, culminated at Sinai. The mountain was filled with holy smoke and holy trembling. But we did not care. We knew it was better than being with Pharaoh. We assented, in a blank check, to the new rules of YHWH because we knew they would be better than the old quotas of Pharaoh (Exod 19:8). Right from the mountain we heard the holy voice of covenant speak to us ten times about the love of God and love of neighbor (Exod 20:2-17). We pledged our loyalty and in that instant were converted from a company of weary slaves to a people summoned to neighborliness (Exod 24:3, 7). It was a transformation wrought by the holy power of YHWH, but we gladly signed on.

The most interesting facet of our treasured narrative memory is how we got from the waters of Egypt to the trembling of Sinai. We had to trek all of three long chapters to get there, and we were without water or bread or meat on the way (Exod 16–18). In response to our constant griping, Moses and then YHWH answered with the surprise of life. We had thought there were no viable life-support systems in the wilderness. But it turns out that even there the God of covenantal freedom could perform an economic act of bread: enough for all, not too much, and even a provision for seventh-day bread so that we did not need to work on Sabbath (Exod 16:13-36).

This is the narrative memory we deeply treasure. We treasure it so much that we teach our kids and we regularly perform it in order to recall why this night is different from all other nights. It is the night of death and of new life. It is the night of departure. It turns out to be the event of abundant bread. And before we finished, the narrative led us to new promises and pledges of loyalty to neighborly justice. The trek from *slavery* through *abundance* to *covenant* is one we made in wonder. And we keep making it, always again in wonder. And every time we perform it well, it is yet again an awesome miracle that we can hardly trust.

It turns out, for us, that there is a familiar U.S. version of that narrative memory shared by Catholics, Protestants, Jews, and secularists in a Euro-white casting.[1] It continues to be a narrative of departure from religious oppression for a better economic opportunity; and the replay features YHWH as the God of liberty and the new community of possibility. We can recite Columbus and the Mayflower and Jamestown and the Pilgrims and the Puritans and the "city set on a hill," and we have no doubt at all concerning our national connection to the God of the promised land:

> O beautiful for pilgrim feet, whose stern impassioned stress
> A thoroughfare for freedom beat across the wilderness!
> America! America! God mend thine every flaw,
> Confirm thy soul in self-control, thy liberty in law! . . .
> O beautiful for patriot dream that sees beyond the years
> Thine alabaster cities gleam, undimmed by human tears!
> America! America! God shed his grace on thee
> And crown thy good with brotherhood from sea to shining sea![2]

We sing this belated version of our manifest destiny. It is a serious reuse of the older narrative, and we do not doubt that the God of liberty and covenantal justice and mercy and compassion continues to be the primal agent in our history. That version was primarily Protestant; we have all, however, appropriated it. We have gathered around it a mix of deep faith and patriotic pride, sure that this radical God willed a revolution in public power that ends in practices of peace and prosperity with liberty and justice for all.

II

It was not easy in ancient Israel to continue to perform this treasured narrative memory in a faithful way; that performance required a great deal of courage and passion to enact the memory in contemporary life. Israel had been called by God, chosen to be a holy, peculiar people in the world. But the Israelites could readily observe that other ways in the world worked very well, often better than their own. They noticed the way of technological religion that they called "Canaanite," and the ways of power politics. They wanted, they said, to be "like the other nations" (1 Sam 8:5, 20). They were ready to compromise their distinctive way in the world in order to sign on for other ways that seemed more effective. It depends on how you line it out. You could say that energy for their treasured narrative memory slowly *eroded* over time. Or you could say that the performance of the memory was *abruptly interrupted*. Either way, it is King Solomon who is presented in the Bible as the great eroder or the great interrupter who experimented with a more ordinary way in the world.[3]

Perhaps he learned something of the new way from his own father, David, who is a multivalent figure in ancient Israel. More likely he learned a great deal from his father-in-law, Pharaoh. He learned about bureaucratic administration and organizational complexity, about harnessing religion to the aims of power, and about transposing ideology into propaganda into liturgy. The outcome of his new venture was to establish a governance in Jerusalem that would rival the other great governances in his world, to be like the other nations and even to outdo the other nations.

The goal of such governance, he observed from his father-in-law and from the other models close at hand, was accumulation. The Israelite story had begun in Pharaoh's accumulation, and now the same practice emerged within Israel itself. Thus we are told that Solomon accumulated horses and chariots (arms), gold and silver, wives and concubines (1 Kgs 10:23–11:3). He accumulated thousands of proverbs so that he gained a near monopoly on wisdom (1 Kgs 4:29-34). He applied much of the gold he had accumulated to his new temple, which was a structure of aggrandizement for the regime. He borrowed the pattern for the temple from outside Israel. It was a three-chambered complex with degrees of holiness that reflected the stratification of his urban society (1 Kgs 6:1-6). The outcome of it all was breathtaking. Indeed, we are told that when the Queen of Sheba came to Jerusalem on a trade mission and saw his achievements and his accumulations, "there was no spirit within her" (1 Kgs 10:5). Or better, it took her breath away!

In his new venture of acquisitiveness, moreover, the old treasured narrative memory was something of an embarrassment and an unwelcome restraint. For it smacked of the particular, and Solomon wanted to stifle *the particular* in his pursuit of *the generic*. More specifically, we are told that he "loved many foreign women" who brought with them to Jerusalem their many gods (1 Kgs 11:1). Solomon was a very religious guy, but it was religion that suited his passion for accumulation. And the verdict is rendered:

> For when Solomon was old, his wives turned away his heart after other gods; and his heart was not true to the LORD his God, as was the heart of his father David. (1 Kgs 11:4)

That is, he forgot the first commandment concerning "no other gods." He forgot the God who stood behind that first commandment, the one who "brought you up out of the land of Egypt, out of the house of bondage." He forgot the God of the exodus and he forgot that exodus. He forgot the God of the first commandment and the covenant of Sinai. He forgot the old treasured narrative memory and ceased to perform it. He forgot it by carelessness; or he scuttled it deliberately because it did not serve his ideology of acquisitiveness. We may, then, record Solomon as the *great forgetter* and note the Solomonic disease of amnesia concerning the old treasured narrative memory.

The analogue is obvious in U.S. society. Our own reuse of the treasured narrative memory became truncated in more recent time. There were of course occasional reminders of the old memory from Walter Rauschenbusch and Martin Luther King Jr. and Daniel Berrigan and Jim Wallis and their ilk. But as the U.S. economy has turned the corner toward imperialism and its companion, consumerism, the narrative has become remote from serious discourse. "Pilgrim feet" and "patriots' dreams" and even "alabaster cities" and "brotherhood" seem now remote and archaic, better left to safe spheres like family values in suburban contexts because there are other matters to which to attend, matters of market share and natural resources and stocks and bonds and investments and leverage and welfare reform and market ideology, and all the slogans and practices that put us on the path of unrestrained acquisitiveness that has no patience for the neighborhood. As local ownership yielded to large corporations and as stockholders turned their investments over to anonymous managers, the fabric of covenantal neighborliness disappeared from the public scene and with it the graces of generosity and hospitality.

The treasured narrative memory soon enough yielded to a new account of reality that affirmed that "greed is good," that "there is no free lunch," that your neighbor is a competitor for limited goods or a threat or at least an inconvenience, and you had better look out for number 1. The treasured narrative memory over time was transposed into a narrative of "democratic capitalism," much more capitalist than democratic, and overtaken by a market ideology and an aggressive practice of market control and a monopoly of natural resources. In a season of amnesia about the old narrative memory, the president of the United States can and must regularly sign off, "God bless America." But of course that mantra must remain without exegesis and remain completely generic because to tie it to Sinai demands or any specificity would offend the generic sensibility of the managers of the new economy. Solomon managed the necessary amnesia to shift Israel away from its foundational narrative. And we, in our society, come close to a parallel amnesia. Without that energizing, restraining memory, everything becomes possible, everything except neighborliness.

III

There will be a reckoning, says the treasured narrative memory, for rapacious, acquisitive economics. The model is the disaster that befell Pharaoh in the exodus narrative. He could not sustain his practice in the face of YHWH's will for emancipation. In the covenantal judgment on Solomon and his ilk, his reckoning is figured as *divine judgment*:

> Then the LORD was angry with Solomon, because his heart had turned away from the LORD, the God of Israel, who had appeared to him twice, and had commanded him concerning this matter, that he should not follow other gods; but he did not observe what the LORD commanded. Therefore the LORD said to Solomon, "Since this has been your mind

> and you have not kept my covenant and my statutes that I have commanded you, I will surely tear the kingdom from you and give it to our servant." (1 Kgs 11:9-11)[4]

In the case of Solomon it took four hundred years to implement fully the divine judgment, but the arc of Gods' governance is long, even as God's poets are patient.

Such a way of speaking in our time strikes many of us as silly supernaturalism. As a result, we do not speak that way. But the reckoning will nonetheless come. We call it, as it comes, an *economic collapse*. We are, nonetheless, able to see that the basis for the collapse is greed, corruption, and dishonesty, the very affronts that in the ancient world evoked divine judgment. It is, I suppose, an open question whether "economic collapse" can function as a synonym for "divine judgment." It is not, among us, an open question whether there is to be a reckoning. For it is plain for all to see. If we agree that there is some kind of moral accountability in the public process, then a reckoning is an inescapable reality, now as then.

IV

These three claims provide background for consideration of our topic of economic crisis and conversion:

- a *treasured narrative memory* of emancipation and covenant;
- an *erosion or an interruption* of that narrative in the form of accumulative acquisitiveness;
- a *reckoning* upon such acquisitiveness.

That much is an unargued assumption of a covenantal-prophetic read of the Bible. But that leaves important questions to face:

- Is it too late to avert the reckoning?
- What can be done in the face of the reckoning?

I will focus on the contemporary immediacy (or the immediate contemporaneity) of the treasured narrative memory.

In the Old Testament that immediacy and contemporaneity to the old narrative memory was offered in the tradition of Deuteronomy, which I judge to be the central text for our general topic of economics. In the

Bible itself, the book of Deuteronomy is situated as a late, final address of Moses to Israel, after forty years of wilderness wandering, just as they were to cross the Jordan River into the land of promise. The address at the river is Moses' restaging of the Sinai covenant in a way that is pertinent to the new situation in the land of promise.

As you may know, on critical grounds the book of Deuteronomy is brought to visibility in 621 BCE in the time of King Josiah when the scroll found in the temple—in critical judgment, at least the law code of Deuteronomy—became the urgent basis for a great reform instigated by the king (2 Kgs 22). We may take it on either traditional or on critical grounds as a reform document in which it is insisted that the old memory has important currency in the new circumstance of the land. The book of Deuteronomy thus is the central biblical model for the continuing relevance of the tradition in a way that we might term "progressive revelation," that is, the continued contemporary interpretation and application of old tradition. The work of contemporaneity is signaled by Moses in Deuteronomy:

> Not with our ancestors did the LORD make this covenant, but with us, who are all of us here alive today. (Deut 5:3)

It is affirmed that Sinai is not an ancient memory; it is rather a current mandate. In that same chapter 5, Moses reiterates the Ten Commandments that then become the ground for the more specific commandments that follow (Deut 5:6-21). In this extended address, Moses shows how the *tradition of covenant* is to be practiced in *a land of enormous wealth and prosperity*. In sum Moses exposits two programmatic convictions.

On the one hand, the land of well-being and prosperity is enormously *seductive*; if you are not alert, the wealth of the land will talk you out of your identity. You will forget who you are and you will become simply another affluent Canaanite. Thus the speech of Moses is filled with warning: "Take heed." The warnings are particularly against amnesia, for affluence produces amnesia:

> When the LORD your God has brought you into the land that he swore to your ancestors, to Abraham, to Isaac, and to Jacob, to give you—a land with fine, large cities that you did not build, houses filled with all sorts of goods that you did not fill, hewn cisterns that you did not hew, vineyards and olive groves that you did not plant, and when you have

> eaten your fill, take care that you do not *forget* the LORD, who brought you out of the land of Egypt, out of the house of slavery. (Deut 6:10-12)
>
> For the LORD your God is bringing you into a good land, a land with flowing streams, with springs and underground waters welling up in valleys and hills, a land of wheat and barley, of vines and fig trees and pomegranates, a land of olive trees and honey, a land where you may eat bread without scarcity, where you will lack nothing, a land whose stones are iron and from whose hills you may mine copper. You shall eat your fill and bless the LORD your God for the good land that he has given you.
>
> Take care that you do not *forget* the LORD your God, by failing to keep his commandments, his ordinances, and his statutes, which I am commanding you today. When you have eaten your fill and have built fine houses and live in them, and when your herds and flocks have multiplied, and your silver and gold is multiplied, and all that you have is multiplied, then do not exalt yourself, *forgetting* the LORD your God, who brought you out of the land of Egypt, out of the house of slavery, who led you through the great and terrible wilderness, an arid wasteland with poisonous snakes and scorpions. He made water flow for you from flint rock, and fed you in the wilderness with manna that your ancestors did not know, to humble you and to test you, and in the end to do you good. Do not say to yourself, "My power and the might of my hand have gotten me this wealth." But remember the LORD your God, for it is he who gives you power to get wealth, so that he may confirm his covenant that he swore to your ancestors, as he is doing today.
>
> (Deut 8:7-18)

The land is filled with Canaanites, with Canaanite fruitfulness, Canaanite production, and Canaanite religion, all of which are seductive. It is not necessary to think that everything Canaanite is degenerate. No, rather things "Canaanite" are self-contained without reference to anyone more ultimate outside the system. Because the Canaanite system was so attractive, it functioned to seduce Israel.

On the other hand, says Moses, the land of Canaan is *transformable*. That is why the commandments are issued with such urgency. The land that is so prosperous and inviting can indeed be transformed into a viable working neighborhood. That is the import of the commandments that follow. They are specific disciplines to be taken seriously as concrete steps for societal transformation.

Given both the *warning about seduction* and the *affirmation about transformation*, the tradition of Deuteronomy itself is an *antidote to amnesia*, a sustained act of remembering:

> Keep these words that I am commanding you today in your heart. Recite them to your children and talk about them when you are at home and when you are way, when you lie down and when you rise. Bind them as a sign on your hand, fix them as an emblem on your forehead, and write them on the doorposts of your house and on your gates. (6:6-9)

I call this "saturation education," when the learning community is surrounded by signs and reminders of a particular work to do and a peculiar destiny to live.[5] The tradition of Deuteronomy believes that concrete, intentional acts of obedience are the way to fend off Canaanite amnesia. Thus Deuteronomy is an anticipation of the fine exposition recently offered by Michael Fishbane of the disciplined practices of Judaism in his book, *Sacred Attunement*.[6] His thesis is that the characteristic disciplines of Judaism serve to keep one "attuned" to the truth of God, to keep one "mindful" of being a Jew. Fishbane avers that such mindfulness is of enormous importance in a society that is increasingly "mindless." So it was in the ancient world. Moses proposed that *covenantal mindfulness* is the ground for resisting Canaanite amnesia and for the emancipated actions that can convert an acquisitive economy into a neighborly fabric.

Here I will consider five specific commandments from the corpus of Deuteronomy that serve to keep the old narrative memory current. I shall follow Norbert Lohfink and Dean McBride in their notion that Deuteronomy functions something like a "constitution," a way to order and practice public power.[7] In the preaching of Deuteronomy Moses seeks to transpose the old narrative memory into a workable practice of policy. Here are five proposals for *policy* derived from *narrative:*

1. Moses provided the conditions for *a king* in Israel who would administer power in covenantal ways. Negatively, Moses precluded any king who would be an accumulator:

> He must not acquire many horses for himself or return the people to Egypt in order to acquire more horses, since the LORD has said to you, "You must never return that way again." And he must not acquire many wives for himself, or else his heart will turn away; also silver and gold he must not acquire in great quantity for himself. (17:16-17)

The terms are a direct reference to Solomon. The king must be *unlike* Solomon. Positively the king must be a torah reader, focused on the treasured memory of Israel and specifically upon these Deuteronomic provisions:

> When he has taken the throne of his kingdom he shall have a copy of this law written for him in the presence of the levitical priests. It shall remain with him and he shall read it all the days of his life, so that he may learn to fear the LORD his God, diligently observing all the words of this law and these statutes. (17:18-19)

The contrast between *accumulation* and *torah study* is programmatic in Israel. The tradition assumes that if one stays fixed on torah, there will be no excessive accumulation of power. Conversely, if one's energy goes to accumulation, the hopes and summons of torah will be promptly forgotten and neglected. In the context of torah, public power is taken differently. The text poses the question, then and now, whether public power can be differently construed.

2. Moses provided a covenantal characterization of *worship*, which is so important because worship is the venue wherein Israel imagines and performs shared life differently. In Deuteronomy 16:1-17, focus is upon the three great festivals of Israel's liturgical calendar, Passover, Weeks, and Booths. There is a great deal of specificity about proper protocol. The Festival of Weeks is supplied by a free will offering that will be shared with the entire community:

> Rejoice before the LORD your God—you and your sons and your daughters, your male and female slaves, the Levite resident in your towns, as well as the strangers, the orphans, and the widows who are among you. (Deut 16:11)

It is no wonder that the guideline concludes with a narrative reference:

> Remember that you were a slave in Egypt and diligently observe these statutes. (16:12)

Concerning the festival of Booths, Moses provides:

> Rejoice during your festival, you and your sons and your daughters, your male and female slaves, as well as the Levites, the strangers, the orphans, and the widows resident in your towns . . . you shall surely celebrate. (16:14)

The summons at harvest time is to share the produce of grain and wine with the entire community, most especially the vulnerable. The summary admonition is this:

> They shall not appear before the LORD empty-handed. (16:16b)

The festivals are a performance of blessed materialism in which the community at worship reiterates and emphasizes the intense solidarity between haves and have-nots. The reference to exodus in the Festival of Weeks and the fact that Passover is recital of exodus shows how the ordering of worship is a reiteration of the treasured narrative. Worship rooted in God's generosity in creation and God's emancipation in history intends to evoke the generosity and emancipation of Israel in ways that are congruent with divine generosity and divine emancipation.

There is no doubt that this defining theme for worship is reiterated in the familiar poetry of Isaiah 58. The positive mandate that we recite in lent is about the materiality of communal solidarity:

> Is not this the fast that I choose:
> to loose the bonds of injustice,
> to undo the thongs of the yoke,
> to let the oppressed go free,
> and to break every yoke?
> Is it not to share your bread with the hungry,
> and bring the homeless poor into your house;
> when you see the naked, to cover them,
> and not to hide yourself from your own kin? (Isa 58:6-7)

The negation warns against going through the motions of worship without corresponding economic practices:

> "Why do we fast, but you do not see?
> Why humble ourselves, but you do not notice?"
> Look, you serve your own interest on your fast day,
> and oppress all your workers. (Isa 58:3)

The poem is impatient with worship that is not rooted in and informed by practices of material covenantal solidarity.

3. Moses provides that *agriculture* should be practiced in communitarian ways:

> When you reap your harvest in your field and forget a sheaf in the field, you shall not go back to get it; it shall be left for the alien, the orphan and the widow so that the LORD your God may bless you in all your undertakings. When you beat your olive trees, do not strip what is left; it shall be for the alien, the orphan, and the widow. When you gather the grapes of your vineyard, do not glean what is left; it shall be for the alien, the orphan and the widow. Remember that you were a slave in the land of Egypt; therefore I am commanding you to do this.
>
> (Deut 24:19-22)

The commandment names the three great money crops of Judean agriculture. In each of them it provides that the farmer must leave a residue of the crop in the field for the vulnerable and the disadvantaged, the three groups of the disinherited: widows, orphans, and immigrants. The vision of these commandments is against the more recent, more modern "laws of enclosure" that prohibit the poor from foraging on the land of the owners.[8] The commandments provide an alternative to the tight notion of "private property" that is the bottom line of modern economics, and allows that property held privately is held in the midst of communal reality. The threefold commandment, moreover, concludes with a not unexpected assertion:

> Remember that you were a slave in the land of Egypt; therefore I am commanding you to do this. (v. 22)

The laws provide access to the communal resources in a concrete way, so that the exodus *narrative* produces *policy.* Every time a farmer leaves a part of the produce for the needy, the farmer is enacting *a miniature exodus* whereby the neighbor may enjoy a moment of emancipation. The task of interpretation is to see how such policies from a small face-to-face agrarian economy can be performed in a complex urban environment.

4. Moses provides an alternative way to think about *money management*. Perhaps in that simple economy there were not yet banks, but they were, no doubt, on their way to a banking industry. Moses' work is to provide the kind of banking regulations that will assure that the policies and practices of the bank are directed toward the common good. I cite two regulations that subordinate banking practices to neighborly commitments. First concerning usury:

> You shall not charge interest on loans to another Israelite, interest on money, interest on provisions, interest on anything that is lent . . . so that the LORD your God may bless you in all your undertakings in the land that you are about to enter and possess. (Deut 23:19-20)

Generosity toward the neighbor evokes divine blessing of a material kind. Sandwiched between these two claims is a footnote:

> On loans to a foreigner you may charge interest, but on loans to another Israelite you may not charge interest . . .

No interest on loans to *members* of the covenant; interest on *nonmembers*. The distinction poses the resilient question, who is a fellow member of the covenant? Who is my neighbor? Of course the question continues to haunt the biblical tradition, with the emerging consensus that all are neighbors.[9]

A second banking regulation concerns securing loans. Obviously they were not yet troubled about subprime loans. What is interesting is the fact that the commandment makes a distinction for the poor who cannot provide loan collateral:

> When you make your neighbor a loan of any kind, you shall not go into the house to take the pledge. You shall wait outside, while the person to whom you are making the loan brings the pledge out to you. If the person is poor, you shall not sleep in the garment given you as the pledge. You shall give the pledge back by sunset, so that your neighbor may sleep in the cloak and bless you; and it will be to your credit before the LORD your God. (Deut 24:10-13)

> You shall not deprive a resident alien or an orphan of justice; you shall not take a widow's garment in pledge. (v. 17)

The central premise is that you cannot enter private property to seize collateral. But the subordinate premise is that you must treat the poor differently. If you take the only coat of a poor person as collateral, then that person will freeze at night. For that reason, at sunset each night the creditor must return the coat to the poor to sleep in and may pick it up for collateral again the next morning. I suggest that the intention is to make it uncommonly inconvenient to hold the coat as collateral. Imagine on a thirty-year loan needing to pick it up every morning and return it each evening! It is simpler to let the poor have the loan and keep the coat. It is then an unsecured loan, but it is to a neighbor. The second of these commandments, moreover, ends with a now familiar affirmation:

> Remember that you were a slave in Egypt and the LORD your God redeemed you from there; therefore I command you to do this. (v. 18)

The *narrative* pushes directly into *policy*! The entire economic practice of Israel is to reperform in an institutional way the exodus event, so that Moses envisions an economic emancipation. The verse uses the term "redeem": "The Lord God redeemed you from slavery." The term "redeem" is an economic term, "to buy back, to buy out." Economics and therefore banking regulations are for the redemption of those who have been held in bondage through standard economic processes.

5. This notion of reperformance of the exodus narrative as economic practice is nowhere more evident than in the commandment on the "year of release" in Deuteronomy 15:1-18 that concerns *debt management*. I end my discussion of specific commandments in the Deuteronomic tradition of contemporaneity with reference to this text because this text is commonly regarded as the pivot point of the teaching of Deuteronomy, making the most daring, most demanding, and most dangerous requirement in covenantal economics.

The commandment provides that at the end of every seven years there will be a time of debt cancellation. The thought, apparently, is that in the rough and tumble of economics, the social fabric is frayed, and neighborly relations become skewed. Reaching back to the principle of Sabbath, the commandment provides a time to take a deep breath about the economy and a time to return focus to the neighborhood. The focus of the law is particularly upon the economy of the poor. Here I want to call attention to four remarkable features in the rhetoric of the commandment that will tell us a great deal about economic thinking in covenantal perspective:

a) The law has an eye on the poor who are always on the short end of the economy. Imagine focusing on the economy of the poor! In v. 11, Moses asserts:

> Since there will never cease to be some in need on the earth, I therefore command you, "Open your hand to the poor and needy neighbor in your land." (15:11)

You may recognize that this is the statement that Jesus quotes in Mark 14:7 when the woman pours costly oil over his feet. Taken by itself the statement seems to sanction resigned indifference to the poor. But the urging of the verse is in fact to the contrary. There will always be poor people; for that reason generous acts must be performed. This v. 11 is matched by v. 4 that affirms that the intense practice of debt cancellation makes it possible that there need be no poor in the community:

> There will, however, be no one in need among you, because the LORD is sure to bless you in the land that the LORD your God is giving you as a possession to occupy. If only you will obey the LORD your God by diligently observing this entire commandment that I command you today.
>
> (15:4-5)

Poverty can be eradicated! It is important to keep the urgency of v. 11 and the assurance of v. 4 closely related to each other.

b) In this commandment Moses six times utilizes a peculiar grammatical construction in Hebrew: the infinitive absolute. This device serves to intensify the verb by repeating the verb as an adverb. Thus "really give" is offered in the Hebrew as "give give." It is remarkable that in this commandment there are seven infinitive absolutes, more than I know in any other text:

v. 4 "sure to bless" . . . bless bless;

v. 5 "diligently observe" . . . observe observe;

v. 8 "rather open" . . . open open;

v. 8 "willingly lend" . . . lend lend;

v. 10 "Give liberally" . . . give give;

v. 11 "Open" . . . open open;

v. 14 "Provide liberally" . . . provide provide.

The accumulation of infinitive absolutes evidences the intensity of the act. It is as though the rhetoric indicates that this is the most urgent provision in the whole of the Torah. There is a lot of one-issue politics and one-issue religion around. This might suggest that Moses is a one-issue man. Torah teaching is focused on that single issue: the redress of economic imbalance through debt cancellation.

c) It is clear that the commandment evoked resistance among those who could recognize at a glance that the requirement is expensive:

> Do not be hard-hearted or tight-fisted toward your needy neighbor. . . . Be careful that you do not entertain a mean thought, thinking, "The seventh year, the year of remission is near," and therefore view your needy neighbor with hostility and give nothing; your neighbor might cry to the LORD against you, and you would incur guilt. (15:7b, 9)

I cite this only to indicate that there is resistance to the commandment that is based in economic interest. Moses knows about the compulsion to choose self-interest over neighborly good. The teaching dares, however, to imagine that the covenantal narrative memory is powerful enough to convert the imagination of Israel and thereby to transform economic practice.

d) It does not surprise that the commandment concludes with yet one more appeal to the exodus:

> Remember that you were a slave in the land of Egypt, and the LORD your God redeemed you; for this reason I lay this command upon you today. (15:15)

Indeed the year of release is a *policy provision* that replicates the *narrative memory* of the exodus. As exodus was to deliver the slaves from a hopeless rat race of production, so the legal provision is to deliver the poor from a hopeless pursuit of debt payment. The commandment knows that radical steps must be taken to prevent the formation of a permanent underclass in Israel. The only way to do that is to order the economy so that it is subordinated to and in the service of the neighborhood.

To be sure, there are commandments in the corpus of Deuteronomy that do not so directly serve my argument. If, however, we focus on these five accent points, Moses advocates that *power* (17:14-20), *worship* (16:1-17), *agriculture* (24:19-22), *banking* (23:19-20; 24:10-13), and *debt management* (15:1-18) can be construed and practiced differently, according to the memory of the exodus covenant. It is striking how consistently the motivation for these commandments is the remembered exodus that through these provisions can be a contemporary transformative practice:

- The provision for kingship in 17:14-20 does not mention the exodus, but it does say, concerning trading for horses (arms) with Egypt, not to "return that way again." It is as though traffic with Egypt in arms is the undoing of the exodus.

The law on worship concludes in 16:12:

> Remember that you were a slave in Egypt, and diligently observe these statutes.

The commandment on agriculture concludes in 24:22:

> Remember that you were a slave in the land of Egypt; therefore I am commanding you to do this.

The regulation for banking ends this way in 24:18:

> Remember that you were a slave in Egypt and the LORD your God redeemed you from there; therefore I command you to do this.

The practice of debt cancellation appeals in 15:15:

> Remember that you were a slave in the land of Egypt, and the LORD your God redeemed you; for this reason I lay this command upon you today.

The legal imagination of Israel is permeated with the exodus.[10] The exodus is no remote memory. It is present mandate that requires not only deep resolve but also ongoing imaginative energy that can transpose ancient memory in a simple economy into a durable public practice in a complex economy. Where the narrative is forgotten there will be no covenantal economics. It remains the mandate of the church and the synagogue to supply not only the memory but also the imagination that makes a transposition possible from narrative to policy, from ancient to contemporary, from simple to complex. Moses himself is at that task in the tradition of Deuteronomy.

V

I wish to draw two sorts of conclusions from this argument:

1. The emancipatory, covenantal memory keeps beating in our ears, requiring that we continue the imaginative task of transposing ancient narrative memory into contemporary policy formation. There is no doubt that the memory continues to resound in the ears of the early church. That is nowhere more evident than in the narrative of Luke, from which I will cite four familiar texts:

A. Mary's song is clearly an act of revolutionary imagination. She sings of the economy and imagines a turn of affairs at least as radical as the year of release:

> He has brought down the powerful from their thrones,
> and lifted up the lowly;
> he has filled the hungry with good things,
> and sent the rich away empty. (Luke 1:52-53)

B. When Jesus is in the wilderness, the tempter comes to talk him out of his vocation. The tempter is for Jesus a seduction as the land of Canaan was a seduction from vocation to the Israelites. It strikes me as most important that in each of Jesus' responses to the tempter, his reply is a quote from Deuteronomy, for Deuteronomy is the teaching tradition that most powerfully resists the tempter:

Concerning turning stones to bread:

> He humbled you by letting you hunger, then by feeding you with manna, with which neither you nor your ancestors were acquainted, in order to make you understand that one does not live by bread alone, but by every word that comes from the mouth of the LORD. (Deut 8:3; see Luke 4:4)

Concerning worship of the tempter:

> Hear O Israel: The LORD is our God, the LORD alone. You shall love the LORD your God with all your heart, and with all your soul, and with all your might. (Deut 6:4-5; see Luke 4:8)

Concerning jumping from the temple spire:

> Do not put the LORD your God to the test, as you tested him at Massah. (Deut 6:16; see Luke 4:12)

C. In that same Luke 4, in the synagogue in Nazareth, Jesus quotes the book of Isaiah concerning "the year of the Lord's favor" (Luke 4:19). As you will know, that quote from Isaiah 61 concerns the Jubilee year, the "year of release" writ large. The quote suggests that Jesus is to enact that ancient commandment, thus reiterating the economic revolution whereby the narrative was to become new policy.

D. Eventually, in Acts 2:45, the early Pentecostal church became a living sign of the new covenantal economy:

> All who believed were together and had all things in common; they would sell their possessions and goods and distribute the proceeds to all, as any had need. Day by day, as they spent much time together in the temple, they broke bread at home and ate their food with glad and generous hearts, praising God and having the good-will of all the people. (Acts 2:44-47)

The New Testament witness to the Jesus movement concerns the new economy.

2. I have proceeded in my argument by way of analogy:

I have suggested *an analogue* between the foundational narrative of exodus-Sinai and the primal narrative of U.S. society. It is admittedly a Euro-white construct, but it is so engrained now in the U.S. imagination that all comers must deal with it.

I have suggested *an analogue* between the accumulative acquisitiveness of Solomon and the accumulative acquisitiveness of U.S. society. In both cases the accumulative impulse has jeopardized the social fabric.

I have suggested *an analogue* in terms of reckoning, between divine judgment and economic collapse. I have entertained the thought that they are fundamentally synonymous, whether or not they are expressed in supernaturalist language.

It remains now to consider how the imaginative summons of the tradition of Deuteronomy could serve, *by analogy*, as an antidote to amnesia in our society. I do not underestimate the difficulty of moving from Deuteronomy to our complex economic crisis. And yet, I suggest that Deuteronomic imagination concerning neighborliness and the restoration of the neighborly fabric is exactly central to biblical faith and exactly urgent in our time and place. It remains for the faithful church to muster imaginative interpretation to make the case for a neighborly economy.

I dare suggest to you two aspects of such a task. First, *the public agenda* of such a church is to bear witness to a neighborly economy that is an alternative to a market economy of competitive devouring. For the most part, it is assumed among us that the market economy is a given. I see no point or any possibility in abstract debate about socialism and capitalism. What needs to be championed, in my view, is how the economy can be ordered to serve the neighborhood. I suppose, moreover, that this requires not a grand strategy but intentional incremental steps.

Second, I believe that there is also *an in-house* task for the church. My sense is that the Western Church (and here I speak of the church as I know it and not with particular reference to the Roman Catholic Church) has been captured and detained in a privatized sacramentalism that distorts the gospel and that siphons energy away from the main claims of the good news. That is, there is huge nurture and education to be done to see that the practice of a neighborly economy is the primal agenda of the gospel news. This has been so since the exodus. Jesus, moreover, was not crucified by the empire because he had odd views on sexuality. He was executed because he challenged the socioeconomic-political power arrangements of his time and place. The in-house work is to help folk see the chance to be a participant in that divine resolve. I suspect, moreover, that almost everyone with whom we minister (not unlike ourselves) is ambiguous about that chance; that point of ambiguity is precisely the rich venue for the transformative spirit of God. The narrative must be remembered; the policy must be reimagined. Michael Walzer, the Jewish political philosopher, has written of the primal narrative:

> So pharaonic oppression, deliverance, Sinai, and Canaan are still with us, powerful memories shaping our perceptions of the political world. . . . We still believe, or many of us do, what the exodus first taught, or what it has commonly been taken to teach, about the meaning and possibility of politics and about its proper form:
>
> –first, that wherever you live, it is probably Egypt;
>
> –second, that there is a better place, a world more attractive, a promised land;
>
> –and third, that "the way to the land is through the wilderness." There is no way to get from here to there except by joining together and marching.[11]

I dare imagine we are in a moment of acute readiness for such *remembering* and *reimagining*. Where else could we turn?

12

THE GOD WHO GIVES REST

An expansive theological exposition of the book of Exodus is neither obvious nor easy because the book is quite complex. Critical issues of two kinds contribute to that complexity. On the one hand, the book consists in a sequence of quite distinct themes that do not readily cohere. It is probable that these themes arise from different interpretive venues and perspectives, so that they voice different theological convictions that are at variance with each other. The themes themselves are readily identified and provide an outline of the contents of the book. Each such theme voices a distinctive characterization of YHWH:

The exodus deliverance (Exod 1–15);

The wilderness sojourn (Exod 16–18);

The covenant of Sinai (Exod 19–24);

The authorization of the tabernacle (Exod 25–31);

The violation of the Sinai covenant (Exod 32–34);

The completion of the tabernacle (Exod 35–40).

Each of these thematic expressions has its own theological voice and its own articulation of YHWH, the God of Israel, in a distinct way appropriate to the intent of the theme.

On the other hand, the tradition is complex because it consists in different materials (that heretofore have been taken variously as "documents" or "sources"). In critical jargon the old "documentary hypothesis" reflects a dynamic tradition with many layers of interpretation, each of which reflects a particular circumstance, a particular theological need, and a particular interpretive response to that need. Specifically the materials in chapters 25–31, 35–40 are very different from those of the earlier narrative and are uniformly assigned to the Priestly tradition that had its own theological perspective. There is no way to fit all of these distinctive propensities into a harmonious whole.

Given the thematic differences and layers of interpretive tradition, we are able to see that the whole of the book is a sustained act of imagination in which YHWH is variously rendered (imagined). There is an elemental constancy that focuses upon YHWH, but that constancy is handled with great flexibility and interpretive freedom. My task here is to elucidate that constancy-cum-flexibility to see how God is rendered in the book. Because we have many fine expositions of God in the book of Exodus, notably by Donald Gowan and by my friend Terry Fretheim, I do not need to cover all of those bases.[1] Thus I take the liberty of proposing and exploring a different way of reading constancy-cum-flexibility. My thesis for what follows is that the God given us in the book of Exodus is the God who gives rest; who authorizes, permits, and insists upon Sabbath; and who wills emancipation from social arrangements that refuse Sabbath. It is clear that Sabbath authorization-permission-insistence is not reducible to a religious practice or discipline. It is rather an icon for a socioeconomic-political arrangement of social power in a distinctive way that is critical of and an alternative to other social arrangements that are authorized by other gods. Sabbath thus becomes, in the tradition, a way of indicating and enacting an alternative society that stands outside of the predatory anxiety that requires endless production and performance. From the linkage between *the God of this tradition* and *social practice* emerges an alternative social possibility of neighborliness that is inimical to limitless acquisitiveness.[2]

I

At the center of the book of Exodus is the Sinai pericope, the narrative account of YHWH's and Israel's entry into a covenant of mutuality between lord and subject (Exod 19–24). At the center of this textual unit is the initial declaration of YHWH that functions as a pivot point for the book of Exodus:

> I am the LORD your God, who brought you out of the land of Egypt, out of the house of slavery; you shall have no other gods before me.
>
> (Exod 20:1-2)

The utterance is directly from YHWH; the speech declares the identity of YHWH and the will of YHWH. The identity of YHWH is by way of allusion back to the exodus narrative of Exodus 1–15. The God who meets Israel at Sinai is the God who delivers and emancipates:

> I am the LORD, and I will free you from the burdens of the Egyptians and deliver you from slavery to them. I will redeem with an outstretched arm and with mighty acts of judgment. I will take you as my people, and I will be your God. You shall know that I am the LORD your God, who has freed you from the burdens of the Egyptians. (6:6-7)

This God has the capacity to override the rule of Pharaoh and so to veto the claims of Pharaoh and his gods. This God, moreover, has the will to create a *novum* in human history, a people formed out of a slave company, a newness for those who had been "no people."

What follows in the Decalogue is a disclosure of the will of YHWH that will serve to anticipate and organize an anti-Pharaoh community. The first step in such newness is the contradiction of "other gods." The other gods are not named here and thus may be a reference to the many gods present in the culture Israel faced. But the reference just above to Egyptians may suggest that the other gods are particularly the gods of Egypt, the ones who authorize the predatory social system of Pharaoh (see Exod 12:12). Thus if Israel is to have the anti-Pharaoh society here envisioned, it must remain free of the requirements and penchant of the Egyptian gods for production and performance. Along with the exclusionary religious claims of YHWH are the exclusionary social practices that resist pharaonic social power.

The mutuality of this covenant is one of command and obedience. We notice, moreover, that in Exodus 19:8, Israel readily agrees to the commands of YHWH, consents even before the commands are voiced or known. It surely is the case that Israel's consent is in the awareness and confidence that whatever will be given as commands of YHWH in chapter 20 are better than and preferable to the commands of Pharaoh that concern endless production. Thus the commands of YHWH are designed to order life outside the control of the exploitative system.

The second and third commandments (Exod 20:4-7) voice central requirements for relating to YHWH. In doing so they characterize YHWH and by implication characterize the other gods who must remain expelled. The prohibition against images is in the interest of the freedom of YHWH who will not be reduced to a manageable image. This prohibition thus suggests that the other gods, the gods of Egypt, are indeed reducible to image, that is, are manageable and can be recruited to legitimate Pharaoh's exploitative system. The third commandment provides that because YHWH is free and unfettered by any such system, YHWH cannot be recruited for or harnessed to any lesser project. YHWH's name and identity are not "usable" because YHWH is singularly available only for YHWH's own enterprise that is here the formation of an alternative community of covenant. By contrast, the gods of Egypt have names (and identities) that can be readily mobilized for "reasons of state" or any other reason by those who manipulate the image. YHWH will not be enmeshed in such human enterprise; by contrast the gods of Egypt, expressed in image and harnessed in utterance, can be made to be players in the exploitative system, thus an object rather than an agent.

But it is the fourth commandment on Sabbath that concerns us. As Patrick Miller has discerned, this commandment occupies the central position in the Decalogue, looking back to the God who rests and looking forward to the neighborly community that is compelled to rest.[3] The restfulness of God foresees social practice in which social relationships are not reduced to "work," to coercive production. Indeed the remainder of the Decalogue attests to a neighborly community in which respect reigns and encroachment against a neighbor is limited or excluded.

"Rest" here means the regular, disciplined, public, visible stoppage of work. It is an act that assured that the life of the community is not defined by work or production but by the time and space and freedom for life apart from coerced production. The ground for such social practice, moreover, is found in YHWH's own life. The linkage of YHWH and Sabbath suggests, on the one hand, that YHWH is unlike the rejected gods who endlessly compete for honor and control, for YHWH has no such compulsive anxiety. On the other hand, the reference is quite exactly to the rest of the creator God in Genesis 2:2-4a. Thus the God who rescues and now commands Israel is the creator of heaven and earth, the one who has not only blessed the seventh day but who has blessed the earth and assured its life-giving generativity. Thus a rhetorical line is drawn to connect creation wrought by this unanxious God and deliverance from the unbearable regime of Pharaoh.

It is clear that the first four commandments are at the same time a *sketch of a God* who is uninvolved in the endless anxiety of world-making by effort and *a sketch of a society* (world) that is not propelled by such anxiety. The remainder of the Decalogue delineates social relationships in a community that is situated outside the requirements and expectations of "Egypt." The concluding commandment in v. 17 forbids acquisitiveness. It is impossible to imagine a prohibition that would more frontally contradict the ways of Pharaoh, who is the great coveter and the great accumulator and is insatiable in his needs and desires (see Gen 47:13-26). That commandment, moreover, uses the term "neighbor" three times:

> You shall not covet your neighbor's house; you shall not covet your neighbor's wife, or male or female slave, or ox, or donkey, or anything that belongs to your neighbor. (Exod 20:17)

The resounding cadence indicates a commanding God who wills neighborliness, who anticipates a neighborhood, and who intends life kept out of the reach of acquisitive Pharaoh. Thus it is clear that the Sabbath command not only stands at the center of the Decalogue; it provides a way to read all the commandments that are given by this God who wills a distinctive society that is free of coercive performance.

The "if" of Exodus 19:6 has often been understood to indicate the "conditionality" of this covenant. Beyond that, the "if" also serves to connect YHWH with social practice. At Sinai Israel was invited to life with YHWH, to be YHWH's covenant partner. The "if" assumes that YHWH is not available simply as a religious object to be engaged in religious practices of piety and worship. YHWH comes with YHWH's commandments, and YHWH's commandments concern the ordering of social power. Thus as the Egyptian gods gave legitimacy to Pharaoh's social policies, so too does YHWH give legitimacy to an alternative. The alternative God is involved with and committed to alternative social relationships. This God comes only with these commandments. The right ordering of social relationship is then the sine qua non of the life with YHWH to which Israel has signed on. Thus Sinai is not only a religious meeting but also a social vision of an alternative society.

As the book of Exodus is organized, the first wave of interpretation of the Decalogue is given in chapters 21–23, dubbed by scholars the "Covenant Code." It is surely the case that this brief collection of laws came from elsewhere and was engrafted into the text, so that its linkage with the Decalogue is at best secondary. We may nonetheless notice two specific stipulations in this corpus. First, the lead commandment in 21:2-11 concerns the emancipation of slaves. It is of enormous importance that

Israel organized this material so that the first provision is for such an emancipatory act. The placement of the commandment indicates that such emancipation is on the mind of the community, together with the awareness that the emancipation undertaken by the God of 20:2 is unfinished business that continues to require attention:

> When you buy a male Hebrew slave, he shall serve six years, but in the seventh he shall go out a free person, without debt. (21:2)

The terse provision culminates with three powerful terms: "go out," a characteristic exodus term, "free person," a particular social identity, and "without debt," that is, unencumbered. The statute acknowledges that there is still slavery, no doubt debt slavery for those who could not pay their debts. But the law sets a limit on such bondage. The beginning of the statute, moreover, is matched at the end, in v. 11, again with a cluster of intense terms, "go out," "unencumbered," and "with no cash payment." The great cost of freeing a slave is a cost that is necessary to the maintenance of an emancipatory society, the same cost slave owners since Pharaoh have experienced with such loss of cheap labor.

At the end of the corpus in 23:10-17 we are offered a festival calendar in which the lead reference is to the Sabbath. The "six-year" provision for Sabbath matches that of the provision on slaves in 21:1. The Sabbath regulation given here is quite remarkable:

> It is rest for the land;
>
> It is for the well-being of the poor;
>
> It pertains to wild animals;
>
> It pertains to agricultural land;
>
> It concerns domesticated animals;
>
> It pertains to slaves, as slavery is curbed a bit.

That is, it connects Sabbath to every facet of economic life and to the entire community; and it has in purview the well-being of all of creation. As a result, the Sabbath connects Israel's life and the large scope of creation, all readily at rest.

The conclusion of v. 13 is striking. It summons Israel to attentiveness. Sabbath compels attention! The reference to other gods—the gods of Egypt?—may suggest that the gods of Egypt, in their zeal for accumulation, would not only not invest in Sabbath, but would seduce Israel away from Sabbath. Because if Sabbath can be negated, then the entire life of the community can be reshaped according to the will of the Egyptian gods who evoke and legitimate Pharaoh's system, a system of acquisitiveness without limit or restraint.

Provision for the emancipation of slaves (21:1-11) and the Sabbath (23:10-13) are the pivot points of the corpus, and the entire Covenant Code is to be read through them. We are able to see the connection of the commandment on *slavery* (with an eye on 20:2) and *Sabbath* (with an awareness of 20:8-11), two issues that are crucial for the covenant community. They are crucial for the community because they are definitive for YHWH who gives the commandments. It is YHWH who *keeps Sabbath* and YHWH who *frees slaves*. Sabbath is the culminating command of the Covenant Code, even as it is central to the Decalogue. The God met at Sinai commands Sabbath as an icon for an alternative way of organizing all social relations. Without such a practice of Sabbath, one can imagine that there is no limit to the acquisitiveness that will destroy every community. Sabbath becomes a practice that makes neighborliness possible. It is no wonder that this provision comes with such a warning about the other gods!

II

The God of Sinai has placed the Sabbath command at the center of the Decalogue, the foundation of covenantal obedience (Exod 20:8-11). The accent on Sabbath, moreover, has been reiterated in the first "exposition" of the Decalogue in Exodus 23:10-13 as the lead item in the festival calendar. The God of Sinai issues commands quite intentionally in the wake of the exodus. This God can vividly recall the "house of slavery" that initially had evoked YHWH's attention and concern. Thus the first divine utterance at Sinai is with reference to the exodus:

> You have seen what I did to the Egyptians, and how I bore you on eagles' wings and brought you to myself. (19:4)

Everything begins in exodus deliverance. That deliverance of course is recalled at the outset of the Decalogue as the identifying mark of YHWH who gives the commandments (20:2). The memory of Egyptian slavery is twice recalled in the Covenant Code as motivation for covenantal obedience in time to come:

> You shall not wrong or oppress a resident alien, for you were aliens in the land of Egypt. (22:21)
>
> You shall not oppress a resident alien; you know the heart of an alien, for you were aliens in the land of Egypt. (23:9)

And in the festival calendar the exodus memory is the locus of the "festival of unleavened bread" (23:15). Indeed, the command of YHWH cannot be understood except in the wake of the exodus.

To appreciate the interface of exodus and Sabbath, it is essential to probe the pharaonic system of Egypt as the matrix in which the God of the book of Exodus is situated. It is credible to think that slavery, which is the assumed social circumstance of the book of Exodus, has arisen through the usurpacious land/food policies of Pharaoh as voiced in Genesis 47:13-26. That is, slavery is not simply a social "given." It is a social arrangement effected by particular economic policies: those policies aimed at producing wealth for the royal court of Pharaoh. The outcome is a predatory system that enriched Pharaoh and his court at the brutalizing expenses of the slaves, who were economically impotent but who produced the wealth of the land.

The particular work assignment of the slaves was the construction of "supply cities" for Pharaoh (1:11), that is, great storage centers that in the ancient world held surplus grain (a vehicle and emblem of wealth) that might have its contemporary equivalent for us in banks or perhaps corporations. The extent of such storehouse cities was limitless and the demand for them was insatiable because the greedy policies of the regime knew no restraint. Because of that insatiable need, the labor force is pressed to the limit of its productive capacity.

We are given two glimpses of such aggressive labor policies. In chapter 1, the report is terse:

> The Egyptians became ruthless in imposing tasks on the Israelites, and made their lives bitter with hard service in mortar and bricks and in everything of field labor. They were ruthless in all the tasks that they imposed on them. (1:13-14)

In chapter 5 the policies of Pharaoh are given fuller expressions, albeit not in courtly cadence but in narrative rhythms that surely reflect the perspective of the underlings who constitute the supply of cheap labor. We might delineate the demands of Pharaoh in this sequence:

> Get to your labors (v. 4);
>
> You shall no longer give the people straw to make bricks as before; let them go and gather straw for themselves. But you shall require of them the same quantity of bricks as they have made previously; do not diminish it, for they are lazy. That is why they cry, "Let us go and offer sacrifice to our God" (vv. 7-8);
>
> Let heavier work be laid on them; then they will labor at it and pay no attention to deceptive words (v. 9);
>
> Go and get straw yourselves where you can find it; but your work will not be lessened in the least (v. 11);
>
> Complete your work, the same daily assignment as when you were given straw (v. 13);
>
> Why did you not finish the required quantity of bricks yesterday and today, as you did before? (v. 14);
>
> Make bricks (v. 16);
>
> Go now and work (v. 18);
>
> You shall deliver the same number of bricks (v. 18);
>
> You shall not lessen the number of bricks (v. 19).

The narrative is a mix of direct quotation, narrative commentary, and response, all of which is stated in hyperbolic fashion. But the accent point is unmistakable. The slaves are to engage in an endless, demanding production of bricks that are to satisfy the economic goals of Pharaoh. There is, in this regime, no rest, no respite, no relief, no Sabbath. It is impossible to imagine that anyone in Egypt—from the slaves to the taskmasters to the supervisors, even to Pharaoh—ever had occasion for Sabbath rest.

Given the arbitrary way in which I have delineated the substance of chapter 5, it is possible, as I have done, to divide the content of the chapter into ten units, which correspond to the Ten Commandments. The insistent, repetitious commands of the regime thus reduce all of life to production.[4] The text is at pains to delineate the predatory system of Pharaoh and to call attention to the cost of that system for the labor force. Not surprisingly, such exploitative policy evokes a reaction from those who bear its costs, as such exploitative policy inevitably does. In the transition from one king to another, we get this:

> After a long time the king of Egypt died. The Israelites groaned under their slavery and cried out. (2:23a)

The cry of the Israelites was the most elemental act of bringing unbearable pain to public expression. The cry and the groan are so elemental that they are not addressed to anyone. No surprise in that! What surprises is that the next line tells us,

> Out of the slavery their cry for help rose up to God. (v. 23b)

In our study of the God of the exodus, we are bound to notice that until this moment in the narrative, there was no appearance of YHWH in the text. YHWH is evoked by the cry of pain (even as YHWH in the exposition of 22:21-27 promises to respond vigorously to such a cry).

Thus the narrative is designed to show that *the cry from below* will evoke *divine attention from above:*

> God heard their groaning, and God remembered his covenant with Abraham, Isaac, and Jacob. God looked upon the Israelites, and God took notice of them. (vv. 24-25)

And from that notice: the God evoked by human cries of injustice is moved to make history-redefining promises:

> I have observed the misery of my people who are in Egypt; I have heard their cry on account of their taskmasters. Indeed, I know their sufferings, and I have come down to deliver them from the Egyptians, and to bring them up out of that land to a good and broad land, a land flowing with milk and honey, to the country of the Canaanites. . . . The cry of the Israelites has now come to me; I have also seen how the Egyptians oppress them. (3:7-9)

YHWH in principle is an adversary of all such exploitative systems!

But then, surprisingly, the God of emancipatory resolve hands off the work of emancipation to a human agent, Moses:

> So come, I will send you to Pharaoh to bring my people, the Israelites, out of Egypt. (v. 10)

YHWH has promised to deliver, to "bring them up out of that land" in response to the cry. Moses is now to implement that divine resolve.

The remainder of the exodus narrative exhibits the tension between competing historical possibilities. The narrative is a life-or-death contest

between Moses and Aaron and the Egyptian "magicians";

between the prospect of an alternative land and the exploitative system;

between YHWH and the "Egyptian gods" who legitimate Pharaoh's oppressive regime.

The work of emancipation is carried on by Moses and Aaron, but the narrative leaves us no doubt that YHWH is the key actor in the narrative. Thus the God who would *give rest* is the one who must overcome the regime of *restless productivity*. The actual staging of the contest, moreover, features a massively impressive, powerful, learned regime juxtaposed to these uncredentialed representatives who can claim no more than, "Thus saith YHWH."

The initial challenge together with Pharaoh's prompt refusal is dramatically presented in 5:1-2:

Moses and Aaron: Thus says the Lord, the God of Israel, "Let my people go, so that they may celebrate a festival to me in the wilderness."

Pharaoh: Who is the Lord, that I should heed him and let Israel go? I do not know the Lord, and I will not let Israel go.

Moses and Aaron: The God of the Hebrews has revealed himself to us; let us go a three days' journey into the wilderness to sacrifice to the Lord our God, or he will fall upon us with pestilence or sword.

Pharaoh: Moses and Aaron, why are you taking the people away from their work?

The request is to commit an act of festival and to offer a sacrifice. The proposal is simply for "liturgical leave." We are given no detail about the nature of the proposed festival or sacrifice. What all parties recognized, however, is that such a liturgical act is no innocent act of piety. It is rather a performance of an alternative allegiance that would substantively delegitimate Pharaoh. It is not a wonder that Pharaoh refuses the request. His alternative to festival and sacrifice is more work. As such a *festival and sacrifice* would have credited YHWH, *oppressive and demanding work* is the totem of Pharaoh's authority. Thus the contrast between *festival* and *work*! The appeal of Moses and Aaron, throughout the narrative, is variously, "Let them serve (worship) me," or "Let them make a festival to me." The point of the two variant statements is the same. Let them embrace YHWH and reject Pharaoh!

The narrative shows that YHWH has a commitment to defeat Pharaoh that serves two purposes. On the one hand, the defeat of Pharaoh is in order that "I may gain glory over Pharaoh" (14:4, 17). It is all about YHWH's glory that can be established only by the wholesale defeat of the regime of Pharaoh. The narrative that follows concerns the glorification and enhancement of YHWH, slowly, scene by scene, together with the diminishment of Pharaoh. On the other hand, the only way in which YHWH can assert such glory is by the emancipation of Israel. Thus YHWH's positive commitment to the slave community is affirmed (see 14:14, 25, 30-31). It is conventional to accent the freedom won for Israel through this narrative. We should not, however, neglect that the victorious performance is for the glorification of YHWH. *YHWH's glory* is tied to *the freedom of Israel*!

The force of the narrative serves to exhibit the impotence of Pharaoh's system and therefore its lack of legitimacy. This narrative rendering of that impotence reaches its pivot point in 8:18 in the report that the Egyptian technological apparatus (the magicians) is unable to match the performance of Moses and Aaron in the production of gnats. In that instant the mighty kingdom of Pharaoh reaches its technological limit and is outflanked by the agents of YHWH. The denouement of the narrative is reached in the final exchange between Pharaoh and Moses in which Pharaoh is reduced to helplessness and pleads with Moses to depart before more deathly troubles are performed against the empire. The pathos of Pharaoh's petition to Moses is voiced in his final words, "Bring a blessing on me too!" (12:32). In that moment Pharaoh concedes that YHWH, via Moses, presides over the power for life and blessing and that Pharaoh has been reduced to a needy suppliant.

The victory song of Moses in 15:1-18 manages to hold together, in doxological exuberance, the two accent points of the narrative. On the one hand, the emancipated people are led in triumph through the territory of the enemies until they are "planted" in their own land, the land anticipated already in 3:7-9. But, on the other hand, the song is one of praise to glorify YHWH. It is all about YHWH's massive defeat of Pharaoh and Pharaoh's production apparatus. The poem pauses at midpoint to celebrate the incomparability of YHWH (15:11). There is no god like YHWH, certainly not among the Egyptian gods! The poem culminates with a formula of divine enthronement:

> The LORD will reign forever and ever. (v. 18)

The God who set out to get glory has now gotten glory, precisely over Pharaoh!

The narrative makes clear that YHWH is the determined, effective opponent of a predatory system of labor and intends to provide an alternative to the predatory system. This is of course the narrative of Israel, and the narrators take deliberate steps to connect this narrative to the durable promises of Genesis. At the same time, however, the narrative allows that the company of slaves set on its way out of Egypt en route to Sinai was no definable ethnic community, but rather was a "mixed crowd" of suffering people. This is first of all a narrative of Israel, and yet it is a narrative out beyond Israel for other suffering captives. YHWH is first of all the God of Israel, but then is God out beyond Israel to be the God of suffering people beyond Israel. YHWH invites Israel to an alternative way in the world; and then out beyond Israel others are invited to that same alternative way in the world.

It is no wonder that the God who commands at Sinai does so with vivid recall of the exodus and the groans emitted from the "house of slavery." It is no wonder, moreover, that this God has set the Sabbath at the center of new covenantal obedience, for Sabbath becomes the icon of contradiction that contradicts the predatory economy of production and performance that defines Pharaoh. Sabbath, moreover, becomes the icon of contradiction against every predatory regime and every predatory arrangement of power.

But we may notice, in the wake of Pharaoh, an odd fact about the Sabbath commandment in Exodus 20. Unlike its counterpart in Deuteronomy 5:12-15, the Sabbath commandment in Exodus 20 makes no mention of the exodus. Rather it alludes to YHWH's rest on the seventh day of creation (Gen 2:2-4a). This rootage of Sabbath in creation permits us a second glimpse into the exodus narrative. Terence Fretheim has detailed the way in which Pharaoh is the great de-constructor of creation.[5] Fretheim has noted how the narrative repeatedly employs the term "all" to stress the lethal reach of Pharaoh as a destroyer of all of creation. Thus the Sabbath-giving God contradicts not only the historical-economic practice of enslavement but also the creation-destroying impulse of Pharaoh. The Sabbath is not only rest for slaves; it is rest for creation given by the creator as an alternative to Pharaoh's exploitation of creation. It is for that reason, perhaps, that in the exposition of 23:10-13, before the seventh day for "rest" and "relief" is mentioned, the seventh year is mentioned for the land to "rest and lie fallow." The God of Sinai makes provisions that will be restorative of human community and equally restorative of the land on which the human community relies. In both cases of historical deliverance and restoration of creation, Sabbath contradicts rapacious practices grounded in the hubris of Pharaoh who claims,

> "My Nile is my own;
> I made it for myself." (Ezek 29:3c)

This lord of the Sabbath disrupts the story of predation; rest must disrupt the exploitation of creation. This is the God of rest who has wrested both the historical economy and creation away from the restlessness of Pharaoh. Thus the move of the narrative from Egyptian oppression in the interest of production to covenantal commandments is a manifestation of a new reality:

> Once there was no Sabbath / Now there is Sabbath rest![6]

III

The exodus deliverance from a "no Sabbath" milieu (1–15) and the Sinai covenant with its Sabbath command (19–24) are intimately and intentionally connected to each other as contrasting models of human community. But the book of Exodus does not move directly from Egypt to Sinai. It pauses in chapters 16–18 for narratives in the wilderness that is portrayed as a "no man's land" that must be traversed before Israel can come to the mountain to make a covenant with YHWH. The wilderness is presented as a place without viable life-support systems. In the narrative rendering of Israel it turns out, surprisingly, that even in such a context YHWH counters its barrenness with a readiness and a capacity to provide for Israel meat (16:13), bread (16:14), and water (17:1-7), all the staples of life.

For our purposes, in addition to the wonder of "bread from heaven," three matters in the manna narrative of Exodus 16 may claim our attention. At the very outset of the narrative, in 16:2-3, only two verses into the wilderness, Israel resists its wilderness context and wants to return to Egypt. In their desire to return, Israel does not remember the hard labor required in Egypt but only the capacity to eat "our fill" there. But then, that is the enduring, seductive attraction of a "no Sabbath" environment. Such an environment is dominated and sustained by a narrative of security: Pharaoh will provide bread! When in the wilderness, murmuring Israel accepts the unspoken trade-off of bread for hard labor. A "no Sabbath" environment will always offer bread in exchange for hard labor. At the outset of the narrative, Israel found the requirements of the sojourn toward Sinai too demanding, judging it, on the way, as more unbearable than the previously unbearable pain of Pharaoh's predatory system.

But that initial complaint is abruptly interrupted. Israel, in its departure, had thought that all the "glory" of power and majesty was the property of Pharaoh. After all, Pharaoh had taken great pains to exhibit the wonder of his rule. A hint of that exhibit is offered in the Joseph narrative where the crowd could be spectators to the passing of royal glory:

> See, I have set you over all the land of Egypt. Removing his signet ring from his hand, Pharaoh put it on Joseph's hand; he arrayed him in garments of fine linen, and put a gold chain around his neck. He had him ride in the chariot of his second-in-command; and they cried out in front of him, "Bow the knee!" Thus he set him over all the land of Egypt. (Gen 41:41-43)

In our narrative, however, they reluctantly moved into the wilderness, perhaps backing in as they kept a wistful eye on the glory of Pharaoh and his "no Sabbath" society, but they eventually had to turn to face the wilderness. And then, we are told,

> They looked toward the wilderness, and the glory of the LORD appeared in the cloud. (Exod 16:10b)

The double reference to "glory" and "cloud" bespeaks a settled, nearly passive cultic divine presence that will be more central in later Exodus texts that we will consider.[7] The narrative witnesses that the awesome, sovereign splendor of YHWH is on exhibit in the wilderness, exactly where it would be least anticipated. Such a presence attests that the wilderness is not what Israel had thought it was; it is now occupied and governed by the Sabbath-authorizing God who overpowered the glory of Pharaoh. YHWH had resolved to "get glory over Pharaoh," and now this newly won glory is on exhibit as the defining reality of the wilderness. I understand very well that the glory sought by YHWH in Exodus 14:4, 17 and the glory witnessed in the wilderness in 16:10 are two very different matters. The former has to do with a dramatic victory that established YHWH as the "winner" over Pharaoh. The latter is a cultic presence that is more or less static. Nevertheless, these usages of the same term suggest a continuity between the two. The God who has been *victorious* in defeating the "no Sabbath" system is now an *abiding presence* in Israel that transforms Israel's bereft wilderness into a matrix for life.

The testimony to YHWH's glory in 16:10 is abruptly followed in vv. 11-12 with a dramatic promise of meat and bread. This transition from v. 10 to vv. 11-12 has evoked a scholarly conclusion that we are dealing with distinctive interpretive voices ("sources"). Perhaps so. But now they run seamlessly from the one to the other. It is the God who abides in splendor who will guarantee sustenance for life in a place seemingly without sustenance. It is the presence of YHWH's glory that transforms the circumstance of Israel.

Then follows the narrative of bread from heaven. The bread was given inexplicably. The Israelites responded in wonder and uncertainty: "What is it?" The answer from Moses is:

> It is bread that the LORD has given you to eat. (16:15)

His answer is terse and explains nothing. The narrative that follows includes four notes about the inexplicable bread given by YHWH:

> There was enough and no shortage of bread;
>
> They were warned not to horde the bread or try to store it up for the next day;
>
> They did not listen and stored it up;
>
> What they stored up in their anxiety did not last, but "bred worms and became foul" and eventually "melted."

The Israelites, not surprisingly, did not trust the gift of bread; they tried to secure their own bread supply. In doing so, they replicated the bread policies of Pharaoh, attempting to accumulate and so secure themselves. The bread of heaven is unlike the bread of Pharaoh: Pharaoh's bread is all about surplus and storage, whereas the bread of heaven is about faithfulness and trust. Israel is not permitted to look beyond the needs of the day.

Given that defining plotline about bread, we are scarcely prepared for the surprising turn in the narrative. YHWH makes special allowance for the Sabbath, allowance that leads to a departure from (violation of) the one-day-at-a-time limit. Now, because of pending Sabbath, Israel is permitted to gather an extra day's worth of bread so that it can eat without gathering (working) on the Sabbath:

> This is what the LORD has commanded: "Tomorrow is a day of solemn rest, a holy Sabbath to the LORD; bake what you want to bake and boil what you want to boil, and all that is left over put aside to be kept until morning." So they put it aside until morning, as Moses commanded them; and it did not become foul, and there were no worms in it. Moses said, "Eat it today, for today is a sabbath to the LORD." (16:23-25)

Not only is Israel not to gather on the Sabbath but no bread will be given, perhaps suggesting that the creator God will not do the work of providing bread on that day. Both parties take a Sabbath break from supplying bread, YHWH from giving it and Israel from gathering it.

But as they disobeyed in v. 20 by seeking a surplus of bread for themselves, so now on the Sabbath day some disobeyed and refused the Sabbath provision:

> On the seventh day some of the people went out to gather, and they found none. The LORD said to Moses, "How long will you refuse to keep my commandments and instructions? See! The LORD has given you the Sabbath, therefore on the sixth day he gives you food for two days; each of you stay where you are; do not leave your place on the seventh day."
> (vv. 27-29)

They did not practice Sabbath; they did not trust the Sabbath supply; they did not rely on the Sabbath-supplying God. Their mistrust is bespoken by their readiness to work on the Sabbath day, proposing that work rather than rest could secure their lives.

This matter of Sabbath provision and mistrust of Sabbath provision voices an astonishing narrative disclosure. Because wilderness is a place of scarcity, one will have taken it as necessary to keep gathering food every day. Of course! This is what the Israelites thought. But because of YHWH's will for Sabbath rest, even in this most barren of circumstances, Sabbath prevails. It prevails because YHWH provides what is needed. It prevails because trusting Israel counts on the bread of heaven and does not try to secure its own supply of bread. There is, then, no circumstance of scarcity in which Israel will not keep Sabbath because there is no circumstance in which YHWH will not provide what is needed. It is rest that is the supreme enterprise for YHWH, the very reason for the exodus deliverance in the first place!

This claim is so perfectly counterintuitive that some in Israel could not believe it; they thought it worth violating Sabbath to secure their own bread supply. Clearly those who take such Sabbath-violating action imitate what they had learned in Egypt from Pharaoh. They were unwilling or unable to trust the God who would give them rest. They were inured to the restless system of self-securing that had no time or energy for Sabbath keeping. As much as they could, they would distort a Sabbath-governed wilderness into the commodity pursuit of Pharaoh. As Sabbath contradicts the ideology of Pharaoh, so the relentless gatherers now contradict the command to trust the Sabbath-governing, rest-giving God whose glory transposes the wilderness.

IV

The Sinai pericope ends in Exodus 24:9-18 with accounts of visions of YHWH upon Mount Sinai. After the appearance of YHWH to the seventy elders (vv. 9-11), Moses goes further into the cloud (see 16:10) where there was an appearance of YHWH's glory "like a devouring fire." Here the narrative ends. The text moves from narrative to instruction in the form of divine command. In chapters 25–31, an extended instruction, YHWH authorizes Moses to design, construct, and decorate the holy place that will be a suitable habitat for YHWH's glory. By reference to the "cloud" in 24:16, as in 16:10, it is clear that the glory won over Pharaoh is now transposed into a cultic presence. Thus these chapters concern hosting the God of exodus as an abiding cultic presence. Concerning these chapters we may notice three matters that pertain to our theme.

First, scholars have noticed that YHWH's address to Moses is divided into seven speeches, each of which has an introductory formula, "The Lord said to Moses" (25:1; 30:11, 17, 22, 34; 31:1, 12).[8] Although the first of these speeches is by far the longest, the full complement of seven is important. The text concerns much detail about cultic furniture and arrangement and the priesthood that is qualified to manage the new place, but the force of the text is in the sum of the parts. In the liturgical imagination of Israel, the temple in Jerusalem is an imitation of the heavenly temple. In the tradition of Exodus, moreover, the tabernacle is an anticipation of the temple in Jerusalem. Understood in its mythic, poetic force, these chapters present a properly ordered sanctuary that is in fact a properly ordered world, that is, a new creation. As a result, the sum of the seven speeches of YHWH to Moses constitute a parallel to the seven days of creation in Genesis 1:1–2:4a, and the outcome is a completion, a "finish" of a perfectly ordered sanctuary (creation) where the glory of YHWH may dwell in the midst of Israel.

If this text is dated, as is often thought to be the case, in the chaotic days of exilic displacement, then this liturgically imagined universe functions as an alternative universe, alternative to the disorder of lived historical reality. And indeed, for many persons among us, "going to church" is exactly an experience of leaving, for a time, the unbearable disorder of historical existence and entering into an alternative world that is properly ordered, aesthetically healing, and restorative for the community. For that reason the liturgical place and its legitimated conduct must be symmetrical and well ordered as a contrast to the disorder known elsewhere. Unlike the disordered world of Jerusalem, which YHWH, according to Ezekiel, had to flee because it was "abominable," this constructed/imagined world is appropriate in order, beauty, symmetry, and grandeur to the character of YHWH who may dwell there.

Second, once we have noted the seven speeches of YHWH to Moses, it is especially important that the first six speeches concern the holy place, its order, and its management by the priests. But the seventh speech leaves off interest in the holy place and instead is preoccupied with holy time, namely the Sabbath that requires no priestly oversight (31:12-17). Thus the seven speeches end with Sabbath as do the seven days of creation in Genesis 2:2-4a. There can be no doubt that this reference to Sabbath is a deliberate appeal to the rest of YHWH in Genesis 2:1-4a, the same appeal that is made in the command about Sabbath at Sinai in 20:8-11. The tabernacle, with its detailed characterization, culminates with rest for YHWH–and for Israel! This provision for Sabbath as "the last word" in this sequence concerning an alternative world contains three interesting notes that relate to our topic.

A. Sabbath is a "perpetual covenant" between "me and my people," a "sign forever." The conditional "if" of 19:4 has been completely overcome. Now the covenant is guaranteed, so that "rest" practiced on Sabbath is an act of solidarity with and fidelity to the rest-giving God.

B. We notice the urgency of this commandment:

> Whoever does any work on the Sabbath day will be put to death. (31:15)

Sabbath has become a rigorous norm for membership in the covenant community of Israel. We may gather that this text reflects times when Israelite-Jewish identity was in jeopardy, as members of the community easily slid into conventional cultural practices of production and performance, that is, back into pharaonic modes of existence.

C. The concluding note is astonishing: On Sabbath YHWH is "refreshed"! The reflexive verb is from the noun *nepeš*, "self, soul." In Sabbath rest YHWH's depleted self—exhausted from the work of creation?—is replenished. As with YHWH, so with Israelites who keep Sabbath. Their depleted selves can be restored. Their diminished Jewish identity can be recovered. The intent of this alternatively imagined world is rest that is shared by YHWH and YHWH's people, rest that draws a line against any ideology of production and performance that recruits persons into bondage.

The third matter we notice is that this extended text is not in any intense way connected to the exodus tradition and likely was formulated in a very different context. In one reference, however, the connection of this dwelling God to the exodus tradition is made explicit:

A. The text reiterates the "covenant formula" in Exodus 29:45 that will be much used in the exilic period by Jeremiah and Ezekiel. This is the God who made covenant with Israel at Sinai. It is this God who rests and summons to rest.

B. The God who speaks here is a God manifested in "glory" who "dwells" among the Israelites (v. 43).

C. The God who dwells in glory as a covenant-maker is the God of the exodus:

> And they shall know that I am the LORD their God, who brought
> them out of the land of Egypt, that I might dwell among them.
> I am the LORD their God. (v. 46)

The purpose of the exodus is for this dwelling presence! The formula is not unlike the introductory formula of the Decalogue in 20:2. Thus even in this act of intense liturgical imagination, this is the God who triumphed over Pharaoh in order to end enslavement. In long-term cultic practice, keeping Sabbath is a disciplined act of rest, enacted even by

YHWH as a protest against pharaonic enslavement and as a deliberate summons to an alternative. While there is no doubt that this priestly material arose out of a very different sphere, it is astonishing that it continues to connect this core discipline of the Decalogue both to *emancipation* from Pharaoh and to an assured *sacramental practice.*

V

When the narrative of Exodus 24:15-18 resumes in 32–34, Moses is still on the mountain. He is the protector and guarantor of the covenant that was a demanding alternative to pharaonic life. In his absence, Israel was again seduced into a life of commoditization. The *calf* of *gold* "produced" by Aaron reenacted all the false assumptions and practices of a commodity-oriented enterprise:

It was a calf (bull!), emblem of productive vitality, interpreted by Israel's stringent covenantal traditions as the quintessence of self-sufficiency.

It was gold. When gold is taken as an object of desire and therefore worship, it is a violation of covenant.

It was a calf of gold produced by priestly effort:

> He took the gold from them, formed it in a mold, and cast an image of a calf. (v. 4)

Aaron violates the second commandment of Sinai, and fashions a god who is object and not subject. More than that, he assigns to his "produced" god credit and agency for the exodus deliverance:

> These are your gods, O Israel, who brought you up out of the land of Egypt! (v. 5)

The crisis instigated by Aaron consists in the offer of a domesticated god who was produced and controlled, lacking in freedom, power, sovereignty, or agency, and surely lacking in glory. This ersatz god will never "get glory" by performing any emancipatory wonder. The act of Aaron and the uncritical response of Israel (see v. 6) constitute a total misconstrual, violation, and rejection of the covenant of Sinai and the God who initiated it. For due cause the Sinai covenant is terminated!

Then follows the anguished way in which the broken covenant is reconstituted as YHWH and Israel (via Moses) walk back into covenantal fidelity. In chapter 33, YHWH and Moses choreograph a delicate negotiation. This turns variously on the divine glory, the divine goodness, the divine name, and the divine face, and culminates with the divine mercy (33:17-34). Moses wants to see the glory of YHWH (v. 18). The narrative turns on the tricky readiness of YHWH to be seen and the insistence of YHWH on remaining hidden. Thus *seen* and *hidden*! Perhaps Moses wanted to see the glory in order to be sure that the God with whom he deals is the one who got glory over Pharaoh and who transformed the wilderness. By the end of the narrative, YHWH's glory does pass by—but only the backside! This is still the God who is free, faithful, powerful, and transformative.

In the crucial text of 34:6-7, that seen, hidden God is further exposited in the generous, rigorous categories of covenant. The glory is voiced in relational terms. From that relational self-giving, Moses submits (34:8-9) and YHWH grants renewed covenant (34:10). The God who recommits to Israel promises to do "marvels" and an "awesome thing," terms that are reminiscent of the exodus deliverance. YHWH will do in time to come what YHWH has done!

Then follows, as in Exodus 20, a new set of commandments that some regard as a second version of the Decalogue (34:11-26). Care is taken to distinguish Israel from the other peoples (vv. 12-16). The making of gods is prohibited (v. 17). And finally in the festal calendar Sabbath stands as an abiding requirement of covenant:

> Six days you shall work, but on the seventh day you shall rest; even in plowing time and in harvest time you shall rest. (20:21)

The second sentence of reinforcement indicates that there is no crisis in an agricultural economy that justifies the violation of Sabbath. The reconstituted covenant, like the original at Sinai, provides that Israel must regularly and visibly desist from production. It is possible to juxtapose the *rest* of Sabbath and the *making* of gods, the symbolic act of producing one's own life. The active verbs for "making gods" are "form" and "cast," efforts at self-sufficiency. Sabbath as alternative is to give one's life over to the creator God, who will continue, in glory, to perform miracles that undo bondages.

VI

The final section of the book of Exodus, chapters 35–40, reports on the obedience of Moses to the commands of YHWH in chapters 25–31, with the construction of an adequate dwelling place for YHWH's glory. Two matters claim our attention in this text, which is largely a reiteration of the materials of 25–31. First, the completion of the construction process is twice reported:

> In this way all the work of the tabernacle of the tent of meeting was *finished*; the Israelites had done everything just as the LORD had commanded Moses. (39:32)

> So Moses *finished* the work. (40:33)

Interpreters have noticed that the use of the verb "finish" in both cases closely parallels the "finish" of creation in Genesis 2:1.[9] As creation is "finished" in Genesis, so the tabernacle as new creation is completed according to the specifications of the holy God. The parallel to and echo of the creation text is unmistakable. This ending of the narrative asserts that the entire project is a new creation of order, beauty, and most especially divine presence, a creation not scarred by the anticreation efforts of Pharaoh.

As a result, the glory of YHWH in the cloud is now able to occupy the tabernacle; the dwelling of YHWH is with Israel (see Ezek 37:27). If we trace the parallels between the command of 25–31 and the enactment of 35–40, we are able to notice that we have no exact parallel to the seventh speech of YHWH in 31:12-17 concerning Sabbath. Instead of a parallel we have the entry of the glory of YHWH into the tabernacle. That now takes the place of Sabbath rest, or offers a new form of Sabbath rest. Now the glory of God rests securely and abidingly in the tabernacle as emblem and assurance of a new ordered creation. We are able to see the completion of the journey of YHWH's glory all the way from the exodus contest (14:4, 17) through the wilderness (16:10) to the mountain (24:16-17), into the negotiation for renewed covenant (33:17-23), and now to be at rest. YHWH's glory at rest is no longer in a struggle with Pharaoh but has prevailed. YHWH's restfulness then is a counterpoint to the Sabbath rest of Israel commanded in 31:12-17. This is not a God or a people in a world that is in contestation. There is no slavery. There is no need to compete or to produce. There is no restlessness. All is well . . . and all manner of things shall be well!

VII

Theological exposition of biblical texts must, I believe, send out lines of contemporary connectedness. For that reason I finish with three observations:

1. When the exodus tradition is carried toward the Christian New Testament, perhaps the most poignant text is the teaching of Jesus in Matthew 11:28-30:

> Come to me, all you that are weary and are carrying heavy burdens, and I will give you rest. (v. 28)

Jesus contrasts his way of life in obedience to God with the heavy "yoke" imposed by the world, perhaps here the "yoke" of Roman taxation or the "yoke" of demanding religious performance. Either yoke was a burden of production and performance. It is not happenstance that this teaching is followed, in the sequence of Matthew, by a teaching reflection on the Sabbath. In Matthew 12:1-8, Jesus is said to be "the lord of the Sabbath" (v. 8). That is why he can declare that "my yoke is easy and my burden is light" (11:30). This teaching only makes sense when seen in the context of the ancient alternative that Sabbath is to every Pharaoh.

2. Charles Ferguson has recently published his analysis of the U.S. economic "meltdown" of 2008. He has knowingly titled his analysis, *Predator Nation*.[10] His title of course refers to the aggressive greed of the financial community in collusion with the government that is managed by the same cast of characters who constitute an unrestrained oligarchy. The wake of the meltdown of course has resulted in huge suffering for the economically vulnerable, while the alliance of corporation and government protects only the interests of the 1 percent.

It requires no imagination at all to see that this contemporary practice of "legitimated" predation is a strong parallel to the predatory policies of Pharaoh in the ancient narrative. In ancient and contemporary form, the acquisitive (coveting) society enacts lethal costs on the politically dominated and the economically vulnerable. It is precisely in such a predatory society that Sabbath emerges as a way in which the alternative God of covenant "gets glory" against the glorification of wealth, power, control, and virility that dominate our society.

3. Michael Fishbane has offered a compelling exposition of the Jewish disciplines of mindfulness that counter the mindlessness of our society in its acquisitive insanity. Central to his analysis is Sabbath, the

observance of which "may cultivate a theological mindfulness."[11] Fishbane sees that Sabbath is a "divestment" from the ordinary world, the observance of which

> trains the mind to move from the habitude of action to the ultimate borders of imaginable immensity, where one can only put oneself in mind of a reality altogether exceeding normal activities and objects. This reality, as we may imagine it, is a realm of conjunctive interaction, where the actuality of all possibilities embraces in the loving heart of God.[12]

It is exactly that divestment that was the work of the exodus when Israel, with YHWH, departed the "normal activities and objects" of pharaonic society. The alternative of "some supernal balance or repose" is evident in the settled glory of YHWH in the tabernacle (40:34-38).[13] When one considers our predatory nation with its mindlessness, the alternative of Sabbath is an acute summons. The "glory" of Pharaoh, now as then, is only disrupted when the divine command is humanly uttered in the face of such predation, "Let my people go."

13

COVENANTAL RISKS AND REWARDS

The codification of holiness is indeed present in the Bible, and so has become a treasured assumption in the church. That codification, either wittingly or not, has provided the script for the reduction of faith to a commodity transaction with all the costs, benefits, and risks of such transactions. In the ancient world, Israel's attraction to such codification of commodity transactions was in imitation of its cultural milieu in which a variety of competing gods were hungry, demanding, and ready to bargain. In our contemporary world we are not drawn to such codification and reduction of faith in commodity transactions by the imitation of other gods. It is rather, I propose, an imitation of market ideology that draws us to such commoditized religion. As the faith of ancient Israel was distorted by imitation of the gods, so contemporary church faith is distorted by the imitation of the market ideology and the reduction of church operations to a business model.

I

There are many such distortions, seductions, and reductionisms in the Bible. I will mention three that are more or less familiar:

1. The poet Amos chides his contemporaries for their zealous devotion to such performances of commodity transactions:

> Come to Bethel—and transgress;
>   to Gilgal—and multiply transgression;
> bring your sacrifices every morning,
>   your tithes every three days;

bring a thank offering of leavened bread,
and proclaim free will offerings, publish them;
for so you love to do, O people Israel, says the Lord God. (Amos 4:4-5)

Amos identifies two major sanctuaries to which there must have been many pilgrimages. Hans Walter Wolff, among others, has suggested that his opener, "Come to Bethel . . . to Gilgal" is an imitation of a summons or call to worship.[1] But there is a quick reversal of rhetoric:

. . . to Bethel *and transgress;*
. . . to Gilgal *and multiply transgressions.*

The more you do it, the more you sin. The double use of "transgress" undermines the summons to worship and indicates that such worship produces exactly the opposite of what one expects. The middle portion of the verses indicates that the poet is quite familiar with the encoded practices:

sacrifices every morning;

tithes every three days;

thank offerings (*tôdâ*) of leavened bread;

free will offerings.

He names enough specifics to serve as a summary inventory of the practices. And then he adds a biting last line, "Thus you love to do." You enjoy it. You indulge in it. And then, as you know, Amos returns to his dark denunciations and summons to justice. The larger claim of his poetry is that such commodity gestures will never produce what you hope for.

2. In a later text in Isaiah 58, another poet derides Israel for its preferences for such coded gestures. He portrays busy worshippers who are disgruntled that their ritual performances are not effective:

He describes their actions:

Yet day after day they seek me
and delight to know my ways. (Isa 58:2a)

Then he exposes their actions with an "as if" that is contrary to fact.
As if . . . like . . . pretending to be:

. . . a nation that practiced righteousness,
and did not forsake the ordinance of their God. (v. 2b)

The "as if" means, to the contrary, that they do not do righteousness, they do in fact abandon justice. These two lines are sandwiched between the double use of "delight," which means that their worship performance is an act of self-indulgence. They do what they like to do because it is pretend faith that requires of them nothing serious.

He exposes their disappointed expectations about outcomes, thus a performance designed to secure something from the God to whom the sacrifice is offered:

> "Why do we fast, but you do not see?
> Why humble ourselves, but you do not notice?" (v. 3a)

Then the poet, with a double "behold," exposes the way in which their coded holiness is linked to social oppression:

> Look, you serve your own interest on your fast-day,
> and you oppress all your workers.
> Look, you fast only to quarrel and to fight
> and to strike with a wicked fist. (vv. 3b-4a)

Ergo, says v. 4b, your fasting will not get God's attention.

This remarkable poem—that we always skip before rushing on to the more familiar text about a "good fast"—is a shrewd deconstruction of the ritual performance:

It is self-indulgent and self-serving;

It is ineffective;

It is contradicted by bad economic practices.

Coded holiness is dismissed as illusionary.

3. In his parable on prayer in Luke 18:9-14, Jesus contrasts two prayers. Our interest here is in the prayer of the Pharisee, the one who knows the codes. John Donahue has observed that the prayer of the code manager is dominated by first-person pronouns:

I thank,

I am not like others,

I fast,

I tithe,

I possess.[2]

The Pharisee is self-absorbed and uses the code to voice and exhibit his self-absorption. Indeed he is introduced in the parable as one who is "righteous" and "regards others with contempt." He has confidence in his commoditized self and proposes to use his commodity vis-à-vis God to his advantage. The outcome of the parable is that he is not "justified," for his performance of the code will not yield anything for him. The dramatic presentation of the Pharisee begins with his high self-regard as he counted on his righteousness. It continues by an accent on his thanks (*eucharisto*) and it ends with his not being justified. The sequence is *righteous-thanks-not justified.*

By contrast the second character in the parable, the tax collector, gets only half a sentence: "Be merciful to me a sinner." That is all he could say. He had no credible commodity to offer. He appealed, outside the code, to the generosity of God; he humbled himself, looking down and beating his breast. More than that, he has been humiliated by the Pharisee who "regarded others with contempt." People inside the code have little patience with those outside the code! Donahue comments on the tax collector:

> He does not unroll a catalogue of sins, like the Pharisee's catalogue of virtues, nor does he compare himself with others. His hope is in God alone. Like the other powerless outsiders in Luke and the OT—the poor, the widow, the stranger in the land—he casts his lot with God.[3]

In the end, it is mercy, not commodity transaction, that causes exaltation before God. God's exaltation occurs outside the codes of holiness, not within them or because of them!

So here are three sketches of coded confidence:

1. Amos' contemporaries at Bethel and Gilgal;
2. Isaiah's self-important, demanding fasters;
3. the Pharisee who was self-confident.

The portrayal is consistent. They each know the code and the cost of "doing business" with God.

II

But here is the news! The system of codified holiness that scripts commodity transactions can be and is dramatically interrupted in ways that permit transformative, emancipatory, reconciling alternatives. The interruption is the stuff of action, gesture, and utterance. It is the stuff of human interaction that is evoked by the combination of unbearable pain and unbending hope. When that uncredentialed combination of unbearable pain and unbending hope is enacted, it is readily and often understood to be a divine act, a disclosure of divine resolve and fidelity that transforms the human drama. In the end, the Bible attests that God will refuse to be held in any system of commoditized transactions, no matter the decorous attractiveness or the careful legitimation of the code.

Here I will review nine instances in which the coded system is disrupted by Holy Resolve. Many more examples could be cited, but these will suffice as a representative inventory. After I have reviewed this inventory, I will conclude by reflecting on what is offered in place of the coded system, which will be, in many variant expressions, the enactment of risky fidelity that creates neighborly possibility, the very possibility that Hosea had in mind with his focus on steadfast love and knowledge of God in Hosea 6:6.

1. *The Baal system* of commodity exchange legitimated an economy in which everything could be reduced to a commodity. That is what is at issue in Elijah's contest at Mount Carmel (1 Kgs 18). The links to the economy are not clear until the narrative of 1 Kings 21 concerning Naboth's vineyard. In that narrative King Ahab wants to buy Naboth's vineyard. He believes that property, like everything else, could be bought and sold. And of course Naboth replies to the king:

> "The LORD forbid that I should give you my ancestral inheritance." (21:3)

We should not miss the verbal interface that pervades the narrative. Ahab and Jezebel speak always of "possession":

> "Go, *take possession* of the vineyard of Naboth the Jezreelite, which he refused to give you for money; for Naboth is not alive, but dead." As soon as Ahab heard that Naboth was dead, Ahab set out to go down to the vineyard of Naboth the Jezreelite, to *take possession* of it. (vv. 15-16)

The term reflects a commodity transaction. Naboth, by contrast, speaks of inheritance:

> I will not give you my ancestral *inheritance*. (v. 4)

The two terms disclose two economic theories that have behind them two notions of human community that are grounded in theological conviction. Jezebel's rhetoric is all about the transfer of property:

> His wife Jezebel came to him and said, "Why are you so depressed that you will not eat?" He said to her, "Because I spoke to Naboth the Jezreelite and said to him, 'Give me your vineyard for money, or else, if you prefer, I will give you another vineyard for it'; but he answered, 'I will not give you my vineyard.' " His wife Jezebel said to him, "Do you now govern Israel? Get up, eat food, and be cheerful; I will give you the vineyard of Naboth the Jezreelite." (vv. 5-7)

And of course Jezebel prevails. By a cunning plot of staged false witnesses, Naboth is executed as an enemy of the regime because he has "cursed God and the king." Clearly the commodity system has prevailed, and Naboth is helpless before it.

Until v. 17 when the narrative turns decisively:

> Then the word of the LORD came to Elijah the Tishbite, saying, Go down to meet King Ahab of Israel, who rules in Samaria; he is now in the vineyard of Naboth, where he has gone to *take possession*. You shall say to him, "Thus says the LORD: Have you killed, and also *taken possession*?" You shall say to him, "Thus says the LORD: In the place where dogs lick up the blood of Naboth, dogs will also lick up your blood." (vv. 17-19)

Elijah twice uses Jezebel's term "possession." Only now he uses it not as a promise to the king but as an indictment of the king. The king has violated the public morality of the village economy. He has enacted the usurpatious power of his throne and has failed to respect ancient land arrangements in the village economy. YHWH, moreover, is preoccupied with the case. There follows a condemnation of the king by the prophet. It turns out, in this case, that the economics of commodity is not the final word. The last word is that of YHWH who is committed to relational economics that make a neighborhood viable.[4] The alternative to the "possession" policy of Ahab and Jezebel is the role of transformative abundance enacted by Elisha. Given his presence, the land is no longer at the behest of the king and so can become a venue for life that is transformed by the word of the Lord.

2. *The pyramid club of Pharaoh* was completely committed to commodity. The specificity concerns bricks, but the bricks are in the service of storehouse cities, and the storehouse cities are a vehicle for commodity accumulation. Pharaoh knows that food is power and food is a weapon. The commodity system proceeds with ruthless brutality to impose impossible production quotas on the workforce:

> Then the Israelite supervisors came to Pharaoh and cried, "Why do you treat your servants like this? No straw is given to your servants, yet they say to us, 'Make bricks!' Look how your servants are beaten! You are unjust to your own people." He said, "You are lazy, lazy; that is why you say, 'Let us go and sacrifice to the LORD'; Go now, and work; for no straw shall be given you, but you shall still deliver the same number of bricks." The Israelite supervisors saw that they were in trouble when they were told, "You shall not lessen your daily number of bricks."
>
> (Exod 5:15-19)

The arrangement is quite conventional and hardly to be noticed. Except that it is interrupted. It is interrupted from below. The slave labor force cries out:

> After a long time the king of Egypt died. The Israelites groaned under their slavery, and cried out. (Exod 2:23)

The moans and groans concern impossible work conditions and impossible production quotas. The slaves found voice that could not be silenced by the totalizing power of Pharaoh.

But of course the narrative has staying power because the system is assaulted from above. In the burning bush, the fugitive Moses is addressed by holy resolve. The God who speaks is the God of Genesis who creates worlds and who generates heirs. And now this same holy voice pronounces a decisive turn in the economy when the pyramid club is challenged:

> I have observed the misery of my people who are in Egypt; I have heard their cry on account of their taskmasters. Indeed, I know their sufferings, and I have come down to deliver them from the Egyptians, and to bring them up out of that land to a good and broad land, a land flowing with milk and honey. . . . The cry of the Israelites has now come to me; I have also seen how the Egyptians oppress them. (Exod 3:7-9)

The story cannot be told without the resolve of God. Except that that resolve is handed off to human agents. The next verse has this:

> So come, I will send you to Pharaoh to bring my people, the Israelites, out from Egypt. (3:10)

Moses is mandated to enact God's holy resolve that the future belongs to those who step outside the commodity system in order to live in a world of inexplicable gifts.

What follows is a contest between Moses (and Aaron) and the Egyptian "magicians," that is, the intelligence community of the empire that knows how to manage finance, how to ensure production, how to administer the workforce, how to control. This human struggle for the future is an unequal struggle between the formal apparatus of the commodity system and the force of wounded bodies that will no longer be silenced. The narrative reaches its turning point with the third plague wherein Moses produced gnats and the Egyptian intelligence community cannot match his act:

> The magicians tried to produce gnats by their secret arts, but they could not. (8:18)

In that instant the narrative reached the extreme limit to the capacity of the commodity system. The rest of the narrative is a mop-up action. It is a triumph of Moses over the magicians.

Except that the contest is in fact a theological contest between the gods of commodity and the God who attends to human persons and human possibility. The interruption *from above* is to be enacted *from below*, by human agents. But YHWH never cedes action to human agents. Thus the topic becomes one of Pharaoh and Israel "knowing" or "not knowing" YHWH:

> But Pharaoh said, "Who is the LORD that I should heed him and let Israel go? I do not *know* the LORD, and I will not let Israel go." (5:2)

> From this time I will send all my plagues upon you yourself, and upon your fields, and upon your people so that you may *know* that there is no one like me in all the earth. . . . Moses said to him, "As soon as I have gotten out of the city, I will stretch out my hands to the LORD; the thunder will cease, and there will be no more hail, so that you may *know* that the

> earth is the LORD's. But as for you and your officials, I know that you do not yet fear the LORD God." (9:14, 29-30)
>
> I have hardened his heart and the heart of his officials, in order that I may show these signs of mine among them, and that you may tell your children and grandchildren how I made fools of the Egyptians and what signs I have done among them—so that you may *know* that I am the LORD. (10:1b-2)
>
> I will take you as my people, and I will be your God. You shall *know* that I am the LORD your God, who has freed you from the burden of the Egyptians. (6:7)
>
> The Egyptians shall *know* that I am the LORD, when I stretch out my hand against them and bring the Israelites out from among them. (7:5)
>
> By this you shall *know* that I am the LORD (7:17).
>
> But on that day I will set apart the land of Goshen, where my people live, so that no swarms of flies shall be there, that you may *know* that I the LORD am in this land. (8:22)
>
> I will gain glory for myself over Pharaoh and all his army; and the Egyptians shall *know* that I am the LORD. (14:4)

Pharaoh, the commodity dealer, does not know YHWH. He cannot because his knowledge is confined to his commodity system. Surely it is this same "knowledge of God" about which Hosea spoke in Hosea 6:6:

> Knowledge of God is preferable to burnt offerings!

Acknowledgment of YHWH's singular resolve for righteousness is preferable to commodity transactions. The narrative is a harsh teacher for the pyramid managers, as it reaches to mediate an alternative life outside of that system.

3. *The Jerusalem system of dynasty and temple*, epitomized by Solomon, is a commodity system. The temple functioned to legitimate the dynasty, and the force of the dynasty attested to the truth of temple faith. But of course that cozy arrangement is interrupted. It is interrupted by prophetic utterance. These poets are uncredentialed and without pedigree from the commodity system of dynasty and temple. They know, nonetheless,

that the substructure of neighborliness cannot be disregarded, no matter how much money, power, and control may be mustered. Thus Jeremiah, in belated time, by his utterance places that entire system in jeopardy. In his famous temple sermon, he mocks the self-assured liturgical repetitions of the commodity system:

> Do not trust in these deceptive words: "This is the temple of the LORD, the temple of the LORD, the temple of the LORD." (Jer 7:4)

He summons his listeners to a neighborly ethic that echoes the Torah of Deuteronomy. In his summons he pays attention to the economic realities of the vulnerable:

> For if you truly amend your ways and your doings, if you truly act justly one with another, if you do not oppress the alien, the orphan, and the widow, or shed innocent blood in this place. . . . (7:5-6)

And finally he warns that the city, in its self-deception, is at profound risk. His indictment focuses on the violation of Torah commandments, including sacrifices to Baal:

> Here you are, trusting in deceptive words to no avail. Will you steal, murder, commit adultery, swear falsely, make offerings to Baal, and go after other gods that you have not known? (7:8-9)

It is likely that mention of Baal was by this time an anachronism, but one that nonetheless summarized the theo-economic system he was criticizing. By the time he finishes, Jeremiah can imagine the failed city left in ruins. We may take Jeremiah as a representative of the wave of interruption caused by prophetic utterance concerning the Jerusalem system.

It was to be a long time later before the Jeremiah tradition could anticipate a reordered world. But when that act of imagination takes form, it is as a covenant based on glad Torah obedience:

> I will put my law [Torah] within them, and I will write it on their hearts; and I will be their God, and they shall be my people. . . . [T]hey shall all *know* me, from the least of them to the greatest. (31:33-34)

That vision of the future is compellingly contrasted with the failed regime. The important point is that they shall "all know me." This is the covenantal knowledge of God about which Hosea speaks. In a succinct summary that echoes Hosea 6:6, Jeremiah can say:

> Do not let the wise boast in their wisdom, do not let the mighty boast in their might, do not let the wealthy boast in their wealth; but let those who boast boast in this, that they understand and *know* me, that I am the LORD; I act with steadfast love, justice, and righteousness in the earth, for in these things I delight, says the LORD. (9:23-24)

The commodity system specialized in wealth, power, and wisdom of a technical kind. But those passions are inimical to YHWH, who is, alternatively, a champion of justice, righteousness, and steadfast love. Jeremiah voices the contrast with clarity that cannot be misunderstood.

4. Two generations after Jeremiah *the empire of Babylon* was fully and grandly established. With echoes of the old tower of Genesis 11:1-9, Babylon seems guaranteed to perpetuity and beyond challenge in its wealth and power. The poetry of Isaiah traces out the imperious stance of Babylon:

> You said, "I shall be mistress forever,"
> so that you did not lay these things to heart
> or remember their end . . .
> who say in your heart,
> "I am, and there is no one beside me" . . .
> You said, "No one sees me . . .
> I am, and there is no one besides me." (Isa 47:7-8, 10b)

This is a system designed to collect all the wealth of the world. In its wealth, moreover, the empire imagined it was not accountable to anyone at all. The religion of the empire is mocked by the poet:

> Stand fast in your enchantments
> and your many sorceries,
> with which you have labored from your youth;
> perhaps you may be able to succeed,
> perhaps you may inspire terror.
> You are wearied with your many consultations;
> let those who study the heavens
> stand up and save you,
> those who gaze at the stars
> and at each new moon predict
> what shall befall you. (47:12-13)

But of course, in the purview of poetic Israel, such an empire, a combination of religious manipulation and economic indulgence, cannot stand.

The force of historical reality is subsumed in Israel as the claim for YHWH as the true sovereign of history. The commodity system is interrupted by poetry. The poetry is addressed to Israel as a victim of empire, but the poetry itself is a theological act that condemns and dismantles empire. For the occasion the poet assigns a new function for the old word, "news." Now it is "good news." It is good news about the God who, on the lips of the poet, will disrupt all business as usual in the empire:

> Lift up your voice with strength,
> O Jerusalem, herald of *good tidings*,
> lift it up, do not fear;
> say to the cities of Judah,
> "Here is your God." (Isa 40:9)

> How beautiful on the mountains
> are the feet of the messenger who announces peace,
> who brings *good news*;
> who announces salvation,
> who says to Zion, "Your God reigns." (52:7)

The news is that YHWH, in restless resolve, now moves against the system of avarice that flies the flag of empire:

> See, they are like stubble,
> the fire consumes them;
> they cannot deliver themselves
> from the power of the flame.
> No coal for warming oneself is this,
> no fire to sit before!
> Such to you are those with whom you have labored,
> who have trafficked with you from your youth;
> they all wander about in their own paths;
> there is no one to save you. (47:14-15)

5. There is a belated reprise on the kingdom of Babylon, rendered long afterward; the *narrative of Daniel* offers Babylon once more, now a cipher for all such indulgent systems. The system is offered here in the person of Nebuchadnezzar, the one who sits atop the tower of commodity. Nebuchadnezzar is sovereign and supreme, immune to threat.

Except of course he must sleep. In such sleep, even royal sleep, the guard is down. The imperious become vulnerable. The dream penetrates the security system. Royal rest turns out to be acute restlessness, a nightmare that would never happen during wakeful working hours. But that is how it is in the commodity system—expansive, competent, impressive—but jeopardized and at risk beneath the surface of control.

Nebuchadnezzar dreamed a dream. And not all of his hired religious staff could interpret:

> So I made a decree that all the wise men of Babylon should be brought before me, in order that they might tell me the interpretation of the dream. Then the magicians, the enchanters, the Chaldeans, and the diviners came in, and I told them the dream, but they could not tell me its interpretation. (Dan 4:6-7)

His religious sycophants were good at ceremony. But they had no access to the stirrings of the true God. That required a Jew who was skilled in holy discernment.

The nightmare concerns a tree cut down. And Daniel told the truth to the emperor:

> It is you, O king! You have grown great and strong. Your greatness has reached to the heavens, and your sovereignty to the ends of the earth. (4:22)

The dream brings this reading of reality:

> You shall be driven away . . . *until* you have learned that the Most High has sovereignty over the kingdom of mortals and gives it to whom he will. (v. 25)

This is a huge "until" that makes all commodity systems penultimate and unsustainable. Such systems always imagine they are ultimate and designed for perpetuity. But no! Nebuchadnezzar does not ask the Jew for advice; but Daniel gives it to him anyway:

> Atone for your sin with righteousness, and your iniquity with mercy for the oppressed, so that your prosperity may be prolonged. (v. 27)

How remarkable that in the National Security State of Babylon, with all its wealth and power, the Jew speaks righteousness and mercy for the oppressed; these are the terms of sustainable power. With echoes of Hosea, the condition of the imperial project is the practice of mercy to the oppressed. The oppressed, since the pyramid-building slaves of Egypt, have always paid the price for the commodity system. They are not even noticed by Nebuchadnezzar. But they are noticed and brought to speech by Daniel, the Jew.

> The dream comes to reallity. The failed empire lingered in abasement:
> . . . *until* you have learned that the Most High has sovereignty over the kingdom of mortals and gives it to whom he will. (4:32)

And when the "until" was actualized, we are told that Nebuchadnezzar was restored to sanity. He had become insane in his ultimacy, as commodity systems tend to do.[5] But sanity now repositions the empire as penultimate. The last word of the empire in this narrative is a doxology concerning justice that disrupts self-indulgence and truth that disrupts illusion:

> Now I, Nebuchadnezzar, praise and extol and honor the king of
>   heaven,
> for all his works are truth,
>   and his ways are justice;
> and he is able to bring low
>   those who walk in pride. (v. 37)

The Old Testament stretches from Pharaoh to Nebuchadnezzar. All along the line from the one to the other, there is the seduction of commodity. Both Pharaoh and Nebuchadnezzar have plenty of religious verification, gods who sanction self-congratulations and who were coded to receive their share in sacrifice. But the whole is unsustainable, now decisively interrupted!

6. This entire legacy of the commodity system is mobilized for the decisive contrast of mercy and sacrifice as it was enacted on Friday, that day of all truthfulness. In the trial and execution of *Jesus*, the commodity system of Rome, together with the collusion of local officials, was strong and effective. Perhaps the commodity dimension of the transaction is indicated by the "thirty pieces of silver" given to Judas, a small price by which to eliminate a dissenter (Matt 27:3). By sundown on Friday, the commodity system had prevailed.

Except of course, its power was interrupted. The ultimate interruption occurred on Sunday. But a harbinger of that decisive interruption happened, according to Matthew, in the very midst of the state execution:

> At that moment, the curtain of the temple was torn in two from top to bottom. The earth shook, and the rocks were split. The tombs were also opened, and many bodies of the saints who had fallen asleep were raised. (Matt 27:51-52)

The death system could not prevail. The death system could not keep the saints dead. The death system could not keep the lid on the cosmic disorder that came with the execution. The death system could not maintain the arrangement of "graded holiness" whereby the temple curtain was a barrier between the "holy" and the "really holy."[6] The death system could not maintain its empty mystery against the power of steadfast love that he taught and embodied. Although more radical than its antecedents, this massive interruption of the commodity system of the empire stands in close continuity with those antecedents.

7. And now, belatedly, we are watching the most recent interruption of the commodity system in the *Occupy Wall Street movement*. Nobody knows yet about the outcome of that movement, whether it has staying power or whether it can come to political effectiveness. But if nothing more, it is already a huge dramatic interruption of the commodity system that now dominates our economic life and that controls our political discourse. We have arrived, in our society, at the most recent version of the pyramid scheme modeled by Pharaoh. And while Bernie Madoff has paid "the supreme sacrifice," the system goes on unhindered. It is an arrangement of cheap labor through which the commodities flow unhindered to those at the top.

The Occupy Wall Street (OWS) movement is the bodily dissent of those who have come to critical awareness about their subservient role in the system. That enactment of bodily rage is in continuity with the "moan and groan" of the cheap labor force in Egypt, our first remembered interruption of the regime. Our economy, like that ancient economy, is arranged so that the disempowered must offer their long-term sacrifice for the enhancement of the pyramid. And now, as the top grows more and more prosperous and more narcotized, there arise those with courage and candor, an interruption that comes surely *from below*, but no doubt *from above*.

8. The Occupy Wall Street movement is dramatic and singular. Except that it is in fact only a dramatic form of the interruption that occurs all the time, about which *every pastor knows*. Every pastor watches in astonishment, often along with fatigue, for the disruptions of the death system that are as powerful as slave moans or as dramatic as a curtain's rent. Every pastor knows about acts of courage and emancipation, incursions of freedom and daring, ventures in foolishness propelled by dreams, departures from old failed systems. And while the church, perforce, attends as best it can to business matters of membership, dollars, and survival, it is clear, again and again, that the primary discourse of the church is not about commodity. It is about steadfast love that is rooted in knowledge of God, and of his Son, Jesus Christ. Sometimes, to be sure, the church is reduced to commodity because it is closely allied with big imperious systems of demand and exploitation. But not finally, and not at heart.

9. Finally in this series of nine entries, I propose that Psalm 73 is a compelling epitome of the crisis of commodity in the orbit of faith. In that remarkable psalm, vv. 2-16 have the psalmist report on envy for the seductions of the commodity enterprise:

> Such are the wicked;
> always at ease, they increase in riches.
> All in vain I have kept my heart clean
> and washed my hands in innocence. (73:12-13)

Everything except pursuit of commodity is a foolish choice.

But then, in v. 17, the psalmist "goes to church" and receives a dramatic interruption of the system. He discerns in an instant that those inured to commodity have no staying power:

> until I went into the sanctuary of God;
> then I perceived their end.
> Truly you set them in slippery places;
> you make them fall to ruin.
> How they are destroyed in a moment,
> swept away utterly by terrors!
> They are like a dream when one awakes;
> on awakening you despise their phantoms. (vv. 17-20)

And then, in vv. 23-28, the psalmist comes to an alternative, a rediscovery of trust, communion, companionship, and well-being:

> Whom have I in heaven but you?
> And there is nothing on earth that I desire other than you. (v. 25)

The psalm is a perfect sketch of the drama of system, interruption, and new possibility.

III

In each of the cases that I have mentioned, the interruption (of the commodity system based on coerced sacrifice) yields an alternative. I will suggest in this brief reprise that the alternative to the commodity system that is now interrupted is exactly the steadfast love that Hosea accents that is grounded in knowledge of God.

1. In the Elijah–Elisha narratives, the Baal system is interrupted by the force of prophetic transformation. In the narrative of Naboth's vineyard, Elijah intervenes and calls a halt to the exploitation that is conducted under the aegis of Baal. In what follows, the narratives of Elisha evidence a regime of transformative abundance that is in sharp contrast to the parsimony of the sacrificial system. It is Elisha who brings rescuing abundance to a widow who could not pay her mortgage (2 Kgs 4:1-7). It is Elisha who raises the dead son to new life (2 Kgs 4:25-37). It is Elisha who heals the goi leper (2 Kgs 5:8-14). It is Elisha who terminates the war with Syria by the offer of a great feast (2 Kgs 6:23). It is Elisha who brings an end to a lethal famine (2 Kgs 7:16-20).

Elisha is a carrier and agent for YHWH's steadfast love. His very presence makes possible authentic human existence that was increasingly rare in the Baal-legitimated regime of Ahab and Jezebel.

2. Pharaoh's pyramid in Egypt is disrupted from below by the moans and groans of the slaves, from above by a voice in a burning bush. The interruption led to a departure and, eventually, to an arrival in the new land of promise. But the real alternative to Pharaoh's pyramid is arrival at Mount Sinai, the making of covenant, and the receiving of Torah. It is remarkable that in Exodus 19:8, just as they arrived at Sinai, Israel readily signed on for YHWH's commandments. Israel did so in chapter 19, before the commandments were uttered in chapter 20. Israel agreed beforehand because it knew and trusted that YHWH's commands were to be greatly preferred to the commands of Pharaoh. The new commands

of covenant were outside the commodity system, thus no graven images (commodities) (Exod 20:4-6), thus Sabbath rest (life not defined by production) (Exod 20:8-11), thus no coveting, no accumulation, no usurpation of what belongs to the neighbor (Exod 20:17). The commandments are aggressively counter-Pharaoh. As the commands of Pharaoh are anticommunity, so they host the possibility of community. The contrast to Pharaoh is stunning and complete.

3. The alternative to commodity (as practiced by dynasty and temple in Jerusalem) in the prophetic tradition is neighborliness enacted as distributive justice. After his stricture against self-indulgent sacrifices, the prophet Amos moves to political-economic analysis. On the one hand, he condemns those who, in self-indulgence, exploit the poor:

> They hate the one who reproves in the gate,
>   and they abhor the one who speaks the truth.
> Therefore because you trample on the poor
>   and take from them levies of grain. . . . (Amos 5:10-11)

On the other hand, he issues an imperative about neighborly engagement:

> Hate evil and love good,
>   and establish justice in the gate. (5:15)

The same either/or is more familiarly sounded in Amos 5:21-24, which moves readily from an indictment of sinful worship to a neighborly summons:

> I hate, I despise your festivals,
>   and I take no delight in your solemn assemblies.
> Even though you offer me your burnt offerings and grain offerings,
> I will not accept them;
> and the offerings of well-being of your fatted animals
> I will not look upon.
> Take away from me the noise of your songs;
>   I will not listen to the melody of your harps.
> But let *justice* roll down like water,
>   and *righteousness* like an over-flowing stream.

"Justice and righteousness" became a mantra for the prophetic tradition wherein those with socioeconomic resources are summoned to share with those who lack those resources. The new social possibility depends upon social solidarity between haves and have-nots, the very kind of social solidarity that commodity systems tend to preclude.

The prophet Jeremiah sees that the king is at the top of the exploitative economic pyramid. Thus he voices a harsh critique of King Jehoiakim, who specialized in "injustice and unrighteousness:

> Woe to him who builds his house by *unrighteousness*,
> and his upper rooms by *injustice*;
> who makes his neighbor work for nothing,
> and does not give them their wages. (Jer 22:13)

The poem contrasts such a royal commodity system with the way of the king's father, King Josiah, who acted on behalf of the poor and needy, a policy commensurate with knowledge of God, the very knowledge of God commended by Hosea 6:6:

> Did not your father eat and drink
> and do *justice and righteousness*?
> Then it was well with him.
> He judged the cause of the poor and needy;
> then it was well.
> Is not this to know me?
> says the LORD. (Jer 22:15b-16)

Indeed Jeremiah directs the either/or to the monarchy. On the one hand, it is greedy kings (shepherds) who have brought destruction and displacement on Jerusalem:

> It is you who have scattered my flock, and have driven them away, and you have not attended to them. (Jer 23:2b; see Ezek 34)

But, on the other hand, the royal alternative is neighborly solidarity enacted as justice and righteousness:

> The days are surely coming, says the LORD, when I will raise up for David a righteous branch, and he shall reign as king and deal wisely, and shall execute *justice and righteousness* in the land. (23:5)

It is this governance that provides the humane alternative to the commodity system of dynasty and temple.

4. The exploitative system of the Babylonian empire, surrogate in the Bible for all exploitative systems, overreached militarily and economically in its palpable pride and its illusion of autonomy. But such an illusionary reach cannot be sustained because even an all-powerful superpower must come to terms with the limit imposed by the intransigent rule of God.

For a post-Babylonian world, the poet sketches out new social possibility. The tradition of Isaiah acknowledges that the new reality on the ground is Persian, but in theological lyric, the new possibility is in the postempire resolve of YHWH to restore the city of Jerusalem as an epicenter of trade, economic prosperity, and well-being. Thus the great Zion poems of Isaiah 60–62 envision a recovered Jerusalem that flourishes:

> A multitude of camels shall cover you,
> the young camels of Midian and Ephah;
> all those from Sheba shall come.
> They shall bring gold and frankincense,
> and shall proclaim the praise of the LORD.
> All the flock of Kedar shall be gathered to you,
> the rams of Nebaioth that minister to you . . .
> Whereas you have been forsaken and hated,
> with no one passing through,
> I will make you majestic forever,
> a joy from age to age.
> You shall suck the milk of nations,
> you shall suck the breasts of kings;
> and you shall *know* that I, the LORD, am your Savior
> and your Redeemer, the Mighty One of Jacob.
> Instead of bronze I will bring gold,
> instead of iron I will bring silver;
> instead of wood, bronze,
> instead of stones, iron. (Isa 60:6-7, 15-17)

> Go through, go through the gates,
> prepare the way for the people;
> build up, build up the highway,
> clear it of stones,
> lift up an ensign over the peoples.
> The LORD has proclaimed
> to the end of the earth:

> Say to daughter Zion,
>   "See, your salvation comes;
> His reward is with him,
>   and his recompense before him."
> They shall be called "The Holy People,
>   The Redeemed of the LORD";
> and you shall be called "Sought Out,
>   A City Not Forsaken." (Isa 62:10-12)

The lyric of course lacks specificity. There is enough there, however, to see an alternative to the exploitative system of the empire. The poetry clearly imagines a local economy that is freed of imperial taxation for military expenditure, with ample resources shared for the community. While the poetry commends the coming city to prosperity, it imagines a social system that is not held in bondage by the struggle for quid pro quo commodity. The lyrical quality of the poetry itself bespeaks a kind of emancipation that is to be matched by emancipatory social relationships that are not under the quota system. Indeed, in this act of imagination, the calculating quota system of the empire has been shattered; in its place is a new kind of abundance that is not the product of empire but is the generous gift of God.

5. Concerning the narrative about Nebuchadnezzar in Daniel 4, I have already noted the Jewish intrusion of counsel from Daniel, the Jewish seer. It concerns "righteousness" and "mercy for the oppressed." The term rendered "mercy" is different from Hosea's word for "steadfast love." But the intent is the same. In context, it concerns a genuine notice of those who are weak and poor down below by those at the top of the pyramid.

As you will recall, Nebuchadnezzar was struck with insanity. His insanity consisted in his sense of autonomy, of being cut off from his true identity; and so he lived in a world of commodity where he thought he could generate his own identity and his own well-being. Thus Daniel's advice to the great king is a step back toward sanity that consists in the embrace of solidarity that has been broken by the illusions of the commodity system. For good reason, the final doxology of the empire in this narrative, now restored to sanity, is an acknowledgment of the fact that "his ways are justice." When the great king can acknowledge that, he has arrived at Hosea's "knowledge of God" and can resume his governance.

6. Of course it is not different with Jesus of Nazareth. The Roman Empire wherein the gospel narrative is situated is a commodity system. For that reason we get a lot of talk about tax collectors, a vehicle for sustaining the commodity system. The readiness of Jewish collusion with the imperial system that sustained the politics of commodity, moreover, amounts to a practice of bargaining, bribes, and quid pro quo; thus the tricky question of Mark 12:14:

> Is it lawful to pay taxes to the emperor, or not?
>
> It is all about taxes; it is all about "rendering." It is all about what is due in payment, what is owed. The enigmatic response of Jesus honors the question but does not resolve it. What is to be rendered to the masters of the commodity system? What is to be rendered to the gods who sit atop the pyramid of commodity?

Finally, of course, these same questioners want to witness Jesus' execution. He must be eliminated because he did not simply recalibrate the formulae of rendering. He refused the entire assumption behind the familiar formulae. He acted out the abundance of the creator, the one who had said:

> I will not accept a bull from your house,
> or a goat from your fold.
> For every wild animal of the forest is mine,
> the cattle on a thousand hills.
> I know all the birds of the air,
> and all that moves in the field is mine.
> If I were hungry, I would not tell you,
> for the world and all that is in it is mine.
> Do I eat the flesh of bulls,
> or drink the blood of goats? (Ps 50:9-13)

It is that overflow of divine abundance that makes the calculations of the commodity system unconvincing and irrelevant. The reality of abundance generates transformations, reconciliations, and emancipations that are not imaginable in the commodity system, for the commodity system is designed only to maintain equilibrium. It will generate nothing new. But the gospel is exactly the enactment of newness beyond calculation. Thus when they asked him about his messianic identity, he had no close exegetical reasoning with which to answer. He only invited them to notice:

> The blind receive their sight, the lame walk, the lepers are cleansed, the deaf hear, the dead are raised, the poor have good news brought to them. (Luke 7:22)

His response to commodity parsimony is neighborly flourishing, made possible by self-giving that dislocates the commodity system. It is no wonder that in his strictures against the commodity system, he could say:

> Woe to you, scribes and Pharisees, hypocrites! For you tithe mint, dill, and cummin, and have neglected the weightier matters of the law: *justice and mercy and faith.* (Matt 23:23)

The old triad of Jeremiah 9:23-24 is sounded again: *justice, mercy, faith*, a triad that comes full circle to Hosea's either/or. This triad is not an add-on of good works. It is rather the displacement of the commodity system with a neighborhood. It is no wonder that the woe-series in Matthew 23, in which this statement is embedded, ends in vv. 37-39 with a lament over Jerusalem, the epicenter of the commodity system in that ancient tradition:

> Jerusalem, Jerusalem, the city that kills the prophets and stones those who are sent to it! How often have I desired to gather your children together as a hen gathers her brood under her wings, and you were not willing. (Matt 23:37)

7. It is a leap from there to the Occupy Wall Street movement. But as "Wall Street" specifies the culture of commodity, so OWS, however it turns out, voices a yearning sense that the economy could be ordered differently. The problem of course is that the media that cover the movement and the government that contains the movement are largely committed to the commodity system. Any movement has a very tough time in the face of system, a tough time organizing, a tough time centering and articulating. But its point is no secret. In the end, the pyramid cannot be sustained, even if it is supported by patriotic and theological mantras. In the end, neighborliness will prevail and the commodity system will have to accommodate. In the meantime, before that end-time outcome, the movement features those who tell the truth, who place their

bodies in protest against the commodity system, whose very grievances become acts of insistent hope for an alternative.

8. Thus all the alternatives are the same:

Elisha's transformations instead of Baal's possessiveness;

covenantal possibility instead of Pharaoh's pyramid;

reconciling justice from the prophets instead of urban avarice in Jerusalem;

flourishing instead of exploitation;

imperial mercy instead of hubris;

gospel abundance instead of the exploitative impositions of Rome; and

a democratic movement instead of a pyramidic system.

All these statements are fundamentally equivalent. And then we come close to the pastoral reality that is alive in a local congregation:

Here is a college chaplain who stops one night to talk with prostitutes on the street, and undertakes a new ministry;

Here is a teenager who refused confirmation but by her senior year knows God and invests in generative ministry among her peers;

Here is a wife and mother of a household who takes her enormous cooking skills as a transformative venture in hospitality;

Here is a brutalizing father who dissolves in tears of self-awareness and begins a new way in the family;

Here is a retired guy who gives his days over to lobbying in the state capital against union-busting;

Here is a congregation with a lightness of being, living out the truth of Jesus:

> Blessed are you who weep now,
> for you will laugh . . .
> Woe to you who are laughing now,
> for you will mourn and weep. (Luke 6:21-25)

9. It all comes to fruition in Psalm 73 that is for now the paradigmatic narrative of our common life. It is the discovery, somehow, somewhere,

sometime, "when I went to the sanctuary," that commodity system yields nothing that lasts. Rather the defining truth of life is this:

> Whom have I in heaven but you?
> And there is nothing on earth that I desire other than you.
> (Ps 73:25)

IV

We finish with Hosea. He reduced it to a poem of divine hyperbole. God speaks:

> What shall I do with you, O Ephraim?
> What shall I do with you, O Judah?
> Your love is like a morning cloud,
> like the dew that goes away early. (Hos 6:4)

There is no staying power for fidelity among this people that should know better. God asks and ponders, and then in the next verse God answers with a divine response to Israel's fickle disability:

> Therefore I have hewn them by the prophets,
> I have killed them by the words of my mouth,
> and my judgment goes forth as the light. (v. 5)

Divine harshness is evoked by human, covenantal fickleness. YHWH finally will not tolerate antineighborly self-preoccupation. In the purview of Hosea, that divine harshness results in the Assyrian attack on Samaria. And then, so as not to be misunderstood, in the wake of hyperbole and harshness, YHWH clarifies:

> For I desire steadfast love and not sacrifice,
> the knowledge of God rather than burnt offerings. (v. 6)

The non-negotiable divine preference is for covenantal fidelity. "Knowledge of God" here means loyal acknowledgment of the ultimacy of YHWH in the life of the world. Given God's preference for relational durability, the commodity practices of sacrifices and burnt offerings turn out to be flimsy and of no consequence, rather like "morning dew." That clarifying prophetic word is immediate to the crisis in the old capital city of Samaria. But the crisis keeps recurring, until we arrive at our contemporary pyramid club that consists in cynical politics, self-serving religion, and mean-spirited economics, all allied against the neighborhood.

The text suggests that in our contemporary commodity fickleness, divine exasperation runs out of patience. Divine clarity invites us, at this late hour, to regroup. As we regroup, we may reflect on our several collusions with the commodity system and take fresh notice of what has been offered as an alternative. We can see that at pivot points in the Bible, the vocabulary of covenantal fidelity clusters, the vocabulary voiced in our basic text of Hosea 6:6 as "steadfast love . . . knowledge of God." I finish by citing three such clusters of that vocabulary.

1. In the Hosea tradition, the astonishing second chapter moves through YHWH's divorce from Israel because of Israel's infidelity. And then, in a fresh move designed to take our breath away, YHWH declares to this divorced partner:

> And I will take you for my wife forever; I will take you for my wife in righteousness and in justice, in steadfast love and in mercy. I will take you for my wife in faithfulness, and you shall know the LORD.
>
> (Hos 2:19-20)

Here are the five big words of covenantal neighborliness:

> Righteousness,
>
> Justice,
>
> Steadfast love,
>
> Mercy,
>
> Faithfulness.

That is, *ṣedāqâ, mišpāṭ, ḥesed, raḥam, 'emûnâ*. They are all synonyms! They are all about God's reach beyond commodity requirements to interpersonal engagement and solidarity. The terms provide a model for human transactions of interpersonal engagement and solidarity. They are capped, moreover, in this divine generosity by the assurance:

> You shall know YHWH.
> You shall know the LORD.

You shall make covenant; you shall trust; you shall gladly obey; you shall get past commodity to life with all of its wonder and risk. As a result, says the poet, all the needed gifts of life will follow:

> The earth shall answer the grain, the wine, and the oil . . .
> And I will have pity on "not pitied,"
> and will say to "not my people," "You are my people";
> and he shall say, "You are my God." (vv. 22-23)

The NRSV "pity" is the term "mercy." That which YHWH most prefers in 6:6 is what YHWH ultimately promises in 2:23.

2. Long before Hosea, back in Exodus 32–34, Israel experienced its defining commodity crisis, the golden calf, the ingenuity to produce a god out of gold! That crisis caused a caesura in Israel's relation to YHWH and a careful renegotiation of covenant. The outcome of that negotiation is a double use of our rhetoric of covenantal fidelity. In Exodus 33:19 YHWH asserts YHWH's ready freedom to begin again:

> I will be gracious to whom I will be gracious, and will show mercy on whom I will show mercy.

The final word is "mercy"! I will enact mercy if I want to!

And then as a capstone, in Exodus:

> The LORD, the LORD,
> a God merciful and gracious,
> slow to anger,
> and abounding in steadfast love and faithfulness,
> keeping steadfast love for the thousandth generation,
> forgiving iniquity and transgression and sin. (Exod 34:6-7a)

There is, to be sure, a severe warning that follows in the next lines, but my point now is the cluster of covenantal terms, all of which bespeak a durable solidarity in spite of alienation. By the utterance of this cluster of terms, YHWH evidences that YHWH has moved beyond the affront of commodity and is ready, willing, and able to engage in relationship, which is the hallmark of serious life in the world.

3. Long after Hosea, in the depth of exile when Israel was destroyed, displaced, and abandoned in despair, we have this grief poem in Lamentations 3. The poem reaches a nadir of candor in v. 18, judging that Israel's life with YHWH and its life in the world are over:

> So I say, "Gone is my glory,
> and all that I had hoped for from the LORD." (Lam 3:18)

But then, all of a sudden, the poem reverses field:

> But this I call to mind,
> and therefore I have hope. (v. 21)

This is not unlike the reversal in Psalm 73 when "I went into the sanctuary." The voice in this poem remembers what had been forgotten, remembers the great cluster of terms bespeaking durable fidelity, remembers the relationship and those old transformations, and dares to claim that these old durable terms still pertain, even in this abandonment:

> The steadfast love of the LORD never ceases,
> his mercies never come to an end;
> they are new every morning;
> great is your faithfulness. (Lam 3:22-23)

This poem has three of our defining terms: steadfast love, mercy, faithfulness—*ḥesed, raḥam, 'emûnâ*—the first two in the plural. They still pertain! They have staying power beyond commodity. YHWH's constancy is quite unlike that of Israel, not "like the morning dew that goes early away." And therefore, says the poet in v. 24, " 'The LORD is my portion,' says my soul, 'therefore I will hope in him' " (see Ps 73:26).

Thus the cluster of terms recurs,

> in Exodus 34:6-7 after the golden calf;
>
> in Hosea 2:19-20 after the fall of Samaria;
>
> in Lamentations 3:22-23 after the fall of Jerusalem.

All attest to the durable fidelity of God after the failure of the commodity system.

It is no wonder that Jesus could twice quote Hosea 6:6. In both cases he champions covenantal neighborliness over commodity. With reference to work on the Sabbath (Matt 12:1-8) and to eating with the disqualified (Matt 9:10-13), he attends to bodily, neighborly reality that is outside the reach of the commodity system. And now, among us, we are in a life-or-death context to see whether the lethal power of the commodity system can be overcome by the truth we know better, a truth given *from above* in God's utterance of pledge, a truth palpably given *from below* in the form of neighbors who lay down their lives in hope for the give-and-take of fidelity.

PART IV

IMAGINATIVE PROVOCATIONS THAT COMPEL

14

TESTIMONY

In 1977 Elie Wiesel notably wrote,

> If the Greeks invented tragedy, the Romans the epistle, and the Renaissance the sonnet, our generation invented a new literature, that of testimony.[1]

In a contribution to a volume titled *Dimensions of Holocaust*, Wiesel refers specifically to the death-camp survivors who are the surviving witnesses and testifiers to a truth that might otherwise be ignored and forgotten and, in some quarters, vigorously denied. Of course Wiesel, for obvious reasons, overstates the case of new twentieth-century inventiveness. He wants to insist that the entire reality of the death camps is without precedent or parallel. Given that, the consequent act of testimony from the death camps is derivatively also without precedence or parallel. That of course is not factually true; the truth rather is that folk in pain have been forever speaking their truth against the establishment, at least since the slaves in Egypt groaned and cried out when Pharaoh died (Exod 2:23-25).

I

We may therefore take Wiesel's clue to the character of testimony without his historical claim and consider the recurring circumstance of testimony, the emergence of testimony, the truth it carries, and the risk it necessarily entails. At the outset we recognize that "testimony" rings the cadences of a juridical context, as I have argued in my *Theology of the Old Testament*.[2] Witnesses—testifiers, martyrs—appear regularly before the bar of judgment, a bar variously consisting in demanding interrogators, the court of public opinion, or the long-term judgment of history. They do so in order to voice an advocacy about how events are to be understood and eventually about the particular world that has been observed and experienced. I propose that these five elements belong to the offer of testimony and the proposal of truth:

1. Testimony emerges or *erupts in a world of silence*, often a context of enforced silence in which establishment power controls the conversation and does not want the conversation to continue. The enforcer of silence may be variously the empire, because empires survive on the basis of silence, or totalizing coercion in the church, community, or family that is variously authorized by age, race, gender, or other valued social distinctions. Such domination at a micro or macro level invites no "voice from below" and, if possible, permits none.

2. The emerging, erupting witness *refuses the silence. She or he breaks the silence* and offers utterance that contradicts the claims of the dominator. We have seen many such occasions of bold persons and movements in our own contemporary context who have run great risks in breaking silence and who characteristically bring down on themselves the wrath of the silencer. Such breaking of silence is propelled, characteristically, by the reality of pain and suffering, by a dignity that refuses to give in, and by a profound hope that it need not be so.

3. The very utterance of such pain, dignity, and hope in a context that generates pain, overrides dignity, and nullifies hope *puts establishment truth in contestation*. Until there is such testimony, the truth of the dominant system remains uncontested and nobody dares to entertain the thought that it could be otherwise. But once uttered, the supremacy and immunity of establishment truth is placed irreversibly in jeopardy, and eventually negotiation and adjudication must be undertaken in order to find a new arrangement of power and a new articulation of truth.[3]

4. The witnesses do not get to decide the outcome of such articulation and such adjudication. Rather they set in motion processes that run well beyond their own utterance. Their work is to break the silence, to mount a contest, and to insist upon openness to a possibility not heretofore entertained. That *insistence upon openness* will be marked by honesty about pain, nerve about dignity, and resilience about hope.

5. Whereas establishment truth has much credentialing and authorization on its side—most often establishment logic, academic support, data, and footnotes—the witness characteristically *only has a story to tell*, and perhaps *bodily scars* that bespeak both pain and hope. The wonder of such testimony is that it offers a subversion of reality that subverts

established truth. The utterance and its hearing reach below managed explanation and have the chance of human touch to human touch, in order to effect transformation of vision and practice that the establishment can no longer preclude. (It follows, in my rendition, that such witness is never an utterance of establishment truth; no witnesses are needed for that.)

Thus in Wiesel's case in which testimony is "invented," there was for a long time a silence about the death camps with many respected colluders.[4] There has been the breaking of the silence, though it required a generation for the voices from below to form effective ways; there was a challenge to preferred establishment truth, a "new truth" of pain, dignity, and hope. This new truth is a human touch to human touch, and an inevitable, required renegotiation of how truth will be uttered among us concerning that brutality.

II

We may, however, go behind the contemporary reality of such testimony. In the Hebrew Bible, the most dramatic usage of testimony is in 2 Isaiah, in the midst of exile. (In the New Testament, the parallel is found in the Fourth Gospel, on which see Andrew Lincoln.[5]) The poetry of 2 Isaiah reflects the utterance of the Jewish community in the midst of Babylonian hegemony. That hegemony had, for all practical purposes, silenced Jewish hope and eliminated Jewish historical possibility. It was clear that the Babylonian gods had triumphed over YHWH and had legitimated raw imperial power. To some extent, the silencing of Jewish historical possibility was coercive and heavy-handed; but it surely was also the case that the silencing was accomplished by seduction, as some Jews surely colluded with Babylonian power in order to make it in the Babylonian economy. The empire was vigorously totalizing and did not allow thought or utterance or gesture outside that totality.[6] (We have witnessed such totalizing capacity in the twentieth century; in many quarters, moreover, the church has proceeded by a totalizing of its own.[7])

But then, in ways that we do not understand, the silence is broken. The poet, 2 Isaiah, broke the silence in daring, lyrical ways that contest the truth of Babylonian claims. The silence is broken, says the poet, by the instigation of the holy God who finally will not be dismissed but who authorized this speaker to "get you up to a high mountain" (Isa 40:9). This poet three times uses the term "gospel" in a theological way never before employed in ancient Israel. His "testimony" is "news" that breaks the silent totality of Babylon by an "experience" (so he claims) of being present in the council of the gods from which poetry is generated (Isa 40:1-11). In his claim, he of course replicates Isaiah of Jerusalem, who in Isaiah 6 "experienced" a vision of God surrounded by God's heavenly acolytes.[8]

From that "experience," the poet bears witness to Jews that an alternative to the empire is possible, that life outside the empire is livable, but that achieving this alternative will require a willful, risky departure from empire. The veracity of his defiant utterance, in which he calls other Jews to risk, is based only in his hidden experience to which no one else has access. From that "experience" comes the threefold utterance of the "gospel":

> Get you up to a high mountain,
> O Zion, herald of *good tidings*;
> lift up your voice with strength,
> O Jerusalem, herald of *good tidings*,
> lift it up, do not fear;
> say to the cities of Judah,
> "Here is your God!" (Isa 40:9)

> I first have declared it to you,
> and I give to Jerusalem a herald of *good tidings*. (Isa 41:27)

> How beautiful upon the mountains
> are the feet of the messenger who announces peace,
> who brings *good news*,
> who announces salvation,
> who says to Zion, "Your God reigns." (Isa 52:7)

The testimony, rooted in hidden experience, yields an articulation of the power and reality of God amid empire:

> "Here is your God."
> "Your God reigns."

In this utterance based on hidden experience, the poet as witness opens up a large, lyrical alternative world in which Jews are invited to recover enough of their identity in order to act, according to their destiny, against the will of the empire. The sequence of *hidden experience*, *poetic utterance*, and *engagement in contestation* with imperial truth becomes paradigmatic for Israel's faith, replicated by Jesus before Pilate and by the apostles in the book of Acts. Everything depends upon the poet.[9]

But then, remarkably and unexpectedly, the poet as witness recruits his addressees to join the practice of testimony. He imagines a trial in which truth is contested. (All good poetry, I propose, is a contestation between the good news and the deathly option of silencing hegemony.) In Isaiah 43:8-13:

The poet mocks the empire by inviting the empire to dispatch witnesses to the trial to make a case for the empire:

> Let them bring their witnesses to justify them,
> and let them hear and say, "It is true." (43:9c)

The poet summons his Jewish audience:

> You are my witnesses, says the LORD,
> and my servant whom I have chosen. (v. 10a)

The purpose of the recital, it turns out, is not to persuade the Babylonians but for the Jews to take themselves, by their own poetry, into an alternative future:

> so that you may know and believe me
> and understand that I am he. (v. 10b)

The poet has YHWH give the witnesses their testimony, what they are to say on behalf of YHWH, the new truth that yields a new reality in the world:

> Before me no god was formed,
> nor shall there be any after me.
> I, I am the LORD,
> and besides me there is no savior.
> I declared and saved and proclaimed,
> when there was no strange god among you. (vv. 10c-12a)

After such a lyrical self-announcement for YHWH on the lips of the witnesses, the mandate is reiterated:

> You are my witnesses, says the LORD. (v. 12b)

The poetry culminates in the self-doxology of YHWH that will give the witnesses energy and courage:

> I am God, and also henceforth I am He;
>   there is no one who can deliver from my hand;
>   I work and who can hinder it? (v. 13)

The poem moves between *recruitment of witnesses* and the *substance of their testimony*. For those who believe the testimony (and preserve the poetry), a new world comes into being in the moment of utterance.

III

There is no direct or obvious move from that ancient utterance to our contemporary utterance. But the preacher makes such a move intuitively in what James Sanders calls "dynamic analogy."[10] I propose, in rather simplistic fashion, that as 2 Isaiah and his recruited witnesses contested Babylonian truth on behalf of the God who is the subject of this poetry, mutatis mutandis, the current contestation of truth in the U.S. church is between the ideology of the National Security State that I have elsewhere termed "military consumerism" and the narrative of the Triune God, Father, Son, and Spirit, that is fleshed in the tale of Jesus. That is of course a huge mutatis mutandis. It is, however, a mutatis mutandis that must be made, and regularly is made, if we are to attend to *experience*, to *utterance*, and to *credible contestation*. By making such a connection between ancient text and contemporary context, the ancient text can serve as a warrant for how we are to make our own testimony.

I propose that those who would be witnesses for the gospel in the United States can reflect on the truth of the gospel in our own lives in the context of the totalizing claims of the narrative of the consumer economy that is backed by military force and that serves a sense of entitlement rooted in the exceptionalism of being God's most recently chosen people. Of course we do not articulate the crisis so directly; we assume, for the most part, our entitlement to our standard of living, our legitimate monopoly of markets and resources, and the nobility of democratic capitalism without thought about the blowback on us and on those who depend upon us. I will take that common assumption as a given, though we may quibble about the details and its particular articulation. The important point to recognize is that this totalizing narrative is everywhere operative and assured, although rarely acknowledged.

That totalizing narrative, like the ancient Babylonian one, presumes to make us safe and happy. The "safe" part is the military security system that depends upon deep waves of anxiety and fear. The proud exhibit of military force, the dazzling of military technology, the endless exhibit of police patrols, the tightening of the borders, the busy charade of airport security: all attest to a "Dick Cheney" strategy of bottomless fear that is matched by entitlement exceptionalism.

The "happiness" part is the pervasive reach of the advertising game, most especially body care and cosmetics, plus the aura of sports spectacles that offer a public that is endlessly at ease and not inconvenienced. This required public is capable of being constantly entertained, so that critical thought becomes neither necessary nor eventually possible.

The current ideology of "safety and happiness" is evidently a new version of the old imperial offer of "bread and circuses." The wonder is that no one has to pay for it. It is all free because taxes are anathema in response to the offer. I propose, not unlike 2 Isaiah in ancient Babylon, that the preacher has to break the silence in the midst of this totalizing narrative upon which not many companions have used much critical energy. The preacher as witness must, perforce:

Break the silence on which the dominant ideology depends;

Articulate an alternative that puts the truth of the National Security State in contestation;

Find grounds of credibility in text and in life; and

Invite to a fresh adjudication of truth and power.

Christian testimony has a few programmatic themes. Paul Tillich describes the work of God's rescue in Jesus Christ as our *emancipation from bondage* or our *reconciliation from alienation*.[11] Or as my United Church of Christ's Statement of Faith recites about the work of Christ, it is "conquering sin and death and reconciling the world to God's self." The preacher has those familiar, jaded categories that she can transpose into "safety and happiness," safety as emancipation and happiness as reconciliation. The preacher cannot get free of the ancient text that provides the categories and discloses the Holy Source of testimonial, poetic freedom. At the same time, of course, the preacher lets the old testimony against the ancient empire become the contemporary testimony against the dominant contemporary ideology, whereby the old, old story becomes the new, new song.

The preacher, out of personal experience and out of wider contemporary experience, has the two tasks, the same two tasks as the ancient poet. On the one hand, the preacher must tell tales of the deep dysfunction and falsehood of the dominant story in order to disclose that the imperial gods are powerless to provide either safety or happiness; these gods, powerless as they are, can neither emancipate nor reconcile. The second, more important task, however, is to give testimony, personal and beyond personal, from contemporary life where the God of the gospel issues safety that the world does not expect and provides happiness that the world thinks impossible. In our evangelical testimony, it is known that safety comes by entrusting ourselves to the neighbor-making fabric of companionable existence in which we are not abandoned to the vagaries of death. It is known, in our evangelical testimony, that happiness comes by the participation in a missional life of self-giving. Both this entrustment of self to the neighborly fabric that yields safety and this participation in a missional life of self-giving that offers happiness are profoundly countercultural and counterimperial. The utterance of such testimony is, for that reason, a disruptive contestation whereby the congregation is summoned to negotiate between this new truth and the old, jaded truth of empire that daily summons us and surrounds us.

I have no doubt that personal testimony and other contemporary testimony are important in the preaching task. But with these caveats:

Such testimony is not primarily designed to be cute or entertaining or trivial because it mediates a life-or-death contest.

Such testimony can be too closely personal and, very soon, not interesting or compelling; it needs, rather, to draw personal testimony from others in the awareness that the truth of pain and the reality of hope are often more palpable on lips other than our own.

Such testimony can be excessively privatized and personalized until the deep, implied ideological contestation in the utterance is played out.

Such testimony is not "illustration" but a venue for the redescription of the truth of the world.

When these caveats are honored, I have no doubt that experience-rooted testimony carries enormous authority and transformative credibility in shaking the foundations and opening new futures.

The gospel of Mark is a model for linking main claims to personal testimony. In Mark 1:14-15, there is a programmatic declaration of the gospel that echoes 2 Isaiah:

> Now after John was arrested, Jesus came to Galilee, proclaiming the good news of God, and saying, "The time is fulfilled, and the kingdom of God has come near; repent, and believe in the good news."

This declaration is immediately followed in Mark by concrete narratives of testimony about transformations: an unclean spirit, a cleansed leper, a healed paralytic. It is telling that these concrete gospel acts about which testimony is made immediately evoke opposition from the hegemonic company:

> Now some of the scribes were sitting there, questioning in their hearts, "Why does this fellow speak in this way? It is blasphemy! Who can forgive sins but God alone?" (Mark 2:6)

> The Pharisees went out and immediately conspired with the Herodians against him, how to destroy him. (3:6)

It was not the grand claim that got Jesus in trouble. It was concrete testimony that evoked lethal opposition. Such personal testimony that subverts is urgent in our preaching.

IV

I finish with one more text. When we genuinely understand testimony as narrated truth that subverts dominant, settled truth, testimony is seen to be serious, risky business. So it was in the ancient world. Quite clearly Jews in Babylon quaked at telling an alternative truth. The poet has God say to Israel as witness:

> Do not fear, or be afraid:
>   have I not told you from of old and declared it?
>   You are my witnesses!
> Is there any god besides me?
>   There is no other rock; I know not one. (Isa 44:8)

The juxtaposition of "You are my witnesses" and "Do not fear" constitutes an awareness that witnesses can be frightened in their contestation with settled truth. I can think of two such scenarios:

1. A corporate whistle blower, at the last minute, cringes from courtroom testimony because it is too risky; she might lose her pension or endanger her family. Her attorney must remind

her that everything rides on her testimony and she must have courage.

2. A raped woman is about to testify against the rapist; at the last minute she does not want to testify because it is too shameful and too sordid. A loved one reminds her that the whole case depends on her experience-rooted truth-telling.

That is how it must have been in ancient Babylon; consequently God must reassure: "You are my witnesses . . . do not fear." To be a witness to alternative truth is a risky venture. That is why, since that ancient poem, serious witnesses must be surrounded by "Do not fear," an assurance rooted in the steadfastness of the God of all truth. It is this one who finally is the witness. Thus Luke has Jesus say:

> But before all this occurs, they will arrest you and persecute you; they will hand you over to synagogues and prisons, and you will be brought before kings and governors because of my name. This will give you an opportunity to testify. So make up your minds not to prepare your defense in advance; for I will give you words and a wisdom that none of your opponents will be able to withstand or contradict. You will be betrayed even by parents and brothers, by relatives and friends; and they will put some of you to death. You will be hated by all because of my name. But not a hair of your head will perish. By your endurance you will gain your souls. (Luke 21:12-19)

Witnessing can become as jaded, routine, and trivial as every other mode of discourse. Its lively urgency depends upon the recognition of the high stakes of the contestation.

15

OBEDIENCE

Martin Luther King Jr., assassinated before most of you were born, marched to a different drummer, lived boldly outside the box, and dreamed dreams that defied present reality. We mark him on his special day in order to honor him and to give thanks for his daring life and witness. But my purpose with you is not simply to honor him and give thanks for him; it is rather to invite you to think with me about how we live our lives differently in his wake, how we hear and heed the drummers for social and economic justice, how we think outside the box of greed and violence, and how we may dream dreams that refuse the system of death in which our society is organized.

In living as he did, Martin Luther King Jr. lived out of the trajectory of the great prophets of the Old Testament, the ones dispatched by God who refused to accept the world the way it was shaped and given by the systemic powers of the day. And because he stood in the line of the prophets, I thought it useful to consider Moses, the first and paradigmatic prophet in ancient Israel. I will speak of Moses and you may hear me speaking about Martin who is a replica of Moses in his vision and in his boldness.

In his remarkable book on the rhetoric of Moses in the political discourse of the United States, Bruce Feiler concludes that Martin is another Moses.[1] Feiler shows how King clearly and intentionally alluded to the exodus, to Moses, and to that ancient emancipation as a code for his own emancipatory vision. In his great "I Have a Dream" speech Martin was all about emancipation, emancipation of slaves, emancipation of workers from low wages, emancipation of racial-ethnic minorities from discrimination, emancipation of the old and the young and the disabled and women and gays from the circumstance of oppression and abuse, emancipation of the earth from the bondage of chemical aggressiveness. He said it lyrically:

> Let freedom ring from the prodigious hilltops of New Hampshire.
> Let freedom ring from the mighty mountains of New York.
> Let freedom ring from the heightening Alleghenies of Pennsylvania!
> Let freedom ring from the snowcapped Rockies of Colorado!
> Let freedom ring from the curvaceous slopes of California!
> But not only that, let freedom ring from Stone Mountain of Georgia!
> Let freedom ring from Lookout Mountain of Tennessee!
> Let freedom ring from every hill and molehill of Mississippi.
> From every mountainside, let freedom ring.[2]

And it ended, "Free at last, free at last, Thank God almighty, free at last."

I

The freedom Martin has in mind is not freedom to devour the neighbor. It is not a deregulated society in which the strong can consume the weak. It is not a world where each seeks her own advantage against all the others. It is rather freedom for the neighborhood, for the common good. I will walk with you through four questions Moses raised that Martin has entrusted to us. Martin's big question is this one: what would it mean to be genuinely free?

1. The first question left for us by Moses and by Martin is, "What is outside and beyond the kingdom of Pharaoh?" Pharaoh presents a totalizing system that explains everything, that envelops everything, that demands complete loyalty and obedience, and that does not permit a thought or an act or a notice outside that system of totality.

In ancient Egypt, the slave community could not think a thought or breathe a breath beyond Pharaoh's production system of making more bricks on the backs of cheap labor. In the New Testament, the totalizing system was that of the Roman Empire with which some Jewish leaders had colluded. Rome came to control everything, and for that reason it was urgent to ask what to render "unto Caesar" (Mark 12:13-17).

But Moses, led by God's burning bush, dreamed otherwise. He dreamed of a land flowing with milk and honey, that is, with extravagant, luxurious well-being (Exod 3:1-9). It is a land promised out beyond, and Pharaoh was helpless before the dream. It will be, according to the promise, an order of shalom, of well-being, of equity, compassion, and mercy. And Jesus, in reference to that land of promise, used the phrase "kingdom of God," God's regime that is not off in heaven for when we die. It is a socioeconomic arrangement in which all the neighbors have a stake; all are honored and supplied the resources necessary for life.

Martin embraced that dream given him by Moses and Jesus. He trusted that dream against all the harsh circumstances that were in front of him. He never doubted that the dream was a worldly possibility because the dream is the resolve and promise of God who makes all things new. That is why we pray, "Thy kingdom come on earth as in heaven," a governance of well-being that is promised and therefore taken as sure.

And now, as heirs of Moses and Jesus and Martin, we dream out beyond present circumstance. We dream of a world of peace and justice, of laws of equity and financial arrangements of mercy and compassion for all. The dream is the deep conviction that the world can and will be ordered differently; it is not to remain in the disabled condition of Pharaoh.

Long ago Lillian Smith wrote a novel called *Killers of the Dream*.[3] It concerns the power of violent racism and the way in which the pharaonic power of racism kept the land and its inhabitants in social disability. Pharaoh always wants to kill the dream because people who hope are dangerous people, dangerous to the status quo. So Martin, like Moses in his time, believed that the dream was a this-worldly possibility that is defining for how we are to live. The reason that Moses and Martin dreamed in demanding cadences is that the regime of Pharaoh that is totalizing does not in fact contain all social possibility. There are other social possibilities that Pharaoh does not want us to acknowledge. They exist because the God who has created the world is not captive to Pharaoh's system of exploitation and violence and inequity.

2. The second question left by Moses and Martin is, "How are we to get beyond Pharaoh to the fullness of the dream?" I do believe this is the overriding question for all of us, most poignantly for you who are now deciding about the direction of your lives. The answer is, we have to depart Pharaoh's system. The word "exodus" is the term "exit." The great narrative of the Old Testament is that the slaves exit from Pharaoh's land of brutal exploitation and from his totalizing system that claims all meaning for itself. They depart the regime by walking, by mobilizing, by taking initial steps. So imagine, in the wake of Moses and Martin, that the vocational task is the departure in order to arrive at a livable alternative.

It is not easy to depart Pharaoh; indeed, it is not easy even to imagine departure, and it is hardly possible. The exodus narrative back in the Old Testament is about the departure. At the outset Moses can think of many reasons why it will not work:

Moses protests, I am a nobody and cannot really do this. And God answers, "I will be with you" (Exod 3:11-12).

Moses says, They will want to know who authorized me to lead the departure. And God says, I am God; I am God who will be; I am God who creates new worlds out beyond Pharaoh (Exod 3:13-17).

Moses says, They will not trust me or follow me. And God says, I will give you compelling authority that will dazzle them; they will be persuaded of your legitimacy (Exod 4:1-9).

Moses says, I am not eloquent and cannot talk very well. And God says, Shut up and get moving. Well, what he says is this:

> Who gives speech to mortals? Who makes them mute or deaf, seeing or blind? Is it not I, the LORD? Now go, and I will be with your mouth and teach you what you are to speak. (Exod 4:11-12)

Moses says, "Please send someone else." And God says, You do not have to go alone. You can take Aaron, your brother with you, and he will hold up your hands in power (Exod 4:13-17).

As a result, Moses prepared to depart. But before he could leave, he had to perform this contest of strength and authority in order to demonstrate his own power and the power of the God who would liberate. He had to perform the dream, to show that the dream from YHWH was stronger than the visible power of Pharaoh. The contest is what we call "the plagues" that concern gnats and frogs and hail, a whole series of miracles (Exod 6–11). As the narrative proceeds, we can see the authority of Pharaoh waning as his violent system loses power and authority. We can see that the movement of the dream grows in power and authority until Pharaoh is defeated.

Well, Martin had to do it all over again. He had to engage in the same contest in order to establish legitimacy and authority for the dream, to see if the dream was stronger than the system of Pharaoh. His marches and demonstrations and acts of civil disobedience were miraculous shows of power. Imagine, this nobody of a black preacher could give a speech in the National Mall, facing the Capitol, the most important public address among us since the Gettysburg Address by President Lincoln. Imagine that at the bridge in Selma the dreamer was stronger than the police dogs and the fire hoses. Imagine the courage of the college students who conducted the sit-ins while the thugs taunted them and the police only watched, and the students prevailed. Imagine that the black children in Little Rock turned out to be stronger than the mob that tried to intimidate them on their way to school. Imagine that Moses, walking through the water, was stronger than Pharaoh. Imagine that Jesus, facing the Roman governor, turned out to be the stronger of the two.

So the vocation of Martin was to depart. But the departure is not easy or obvious. There are debts to be paid and mortgages to be honored and jobs to be pursued, and those are all in the zone of Pharaoh. But what if, in the midst of taxes and debts and mortgages, the long-term work is departure from the system of greed and anxiety? The departure depends on courage and tough freedom. It depends upon not being addicted to the addictions of our society, addictions of consumer goods or fast cars or luxurious living or security that only Pharaoh can give in the name of shallow religion that covers over cheap labor.

Departure requires patience and discipline and stamina and courage and resolve. And in the midst of that, it does not hurt to have a good critical education, learning to spot the power of Pharaoh where it occurs, learning to see the open daylight of alternative that we might miss unless we are vigilant, learning to see that truth is closely allied with justice, learning to recognize that much of what we celebrate in Pharaoh's system is in fact a contradiction of the truth of the neighborhood. Education in the training of Moses and Martin is about coming to self-awareness of our bodies as carriers of pain and of possibility, and not letting our bodies be coopted by the false truth of a system that does not want us to notice or to feel or to care. The mark of such an education is to arrive at intelligent, informed, moral freedom that is bent toward the dream of a world other than the one now so visible among us.

3. The third question left for us by Moses and Martin is this: "What resources are available for the departure toward the dream?" The problem with departure from Pharaoh's system is that he has all the goodies on which we have come to rely. He controls the food supply since our brother Joseph acquired a monopoly of food for him in Genesis 47. He manages the flow of money with an early form of the World Bank; he

surely determines interest rates for our loans, the cost of loans, and all the rest. Besides that, he is the primary employer who administers all the jobs in the world of cheap labor.

This departure, then, is a departure from an assured, secure existence that has a liberal food supply. There is a curious note in the exodus narrative that is mostly overlooked. Three times it is reported that as the slaves left Egypt, they took with them some silver and gold that belonged to Pharaoh (Exod 3:21-22; 11:2; 12:35-36). We can imagine the slaves rushing in to the royal dining room as the plagues struck Pharaoh's house and appropriating some of the silverware; they did not leave empty-handed. I think that little note, reported three times, is a narrative joke on Pharaoh. Even so, you cannot eat silver and gold!

What they took from Pharaoh was not enough to make the departees secure. When they left the land of Pharaoh, they quickly discerned that they could not be immediately in the land of promise, any more than the end of apartheid in South Africa immediately delivered South African blacks into quick well-being. Rather, they were in the wilderness, a place without viable life supports. The "wilderness," in the narrative, is a geographical locus, out in the desert where there is no food. But it is also a mind-set of deprivation and scarcity that puts their lives at risk. We are told that not more than two verses into the wilderness in Exodus 16, they began to complain against Moses and against God (vv. 2-3). More than that, they wanted to go back to Pharaoh's fleshpots. They were ready to trade their freedom for a good meal that Pharaoh could supply. The said:

> If only we had died by the hand of the Lord in the land of Egypt when we sat by the fleshpots and ate our full of bread. (Exod 16:3)

Or a little later:

> If only we had meat to eat! We remember the fish we used to eat in Egypt for nothing, the cucumbers, the melons, the leeks, the onions, and the garlic; but now our strength is dried up, and there is nothing at all but this manna to look at. (Num 11:4-6)

But they could also remember that the bread they ate in Egypt was "the bread of affliction" (see Deut 16:3; 1 Kgs 22:27). It was the bread of quarreling and humiliation; every bite of it reminded them that they were slaves. They were the cheap labor without good health care coverage; it turns out that the bread they ate in the fleshpots tasted bitter, even if it was supplied to them in a reliable way.

As they lingered in the wilderness in their grumbling after a few days, a strange thing happened to them. They woke up in the morning and they saw a "fine flakey substance" all around on the ground (Exod 16:14). They were puzzled and they said, "What is it?" (v. 15). That question in Hebrew is *mān-hû'*, from which we get the term "manna." Thus there is new bread from God that is called "What is it?" They wondered and it turned out to be wonder bread. It was given bread, not by Pharaoh but by God from heaven, from the creator of the heavens and the earth.

Now this is a fanciful story, this business about bread from heaven. That bread and that narrative are both "flakey," and some thought such bread was not a good tradeoff from Pharaoh's reliable bread supply. It is, however, gift bread; it attests to the claim that those who run the risk of departure from Pharaoh find themselves strangely sustained by bread from other sources that enact the goodness and generosity of God. It turns out that God is the provider beyond the provisions of Pharaoh. More than that, there was enough for everyone: some took a little, some took a lot, all had enough (v. 18). They could not store it up because stored bread would replicate the hoarding policies of Pharaoh that lead to new waves of abuse, as we now witness in large concentrations of bread. But there was enough for the day because God's good gifts are given to those who pray for daily bread.

It was not different with Jesus. We are told these strange narratives of Jesus. He came upon a hungry crowd in the wilderness. And as soon as we read "wilderness," we see that Jesus is reenacting in his own life the manna story for his own time and context. We are told twice that he took bread, he blessed it, he broke it, and he gave it to the hungry ones (Mark 6:41; 8:6). He conducted a communion service right there in the wilderness. Holy communion, whenever we eat such bread that is not the bread of affliction, is an act of witness and defiance. The ones who depart Pharaoh no longer depend on the bread of affliction; they are nourished by the abundance of God that is real bread and real wine and real food for real bodies that live in real community.

It is no wonder that Jesus tells his disciples to travel light. Do not take too much stuff with you, "no purse, no bag, no sandals" (Luke 10:4). Travel light, and have authority and transformative power. Bring too much stuff and you will be immobilized as was Pharaoh. This is a most remarkable teaching that we have to learn yet again in a consumer society. When we are loaded with stuff, stuff that Pharaoh wants to give us, we lose our freedom and our capacity for courage and risk and venture. Pharaoh prefers that we be burdened down. But the ones who have departed Pharaoh have always traveled light, and have discovered that the gifts of Pharaoh are not needed when there are the gifts of the God of the promise who presides over the wilderness.

It was not different for Martin. If you have ever been to the King Center in Atlanta, what strikes one is that he did not have much: a couple books, a worn-out robe, a pair of glasses, and not much more. He traveled light, unencumbered by Pharaoh, not beholden to the system, and so free for his obedience to his vocation of freedom.

I do not need to tell you, do I, that since the days of Martin, before most of you were born, we now have much more stuff to carry along that seems indispensible to us, more electronic stuff of every kind, more phones, more computers, more iPods, more equipment, more technology, more surveillance, more weapons, more oil, more consumer goods, more stuff that makes life busy and complicated, more violence, more spectator sports, more advertising, more to keep the engine of Pharaoh running prosperous among us. I would not imagine you would give it up. Except that the trajectory of freedom keeps inviting us to travel light, to be unburdened, to be agile and on the move, and to make sure that the stuff on which we rely is not finally in possession of us.

4. The fourth question left for us by Moses and Martin is, "How shall we live once we have departed Pharaoh?" Conduct in Pharaoh's regime consists in conformity, production, and success. It all boils down to meeting quotas, beating deadlines, making bricks, becoming number one, being the best, having more, staying young and beautiful. It is a way of life that commits one to endless anxiety because one is never on top of the heap in any safe way. More than that, it is clear that Pharaoh intends us to remain anxious because anxious people are more easily persuaded and readily administered. Thus Pharaoh keeps summoning us, on orange alert, to be afraid, to be very afraid. Be afraid of bombs and attack. Be afraid of failure. Be afraid of not being on top of the heap.

But the summons to anxiety is not an adequate mode of conduct or life. The whole point of departure from Pharaoh is to exit his kingdom of anxiety. So Moses led his people, through the wilderness, to Mount Sinai. There they scuttled Pharaoh's commandments to make bricks for the regime and there they received other commandments, ten of them. The Ten Commandments are not rules that exist in a vacuum. They are, rather, an alternative to Pharaoh's commandments and so are a mandate for a different kind of life in the world. The commandments affirm God in God's holiness in a way that keeps everything else in our lives penultimate and not worthy of our worship. The commandments affirm that our neighbors are ends and not means, so that the prohibitions against killing and stealing and committing adultery are protections for neighbors who are not to be violated by our seductive desires.

I suggest that two of the "Big Ten" might be peculiarly important in our present moment as they were important to Martin. At the center of the commandments is the one on Sabbath keeping. Sabbath keeping is the discipline of breaking the pressure of the rat race and being in a receptive mode for the gifts that God wants to give. Sabbath is the visible reminder that our lives do not consist in production and consumption, in working and controlling, and having our way. Rather our lives consist in yielding to what is larger and deeper than ourselves and in being on the receiving end of life-making good gifts. There are no Sabbaths in Pharaoh's regime. There are no Sabbaths in the rat race of greedy anxiety. There are no Sabbaths in the endless round of addictions of shopping and spectator sports. The mandate of Sinai is to live differently.

At the end of the Ten Commandments is this tenth one: "Thou shalt not covet." The commandment does not concern petty acts of envy; rather it is concerned with an acquisitive society that always desires more and creates false desires for more, a desire that drives the consumer economy and eventually the aggressions of the military in the quest for more.

As Moses summoned the departees at Sinai to live differently, he called them to economic justice. His great work in the book of Deuteronomy is all about justice for widows and orphans and other vulnerable persons in society who lack normal legal protections (Deut 24:17-22). In that teaching Moses is concerned for the poor, for the reshaping of the economy, and for the practice of the economic good of all the neighbors that interrupts the predatory practices of Pharaoh (Deut 15:1-18). The long-term intent of Moses is now called "The Common Good," a community that takes neighborly form.[4]

And of course Jesus summons his disciples to a different life in the world. He invited his followers out beyond the anxiety generated by Rome. He said to them:

> You cannot serve God and wealth. (Matt 6:24)

You cannot have it both ways. You cannot rely on God's goodness and at the same time participate in an economy of savage greed. And then he observed in rather innocent fashion that God, the Heavenly Father, supplies what is needed by us, even as God supplies what is needed by the birds and the flowers. The mandate is to depart the anxiety and live in the friendliness of God's generosity.

And then, as you know, he delivered his ultimate mandate for an alternative life: "Love one another" (John 13:34). Be committed to the neighbor, not in maudlin ways but by creating common life for an equitable arrangement of goods, power, and access. In all of this Jesus echoes Moses.

Moses and Jesus imagine the world differently organized. And of course Martin did as well. Martin was not a romantic. He knew that economic greed and military aggressiveness and abuse of the environment make a good life impossible. By his life, he invited those after him to invest in the difference, to live as neighbors for the neighborhood, to recognize that personal well-being depends upon having policies, structures, and procedures that protect the neighborhood from the distorting power of greed.

Thus from these three—Moses, Jesus, and Martin—we get this:

1. Dream.
2. Depart.
3. Travel light with easy bread.
4. Live for the neighborhood.

II

Consider then the world in which we may act out the mandate of Moses that is the mandate of Jesus that is the mandate of Martin. The world is as it was when Martin was assassinated . . . only more so. He saw that the world was shaped by deep *discrimination* that was powered by *fear* and that was enacted by *violence.* When we consider that triad of qualities of the system left to us, it is still a regime of *discrimination*, *fear*, and *violence*. For good reason, Pharaoh from ancient Egypt is an adequate representative of that system of discrimination, fear, and violence.

It is Pharaoh who discriminated against the Hebrew slaves, the term "Hebrew" being a sociological term for those left outside the benefits of the system, cast in the role of cheap labor. And now the force of such discrimination is powerful among us. It takes the form of racial and ethnic exclusion. But as Martin saw clearly, the deeper discrimination is economic; the rich have more and more advantages and the poor are consigned to hopelessness, cast in a role of disadvantage from which they are not likely to be emancipated. Our government has been occupied by corporate wealth all the way to the court system. The outcome of such systemic discrimination is more and more cheap labor in the service of more and more accumulation and concentration of wealth. Thus the urge to destroy the power of labor unions that are a line of resistance against such predation.

The system has a deep stake in fostering fear, so that genuine social interaction and the formation of community become increasingly difficult. The National Security State that supervises our common life wants us to stay deeply fearful and endlessly anxious in a way that produces conformity. That same system offers an endless agenda of sports and shopping, so that eventually there is neither will nor energy left for critical thought or courageous discernment.

That system of anxiety and fear, moreover, is fully prepared for violence, violence against the poor in the form of tax and banking arrangements, violence against racial and ethnic minorities in the form of wholesale imprisonment, making prisons a private for-profit enterprise, violence against the outsider so that the outsider is unwelcome and disqualified from anything except the lowest status in society.

That system of fear, discrimination, and violence, like the ancient system of Pharaoh, is totalizing.[5] It intends to possess all power, to administer all usable knowledge, and to guarantee the only acceptable meanings for public life. That system moreover, like Pharaoh's ancient system, is legitimated and blessed by civil religion that reduces faith to slogans, so that the God of the gospel is reduced to patriotic mantras.

Well, do you think I overstate or engage in hyperbole? One need only "do the numbers" and one can see the willful transfer of wealth from the middle class to the elite urban class, all in a legal way, all truly American, a recipe for social failure that ends in a toxic social order.

That is, the system, now much advanced beyond the scale of Martin's time, is the same system that could not tolerate him. And we, on this day of remembering, are to consider what he was doing. Well,

He was dreaming,

He was departing,

He was traveling light with easy bread,

He was living in obedience for the neighborhood.

That is what he did. He stands in the grand tradition of those who have refused the totalizing system of Pharaoh, who had the will and the courage and the energy to imagine what life could possibly be like outside the system. Like old Moses, he dared to imagine life outside the system because he was committed to the God of freedom and justice and compassion who rejected the totalizing system of Pharaoh.

So Moses had to be abused by Pharaoh before he could leave;

So Jesus had to be executed by the Roman system that would not tolerate his refusal to worship Caesar.

So Martin had to be eliminated by a system that could not bear his dangerous dream.

But that is, as the Bible makes clear, the true shape of the historical process. It is always the absolutizing system that is disrupted, now and then, at the behest of God. And that leaves us, in the wake of Martin, to consider, always again, our place in the totalizing system, and to reflect on our capacity for an alternative that sometimes comes at us as the winds of God blow differently.

It occurs to me that the entire enterprise of higher education is not simply to bestow skills for a job in the system, though there is that, to be sure. But beyond that, there is in higher education a summons to critical thought and to self-awareness about social possibility, not to be labeled as a functionary of the system but to be called otherwise to a life of freedom and justice.

As Martin understood, life in the system is a dangerous business. It is dangerous, on the one hand, if we conform, as our human spirit will shrivel. It is dangerous, on the other hand, if we dissent, because dissent is not welcomed. Except that the dissenters are very often allied with God and end in joy!

It turns out that the agenda of Martin is contemporary for us. It turns out that the ancient exodus story is written and remembered in order to be performed and reperformed here and now by such as us.

Michael Walzer, the great contemporary Jewish political philosopher, has written a book on the exodus narrative.[6] In his book he judges that the exodus narrative has been the taproot of every serious social revolution in modern history, including the revolutions in France, the United States, Russia, and China. He ends his book with this stunning awareness:

—first, that wherever you live, it is probably Egypt;

—second, that there is a better place, a world more attractive, a promised land;

—and third, that "the way to the land is through the wilderness." There is no way to get from here to there except by joining together and marching.[7]

Martin, I think, would have us consider Walzer's last line, which declares that we can only get to the dream land of shalom by marching. So his marches. His march in Selma, and in Chicago, and in DC and finally in Memphis. And after him, Mandela and Tutu. We have sung, "We shall overcome." They sang, "We are marching in the light of God." So there is marching.

Marching by being on the street. Marching by being in the library and reading and studying and learning. Marching by growing into maturity as a justice-caring adult. Marching by deciding where to put your body and how to use your body in the great, continuing contest for truth and justice. Martin is a recent voice and a recent body among those who marched, who said by their talk and by their walk,

Free at last,
Free at last,
Thank God almighty, free at last.

His cadences echo among us, especially on this day of remembering. If we listen, we can sense the beat. We notice our feet pulsing to march, and we imagine the freedom and justice that will come in no other way, his way:

To dream,

To depart,

To travel light with easy bread,

To live in obedience for the neighborhood.

16

SLOW WISDOM

It was very late in the seventh century BCE for the ancient city of Jerusalem. It was very late, only a few years before the destruction of the city when its walls were breached, the temple destroyed, the king deported along with the royal family, and the political state of Judah ended.

It was very late for the ancient city of Jerusalem because the city was being devoured by greedy corruption, of which the poet Jeremiah could say,

> From the least to the greatest of them,
>   everyone is greedy for unjust gain;
> and from prophet to priest,
>   everyone deals falsely.
> They have treated the wound of my people carelessly,
>   saying "Peace, peace,"
>   when there is no peace.
> They acted shamefully, they committed abomination;
>   yet they were not ashamed;
>   they did not know how to blush. (Jer 6:13-15)

It was very late for the ancient city of Jerusalem because the city was under threat at the hands of the aggressive Babylonian armies, of which the poet Jeremiah has God say:

> I am going to bring upon you
>   a nation from far way, O house of Israel, says the LORD.
> It is an enduring nation,
>   it is an ancient nation,

> a nation whose language you do not know,
>   nor can you understand what they say.
> Their quiver is like an open tomb;
>   all of them are mighty warriors.
> They shall eat up your harvest and your food;
>   they shall eat up your sons and your daughters;
> they shall eat up your flocks and your herds;
>   they shall eat up your vines and your fig trees;
> they shall destroy with the sword
>   your fortified cities in which you trust. (Jer 5:15-17)

This is only poetry. And the poet does not even name the coming enemy evoked by the will of God. The description of "a language you do not know" that will "eat up" all that you have sounds like al-Qaeda; but it is likely, in context, Babylon.

More than identifying greedy corruption and external threat, the poetic tradition of Jeremiah dares to connect the two; *because* of greedy corruption, *therefore* the enemy threat; the God who presides over the historical process, in prophetic imagination, connects and enacts what we would analyze differently. The outcome of such odd reasoning is that *internal antineighborliness* yields *external risk and danger.*

I

It is very late in Jerusalem, according to prophetic anticipation, and if one were such a poet, if one were Jeremiah, what would one say after the poetry about greedy exploitation and after the poetry of external threat dispatched by holy resolve? Well, this is what the poet Jeremiah says in the midst of that lateness:

> Do not let the wise boast in their wisdom, do not let the mighty boast in their might, do not let the wealthy boast in their wealth. (Jer 9:23)

The poet focuses on the great triad of control and pride, the three facets of having one's way in the world: might, wisdom, and wealth.

- *Might* here means military force (*gebûrâ*), and we all know about that, the capacity to control markets and natural resources.
- *Wealth* means the capacity to manage capital and impose requirements and restraints and leverage on all the others who live

outside the constituency, so that the whole of the global economy is ordered to flow toward us.

But then *wisdom*. We had not expected "wisdom" to come along with might and wealth, especially because our theme in this conference is wisdom and the work of the university is wisdom. Who can speak negatively of wisdom when we remember our great intellectual inheritance from the Greeks? But of course when wisdom is situated amid might and wealth, something decisive happens to wisdom. And of course that is what has happened among us. We have understood with Bacon that "knowledge is power," and we have transposed wisdom into knowledge that could control. That strange interplay between wisdom and knowledge brought the gift of the great scientific revolution in Bacon's time and in its wake the great technological advances that have moved toward control that is never disinterested.

And before we knew it, Walter Isaacson and Evan Thomas wrote *The Wise Men*, which studies six titanic figures who have managed U.S. foreign policy with Niebuhrian "critical realism" and have produced the abiding superpower, ample wisdom, ample might, ample wealth in order to be the chosen race in the modern world.[1] Perhaps inevitably the great universities have signed on with that wisdom and have entered into compacts of wisdom that brought with them to the university the wealth of research grants and the power of connectedness.

And now we are sobered, as we are in this consultation, needing to take a deep breath concerning the way of Enlightenment wisdom/knowledge to which we have been pledged. That "wisdom," which is what Isaacson and Thomas call it, has led to immense power and wealth. But it has led as well to

the sad picture of Lyndon Johnson, in his last days concerning Vietnam, with his head in his hands, completely exasperated about the ineffective power over which he presided;

the verdict of the brothers Bundy, McGeorge and William, architects of the war who could admit in rare moments of retrospective self-criticism, "we were not as good as we thought we were"[2]; they may stand as an epitome of the hubris that has driven policy enwrapped in ideology;

the departure of the Wise Men from the White House after conferring with the president about Vietnam and without a clue of what to do next;

and then the oil spill and the Japanese nuclear crisis and the widespread suspicion that our technology has outrun our capacity to manage it or even to think clearly;

and us now with deep anxiety that seeks scapegoats, along with zeal to dispose of "the other" among us, if necessary, by violence.

And the poet says,

> Do not boast about your might;
> Do not boast about your wisdom;
> Do not boast about your wealth.

II

But what then? Well, if we take the antithesis of "might, wisdom, wealth," we might come up with a triad of "weakness, foolishness, and poverty." And of course that is what we get in Jesus of Nazareth:

> For God's foolishness is wiser than human wisdom, and God's weakness is stronger than human strength. (1 Cor 1:25)

> For you know the generous act of our Lord Jesus Christ, that though he was rich, yet for your sakes he became poor, so that by his poverty you might become rich. (2 Cor 8:9)

It turns out that the life of the Crucified One, in his body, exhibits the counterpoint to the great seduction of Jerusalem. He is the *embodiment of weakness*, as he stood vulnerable before imperial authority. He is the *embodiment of foolishness*, as Terry Eagleton characterizes him:

> Jesus, unlike most responsible American citizens, appears to do no work, and is accused of being a glutton and a drunkard. He is presented as homeless, propertyless, celibate, peripatetic, socially marginal, disdainful of kinsfolk, without a trade, a friend of outcasts and pariahs, averse to material possessions, without fear for his own safety, careless about purity regulations, critical of traditional authority, a thorn in the side of the establishment, and a scourge of the rich and powerful. . . . The morality Jesus preaches is reckless, extravagant, improvident,

> over-the-top, a scandal to actuaries and a stumbling block to real estate agents; forgive your enemies, give away your cloak as well as your coat, turn the other cheek, love those who insult you, walk the extra mile, take no thought for tomorrow.[3]

He is the *embodiment of poverty*, nowhere to lay his head, no property or even health care.

The remembered Jesus sits amid our posturing and reminds us that the great imperial triad of might, wisdom, and wealth, a triad celebrated in ancient Israel since Solomon, never delivers the security or the happiness that it promises.

III

But I will not linger over that countertriad of *weakness, foolishness*, and *poverty* that waits silently for us. Because that triad is too outrageous and too remote from our business at hand. Instead, I will consider the countertriad that Jeremiah, in his poetry, lines out. His triad is fully congruent with that of Jesus, but it has a kind of available realism that is lacking in Jesus of Nazareth, a realism that permits people like us at least to take it seriously:

> But let those who boast boast in this, that they understand and know me, that I am the LORD; I act with steadfast love, justice, and righteousness in the earth, for in these things I delight, says the LORD. (Jer 9:24)

This countertriad is rooted in the reality of the Lord, the God of Israel, who is celebrated as the great deliverer from slavery and the creator of heaven and earth. And, says the poet, even in the midst of greedy corruption and external threat, some know. They are the ones who boast of my stuff; they know me. They have entered into covenant with me. They have acknowledged my will and my purpose, and they understand me; they can factor out the implications of who I am and what I will. That is what makes the tradition endlessly compelling. They are the ones who give Jerusalem trouble through the night and buoyancy through the day. What they know and understand, says the poet, is that:

> I act with *steadfast love, justice*, and *righteousness;* I delight in those things.

And because I delight in them and am pleased when they appear, this people and this city are under mandate to live them out. Out of the deep covenantal tradition of Israel, the poet offers a *triad of fidelity* that stands counter to the *triad of control* that was destroying Israel.

It is very late in Jerusalem but nobody knows if it is too late. Sometimes the poets, including Jeremiah, said it was too late, too late for the Ethiopians to change their skin, too late for the leopard to change its spots, too late for the Solomonic regime to repent of its might, wisdom, and wealth, too late because of the internal corruption and the external threat (Jer 13:23). At other times, however, these same poets including Jeremiah knew that it was late, but not too late. The urgent task was to move the body politic, with its marching armies and its blessing priests and its cunning scribes, away from the triad of control toward the triad of covenantal fidelity. And when that move is made, a new historical possibility might yet be available; but it is very late.

The university sits in a society where it is very late. The university sits in a society that is in large part committed to the triad of *might, wisdom*, and *wealth*; and in some measure, the university, like the church, has colluded with that triad to its great benefit. The lateness of hour, I suggest, invites the university, like the wayward son in a far country, to come to its senses, to remember its home and its belonging and its vocation, to live alertly and knowingly in a very late moment amid these competing triads of control and fidelity, knowing that both are powerful and compelling and that both are indispensible. But because the triad of control has carried the day in our society without much critical reflection, it may be the great tilt of the university to give privilege and priority to the triad of fidelity that has nearly disappeared from the public face of our society as it had disappeared in the ancient city of Jerusalem. It will be my purpose here to line out, in as many ways as I can think of, *the interface of these two triads* that concerned the poet and that might usefully concern us in a society where it is very late.

With our conference theme of "wisdom," we engage two competing notions of wisdom that will yield two very different worlds: the wisdom of Enlightenment control, on the one hand, and that other ancient wisdom that is rooted in "the fear of the Lord," on the other hand. The wisdom of control we may call *fast wisdom*, wisdom that assumes we are free to manage and shape and administer and master the world according to our own interests, and the wisdom of fidelity I will call *slow wisdom*, wisdom that waits and watches and receives and yields and hopes.[4] Fast wisdom, now paced by electronic urgency, concerns knowing and having and possessing and controlling. Slow wisdom is about serious, engaged relatedness that simply will not be hurried. It matters decisively if the world is "figured" by fast-paced control that breeds greed and resentment or by slow-paced wisdom that hosts complexity and refuses sound bites. The task of the university, I suggest, is to mediate and adjudicate between these triads, and by such mediation and adjudication, to expose the risks and hazards of the triad of control that has, I submit, brought our society to the brink of default that is not only financial but also moral. The ancient city was in a moral default that could not be sustained. It is no wonder that the old poets, given how late it was, wondered if it was too late, or only very late.

IV

Here then, in eight phrasings, is my exposition of the impact and future-generating potential of these two triads,

1. *The triad of control: might, wisdom, and wealth;*
2. The triad of fidelity: steadfast love, justice, and righteousness.

In each case I will, as you would expect, tilt toward the latter that is no doubt, in my judgment, the urgent challenge we face in our belated time.

1. The triad of fidelity focuses on the body, whereas the triad of control focuses, characteristically, on abstractions of power and possession. The couplet of "justice and righteousness" (two of the members of that triad) are concerned with the ways in which the resources of the community are mobilized for the bodily reality of persons and the healthy reality of the body politic. The materiality of the biblical tradition has to do with the quotidian dimension of the vulnerable, the widow, the orphan, the immigrant, and the poor, and the wherewithal to sustain a common life of dignity and well-being.[5] Thus the indictment of the ancient city:

> they have grown fat and sleek.
> The know no limits in deeds of wickedness;
> they do not judge with justice
> the cause of the orphan, to make it prosper,
> and they do not defend the right of the needy. (Jer 5:28)

And the same poet with a summons to possibility:

> If you truly amend your ways and your doings, if you truly act justly with one another, if you do not oppress the alien, the orphan, and the

> widow or shed innocent blood in this place, and if you do not go after other gods to your own hurt, then I will dwell with you in this place.
> (Jer 7:5-7)

Justice concerns seeing to the bodily needs of the vulnerable by ordering the body politic differently. "Righteousness" is weighing in for the well-being of the community. The poetic tradition always cares about food, clothing, and housing. The materiality of the triad of these ancient poets refuses the requirements of "ideas, concepts, theories, and ideologies" that draw energy away from reality of those who stand in front of us. The flight to abstraction is an endless seduction of those in control, so that social reality can be reduced to a program or a budget that depends always upon euphemism to hide the bodily reality of those next door. The seduction of the university, not unlike the government and the church, is to traffic in abstraction, and the challenge of the university is to bring the energy back to that quotidian reality, so that resources and passion may be mobilized differently.

2. The triad of fidelity focuses on the neighborhood, whereas the triad of control is drawn to the club. The "club" is a staging ground and device for exclusion, so that one need deal only with those one chooses, with those most like us. It is a mark of privilege that brings with it the sense of knowing best and being right. It proceeds by exclusion to screen out the other, variously women or blacks and surely the poor, and of course the university, the "best ones," have been no more hospitable than the clubs with their exclusionary quotas.

But the neighborhood takes in all of us who move up and down the street. There is an egalitarian assumption about the legitimacy of all of its members, and the sharing of resources to which all are entitled. Historically, of course, without romanticizing, a rural community, before social stratification, acute division of labor, and the development of surplus value, was a more or less egalitarian community (with the notable exception of the doctor who lived in the big house). But the urban reality of social stratification, the acute division of labor, and the accumulation of surplus wealth has largely destroyed that sense of neighborly egalitarianism.

And of course the university is deeply enmeshed with that crisis. For admission is a ticket to entitlement. We can no longer have affirmative action, the urban elite court has ruled, so that the privileged who come from better schools are better prepared for application and so, on the basis of socially constructed "merit," occupy the space and the fellowships. We produce a class of "manager of social symbols" (of which I am a member), marked out at best by only a vague memory of real "work." The process of privilege and entitlement evokes a stream of influence that eventually culminates in might and wealth based on a certain kind of wisdom. And of course such a trajectory of control will hide behind a hundred defenses of pedigree, certification, gated communities, tenure, and all the rest.

But the cadences of steadfast love concern "the neighbors" who are bound together in common need, common resources, and common destiny, pledged to common goods that will not give credence to these enduring distinctions. I am most taken with the arguments and attestations of Peter Block and John McKnight, my new colleagues, who focus on the mobilization of the neighborhood, by which they mean quite concretely the folk on the block.[6] Their mode of "Asset-Based Community Development" is committed to the proposition that the neighborhood, rightly mobilized, has all the assets necessary for the sustenance of a healthy existence. Their repeated insistence is that it is more adequate to rely on the wisdom of a neighbor than it is to rely on the wisdom of an expert, so that again we come face-to-face with competing modes of wisdom.

Of course I am aware that every college and university has endless program opportunities through which students can participate in and experience the neighborhood on the ground. But we all know, as students know, that such opportunities are marginal and incidental, and at best extraneous to the real requirements and real payouts of education.

But we have, in very recent time, witnessed the failure of the club. We have witnessed it in bail outs in which ordinary tax payers have footed the bill for the privileged who go right on with their excessive privilege. And it will not do! Thus I suspect that a shift of emphasis from one triad to the other is a deep and systemic piece of work in the university, the emergent awareness that the might, wisdom, and wealth of the club has in fact failed, and we fall back on the wisdom of the neighborhood that finds might in vulnerability and health in generosity, vulnerability and generosity that are remote from the culture of the club, which is prone to deny vulnerability and is organized against generosity.

3. The triad of fidelity is deeply situated in the tradition whereas the triad of control traffics in the reasoning of syllogism and memo. Syllogisms reflect controlling reasoning that yields a kind of thin certitude about which there is no argument and nothing of steadfast love. Memos

are unambiguous notes of power, as witness David's memo to Joab that was a death sentence for Uriah (2 Sam 11:14-15) and Jezebel's memo that was a death sentence for Naboth (1 Kgs 21:8-10). Such writing as control is knowingly reflected in Steinbeck's *The Grapes of Wrath* in which the Okies observe that whenever the man with the clipboard writes something down, you own less. Of course that process of writing memos continues in our time—notices from the bank, and so on—all of whose writers would like to be neighborly but whose rules preclude it.

Since the seventeenth century, such reasoning has declared war on tradition.[7] And now that assault on tradition continues in the reduction of reality to sound bites, in the reduction of the praise of the church to "praise hymns," and in the delete button that can erase into innocent amnesia. But communities of steadfast love, justice, and righteousness, by contrast, have long memories and deep hopes and do not believe that instantaneous satisfaction is an adequate displacement for remembering and anticipating.

In the tradition of Jeremiah, the tradition is called "the way":

> Let me go to the rich
> and speak to them:
> surely they know the way of the LORD,
> the law of their God. (Jer 5:5)

> And then, if they will diligently learn the ways of my people, to swear by my name, "As the LORD lives" . . . then they shall be built up in the midst of my people. (Jer 12:16)

> See, I am setting before you the way of life and the way of death. (Jer 21:8)

The latter text is a deliberate echo of Deuteronomy 30:15-20, the way of life and death, the way of blessing and curse. Broadly construed, the way refers to the Torah of the Lord, not only commandments but also instruction and lore. The way is voiced at the beginning of the Psalter:

> Happy are those
> who do not follow the advice of the wicked,
> or take the path that sinners tread,
> or sit in the seat of scoffers;
> but their delight is in the law (*tôrâ*) of the LORD,
> and on his law (*tôrâ*) they meditate day and night. (Ps 1:1-2)

The "way" (*tôrâ*) is the entire legacy of being bound in covenantal fidelity and covenantal obedience to the creator who has ordered the world so that it will not be mocked. This order provides that personal practice and public policy in the life of Israel will cohere with the transcendent purposes of God.

The force of Torah aims to resist autonomy wherein one imagines unfettered freedom without responsibility or restraint, freedom to seize what belongs to another because of more power and freedom to exploit the neighbor who may be vulnerable. In the end, the Torah is Israel's testimony to the covenantal shape of created existence. The world is organized according to steadfast love. The economy is to be engaged according to neighborly justice, which begins with "Thou shalt not covet" (Exod 20:17). The political culture is to be shaped by righteousness that is the work of the common good. The entire purpose of liberal arts is to help the students situate themselves in a summoning tradition that refuses the autonomy of Enlightenment reason with its concomitant of consumer seduction.

The triad of fidelity eschews the seduction of the reasoning of autonomy; it also fends off the countertemptation of absolutism that is so powerful in our society. It refuses absolutism through the ongoing disputatious practice of interpretation. Thus the book of Deuteronomy, the great traditioning background of the poet Jeremiah, is essentially a model and early practice of hermeneutics:

> Not with our ancestors did the LORD make this covenant, but with us, who are all of us here alive today. (Deut 5:3)

The old Torah cannot just be read. Nor can there be recourse, as we are now wont, to "original intention," for such so-called originalism is a complete misconstrual of the nature of tradition. Thus it is the great work of the university to nurture responsible, wise, competent hermeneutists who refuse the easy relativism of popular culture and who refuse, with equal resolve, the temptation to absolutism, whether that of God or country or sect or system. The tradition requires interpretive agility that knows that the memory is a beginning point but never a conclusion, an interpretive assumption made clear by the rabbi who taught, "You have heard it said of old, but I say unto you." Rightly understood, the tradition is always being reformulated in radical contemporaneity, but with deep rootage that is honored and not deleted by interpretation. The ancient paths, the paths trod in the neighborhood and often overridden in the club, give thickness to the human process, a thickness without which we cannot live for very long.

4. The triad of fidelity attends to pain whereas the triad of control specializes in numbness. The interface of pain and numbness is poignantly voiced in the sobbing of failed Jerusalem:

> Is it nothing to you, all you who pass by?
>   Look and see
> if there is any sorrow like my sorrow
>   which was brought on me,
> which the LORD has inflicted
>   on the day of his fierce anger. (Lam 1:12)

The city voices its loss and grief but then notices that bypassers, the other nations, do not acknowledge. Is it nothing to you? The triad of control, like the priest or the Levite on the way to Jericho, in its numbness, does not notice. It passes by on the other side. It has faster errands to run. It has reduced pain to a statistic, suffering to the cost of doing business. The practice of abusive power, exploitative economics, devastating militarism, and the disturbance of the vulnerable earth must continue, even if the pain therein produced requires denial, all in the interest of might and wealth. The denial is based on the race to domination, and we cannot afford to linger very long in the hurt.

When such denial is pushed far enough, it becomes numbness, the frozenness of the human capacity to stand in solidarity. Robert Lifton is our master teacher of what he has termed "psychic numbing," the shutting down of emotional depth in order to survive; circumstance requires that we "quit feeling."[8] Lifton has studied, variously, Hiroshima and Auschwitz and Vietnam veterans and the anxiety over nuclear threat during the Cold War. He devised the phrase "psychic numbing" to describe the strategy of staying sane in a world of insane violence.

The alternative to such numbing is to hear and touch and honor the pain that arises from what Lifton calls "atrocity-producing" policies, systems, and attitudes. It is pain that lives beneath the surface of the world of might, wisdom, and wealth. The triad of fidelity, perhaps, begins in that moment at the start of the exodus narrative. The slaves eventually cry out. They cry out because they suffer abuse at the hands of Pharaoh, a vigorous practitioner of might, wisdom, and wealth. They cry out; and then there is this holy response:

> God heard their groaning, and God remembered his covenant with Abraham, Isaac, and Jacob. God looked upon the Israelites, and God took notice of them. (Exod 2:24-25)

The wonder of this triad is that God hears, God notices, God remembers, God witnesses. God acts in solidarity. The story of faith is the story of divine solidarity with human suffering, an alliance against the drama of control. In that instant of holy notice, the steadfast love of God is evoked. God bends God's self toward the suffering of Israel and, derivatively, toward the suffering of the world. And then God acts in justice and righteousness to sustain steadfast love, an act that challenges systemic covetousness and that terminates the totalizing regime of Pharaoh who is the biblical model for numbness.

But of course this triad of fidelity does not remain at a religious level. We can trace the cry and the holy response as it traverses the world of might and wealth. Just after the Ten Commandments, Moses warns Israel about psychic numbness that receives an economic articulation:

> You shall not wrong or oppress a resident alien, for you were aliens in the land of Egypt. You shall not abuse any widow or orphan. If you do abuse them, when they cry out to me, I will surely heed their cry; my wrath will burn, and I will kill you with the sword, and your wives shall become widows and your children orphans. If you lend money to my people, to the poor among you, you shall not deal with them as a creditor; you shall not exact interest from them. If you take your neighbor's cloak in pawn, you shall restore it before the sun goes down; for it may be your neighbor's only clothing to use as cover; in what else shall that person sleep? And if your neighbor cries out to me, I will listen, for I am compassionate. (Exod 22:21-27)

These two laws focus on the vulnerable who are always our primary candidates for pain. The first law is a generic protection of immigrants, widows, and orphans. The second is a specific warning about extorting the poor with excessive interest on loans. Both laws anticipate that the vulnerable, when abused, will cry out. They will cry out and the totalizing system of numbness and denial cannot silence them. In the first, it is anticipated that God will hear the cry of the abused and will retaliate. In the second, it is anticipated that God will hear and have compassion. Either way, it is the attentiveness of God that will subvert the ordered world of numbness. The future is open to the God who is not numbed.

The university runs the risk of alliance with the interests of might, wisdom, and wealth, a practice of knowledge "from above" that treats the cry as a necessary inconvenience. It is possible, however, that the university may be a venue in which the long history of the subversive cry of pain is hosted, so that the long literature of truth and hurt is received and honored as a contemporary script. Preoccupation with the cry is a natural in the humanities; but it is no less urgent in the social sciences, in economics, and in the earth sciences where the earth itself cries out about the abuse. Given this interface, the question that might haunt the university as it might haunt us all is this: "Is it nothing to you, all you who pass by?" The prophet Amos provides an inventory of the kinds of self-preoccupations that narcotize and keep us busy not noticing:

> Alas for those who lie on beds of ivory,
>   and lounge on their couches,
> and eat lambs from the flock,
>   and calves from the stall,
> who sing idle songs to the sound of the harp,
>   and like David improvise on instruments of music;
> who drink wine from bowls,
>   and anoint themselves with the finest oils. (Amos 6:4-6a)

Amos offers a sketch of affluent self-indulgence. But the accent falls on the indictment that follows:

> but are not grieved over the ruin of Joseph. (v. 6b)

That is, they do not notice that society is practicing an order of death, and so to hell in a hand basket. And then the poetry voices the big, inexplicable leap in anticipation:

> They shall be the first to go into exile. (v. 7)

Those who do not notice will be the ones displaced because the cry pulses in the historical process and the numbing finally will not prevail.

5. The triad of fidelity specializes in dreams that are not held back by circumstance, whereas the triad of control takes life as a present possession to be guarded and kept to perpetuity for the entitled few. The totalizing system of those who make the rules, manage the money, administer the power, and mobilize their wisdom is evident everywhere among us. That totalizing system aims to maintain and enhance advantage over

others. The capacity to control and own to perpetuity through deregulation and by the stacking of the cards by law and by ruthless predatory management finally ends in a society that is short of social possibility. Thus it is that Pharaoh, in his totalizing sovereignty, can finally assert in an illusionary fashion:

> The Nile is my own; I made it for myself. (Ezek 29:3)

He forgets that the Nile, like every proximate source of life, is a gift that can never be possessed.

So it is with Jezebel who says to her pouting husband-king:

> Do you now govern Israel? Get up, eat some food, and be cheerful; I will give you the vineyard of Naboth the Jezreelite. (1 Kgs 21:7)

Are you not king? Are you not entitled? Do you not possess the leverage to have what you want? She imagines that the land is her gift to give to Ahab. And when she has done her nefarious manipulation, she says to her wimpish husband:

> Go, *take possession* of the vineyard of Naboth the Jezreelite, which he refused to give you for money; for Naboth is not alive, but dead. (v. 15)

And the narrator adds:

> As soon as Ahab heard that Naboth was dead, Ahab set out to go down to the vineyard of Naboth the Jezreelite, to *take possession* of it. (v. 16)

It is all about possession, what we may call "realized eschatology": that what we have is permanent, to be secured through seizure and then protected through entitlement.

And from beneath the world of possessions comes the cadence of dream. Dream is always inherently subversive of the present arrangement. The dream already intruded into the sleep of ancient Pharaoh who had everything. And then he dreamed seven lean, sickly cows and seven blighted shocks of wheat, which together signified seven lean years of famine to come (see Gen 41:1-32). No less Nebuchadnezzar, who had it all; it was during the night by the dream of a tree cut down that he was driven by his power to insanity (Dan 4:19-33). The dream was enough to destabilize the most stable of regimes.

The prophets, who do not "predict," are the voices of God's dream. They say with some frequency, "In that day . . . ," or "The days are surely coming. . . ." The day to come is a day of disarmament when they shall beat their swords into plowshares and their spears into pruning hooks (Isa 2:4); they will not learn war anymore. The days are coming when the Lord will act against all hubris:

> For the LORD of hosts has a day
> against all that is proud and lofty,
> against all that is lifted up and high;
> against all the cedars of Lebanon,
> lofty and lifted up;
> and against all the oaks of Bashan;
> against all the high mountains,
> and against all the lofty hills;
> against every high tower,
> and against every fortified wall. (Isa 2:12-15)

The days are coming, say the dreamers, and they cannot be stopped. They are powered by a holy resolve that stands outside our possession in a way that is incessantly subversive. If we trace the dream of subversion far enough, we can follow it to Martin at the Lincoln monument. He said repeatedly, "I have a dream. . . ." The reason we remember the cadences of his "Dream" speech is that we know his dream is the dream of our society writ deep; it is the dream of God for justice and righteousness and steadfast love. Like all such dreamers, Martin had no clue about how to get from here to there. He only knew that the dream had substance and force and authority, and could not be stopped. This trajectory of poets imagines that the dream is still under way, still overcoming apartheid, still working toward dignity for the weak, still demanding equity for the poor, still ensuring an end to the systemic violence that we call policy.

The university is always deciding how much it will serve the forces of possession. In a real world it must do so. But it also must do other than that and more than that because the world is not closed into present arrangements. The world does not stand still simply because we arrive at our preferred arrangement. Francis Fukuyama a while ago opined that with the fall of the Soviet Union that history had come to an end and the force of liberal democratic capitalism had ultimately prevailed.[9] But of course the dreamers know that the world does not end that way. It ends, rather, when the full drama is actualized among us:

> Go and tell John what you have seen and heard: the blind receive their sight, the lame walk, the lepers are cleansed, the deaf hear, the dead are raised, the poor have good news brought to them. (Luke 7:22)

The world is always breaking open beyond possession to dream. The dream is always violating our arrangements of power that we might discover new power from below. The dream is always breaking our wisdom with new awarenesses that arise among the lowly who generate the most poignant poetry. And we, in our entitlements, are always juggling our possessions because the dream has a bite even for us.

6. The triad of fidelity majors in imagination while the triad of control specializes in explanation. Of course we must both imagine and explain. We have known that since the great German hermeneutists, Humboldt and Dilthey. But in a world of technological reductionism and positive reason, explanation comes to contain everything. In a world of explanation, education consists in mastering the rules and procedures for linear clarity in order to get ahead in the current system. Explanation, essential as it is, in the end is a strategy for accumulation of what the system offers. And then the effort is to make it more so—more might, more wisdom, more wealth of the same kind—and life becomes an anxious pursuit of such treasure.

Imagination, by contrast, is the capacity to imagine and host and voice a world other than the one that is in front of us. In my discipline of Old Testament studies, historical criticism, important as it has been, has been a long-term German enterprise of management, containment, and accommodation, making the text fit the reason of this age. Happily, in a postcritical move, we now have ventures in Scripture study that do not force the text into an explanatory strait-jacket, but can hear that the text, in some great measure, is an act of subversive imagination that hosts and brings to voice another world, a world other than the one that is in front of us.[10] That is why preaching is so politically dangerous, and why regimes must keep a lid on Scripture. And that is why, in the end, the triad of control in our modern world has preferred historical critical approaches that keep the dangerous force of such imagination in the remote past.

But it turns out, as Michael Walzer, the great Jewish political philosopher, has seen, that the exodus narrative is not a report on an ancient emancipation.[11] It is rather is a narrative anticipation of many liberations that are yet to be acted. It turns out that Pharaoh is neither Rameses II nor Merneptah; Pharaoh is whoever sits atop the pyramid of might, wisdom, and wealth to the disadvantage of the laborers who are treated ruthlessly. It turns out that the exodus event was a divine stirring in South Africa where there was no chance against the apartheid regime, and the leadership for steadfast love had Egyptian names like Nelson and Desmond. It turns out that the script of steadfast love, justice, and righteousness that eventuates in freedom, dignity, and equity is a script that continues to be performed in bodily dramas of courage and hope.

It turns out that the manna story is not simply a report on an ancient heaven-sent miracle, though it is that. It is, in a postcolonial reading, an act of recognition that all the bread needed—Bread for the World—is not the property of the cartel that stores the grain and owns the bakery. It turns out that the only Bread for the World that will meet the hunger of humanity is broken bread, bread that has shattered the citadels of might and wealth, bread that by its abundance and its generosity refuses imperial production and elitist distribution.

Explanatory education reads backward to tell us how it was—and how it will be world without end. Imaginative education reads forward toward unthought of possibilities, not fantasy, not escapism, not denial of what is, but the complex, irrefutable surging of newness that is inherent in God's ordering of creation. It will not do much good to debate evolution. But it will do much good to notice the pulsing of new possibilities of steadfast love, justice, and righteousness that all the dogs and the surveillance and the weapons cannot stop.

Michael Walzer has written in his book on the exodus narrative:

> first, that wherever you live, it is probably Egypt;
>
> second, that there is a better place, a world more attractive, a promised land;
>
> and third, that "the way to the land is through the wilderness." There is no way to get from here to there except by joining together and marching.[12]

Walzer has offered an interpretive possibility that has been enacted many times in our own lifetime among those not enthralled by might, wisdom, and wealth. Our contemporary "marching" has run from the Freedom Rides to the Velvet Revolution to Yeltsin atop the tank and the March from Selma to the hope-filled in Cairo and among the victims of apartheid who keep singing, and now with the 99 percent on Wall Street:

> We are marching in the light of God,
> We are marching in the light of God.
> We are marching in the light of God.
> We are marching, we are marching in the light of God.[13]

But the narrative of emancipation is performed not only in the streets. It is performed wherever the rule of law tames the predators; it is evident in the Universal Declaration of Human Rights; it is enacted in government initiatives and private-sector initiatives that break the patterns of exploitation. What kind of a "school of imagination" is it that has produced such marchers, such advocates as the awesome people in the book of Acts who keep appearing before imperial authority to testify to the surge of new life that they have glimpsed in Easter? What kind of education nurtures so that explanation does not default on the possibilities of newness that have been entrusted to us? We have narrative models, but we have no blueprints because blueprints run almost immediately to explanation.

7. The triad of fidelity invites us to a vocation, whereas the triad of control envisions a career. The trajectory of might, wisdom, and wealth is all about joining the firm, fitting in, and advancing. It is about the good fortune of having someone at the club or in the admissions office saying, "You will want to look out for this young lady." Such connectedness of course is not bad, and we all would wish for it. But it is, almost invariably, an invitation to go along and get along. By contrast, a vocation, when it is authentic, is a summons outside the box, a calling from someone with deep authority who calls and summons and propels beyond one's own intention to larger purpose. And of course human history is made by those called, all the way back to Moses who was addressed from the bush.

The pressure in higher education now is all about career and practical study in order to make a good living. The university, moreover, must justify itself in terms of earning power. But of course the university at its best is not just about making a living but about making a life that is deeper and more serious than the next advancement in might and wealth.

The best case study I know for this interface of career and calling is the young Daniel, a Jew who lived amid Babylonian (or Persian or Hellenistic) might, wisdom, and wealth. He was recruited into civil service of the empire by Nebuchadnezzar, and he advanced rapidly to great influence. It is astonishing how many of his narrative episodes end with yet another imperial promotion:

> In every matter of wisdom and understanding concerning which the king inquired of them, he found them ten times better than all the magicians and enchanters in his whole kingdom. And Daniel continued there until the first year of King Cyrus. (Dan 1:20-21)

> Then the king promoted Daniel, gave him many great gifts, and made him ruler over the whole province of Babylon and chief prefect over all the wise men of Babylon. . . . Daniel remained at the king's court. (2:48-49)

> Then the king promoted Shadrach, Meshach, and Abednego in the province of Babylon. (3:30)

> Then Belshazzar gave the command, and Daniel was clothed in purple, a chain of gold was put around his neck, and a proclamation was made concerning him that he should rank third in the kingdom. (5:29)

> So this Daniel prospered during the reign of Darius and the reign of Cyrus the Persian. (6:28)

What a career! He made it big in the empire, under Nebuchadnezzar and Belshazzar, the Babylonians, and under Darius and Cyrus the Persian. What is clear, at the same time, is that Daniel's calling to be a faithful Jew in the service of the God of Heaven remained uncompromised. Thus

In chapter 1, Daniel refused imperial food so that he would not be "defiled" (1:8).

In chapter 2, even the king worships Daniel's God to whom Daniel had prayed for wisdom:

> The king said to Daniel, "Truly, your God is God of gods and Lord of kings and a revealer of mysteries, for you have been able to reveal this mystery!" (2:47)

In chapter 3, the three friends of Daniel act defiantly against the empire for the sake of their God:

> O Nebuchadnezzar, we have no need to present a defense to you in this matter. If our God whom we serve is able to deliver us from the furnace of blazing fire and out of your hand, O King, let him deliver us. But if not, be it known to you, O king,

> that we will not serve your god and we will not worship the golden statue that you have set up. (3:16-18)

In chapter 4, Nebuchadnezzar worships the God of Daniel:

> Now I, Nebuchadnezzar, praise and extol and honor the King of heaven,
> for all his works are truth,
> and his ways are just;
> and he is able to bring low
> those who walk in pride. (4:37)

In chapter 6, Darius worships the God of Daniel:

> I make a decree that in all my royal dominion people should tremble and fear before the God of Daniel. (6:26)

No doubt the intention of the Daniel narrative is to make the case that one can be a good faithful Jew and still prosper in the empire. Mutatis mutandis, one can live amid the regime of might, wisdom, and wealth but still be a practitioner of steadfast love, justice, and righteousness.

In the case of Daniel's three friends, the narrative subtly reminds us of the maintenance of an identity and a vocation that do not give into the empire. We know the three friends as Shadrach, Meshach, and Abednego. But those names that are familiar to us are names assigned to these Jews by the empire:

> The palace master gave them other names: Daniel he called Belteshazzar, Hananiah he called Shadrach, Mishael he called Meshach, and Azariah he called Abednego. (1:7)

But those are not their real, Jewish names. The preceding verse attests their real Jewish names:

> Among them were Daniel, Hananiah, Mishael, and Azariah, from the tribe of Judah. (1:6)

And those Jewish names are repeated in Daniel 2:17 as the narrator still remembers.

Thus the struggle for identity. Perhaps we might judge that these four handsome, young Jews maintained a double identity and lived a double life, imperial by day and Jewish by night, imperial in the market,

Jewish in the synagogue. Or perhaps they gave in and forgot their Jewish names and identities. Or perhaps they pretended with their career names but knew their true vocational names. Either way, the matter is complex, now as then. Either way, education may help people who struggle with an identity and a vocation. In our context, it is either the name imposed by consumer ideology or the preservation of a baptismal name assigned to make us, as we say in my church, "Sealed as Christ's own forever." Education is about name and identity, true identity and imposed identity. Clearly the names to which we answer are determined by the triad in which our life is situated: a faith identity amid steadfast love, justice, and righteousness; an empire-given identity amid might, wisdom, and wealth. The issue of identity is complex; it is clear nonetheless that education that aims only at serving the totalizing regime of wealth and might will never yield a covenantal identity that can respond outside the box to the divine impetus for mercy and compassion and generosity.

8. Finally, it is written in Psalm 19:10 concerning the truth and power of God's commandments:

> More to be desired are they than gold,
> even much fine gold;
> sweeter also than honey,
> and drippings of the honeycomb.

We may take this statement as an epitome of the pair of triads I have exposited. The psalm speaks in many synonyms of Torah—decrees, precepts, commandments, fear of the Lord, ordinances—many ways to signify the transcendent purpose of God that orders life toward well-being. This offer is "better," more desired:

> It is better than gold, even much fine gold.
>
> It is better than honey, the drippings from a honeycomb.

Imagine, thick guidance to covenantal existence, preferable to gold or honey. Typically, the proverbial saying of this verse does not say how much better or in what way better, just "more desired," more coveted, more treasured, more to be pursued.

The Torah is the sum of the triad of steadfast love, justice, and righteousness; "gold" is the quick summary of the triad of might, wisdom, and wealth. The task of nurture and socialization is to invite sustained critical reflection on choosing, amid a tradition of folk who have been making that choice forever, sometimes toward death and sometimes toward life.

V

I finish with three conclusions. First, I am in agreement (only this once) with the great U.S. theologian, Donald Rumsfeld. The Secretary of Defense famously quipped in March 2003 that there are knowns and there are unknowns. And of the unknowns, there are known unknowns and unknown unknowns. The comment is wiser than it sounds, and one may wish that Rumsfeld had taken the unknown unknowns more seriously.[14] I have been expositing two kinds of wisdom, the fast known wisdom of might, wisdom, and wealth that ends in control, and the slow unknown unknown of the mystery of God that opens reality out beyond our control and that requires a relational integrity that appears as steadfast love, justice, and righteousness. Education is the disputatious process of reflection on these two wisdoms.

Second, I have offered a list of contrasts and complements that might be supplemented by other pairs of terms concerning *slow* and *fast* wisdom:

body/abstraction,

neighborhood/club,

tradition/syllogism or memo,

pain/numbness,

dream/possession,

imagination/explanation,

vocation/career,

Torah/gold.

These several pairs are roughly synonyms, so the argument keeps coming back to the same point.

It occurred to me that these several word pairs boil down to the possibility of committed relationships of integrity in the neighborhood that make for the common good, vis-à-vis a mode of life that is indifferent or hostile to the common good.[15] Further, it occurred to me that the relational, covenantal narrative is exactly what we might best learn in kindergarten.[16] I will not pursue that, but you can factor it out. How mind-boggling to entertain the thought that what belongs properly to kindergarten continues to belong properly to the work of a serious university, namely, to sustain and evoke relational identity for the sake of the common good.

Third, the poetry of Jeremiah strikes me as profoundly contemporary, as our time, like that of the ancient city, is very short:

We, like that ancient city, are now an anxious society in which "everyone is greedy for unjust gain."

We, like that ancient city, are now a society against which comes an enduring nation whose language we do not know.

We, like that ancient city, are now a society deeply at risk. The poetic response to that risky circumstance seems to me completely pertinent now as then:

> Do not let the wise boast in their wisdom, do not let the mighty boast in their might, do not let the wealthy boast in their wealth; but let those who boast boast in this, that they understand and know me, that I am the LORD; I act with steadfast love, justice, and righteousness in the earth; for in these things I delight, says the LORD. (Jer 9:23-24)

17

BAIL OUT

So far as I know, the Bible says nothing explicit about subprime loans and the financial implications of such risky economic practice. There is a great deal, nonetheless, that the Bible has to say about a crisis such as we now face. I will comment in turn on a biblical perspective for *an analysis of the crisis* and a biblical perspective for *an alternative economic practice.*

I

While the specifics of the current market collapse are peculiarly modern, biblical perspectives are pertinent because the fundamental issues of economics—such as credit and debt, loans and interest, and the endless tension between haves and have-nots—are constant from ancient to contemporary time. We may identify three dimensions of the theological-moral foundations of the current economic crisis:

1. *Autonomy*

A sense of the isolated, self-sufficient economic individual is deeply rooted in modern rationality and comes to full expression in U.S. "individualism" that resists communitarian connectedness and that imagines the individual person to be the primary unit of social reality. Such an individual is completely autonomous, owes no one anything, is accountable to no one, and can rely on no one except himself.

Such a self (perceived almost exclusively as an economic self) is without restraint and is self-authorized to enact Promethean energy to organize life around one's own needs, issues, and purposes. The autonomous, self-sufficient self takes as the proper venue for life "the market," and understands the market as a place of self-advancement at the expense of all others who are perceived either as rivals and competitors or as usable commodities.

This same autonomy is articulated in the Bible under the rubric of "the fool" who says in his heart, "There is no God" (Ps 14:1). The capacity to live without the gift or summons of God has immediate practical implications, for autonomy sets the fool over against the neighbor, most especially the poor neighbor. The one who says in Psalm 10:4, "There is no God," is the one who seeks out neighbors for exploitation:

> they lurk that they may seize the poor;
> they seize the poor and drag them off in their net.
> They stoop, they crouch,
> and the helpless fall by their might.
> They think in their heart, "God has forgotten,
> he has hidden his face, he will never see it." (Ps 10:9-11)

2. Anxiety

But the downside of such theological autonomy is that without the restraint of God, one is also without the resource of God. The self-sufficient person knows down deep that self-securing and self-satisfaction finally are unachievable, because it is life in a world where no gifts are given. The outcome of such autonomy without allies or support is an endless process of anxiety for one never has enough or has done enough to be safe and satisfied. As a result, the autonomous person, championed by current economic theory, is caught in an endless rat race of achievement that produces bottomless anxiety—about the market, about performance, about self-worth. The autonomous person in the end has nothing to do with his anxiety except to "suck it up" and keep moving.

In Leviticus 26:36-37 Moses characterizes the anxiety of a person (or a people) cut off from God and fated to a life under curse:

> The sound of a driven leaf shall put them to flight, and they shall flee as one flees from the sword and they shall fall though no one pursues. They shall stumble over one another, as if to escape a sword, though no one pursues.

Such a person finds threat, danger, and insecurity everywhere. The only sensible response to imagined threat is greater effort, which in turn only produces a new round of anxiety.

3. Greed

The *autonomous* person, beset by *anxiety*, can only resolve to do better, to get more, to arrive at full control of the future by full control of the present. The propulsion to greed in an effort to control generates ravenous acquisitiveness, so that life becomes a passionate pursuit of every form of security and self-worth, most particularly through more money. It is not difficult to understand why those with the most think they do not yet have enough. And those with less imitate the ravenously greedy ones, so that there is a collusion between those who have much and want more and those who have little but long for much. This collusion readily produces subprime loans in which creditors see easy interest income and debtors imagine a better life beyond present deprivation. The end is "tearing down barns and building bigger barns" (Luke 12:18) until all participants in *autonomous, anxious acquisitiveness* end as "fools" engaged in self-destructiveness.

My estimate is that this triad of autonomy/anxiety/greedy acquisitiveness is the story of our recent economic collapse. The theological-ethical issues are how to step out of this hopeless, self-devouring process and how to imagine and enact an alternative way in the world.

II

The Bible is acute in its analysis of self-destructive economics. Beyond that, the Bible is powerfully generative in imagining an alternative economic way in the world.

1. Covenantal Existence

Biblical faith is an invitation away from autonomy to *covenantal existence* that binds the self to the holy, faithful God and to neighbors who are members in a common economy. The biblical construal of reality concerns a covenantal infrastructure whereby one lives from the mercy of God and in turn responds in obedience to the will and purpose of that God. For our topic, perhaps the most compelling text is Deuteronomy 15:1-18, the provision of Moses for the regular cancellation of debts on poor people. The purpose of the commandment is to subordinate "money matters" to the future of the neighborhood. On the one hand, the commandment is rooted in the reality of the God who commands, who has delivered Israel from debt slavery in Egypt. On the other hand, the commandment reflects characteristic resistance to such neighborly economics wherein some are "hard hearted and tight fisted" (v. 7), not wanting to care for the neighbor. Such resistance is the resistance of the autonomous, but Moses has no patience with such resisters, for the reality of God's intent for the neighborhood overrides all such resistance.

2. Divine Abundance

Biblical faith, having vetoed autonomy, is an invitation away from anxiety to *the abundance of God*. The God of the gospel is the God who keeps giving. At the outset of the Bible, it is God the creator who sets creation into its destiny of fruitfulness, so that the world teems with abundance (Gen 1:22-25). It is this same generosity of God that shows up in the wilderness, where there is no visible life-support system. Here it is the "bread from heaven" that feeds the people without resources, so that everyone had what was needed for a viable life (Exod 16:17-18). It is, moreover, the same divine abundance that is in evidence when Jesus feeds crowds with twelve baskets of surplus bread (Mark 6:42-43) and then seven baskets of surplus bread (Mark 8:8-9). Whereas autonomous economics begins with a premise of scarcity, biblical faith is grounded in the generosity of God who wills and provides abundance. And here persons who are members of a covenantal neighborhood respond to divine abundance with generous gratitude, willing to share with sisters and brothers. Those who share, moreover, find in ways they cannot explain that more gifts from God are given. The bread multiplies and loaves abound, a miracle never available to the autonomous. In that world of abundance, covetous greed is inappropriate and incongruous. So Jesus can urge his followers: "Do not be anxious . . . for your heavenly Father knows you need all of these things" (Matt 6:25-32).

3. Generosity

Biblical faith is an invitation away from greed to the neighborly practice of *generosity*. The champions of acquisitiveness regard others as threats and competitors. But in a covenantal frame of reference grounded in God's abundance, others are seen to be brothers and sisters whose life is in a community of solidarity that shares the God-given resources for the well-being of all. The Torah of Moses is especially concerned with generosity toward the most vulnerable in society—the widow, the orphan, the immigrant, and the poor (Deut 24:19-22). A biblical ethic affirms that all members of society—including the poor, even the "undeserving poor"—are legitimate recipients of enough to live in dignity and safety, simply because they are there. Thus the righteous person is one who gives to the poor (Ps 112:9).

It is futile, from a biblical perspective, to engage in disputes about modern theoretical labels such as "socialism" or "capitalism." The Bible does not linger over such labels but insists that every available instrument of well-being—government, charity, private sector—must be mobilized in order to mediate the resources of the community for the sake of the common good. Two important points are evident. First, to desist from the pursuit of more acquisitiveness means that one has more energy for sharing. Second, those who would be effectively generous must utilize many strategic possibilities for sharing, which run all the way from face-to-face neighborly acts to a tax structure, institutional organization, and overall mode of production that serve the common good.

III

This simple sketch suggests that there are, in our present crisis, two large economic possibilities available to us, each grounded in deep but often unrecognized theological assumptions. Given the current failure and challenge, it seems clear to the serious person that our society must move to an alternative way in economics. In broad outline, this is a move,

> from autonomy to covenantal existence;
>
> from anxiety to divine abundance;
>
> from acquisitive greed to neighborly generosity.

This move is the characteristic move of biblical faith. In the New Testament it is the road of discipleship when Jesus summons, "Follow me." He wills his listeners to an alternative way in the world that has acute economic implications. And behind the summons of Jesus there is the exodus narrative. That "narrative of departure" is a model for the way in which human persons are always called to depart the rapacious, anxiety-producing system of Pharaoh that is grounded in acquisitiveness (see Gen 47:13-26) for the covenant of Sinai where God's ultimate commandment is, "Thou shalt not covet" (Exod 20:17). The current crisis among us is a moment ripe for an exodus departure from a system of anxious acquisitiveness that is rooted in pretenses to autonomy. This departure constitutes a radical break that is offered to us in a narrative mode. The reality on the ground is of course more complex and more difficult than the narrative, but it is no less urgent. Biblical faith requires that we look our greedy system of economics in the face and that we linger before God's offer of "a more excellent way." And then comes the risk and the deep reliance upon manna given in the wilderness, en route to a better land, a good city, milk and honey (see Heb 11:16).

18

JUBILEE

The Jubilee year is authorized by Moses in Leviticus 25. It is celebrated in lyrical fashion in Isaiah 61 as "the year of the LORD's favor" (Isa 61:2). It is claimed by Jesus as the shape of his life and the destiny of his ministry:

> Today this scripture [Isa 61:1-2] has been fulfilled in your hearing.
>
> (Luke 4:21)

The biblical provision for the Jubilee year proposes a pause in the rough and tumble of real-life economics. It knows that through predatory action in the economy, some gain at the expense of others and some lose because of their vulnerability, and huge social inequities result. To curb such unsustainable economic arrangements, the Jubilee year provides a regularized occasion when economic property and livelihood is given back by those who have gained to those who have lost. Giving back is a restorative action to maintain a viable neighborly infrastructure. The "give back" is an act of social realism that witnesses against the predatory economics that "takes away."

Given that the Jubilee in biblical provision occurs every fifty years, the fiftieth anniversary of Walmart is a splendid occasion for a Jubilee year among us. Thus it is here proposed that on its fiftieth anniversary, Walmart pause in its rough and tumble of economics to give back for the sake of the neighborhood. Such give back may take many forms: give back to the neighborhoods that the stores tend to diminish; give back to the workers who stay locked into poverty by poor wages; give back hope to those locked into despairing economics. It would be an act of neighborly generosity that would bring health and well-being to the neighborhood to the benefit of all parties.

Naysayers like to ask with a skeptical tone of the biblical Jubilee, "There is no evidence that they ever really practiced it, is there?" We do not know. What we do know is that it is there in the text, in the life of Jesus, and in the vision that faith has for society. Jubilee waits to be enacted now. There is no better agent for such an action than Walmart. Walmart is a master at marketing. It could also be a master at neighborliness. This is the time!

The term "jubilee" comes from the Hebrew term *ybl*, "ram's horn." The Jubilee year begins when the ram's horn is blown. We can listen for it in Walmart stores all across the nation. When it sounds, the neighborhood will dance and sing!

RETROSPECT

This series of essays has developed in my thinking over an extended period of time. The essays have emerged for me in a series of distinct occasions, some of which I have been invited to and some of which seemed inescapable in their urgency. The primary task I have undertaken in each essay is to read the biblical text seriously. To read a text seriously means not only to be alert to its historical context (as best it can be discerned) but also to give attention to the sociopolitical-economic dynamic that operates in the text, often with deliberately elusive rhetoric. It is a dynamic that is, moreover, made additionally complex by the God who inhabits these texts. Thus a serious reading of the text characteristically moves to theological issues about God and the elusive ways in which God is exhibited in the text as a character and as a decisive agent.

Such serious reading of the biblical text readily spills over into contemporary concerns and issues. That of course is a common assumption among those of us who read the text as Scripture. Our common practice, however, is to critique the text according to the best current intellectual criteria that we can muster. Thus historical criticism, on which I count continually, has explored the ways in which the theological claims of the text must be "corrected," toned down, or explained away in terms of our best critical reasoning. My own sense, however, is that the process of criticism must be reversed, so that the elusive, enigmatic insistences of the text can critique our modern assumptions that have in turn issued in such problematic and destructive social relationships. Chapter 4 ("Poems vs. Memos") and chapter 5 ("Biblical Language") constitute my attempt to engage the rhetoric of Scripture that operates with and bears witness to a very different way of speaking in the world.

This biblical rhetoric of "Thou" is an unembarrassed acknowledgment that the world is at bottom a set of relationships that strive for and are committed to fidelity but that often are betrayed into infidelity. This way of thinking affirms that at bottom the "Thou" of God is a lively personal agent who cannot be reduced to a proposition, or a process, or an idea, but is an "I" capable of transformative engagement. That sense of agency of course makes sense only within a community that is committed to this practice of rhetoric. That divine "Thou" who occupies the rhetoric of the text cannot be extracted from that rhetoric, either to universal propositions as favored by fundamentalists or to universal processes as preferred by many progressives. Thus I suppose I am primarily informed by George Lindbeck's "cultural linguistic" perspective, except that I insist in these several analyses that such rhetoric is not a closed system but is always impinged upon by the reality of the world that requires and insists upon reformulation. Once one commits to such a rhetoric and to the theo-social awareness that comes with it, one finds not only that fundamentalist reductionisms are unbearable but also that progressives' universalizing attempts to avoid the particular are equally unbearable.

I have pondered long about how we may move from narrative particularity to policy and practice, and I conclude that there is no easy or obvious or programmatic way to make that move. Except that that move is regularly made by women and men of courage who live in this world of rhetoric. One can see, all the way from the ancient prophets to Martin Luther King Jr. and now to Pope Francis, that this particularity of narrative, song, and oracle presses relentlessly concerning the management of power and the administration of the economy. Thus it was an obvious move for me to travel from my analysis of "testimony" to a consideration of how the testimony of Martin Luther King Jr., to cite one poignant example, eventuated in the transformation of public policy (see ch. 15), and to see that the old proposal of the Jubilee year was indeed pertinent to Walmart on its fiftieth anniversary (see ch. 18). It should not be a surprise that Francis, who inhabits this same narrative, should voice a frontal critique of antineighborly capitalism. Such rhetoric has practical real-world spin-offs, as the Bible itself continues to attest.

The key to such a move from rhetoric to transformative action of course is the practice of imagination that stays fixed on the text while recognizing that the text is not closed to a single meaning but, like all "inspired" art, continues to yield new truth, new assurance, and new summons. My insistent aim, evident variously in these essays, is to resist closure about the text, either the closure of the church with its dogmatic norms or the closure of the academy with its closed Enlightenment rationality. Whereas such closure in church and in academy aims at mastery and eventually control, the text, propelled by the living God who occupies it, refuses such closure. For that reason, it is not surprising that the exodus narrative is paradigmatic of the revolutionary resolve of God to break out of the world of Pharaoh. In important ways the biblical text keeps reperforming that paradigmatic narrative to emancipate us from the enslaving economy and from the enthralling rhetoric and epistemology that sustain such an economy. It is no wonder that Moses urges that the grandchildren must know about this (Exod 10:1-2). They must know that Pharaoh, in all his posturing, ends a fool and is made a fool by the Holy Agent who requires human agency to perform the drama of emancipation. Given the restlessness, amnesia, and despair that are addressed in the text (and derivatively by these essays), it is urgent that our grandchildren not only know these narratives, songs, and oracles but also be able to engage them in the ongoing critical work of living faithfully in our current economy (see ch. 9). Unless our grandchildren know them and know how to reperform them, we will end in violent despair. The chapter on food perhaps makes the stakes most clear (ch. 6). If we set food in the "Thou" world of abundance, we do find more food being wondrously given (manna!). But when food is situated in the narrative world of Pharaoh, that is, in scarcity, we end in a violent contest for "the distribution of scarce resources," which is the mantra of most courses on economics and the unexamined assumption of much of our common life and our political economy.

The news I have tried to exposit in these essays is the affirmation and insistence that it can be otherwise.[1] It can be otherwise in a practice of "Thou" in a world of subversive testimony, in a culture of the poetry of possibility that refuses the memos of certitude.

As I finish I have in mind my five well-beloved grandchildren—Christiana, August, Emilia, Anabelle, and Peter—and the world they must engage. I also have in mind my most beloved student, David Knauert, who died too soon, and his children, Harrison, Lily, and David. And finally I have in mind Davis Hankins, to whom I express my great thanks for bringing these essays to a credible readable form, and his well-beloved children, Miller and Nathaniel. It is no small matter that all of these beloved children and many many more should know that "I made fools of the Egyptians." And from them, perhaps, the parents and grandparents of these beloved children will "know that I am the Lord." Without that knowing, we fall back into the deathliness of denial, despair, and amnesia, and eventually into violence. It could be otherwise.

NOTES

INTRODUCTION

1 The translation can be found in Ernst Pawel, *The Nightmare of Reason: A Life of Franz Kafka* (New York: Farrar, Straus & Giroux, 1984), 158. Brent Strawn first introduced me to this passage from Kafka at Emory University in 2008.

2 Although this introduction does not address it directly, Brueggemann's dogged insistence on relaying his interpretations in the practical-theological vernacular of confessing communities is related to this persistently practical-political character of his work. Throughout his corpus he not only rejects the idea that the practical could be cordoned off as separate or supplemental to the critical but also refuses to relinquish to others the duty of explicating connections between critical interpretation and practical implication.

3 For a good discussion of the issues that focuses on the public university, see Christopher Newfield, *Unmaking the Public University: The Forty-Year Assault on the Middle Class* (Cambridge, Mass.: Harvard University Press, 2008).

4 For an excellent account of this period and the effects of Friedmanite policies, see Naomi Klein, *The Shock Doctrine: The Rise of Disaster Capitalism* (New York: Metropolitan Books, 2007).

5 See David McNally, *Global Slump: The Economics and Politics of Crisis and Resistance* (Oakland, Calif.: PM Press, 2011).

6 For a recent, lucid account of these dynamics, especially of the transformation of the market economy into a market society, see Michael J. Sandel, *What Money Can't Buy: The Moral Limits of Markets* (New York: Farrar, Straus & Giroux, 2012). On postmodernism, see Fredric Jameson, *Postmodernism: Or, the Cultural Logic of Late Capitalism* (Durham, N.C.: Duke University Press, 1991); idem, *The Cultural Turn: Selected Writings on the Postmodern, 1983–1998* (London: Verso, 1998).

7 In fact, as Newfield (*Unmaking the Public University*) shows, the culture wars contributed to such erosion. For an earlier demonstration of the conservative character of identity politics, see Wendy Brown, *States of Injury: Power and Freedom in Late Modernity* (Princeton: Princeton University Press, 1995). In my experience, especially in the late 1990s and early 2000s, Brueggemann's work was overidentified

by some with the diverse but more sectarian ideas being developed by Christian theologians such as John Milbank and especially Stanley Hauerwas and William H. Willimon. While some of Brueggemann's work—such as *Cadences of Home: Preaching among Exiles* (Louisville, Ky.: Westminster John Knox, 1997)—resonates to a certain degree with such perspectives, his work is considerably less necessarily and insistently Christian, and it is not at all as potentially guilty of naively romanticizing premodern forms of social relations. Brueggemann, *Cadences of Home*, 13, explicitly distinguishes his thought from the "sectarian withdrawal" of which Hauerwas and Willimon are often accused.

8 In his widely read monograph *The Prophetic Imagination* (2nd ed.; Minneapolis: Fortress, 2001 [1978]), Brueggemann develops his programmatic opposition between prophetic imagination and royal consciousness. In various works since, he has analyzed the various forms assumed and sociohistorical dynamics created by these two different and opposed ideological tendencies. He calls them "the liberation trajectory" and "the royal trajectory" in Brueggemann, "Trajectories in Old Testament Literature and the Sociology of Ancient Israel," *Journal of Biblical Literature* 98 (1979): 161–85; this article is slightly updated and more connected to the contemporary context in chapter 8, "The Nightmare of Amnesia." See also the many other essays collected in Brueggemann's *A Social Reading of the Old Testament: Prophetic Approaches to Israel's Common Life* (ed. P. D. Miller; Minneapolis: Fortress, 1994).

9 Chapter 4, "Poems vs. Memos," offers another example that is just as clear. There again he extrapolates from the inner-biblical conflict between poetry and memos to reflect on an analogous sphere of contestation that faces contemporary readers.

10 As far as I know, Brueggemann's only citation of Deleuze appears in our coauthored article, Walter Brueggemann and Davis Hankins, "The Affirmation of Prophetic Power and Deconstruction of Royal Authority in the Elisha Narratives," *Catholic Biblical Quarterly* 76 (2014): 58–76.

11 On the distinction between these two differences, see Gilles Deleuze, *Difference and Repetition* (trans. P. Patton; New York: Columbia University Press, 1994), esp. ch. 5.

12 Brennan W. Breed, "Extensive and Intensive Differences in 2 Kings 6:8-23" (paper presented at the annual meeting of the SBL, Chicago, Ill., November 19, 2012).

13 On Deleuze, see Todd May, *Gilles Deleuze: An Introduction* (Cambridge: Cambridge University Press, 2005); and Clayton Crockett, *Deleuze beyond Badiou: Ontology, Multiplicity, and Event* (New York: Columbia University Press, 2013). For a recent, provocative deployment of Deleuze's ontology for theorizing the reception of historical studies of biblical literature, see Brennan W. Breed, *Nomadic Text: A Theory of Biblical Reception History* (Bloomington: Indiana University Press, 2014). Incidentally, Breed joined the faculty to teach Old Testament at Columbia Theological Seminary after Brueggemann retired as professor emeritus.

14 By this I mean those statements that Brueggemann frequently makes, such as in the conclusion to chapter 11, while summarizing his argument, "I have suggested *an analogue* in terms of reckoning, between divine judgment and

economic collapse. I have entertained the thought that they are fundamentally synonymous, whether or not they are expressed in supernaturalist language."

15 This point is developed especially well in chapter 5, "Biblical Language."

16 While YHWH is paradigmatic in this regard, YHWH is but one of many names that Brueggemann uncovers for such productive interstices coursing through the Bible. Consider, for example, his claims about David in *David's Truth: In Israel's Imagination and Memory* (2nd ed.; Minneapolis: Fortress, 2002), 2: "David is no doubt a literary, imaginative construction, made by human hands. . . . But partly that construction is inevitable and unplanned and takes on a force and authority of its own. . . . The power of David endures, and therefore the David that emerges in these narratives is not a helpless, passive product of the artist. Rather, David is like a character in a good drama that takes on a life of his or her own and even surprises the playwright."

17 Walter Brueggemann, *Theology of the Old Testament: Testimony, Dispute, Advocacy* (Minneapolis: Fortress, 1997), 268. This point is also reflected in the title of Brueggemann's partial revision of his *Theology of the Old Testament*, which appeared at the time he was composing the chapters in this volume, *An Unsettling God: The Heart of the Hebrew Bible* (Minneapolis: Fortress, 2009). Unless otherwise noted, all emphases are Brueggemann's.

18 See Ernesto Laclau and Chantal Mouffe, *Hegemony and Socialist Strategy: Toward a Radical Democratic Politics* (2nd ed.; London: Verso, 2001), 112–13; see also Ernesto Laclau, *On Populist Reason* (London: Verso, 2005); and idem, *Emancipation(s)* (London: Verso, 1996).

19 Laclau and Mouffe, *Hegemony and Socialist Strategy*, 113.

20 Laclau and Mouffe, *Hegemony and Socialist Strategy*, 113.

21 In many places Brueggemann himself has dealt with many philosophical and theoretical issues in which his work is implicated. In addition to the many pages addressing such matters in various books, including *Theology of the Old Testament*, he has also explored them in focused monographs such as *Texts Under Negotiation: The Bible and Postmodern Imagination* (Minneapolis: Fortress, 1993) and *Abiding Astonishment: Psalms, Modernity, and the Making of History* (Louisville, Ky.: Westminster John Knox, 1991). Even still, such issues are often more in the background than in the foreground of his work. My sense is that this is at least in part a consequence of his conviction that the line separating the theory and the practice of biblical studies is often artificial.

22 For his own account of this history, see Brueggemann, *Theology of the Old Testament*, 49–60.

23 As my account intends to convey, the many continuities in Brueggemann's work over the years challenges any attempt to hold too rigidly to such a periodization of his scholarship. In addition to the currents discussed above, Brueggemann is also well known for his explorations throughout the 1970s and beyond of the resources available to biblical interpretation—especially of lamentation and the psalms—from insights gained in various currents of Freudian psychoanalysis. See especially, Walter Brueggemann, *The Psalms and the Life of Faith* (ed. P. D. Miller; Minneapolis: Fortress, 1995).

24 See, e.g., Brueggemann, *Cadences of Home*, 12: "Postmodern awareness helps us to consider that there is no 'given reality' behind our several constructs, but even our presumed given reality is itself a rhetorical construct, whether of the cold war, or consumer capitalism, or the 'free world,' or the male hegemony, or whatever." See also Brueggemann, *Texts Under Negotiation*, esp. ch. 1. Of the myriad arguments one could cite to indicate the postmodern background of this claim, suffice it to mention Jacques Derrida's analysis of faith as constitutive of every social relation; see, e.g., "Hospitality, Justice, and Responsibility," in *Questioning Ethics* (ed. R. Kearney and M. Dooley; London: Routledge, 1999), 80: "I do not *see* the other, I do not *see* what he or she has in mind, or whether he or she wants to deceive me. So I have to trust the other—that is faith. Faith is blind." For his part Brueggemann cites Garrett Green, *Imagining God: Theology and the Religious Imagination* (New York: Harper & Row, 1989), 41–60.

25 The formulation can be found in chapter 10, "Double Agency," where he writes, "in the end we traffic in paper gods."

26 Brueggemann, *Theology of the Old Testament*, 65, 66.

27 See Brueggemann, *Theology of the Old Testament*, 83–84.

28 One can easily find such claims advanced and developed throughout Brueggemann's oeuvre. For quick access to a sampling, one can search for those places where he mentions Karl Marx's famous statement from "A Contribution to the Critique of Hegel's Philosophy of Right," in *Early Political Writings* (ed. and trans. J. O'Malley; Cambridge: Cambridge University Press, 1994 [1843]), 58: "It is above all the *task of philosophy*, which is in the service of history, to unmask human self-estrangement in its *secular forms*, once its *sacred form* has been unmasked. Thus, the critique of heaven is transformed into the critique of earth, the *critique of religion* into the *critique of law*, and the *critique of theology* into the *critique of politics*." For references from four(!) different decades, see Brueggemann, *The Prophetic Imagination*, 132; "Israel's Sociotheological Alternatives," in *Old Testament Theology: Essays on Structure, Theme, and Text* (ed. P. D. Miller; Minneapolis: Fortress, 1992 [1985]), 124; *Isaiah 40–66* (Louisville, Ky.: Westminster John Knox, 1998), 86–87; *Ichabod Toward Home: The Journey of God's Glory* (Grand Rapids: Eerdmans, 2002), 11.

29 Using Freud and Marx as patron saints for such reductive approaches—although elsewhere he draws deeply and positively on their much more nuanced work—Brueggemann writes, "With the positive assertions of the truth about Yahweh, biblical faith parts company with the critique of Marx and Freud, for it asserts that the holy, incomparable God of judgment and deliverance is not a projection of our economics or philosophy. This God—true and living—is a free agent who moves toward and against established reality according to his own irreducible purposes." *A Commentary on Jeremiah: Exile and Homecoming* (Grand Rapids: Eerdmans, 1998), 106.

30 See, e.g., Brueggemann, *Theology of the Old Testament*, 268: "Yahweh is a Character and Agent who is evidenced in the life of Israel as an Actor marked by unlimited sovereignty and risky solidarity. . . . *The substance of Israel's testimony concerning Yahweh, I propose, yields a Character who has a profound disjunction at the core of the Subject's life*." In the current volume, see chapter 5, "Biblical Language."

31 Terence E. Fretheim, "Some Reflections on Brueggemann's God," in *God in the Fray: A Tribute to Walter Brueggemann* (ed. T. Linafelt and T. K. Beal; Minneapolis: Fortress, 1998), 27–28. See also Fretheim, *God and World in the Old Testament: A Relational Theology of Creation* (Nashville: Abingdon, 2005), 20–22.
32 Fretheim, "Brueggemann's God," 30.
33 Fretheim, "Brueggemann's God," 33.
34 Fretheim, "Brueggemann's God," 33.
35 See, for example, Brueggemann, *Theology of the Old Testament*, 297: "There is no doubt that the textual witness regards Yahweh as fully capable of such a decision to terminate"; the direct object, stated just before, is "the relationship with Israel, which is tantamount to terminating Israel." Brueggemann makes this point with reference to Numbers 14:11-19, though the following discussion refers to numerous other texts.
36 Brueggemann, *Theology of the Old Testament*, 410.
37 See Walter Brueggemann, "God in Recovery," n.p. [cited November 11, 2013]. Online: http://thecenterforbiblicalstudies.org/2011/god-in-recovery-by-walter-brueggemann/, September 6, 2011, where he explicitly divorces his conception of God "in recovery" (as in a "recovering" alcoholic) from the idea of God in process on the basis both of God's resolve to overcome God's propensity toward violence and of God's capacity to relapse.
38 See Brueggemann, *Theology of the Old Testament*, 329–32.
39 Jacques Derrida, "Force of Law: The 'Mystical Foundation of Authority,'" in *Acts of Religion* (ed. G. Anidjar; New York: Routledge, 2002), 241.
40 Brueggemann, *Theology of the Old Testament*, 410.
41 Brueggemann, *Theology of the Old Testament*, 303.
42 See Fretheim, *God and World*, 20–21, which, in an explicit engagement with the aspect of Brueggemann's theology presently under consideration, argues the precisely inverse case that the language of commitment or fidelity should be abandoned if the commitment could be broken. On the contrary, what could it mean to be faithful in a situation where it is impossible to be unfaithful? To what could one be faithful?
43 Jacques Derrida, *Rogues: Two Essays on Reason* (trans. P.-A. Brault and M. Naas; Stanford: Stanford University Press, 2005).
44 The possibility of God's annihilation raises the issue of the Christian character of Brueggemann's work. Although he typically celebrates what he refers to as the Jewish character of the texts, God, and world over against Western Christian conceptions, Jesus' death is for him a definitive enactment of what he views as a distinctively Jewish view of God as always at risk and under threat of death. Here mention should be made of what is perhaps his single most favorite quotation, which is from George Steiner and occupies the final two pages of Part II of his magnum opus, *Theology of the Old Testament*, 402–3. Steiner suggests that the existential condition shared by Jews and Christians, and indeed by all peoples, is "a long day's journey of the Saturday. Between suffering, aloneness, and unutterable waste on the one hand [Friday] and the dream of liberation, of rebirth on the other [Sunday]." I suppose that the issue dividing Brueggemann from many others is whether the divine realm is safeguarded from or no less

subjected to the reality of Friday. Fretheim's references to an unwavering divine will and unbreakable divine promises render him incapable of accounting for God's absolute brokenness on Friday and utter wavering on Saturday. While Brueggemann's affirmations of the latter are rooted in the Christian tradition, his distance from Fretheim's Christian perspective and his proximity to Steiner's Jewish perspective indicate my sense that his theology is neither limited to nor necessarily Christian.

45 See Walter Brueggemann, "*Theology of the Old Testament*: A Prompt Retrospect," in *God in the Fray: A Tribute to Walter Brueggemann* (ed. T. Linafelt and T. K. Beal; Minneapolis: Fortress, 1998), 314.

46 Walter Brueggemann, *A Pathway of Interpretation: The Old Testament for Pastors and Students* (Eugene, Ore.: Cascade, 2008), 111.

47 Brueggemann, *Pathway of Interpretation*, 111. See also "A Prompt Retrospect," 316: "The text is endlessly polyvalent and . . . its Subject is endlessly elusive and beyond domestication."

48 Norman K. Gottwald, "Rhetorical, Historical, and Ontological Counterpoints in Doing Old Testament Theology," in *God in the Fray: A Tribute to Walter Brueggemann* (ed. T. Linafelt and T. K. Beal; Minneapolis: Fortress, 1998), 11–23. I am sympathetic to and in agreement with much of Gottwald's thoroughly immanent (and not external) critique that aims to preserve the merits of Brueggemann's perspective while surmounting some inconsistencies in his at times dismissive claims about history and ontology. Indeed, Gottwald's article gestures in several theoretical directions that I have tried to develop in this introduction.

49 While I do not have the space here to develop it, I have in mind the account of Slavoj Žižek's ontology, which I think shares much in common with Brueggemann's, by Adrian Johnston, Žižek's *Ontology: A Transcendental Materialist Theory of Subjectivity* (Evanston, Ill.: Northwestern University Press, 2008).

50 See John J. Collins, "Is a Critical Biblical Theology Possible?," in *The Hebrew Bible and Its Interpreters* (ed. W. H. Propp, B. Halpern, and D. N. Freedman; Winona Lake, Ind.: Eisenbrauns, 1990), 1–18.

51 See, e.g., Walter Brueggemann, "Sometimes Wave, Sometimes Particle," *Currents in Biblical Research* 8 (2010): 376–85, which rejects Robert Carroll's "repeated claim that attention to the theological imagination of the text is to be dismissed as 'ideology.' . . . I insist that such attentiveness can be a faithful listening to the text, albeit with a critical sensibility about self and text" (377).

52 See, e.g., Walter Brueggemann and Davis Hankins, "The Invention and Persistence of Wellhausen's World," *Catholic Biblical Quarterly* 75 (2013): 15–31; Brueggemann, *Theology of the Old Testament*, 117–22; and previously, idem, *Abiding Astonishment*.

53 So, e.g., Brueggemann, *Theology of the Old Testament*, 118: "It may well be, in the end, that there is no historicity to Israel's faith claim. . . . And it may well be that there is no 'being' behind Israel's faith assertion. . . . [But] the speech is the reality to be studied."

54 Brueggemann himself prefers to call his interpretive practice postcritical to mark its distance from what has conventionally been treated as biblical criticism. I, however, would prefer not to relinquish the term "critical" to naive

forms of historical criticism and to distance Brueggemann's perspective from others that go under the banner "postcritical."

55 Wendy Brown and Janet Halley, ed., "Introduction," in *Left Legalism/Left Critique* (Durham, N.C.: Duke University Press, 2002), 28. See also Joan Wallach Scott, *The Fantasy of Feminist History* (Durham, N.C.: Duke University Press, 2011), 4.

56 Brown and Halley, "Introduction," 26.

57 See chapter 7, "Departure without Arrival."

58 See, e.g., Brueggemann, *Theology of the Old Testament*, ch. 27 (721–25): "The Constitutive Power of Israel's Testimony."

59 So, e.g., Brueggemann, *Theology of the Old Testament*, 86–87: "It is the great contribution of the entire historical-critical enterprise to indicate that Israel's ongoing life of faith is impinged on and impacted in powerful and discernible ways by circumstance and by experience. . . . Israel's grammar was indeed impinged on by the vagaries of historical experience." See also idem, "A Prompt Retrospect," 314, just after claiming, "I prefer to insist that history follows rhetoric," he admits, "except that acceptance of the testimony creates a circle of affirmation in which it can be subsequently claimed that the rhetoric derives from the history."

60 Brueggemann, *Ichabod Toward Home*, 11.

61 Brueggemann, "Israel's Sociotheological Alternatives," 125.

62 Brueggemann, "Sometimes Wave, Sometimes Particle," 380, is just one of many places where he recognizes that "the route from text to ontology" is an "exceedingly difficult issue."

CHAPTER ONE

* This was originally the first of two lectures to the bishops of the Evangelical Lutheran Church in America in Chicago, Illinois, in March 2011. The second is now chapter 2, "Conflicted Divine Agency."

1 See Daniel Johnson, "Contrary Hopes: Evangelical Christianity and the Decline of Narrative," in *The Future of Hope: Christian Tradition amid Modernity and Postmodernity* (ed. Miroslav Volf and William Katerberg; Grand Rapids: Eerdmans, 2004), 27–48.

2 Throughout this book I follow the English versification.

3 Claus Westermann, *The Living Psalms* (Edinburgh: T&T Clark, 1989), 166–200.

4 John Calvin, *Commentaries on the Books of Psalms*, vol. 1 (Grand Rapids: Baker Book House, 1979), 481.

5 See Samuel E. Balentine, *The Hidden God: The Hiding of the Face of God in the Old Testament* (Oxford: Oxford University Press, 1983).

6 Calvin, *Commentaries on the Books of Psalms*, 494–95.

7 My son, John Brueggemann, a student of Karl Marx, tells me that the statement in my text, while not exactly correct, expresses the sum of Marx's concern. John happily provided me with three quotations from Marx that substantiate the point. Karl Marx, "The Eighteenth Brumaire of Louis Bonaparte," in *Marx: Later Political Writings* (ed. and trans. Terrell Carver; Cambridge: Cambridge University Press, 1996), 32: "Men make their own history, but they do not make it as they please in circumstances they choose for themselves; rather they make

it in present circumstances, given and inherited." Karl Marx, "From the Paris Notebooks (1844)," in *Marx: Early Political Writings* (ed. and trans. Joseph O'Malley; Cambridge: Cambridge University Press, 1994), 80–81: "But even in my *scientific* activity, and in others like that, which I can seldom perform in immediate community with others, I am also *socially* active, because I am active as a *man*. Not only is the material of my activity—in the case of a thinker, the very language in which he expresses himself—given to me as social product, but my *own* existence *is* social activity; and so what I make of myself, I make of myself for society and with consciousness of myself as a social being." And, Karl Marx and Frederick Engels, "The Holy Family," in Marx and Engels, *Collected Works*, vol. 4 (London: Lawrence & Wishart, 1975), 93: "*History* does *nothing*, it 'possesses *no* immense wealth,' it 'wages *no* battles.' It is *man*, real, living man who does all that, who possesses and fights; 'history' is not, as it were, a person apart, using man as a means to achieve *its own* aims; history is *nothing but* the activity of man pursuing his aims."

8 Martin Buber, *On the Bible: Eighteen Studies* (New York: Schocken Books, 1968, 1982), 181.

9 Buber, *On the Bible*, 173.

10 Buber, *On the Bible*, 176–78. In this statement Buber uses the term "encystment," which I had to look up; it means "encapsulated."

11 Jürgen Moltmann, *Theology of Hope: On the Ground and the Implications of a Christian Eschatology* (New York: Harper & Row, 1967).

12 Ernst Bloch, *Atheism in Christianity: The Religion of the Exodus and the Kingdom* (London: Verso, 1972, 2009), 248–49.

13 Bloch, *Atheism in Christianity*, 249.

14 Bloch, *Atheism in Christianity*, 249–50.

15 Michael Walzer, *Exodus and Revolution* (New York: Basic Books, 1985), 115.

16 See Walter Brueggemann, *An Unsettling God: The Heart of the Hebrew Bible* (Minneapolis: Fortress, 2009), 1–17. Martin Buber, *Between Man and Man* (New York: Macmillan, 1965), 209–24, offers an important summary of the history of the "dialogical principle."

17 See Jason Byassee, *Praise Seeking Understanding: Reading the Psalms with Augustine* (Grand Rapids: Eerdmans, 2007).

18 With an appeal to Jacques Ellul, Nicholas Woltersdorff, "Seeking Justice in Hope," in *The Future of Hope: Christian Tradition amid Modernity and Postmodernity* (ed. Miroslav Volf and William Katerberg; Grand Rapids: Eerdmans, 2004), 94–96, exposits prayer as an act of hope for the sake of justice. Prayer is exactly the practice of the dialogic exchange that is elemental for faithful hope.

CHAPTER TWO

* This was originally the second of two lectures to the bishops of the Evangelical Lutheran Church in America in Chicago, Illinois, in March 2011. The first is chapter 1, "Conflicted Human Agency."

1 Abraham Heschel, in *The Prophets* (New York: Harper & Row, 1962), has most effectively and eloquently recovered the pathos of God that in important ways subverts the anger of God.

2 See Phyllis Trible, *God and the Rhetoric of Sexuality* (OBT; Philadelphia: Fortress, 1978), 44–46.
3 See Kazoh Kitamori, *Theology of the Pain of God* (Eugene, Ore.: Wipf & Stock, 1965; 2005), 153.
4 Trible, *God and the Rhetoric of Sexuality*, 45.
5 Trible, *God and the Rhetoric of Sexuality*, 45.
6 Trible, *God and the Rhetoric of Sexuality*, 50–52.
7 This assurance that God may look down and see and remember is reminiscent of the divine response to the slave cry in Exodus 2:23-25.
8 See Renita J. Weems, *Battered Love: Marriage, Sex, and Violence in the Hebrew Prophets* (OBT; Minneapolis: Fortress, 1995); and Julia M. O'Brien, *Challenging Prophetic Metaphor: Theology and Ideology in the Prophets* (Louisville, Ky.: Westminster John Knox, 2008).
9 John Calvin, "I Greet Thee, Who My Sure Redeemer Art," in *The Presbyterian Hymnal* (Louisville, Ky.: Westminster John Knox, 1990), #457.
10 Claus Westermann, *Isaiah 40–66: A Commentary* (OTL; Philadelphia: Westminster Press, 1969), 60.
11 Emmanuel Levinas, *Totality and Infinity: An Essay on Exteriority* (Pittsburgh: Duquesne University Press, 1969).
12 For a remarkable exposition of divine freedom that saves, see Eberhard Busch, *Drawn to Freedom: Christian Faith Today in Conversation with the Heidelberg Catechism* (Grand Rapids: Eerdmans, 2010).
13 See Walter Brueggemann, *An Unsettling God: The Heart of the Hebrew Bible* (Minneapolis: Fortress, 2009).
14 Jürgen Moltmann, *The Crucified God: The Cross of Christ as the Foundation and Criticism of Christian Theology* (New York: Harper & Row, 1974), 243.
15 Alan E. Lewis, *Between Cross & Resurrection: A Theology of Holy Saturday* (Grand Rapids, Eerdmans, 2001).
16 Lewis, *Between Cross & Resurrection*, 343.
17 Lewis, *Between Cross & Resurrection*, 346.
18 George Steiner, *Real Presences* (Chicago: University of Chicago Press, 1989), 232.

CHAPTER THREE

* This chapter also appears in Leo G. Perdue and Archie Lee, eds., *A Postcolonial Commentary on the Old Testament* (T&T Clark, forthcoming). Published with permission.
1 The mocking of Jewishness by the captors is not unlike that reported in Auschwitz.
2 The most important study of these psalms is by my friend, Ben C. Ollenburger, *Zion, The City of the Great King: A Theological Symbol of the Jerusalem Cult* (JSOT Supp. 41; Sheffield: Sheffield Academic, 1987). While I have some disagreement with him on the subject, a disagreement noted in his study, I have learned the most from him about these psalms.
3 Hermann Gunkel, *An Introduction to the Psalms* (trans. J. D. Nogalski; Macon: Mercer University Press, 1998), 29, 35, 55–57, 71. See also Erhard Gerstenberger, "Psalms," in *Old Testament Form Criticism* (ed. J. H. Hayes; San Antonio: Trinity

University Press, 1974), 216–18. For a summary of the theology of this tradition, see Hans-Joachim Kraus, *Theology of the Psalms* (trans. K. Crim; Minneapolis: Augsburg, 1986), 78–84.

4 Barbara Green, *How Are the Mighty Fallen? A Dialogical Study of King Saul in 1 Samuel* (JSOT Supp. 365; Sheffield: Sheffield Academic, 2003), 55–115. Following M. M. Bakhtin, Green nicely shows that genre is not simply a literary classification but a map of social power. In that regard, these psalms do constitute a genre, a map of social power in ancient Israel.

5 See also Samuel Terrien, *The Psalms: Strophic Structure and Theological Commentary* (Grand Rapids: Eerdmans, 2003), 369–74.

6 John Goldingay, *Psalms Volume 2: Psalms 42–89* (Grand Rapids: Baker Academic, 2007), 92. Goldingay's point is persuasive, but the fact that he must make it so extensively indicates a possible ambivalence in the text.

7 Goldingay says "within a whisker."

8 Terrien, *The Psalms*, 385.

9 The NRSV renders as "glorious" (v. 4), "awesome" (vv. 7, 11), and "fear" (v. 12).

10 Some have suggested that these verses are late additions, but we must, of course, take the psalm as it is.

11 Erich Zenger, "Psalm 76," in Frank-Lothar Hossfeld and Erich Zenger, *Psalms 2: A Commentary on Psalms 51–100* (Hermeneia; Minneapolis: Fortress, 2005), 263–64.

12 Zenger, "Psalm 76," 264–70.

13 This is the programmatic thesis of Jon D. Levenson, *Creation and the Persistence of Evil: The Jewish Drama of Divine Omnipotence* (San Francisco: Harper & Row, 1988).

14 See the discussion of Frank M. Cross, *Canaanite Myth and Hebrew Epic: Essays in the History of the Religion of Israel* (Cambridge, Mass.: Harvard University Press, 1973), 12–144, and especially his inimitable term "recrudescence" (135).

15 J. J. M. Roberts, "Mowinckel's Enthronement Festival: A Review," *The Book of Psalms: Compositions and Reception* (ed. P. W. Flint and P. D. Miller Jr.; Leiden: Brill, 2005), 97–115.

16 See Christopher R. Seitz, *Zion's Final Destiny: The Development of the Book of Isaiah: A Reassessment of Isaiah 36–39* (Minneapolis: Fortress, 1991).

17 See Gunkel, *An Introduction to the Psalms*, 275–77; and Brevard S. Childs, *Introduction to the Old Testament as Scripture* (Philadelphia: Fortress, 1979), 517–18. For a summary comment on liturgy as generative of world, see Walter Brueggemann, *Israel's Praise: Doxology against Idolatry and Ideology* (Philadelphia: Fortress, 1988), ch. 1.

18 Karl Mannheim, *Ideology and Utopia* (New York: Harcourt, Brace, 1936). Mannheim entered Old Testament study especially through the work of Paul D. Hanson, *The Dawn of Apocalyptic* (Philadelphia: Fortress, 1975).

19 Ollenburger, *Zion*, does not believe that hope is "misbegotten." He offers a quite positive read of the way in which Zion was an expression of the centrality of justice in the life of the Jerusalem establishment. In other words, he does not find in these texts the hidden but powerful ideology that I think is crucial to their import.

20 Ollenburger, *Zion*, 59–66. While one might trace in critical fashion a distinction between the two traditions, in practice I would think such a distinction is impossible to maintain.

21 On the royal liturgies in the temple, see Aubrey Johnson, *Sacral Kingship in Ancient Israel* (Cardiff: University of Wales Press, 1967).
22 Gerhard von Rad, *Old Testament Theology I* (New York: Harper & Brothers, 1962), 334–47.
23 Walter Brueggemann, *Solomon: Israel's Ironic Icon of Human Achievement* (Columbia: University of South Carolina Press, 2005), 139–59.
24 See H. H. Schmid, *Gerechtigung als Weltordnung* (Tübingen: J. C. B. Mohr, 1968).
25 On the social, historical rootage of Jeremiah, see Robert R. Wilson, *Prophecy and Society in Ancient Israel* (Philadelphia: Fortress, 1980), 231–51.
26 Roberts, "Mowinckel's Enthronement Festival," 111.
27 For a belated act of imagination concerning the flow of consumer goods into privileged Jerusalem, see Isaiah 61:8-13.
28 On the pivotal role of Shaphan, see Oded Lipschits, *The Fall and Rise of Jerusalem: Judah under Babylonian Rule* (Winona Lake, Ind.: Eisenbrauns, 2005), 84–92.
29 See Philip R. Davies, *Scribes and Schools: The Canonization of the Hebrew Scriptures* (Louisville, Ky.: Westminster John Knox, 1998); and Karel van der Toorn, *Scribal Culture and the Making of the Hebrew Bible* (Cambridge, Mass.: Harvard University Press, 2007).
30 Sigmund Mowinckel, *He That Cometh* (Nashville: Abingdon, n.d.), 10–186, has reviewed all the pertinent texts.
31 See Paul Ricoeur, *Freud and Philosophy: An Essay on Interpretation* (New Haven: Yale University Press, 1970). Ricoeur's programmatic mapping of hermeneutics has been elucidated by David Tracy, *The Analogical Imagination: Christian Theology and the Culture of Pluralism* (New York: Crossroad, 1981).
32 For an early use of the phrase, see Paul Ricoeur, *The Symbolism of Evil* (Boston: Beacon Press, 1967), 352. Further, see Mark I. Wallace, *The Second Naivete: Barth, Ricoeur, and the New Yale Theology* (Macon, Ga.: Mercer University Press, 1990).
33 Mark Braverman is deeply involved in a Jewish critique of the ideological claims of the state of Israel that eventuate in military violence. See his book, *Fatal Embrace: Christians, Jews, and the Search for Peace in the Holy Land* (Austin: Synergy Press, 2010).
34 Mark Braverman, "Notes on 'Singing Songs of Zion: Misbegotten Hope' " (private communication), 2.
35 Braverman, "Notes," 4.
36 Braverman, "Notes," 10.
37 Braverman, "Notes," 9.
38 See Mark Braverman, *Fatal Embrace*.
39 Important exceptions are Goldingay, *Psalms 2*, 93–94; and Terrien, *The Psalms*, 375, who writes, "No nation, no church can claim superiority over others. If she believes that 'The Lord of hosts is in the midst of her,' her strength will derive from humble reliance upon the inner stronghold. *Immanuel* is an indictment before it comforts."
40 On the difficulties in rendering this final verse, see Tod Linafelt, *Surviving Lamentations: Catastrophe, Lament, and Protest in the Afterlife of a Biblical Book* (Chicago: University of Chicago Press, 2000), 59–61.

CHAPTER FOUR

1 John D. O'Banion, *Reorienting Rhetoric: The Dialectic of List and Story* (University Park: Pennsylvania State University Press, 1992).
2 O'Banion, *Reorienting Rhetoric*, 15.
3 O'Banion, *Reorienting Rhetoric*, 32–33.
4 O'Banion, *Reorienting Rhetoric*, 35.
5 O'Banion, *Reorienting Rhetoric*, 46.
6 O'Banion, *Reorienting Rhetoric*, 42.
7 The matter of the loss of narrative with particular reference to the Christian tradition has been classically stated by Hans W. Frei, *The Eclipse of Biblical Narrative: A Study in Eighteenth and Nineteenth Century Hermeneutics* (New Haven: Yale University Press, 1974).
8 O'Banion, *Reorienting Rhetoric*, 108–9; for the radical shift accomplished by the Cartesian revolution, see Stephen Toulmin, *Cosmopolis: The Hidden Agenda of Modernity* (New York: Free Press, 1990).
9 O'Banion, *Reorienting Rhetoric*, 138, 140.
10 O'Banion, *Reorienting Rhetoric*, 139.
11 O'Banion, *Reorienting Rhetoric*, 170.
12 See Walter Brueggemann, *Solomon: Israel's Ironic Icon of Human Achievement* (Columbia: University of South Carolina Press, 2005).
13 O'Banion, *Reorienting Rhetoric*, 238.
14 Regina Mara Schwartz, *Sacramental Poetic at the Dawn of Secularism: When God Left the World* (Stanford: Stanford University Press, 2008), 18–24, shrewdly describes the way that sacramental theology developed in the Medieval Church as the *corpus Christi* became the *corpus mysticum*, thereby reducing the mystery of the sacrament to practical politics, a clear example of the alliance of power and holiness.
15 On gradations of holiness, see Philip P. Jenson, *Graded Holiness: A Key to the Priestly Conception of the World* (JSOT Supp. 106; Sheffield: Sheffield Academic, 1992).
16 See Walter Brueggemann, "The Tearing of the Curtain (Matt 27:51)," in *Faithful Witness: A Festschrift Honoring Ronald Goetz* (ed. Michael J. Bell, H. Scott Matheney, and Dan Peerman; Elmhurst, Ill.: Elmhurst College, 2002), 77–83.
17 I deliberately use the term "force" to allude to James Boyd White, *Living Speech: Resisting the Empire of Force* (Princeton: Princeton University Press, 2006), who traces the force of speech when it reflects and serves worldly power.
18 I take my lead concerning the "tent" from the work of Harvey H. Guthrie Jr., *Theology as Thanksgiving: From Israel's Psalms to the Church's Eucharist* (New York: Seabury Press, 1981), 19–25. Guthrie contrasts the mythic hymns of the temple and the songs of thanksgiving from among the peasants. I have carried this in a direction not suggested by Guthrie, but the primary idea is his.
19 I have in mind here the definitive work of James C. Scott, *Domination and the Arts of Resistance: Hidden Transcripts* (New Haven: Yale University Press, 1990). I suggest that poems from the "tents" of Israel constituted acts of resistance and were surely "hidden" from the powers that dominated society. While the poems are theologically serious, they are not politically innocent.

20 For a contemporary notion of "dancing and singing" as a way to create an emancipated community in the face of an abusive system, see John McKnight and Peter Block, *The Abundant Community: Awakening the Power of Families and Neighborhoods* (San Francisco: Berrett-Koehler Publications, 2010), 84–85.

21 Guthrie, *Theology as Thanksgiving*, ties the myths of the great hymns of Israel to the regime of David and the temple.

22 John Athelstan Laurie Riley, "Ye Watchers and Ye Holy Ones," in *The Presbyterian Hymnal* (Louisville, Ky.: Westminster John Knox, 1990), #451.

23 Charles Wesley, "Love Divine, All Loves Excelling," in *The Presbyterian Hymnal* (Louisville, Ky.: Westminster John Knox, 1990), #376.

24 Eleanor Farjeon, "Morning Has Broken," in *The Presbyterian Hymnal* (Louisville, Ky.: Westminster John Knox, 1990), #469.

25 Emmanuel Levinas, *Totality and Infinity: An Essay on Exteriority* (Pittsburgh: Duquesne University Press, 1969).

CHAPTER FIVE

* A previous form of this chapter was read in September 2011 at Hebrew Union College in Cincinnati, Ohio, and published as, "In the 'Thou' Business," *Journal for Preachers* 35 (2012): 21–30. Published with permission.

1 Paul Ricoeur, *The Conflict of Interpretations: Essays in Hermeneutics* (ed. D. Ihde; Evanston, Ill.: Northwestern University Press, 1974), 288, 296–303.

2 Buber's work is defining for the topic of the dialogical; see *Between Man & Man* (New York: Macmillan, 1965); and idem, *I and Thou* (Edinburgh: T&T Clark, 1937).

3 Claus Westermann, *Praise and Lament in the Psalms* (Atlanta: John Knox, 1981), 116–35. His analysis has been greatly supplemented by the extended discussion of Patrick D. Miller, *They Cried to the Lord: The Form and Theology of Biblical Prayer* (Minneapolis: Fortress, 1994), 178–232.

4 It is now fashionable in scholarship to bash the "urban elites" who, in the later period, assembled the Old Testament. No doubt there is such an influence that helped to shape the text. And no doubt the religious practice of ancient Israel was pluralistic. But insofar as ancient Israel was understood as the people of YHWH, such a defining imagination may well have been broad and deep across the spectrum of subcommunities that constituted Israel. There is nothing narrowly elite in such an act of theological imagination.

5 On the impetus of such cultural anxiety, see Susan Bordo, *The Flight to Objectivity: Essays on Cartesianism and Culture* (Albany: SUNY Press, 1987).

6 See Michael J. Buckley, *At the Origins of Modern Atheism* (New Haven: Yale University Press, 1987).

7 Buckley, *At the Origins of Modern Atheism*, 207–8.

8 On the relational risks of fidelity, as contrasted with the flat offer of certitude, see Jürgen Moltmann, *Theology of Hope: On the Ground and the Implications of a Christian Eschatology* (New York: Harper & Row, 1965).

9 Langdon Gilkey, "Cosmology, Ontology, and the Travail of Biblical Language," *Journal of Religion* 41 (1961): 194–205.

10 The misconstrual of biblical testimony in the modern period has led to the exploitation of the earth, on which see Cameron Wybrow, *The Bible, Baconism,*

and Mastery over Nature: The Old Testament and Its Modern Misreading (American University Studies, Series 7, vol. 112; New York: Peter Lang, 1991). Wybrow's argument is important because in recent time the Bible has been credited with the invitation to "have dominion" over the earth. Wybrow shows in a clear way that it is the objectification of nature in the modern period that has provided the impetus for such an abuse of the earth.

11 Philip Goodchild, *Theology of Money* (Durham, N.C.: Duke University Press, 2009), 48, 57, 81, 84, has seen the intimate connection between the instability of the environment and the end of modernity, a connection he sees because modernity depends above all on stability: "The end of modernity will be met by climatic instability, fuel poverty, food shortages, disease, social unrest, conflict, and war. . . . Once nature is no longer stable it cannot be effectively represented and mastered; once concepts are no longer stable, political decisions can no longer be taken according to principles or pragmatic considerations. . . . *Economy and ecology are mathematically incompatible*. . . . The problem of the clash between economic growth and ecological finitude derives from a capitalist system that is based on perpetual growth" (emphasis added).

12 This judgment was made by Max Horkheimer and Theodor A. Adorno, *The Dialectic of Enlightenment: Philosophical Fragments* (Stanford: Stanford University Press, 2002), and more recently by Zygmunt Bauman, *Modernity and Holocaust* (Cambridge: Polity Press, 1991).

13 See my exploration of the theme of "the common good" from a biblical perspective in *Journey to the Common Good* (Louisville, Ky: Westminster John Knox, 2010).

14 See C. B. Macpherson, *The Political Theory of Possessive Individualism: Hobbes to Locke* (Oxford: Oxford University Press, 1962).

15 See Walther Eichrodt, "The Holy One in Your Midst: The Theology of Hosea," *Interpretation* 15 (1961): 259–73.

16 Francis Fukuyama, *Truth: The Social Virtues and the Creation of Prosperity* (New York: Free Press, 1996).

17 Karl Barth, *Commentary on the Epistle to the Romans* (6th ed.; trans. E. C. Hoskyns; Oxford: Oxford University Press, 1977).

18 Robert W. Jenson, *Canon and Creed* (*Interpretation*: Resources for the Use of Scripture in the Church; Louisville, Ky.: Westminster John Knox, 2010), 119–20.

19 Susanne K. Langer, *Philosophy in a New Key: A Study in the Symbolism of Reason, Rite, and Art* (Cambridge, Mass.: Harvard University Press, 1942, 1957).

20 Langer, *Philosophy in a New Key*, 126. Langer cites Sapir with only the reference "article 'Language,' " 157.

21 Langer, *Philosophy in a New Key*, 126.

22 Michael Polanyi, *Personal Knowledge: Toward a Post-Critical Philosophy* (New York: Harper & Row, 1958, 1962), 143.

23 Richard Kearney, *The God Who May Be: A Hermeneutics of Religion* (Bloomington: Indiana University Press, 2001) ponders the generative future of God, based on Exodus 3:14, in a way that takes the self-disclosing utterance of God as generative of new possibilities.

24 Marilyn McCord Adams, *Horrendous Evils and the Goodness of God* (Ithaca, N.Y.: Cornell University Press, 1999), 81.

25 Goodchild, *Theology of Money*, 257–58, connects the dots: "Modern reason, modern politics, and modern economics have been founded on the ideal of autonomy. . . . The modern rejection of political theology consists in the ideal of autonomy: instead of asking how one may serve nature, society or God, one asks how nature and society may be made to serve oneself. The disavowed spiritual energy that gives authority to such an autonomous subject is embodied in money. Money has replaced God."

26 On the violent potential of totalism, see Robert Jay Lifton, *Witness to an Extreme Century: A Memoir* (New York: Free Press, 2011). On pages 67–68, 381, Lifton details the "eight deadly sins" of totalism. One can see such elements in the force and control of late capitalism among us.

27 Terry Eagleton, *Reason, Faith, and Revolution: Reflections on the God Debate* (The Terry Lectures; New Haven: Yale University Press, 2009).

28 On the "Possibilizing God," see Kearney, *The God Who May Be*, 80–100. His argument would be easier and more compelling were there reliance on the dialogical rhetoric of the Bible.

CHAPTER SIX

* A previous form of this chapter was offered as the Heck Lectures at United Theological Seminary in Dayton, Ohio, in May 2011, and published as, "Food Fight," *Word and World* 33 (2013): 319–40. Published with permission.

1 Abraham Maslow is often credited as the person who did the most to draw our attention to the connections among these several needs; see, *Motivation and Personality* (New York: Harper, 1954). But, of course, demonstrations of such connections and tensions recur throughout Freud's work. In, e.g., "Civilization and Its Discontents," in *The Standard Edition of the Complete Psychological Works of Sigmund Freud*, vol. 21 (trans. James Strachey; London: Hogarth, 1957), Freud claims that social reality—civilization—and the subjective ego are historical emergences out of id-level needs and desires, and he credits the former with bringing both pleasure and discontent. He even refers to various cultural advances as "prosthetic gods" that nonetheless cause all sorts of trouble (91–92).

2 Leon R. Kass, *The Beginning of Wisdom: Reading Genesis* (New York: Free Press, 2003), 569, passim.

3 Gerhard von Rad, *Genesis* (OTL; Philadelphia: Westminster, 1972), 398.

4 The note of "alas," here supplied from v. 1 even though it is not in the Hebrew of v. 4, is not a threat but a note of sadness despite its traditional rendering as "woe." The poet speaks as if at a funeral, wanting to bring Israel to an acknowledgment of failure and danger. The address in v. 1 of "Zion" perhaps suggests the oracle was addressed to the south. Alternatively the term "Zion" could refer to any group of urban elites, whether in the north or the south.

5 See John Donahue, *The Gospel in Parable* (Philadelphia: Fortress, 1988), 140. On the violation of food rules, see the difficult but rewarding discussion of Fernando Belo, *A Materialist Reading of the Gospel of Mark* (Maryknoll, N.Y.: Orbis Books, 1981).

6 Martha Nussbaum, *The Clash Within: Democracy, Religious Violence, and India's Future* (Cambridge, Mass.: Harvard University Press, 2007), has made a compelling case

that the "clash" between such views is not between people on different sides; it is, rather, a "clash" within each of us that is variously negotiated and resolved.

7 See Walter Brueggemann, *An Unsettling God: The Heart of the Hebrew Bible* (Minneapolis: Fortress, 2009), 137–61.

8 Isak Dinesen, *Out of Africa and Shadows on the Grass* (New York: Vintage Books, 1985), 126.

9 See Walter Brueggemann, *Israel's Praise: Doxology against Idolatry and Ideology* (Philadelphia: Fortress, 1988).

10 See Michael Fishbane, *Sacred Attunement: A Jewish Theology* (Chicago: University of Chicago Press, 2008); and, Judith Shulevitz, *The Sabbath World: Glimpses of a Different Order of Time* (New York: Random House, 2010).

11 See Frank Moore Cross, *Canaanite Myth and Hebrew Epic: Essays in the History of the Religion of Israel* (Cambridge, Mass.: Harvard University Press, 1973), 44–75.

12 See Sharon H. Ringe, *Jesus, Liberation, and the Biblical Jubilee: Images for Ethics and Christology* (OBT; Philadelphia: Fortress, 1985).

CHAPTER SEVEN

* This chapter was originally published as "Departure, but Not Yet Arrival: Performance in Exodus 15:22-26," *Journal of Scriptural Reasoning* 9 (2010): n.p. [cited January 6, 2014]. Online: http://jsr.lib.virginia.edu/vol-9-no-1-december-2010-the-fruits-of-scriptural-reasoning/departure-but-not-yet-arrival/. Published with permission.

1 On the qualifying "if," see Walter Brueggemann, *Solomon: Israel's Ironic Icon of Human Achievement* (Columbia: University of South Carolina Press, 2005), 136–59.

2 Nicholas Adams, "Reparative Reasoning," *Modern Theology* 24 (2008): 452–53.

3 It is not unimportant that the two other uses of the phrasing occur in the tradition of Deuteronomy. In Deuteronomy 7:15, the special people of YHWH are protected from such diseases. In Deuteronomy 28:60, the culminating curse for violating covenant is return to Egypt (v. 68), with the new affliction of these very diseases. Clearly the exploitative system of Pharaoh has become, in the imagination of covenantal Israel, the antithesis of covenantal well-being.

4 Randi Rashkover, "Introducing the Work of Peter Ochs," *Modern Theology* 24 (2008): 444.

5 Steven P. Kepnes, "Peter Ochs: Philosophy in the Service of God and World," *Modern Theology* 24 (2008): 502–3.

6 Peter Ochs, "Response: Reflections on Binarism," *Modern Theology* 24 (2008): 487–97.

CHAPTER EIGHT

* This chapter was originally offered as the Jarvis Lecture on Christianity and Culture at East Carolina University in January 2010.

1 An example of such expansionist use of the tradition is offered by David M. Gunn, "Colonialism and the Vagaries of Scripture: Te Kooti in Canaan (A Story of Bible and Dispossession in Aotearoa/New Zealand)," in *God in the Fray: A Tribute*

to Walter Brueggemann (ed. T. Linafelt and T. K. Beal; Minneapolis: Fortress, 1998), 127–42.

2 On the recognition that this emancipatory impulse of YHWH extends beyond Israel to other peoples, see Amos 9:7, and my comment on the verse, " 'Exodus' in the Plural (Amos 9:7)," in *Many Voices, One God: Being Faithful in a Pluralistic World* (ed. W. Brueggemann and G. Stroup; Louisville, Ky.: Westminster John Knox, 1998), 15–34.

3 Michael Walzer, *Exodus and Revolution* (New York: Basic Books, 1985).

4 See Walter Harrelson, *The Ten Commandments and Human Rights* (OBT; Philadelphia: Fortress, 1980); idem, *The Ten Commandments for Today* (Louisville, Ky.: Westminster John Knox, 2006).

5 See David J. A. Clines, *Interested Parties: The Ideology of Writers and Readers of the Hebrew Bible* (JSOT Supp. 205; Sheffield: Sheffield Academic, 1995), 26–45.

6 I have proceeded on the assumption that it is Exodus-Sinai and not the Abraham narrative that is foundational for Israel. But when it comes to the legitimacy of the land of promise, the Abraham narrative is drawn into a connection with the Joshua traditions so that the promise to the ancestors is the basis for entry into the land. In the final form of the text, the Abraham narrative thus plays a crucial role in the claim of the whole of the tradition.

7 Garrett Green, *Imagining God: Theology & the Religious Imagination* (San Francisco: Harper & Row, 1989), 73, 140, passim.

8 See Walter Brueggemann, *Divine Presence and Violence: Contextualizing the Book of Joshua* (Cascade Books; Eugene, Ore.: Wipf & Stock, 2009).

9 See Regina M. Schwartz, *The Curse of Cain: The Violent Legacy of Monotheism* (Chicago: University of Chicago Press, 1997), which makes a formidable argument that violence is intrinsic to monotheism and is therefore readily "justified" against any "other."

10 See Walter Brueggemann, *Solomon: Israel's Ironic Icon of Human Achievement* (Columbia: University of South Carolina Press, 2005).

11 The history of the tradition is complex and obscure. The most helpful proposals are those of Frank Moore Cross, *Canaanite Myth and Hebrew Epic: Essays in the History of the Religion of Israel* (Cambridge, Mass.: Harvard University Press, 1973), 195–215; and Robert R. Wilson, *Prophecy and Society in Ancient Israel* (Philadelphia: Fortress, 1980), 135–252.

12 Frank Crüsemann, *The Torah: Theology and Social History of Old Testament Law* (trans. Allan W. Mahnke; Minneapolis: Fortress, 1996), 224–34.

13 Michael Fishbane, in his recent study, *Sacred Attunement: A Jewish Theology* (Chicago: University of Chicago Press, 2008), reflects on the disciplines of "mindfulness" in Judaism that provide an alternative to the "mindlessness" of contemporary society.

CHAPTER NINE

* This essay was originally published as "Antidote to Amnesia," in *Reclaiming the Imagination: Exodus as Paradigmatic Narrative for Preaching* (ed. Dave Bland and David Fleer; St. Louis, Mo.: Chalice Press, 2009), 7–25. Published with permission.

1 It is now generally accepted that one cannot maintain the "historicity" of the exodus narrative. But serious believers have always made a distinction, in any case, between "history" and "memory." See Yosef Hayim Yerushalmi, *Zakhor: Jewish History and Jewish Memory* (Seattle: University of Washington Press, 1982). The alternative to "historical" is often taken to be "paradigmatic," though David Halivni prefers the term "pragmatic," that is, useful to the faith and life of the community of interpretation. See Peter Ochs, "Talmudic Scholarship as Textual reasoning: Halivni's Pragmatic Historiography," in *Textual Reasoning: Jewish Philosophy and Text Study at the End of the Twentieth Century* (ed. P. Ochs and N. Levene; Grand Rapids: Eerdmans, 2002), 120–51.

2 Michael Fishbane, *Text and Texture: Close Readings of Selected Biblical Texts* (New York: Schocken Books, 1979), 81–83.

3 First Maccabees 1:11-15 reports: "At that time there appeared in Israel a group of renegade Jews, who incited the people. 'Let us enter into a covenant with the Gentiles round about,' they said, 'because disaster upon disaster has overtaken us since we segregated ourselves from them.' The people thought this a good argument, and some of them in their enthusiasm went to the king and received authority to introduce non-Jewish laws and customs. They built a sports-stadium in the gentile style in Jerusalem. They removed their marks of circumcision and repudiated the holy covenant. They intermarried with Gentiles, and abandoned themselves to evil ways."

4 On Solomon's impatience with local tradition, see Walter Brueggemann, *Solomon: Israel's Ironic Icon of Human Achievement* (Columbia: University of South Carolina Press, 2005).

5 See the classic exposition of this text by Paul Lehmann, *The Transfiguration of Politics: The Presence and Power of Jesus of Nazareth in and over Human Affairs* (New York: Harper & Row, 1975), 48–70.

6 Michael Walzer, *Exodus and Revolution* (New York: Basic Books, 1985), 149.

7 William T. Cavanaugh, *Torture and Eucharist: Theology, Politics, and the Body of Christ* (Oxford: Blackwell, 1998). On the Eucharist as a sacramental connectedness to common life, see Luise Schottroff and Andrea Bieler, *The Eucharist: Bodies, Bread, & Resurrection* (Minneapolis: Fortress, 2007).

8 On the summoning power of the narrative maintained by the grandparents, see the analogue in James C. Scott, *Domination and the Arts of Resistance: Hidden Transcripts* (New Haven: Yale University Press, 1990). It takes little imagination to see that the exodus narrative functions as a "hidden transcript" for the faithful in a culture that is fundamentally resistant to the claims of that narrative.

9 In addition to placing this text as the frontispiece for his second volume, Gerhard von Rad, *Old Testament Theology*, vol. 2: *The Theology of Israel's Prophetic Traditions* (San Francisco: Harper & Row, 1965), 243–50, shows this text to be pivotal for the newness to be announced in a season of displacement.

10 On the reuse of the exodus tradition in subsequent proclamations, see Bernhard W. Anderson, "Exodus Typology in Second Isaiah," in *Israel's Prophetic Heritage: Essays in Honor of James Muilenburg* (ed. B. W. Anderson and W. Harrelson; New York: Harper & Brothers, 1962), 177–95; idem, "Exodus and Covenant in Second Isaiah and Prophetic Tradition," in *Magnalia Dei: The Mighty Acts of God: Essays on*

the Bible and Archaeology in Memory of G. Ernest Wright (ed. F. M. Cross et al.; Garden City, N.Y.: Doubleday, 1976), 339–60.

11 On the exodus memory "enacted" elsewhere, see Walter Brueggemann, " 'Exodus' in the Plural (Amos 9:7)," in *Many Voices One God: Being Faithful in a Pluralistic World In Honor of Shirley Guthrie* (ed. W. Brueggemann and G. W. Stroup; Louisville, Ky.: Westminster John Knox, 1998), 15–34.

CHAPTER TEN

* This chapter was originally presented to the Exile (Forced Migrations) in Biblical Literature section at the 2010 annual meeting of the Society of Biblical Literature in Atlanta, Georgia.

1 Klaus Koch, *The Prophets: The Assyrian Period* (Philadelphia: Fortress, 1982), 5, 73, 88, 99, 156, passim.

2 It is worth observing that the same term figures twice in pivotal ways in the David narrative. In 2 Samuel 7:15, YHWH "will not take my steadfast love from" David; in 2 Samuel 12:10, "the sword will never depart from [David's] house." The double usage is perhaps intentional as the Davidic house lives between divine fidelity and the sword.

3 In 2 Samuel 11:25, 27 the narrative makes a contrast between "evil in your eyes" and "evil in the sight of YHWH." The inability to distinguish between the two of course vexes the regime forever.

4 Walter Brueggemann, "Heir and Land: The Royal 'Envelope' of the Books of Kings," in *The Fate of King David: The Past and Present of a Biblical Icon* (ed. T. Linafelt, C. V. Camp, and T. K. Beal; LHBOTS 500; New York: T&T Clark, 2010), 85–100.

5 I allude to the remarkable study of James Boyd White, *Living Speech: Resisting the Empire of Force* (Princeton: Princeton University Press, 2006), in which he ponders the phrase "force of empire" from the study of *The Iliad* by Simone Weil. She has seen that *The Iliad* is all about violence, the kind of violence that Nebuchadnezzar exhibited and that YHWH sanctioned.

6 This narrative account of Jehoiakim departs significantly from that of 2 Kings 24; see Leslie C. Allen, "The First and Second Books of Chronicles," *New Interpreter's Bible*, vol. 3 (Nashville; Abingdon, 1999), 654–55.

7 The Jeremiah tradition exposits the interaction of Zedekiah and Jeremiah in some detail; Jeremiah 37:2 summarizes the royal resistance to prophetic summons that is crucial for the *Chronicler.*

8 Langdon Gilkey, "Cosmology, Ontology, and the Travail of Biblical Language," *Journal of Religion* 41 (1961): 194–205.

9 The normative discussion is by Klaus Koch, "Is There a Doctrine of Retribution in the Old Testament?" in *Theodicy in the Old Testament* (ed. J. L. Crenshaw; Philadelphia: Fortress, 1983), 57–87. I am aware that Koch's argument is primarily concerned with wisdom teaching, but the same points pertain to the structure of the Deuteronomic tradition.

10 Bernard M. Levinson, *Legal Revision and Religious Renewal in Ancient Israel* (Cambridge: Cambridge University Press, 2008), 59.

11 Levinson, *Legal Revision and Religious Renewal*, 63.

12 Levinson, *Legal Revision and Religious Renewal*, 67.
13 Levinson, *Legal Revision and Religious Renewal*, 72–84.
14 It is perhaps worth noting that the same term is used in the same way in the famous query of Job 1:9 (see also 2:3; 9:17).
15 It is perhaps not too far-fetched to note that Fredrik Lindstrom, *Suffering and Sin: Interpretations of Illness in the Individual Complaint Psalms* (Stockholm: Almqvist & Wiksell, 1994), makes a compelling case that in the psalms trouble comes because YHWH is absent or indifferent. In a parallel way it is possible to think that Nebuchadnezzar can do what he does in the Jerusalem temple because YHWH is "on leave" for an instant.
16 Perhaps there is some irony in Psalm 137 that the migrants are more passionate than is YHWH about the city and its temple.
17 I am citing the English versification. See the long diatribe of vv. 20-28 that justifies YHWH's harsh action. The punishment is based on the verdict, "It is because they abandoned the covenant of the LORD, the God of their ancestors" (v. 25).
18 On the verb, see Walter Brueggemann, "The Travail of Pardon: Reflections on slḥ," in *"A God So Near": Essays on Old Testament Theology in Honor of Patrick D. Miller* (ed. B. A. Strawn and N. R. Bowen; Winona Lake, Ind.: Eisenbrauns, 2003), 283–97.
19 Levinson, *Legal Revision*, 63, shrewdly uses the terms "devoice" and "revoice" for the ways in which interpretation plays on and against the older tradition. Even the loud, majestic voice of YHWH cannot finally dominate the lived reality of Israel.
20 Benjamin D. Sommer, "Dialectical Biblical Theology: A Jewish Approach to Reading Scripture Theologically," in *Biblical Theology: Introducing the Conversation* (ed. Leo G. Perdue, Robert Morgan, and Benjamin D. Sommer; Nashville: Abingdon, 2009), 1–53. Sommer richly explores the way of biblical theology and interpretation that refuses closure.
21 Jacqueline E. Lapsley, *Can These Bones Live? The Problem of the Moral Self in the Book of Ezekiel* (BZAW 301; Berlin: de Gruyter, 2000), has shown the way in which the tradition of Ezekiel, for example, must move from summons to return to a gift of new heart and new life. The tradition continues to play between the summons and the gift as circumstance requires and permits.

CHAPTER ELEVEN

* This chapter was originally a lecture to the Celebration Publications Conference on Effective Liturgy in Cincinnati, Ohio, in July 2009.
1 On the shared U.S. version of biblical faith, see Will Herberg, *Protestant, Catholic, Jew: An Essay in Religious Sociology* (Chicago: University of Chicago Press, 1983).
2 Katherine Lee Bates, "O Beautiful for Spacious Skies," in *The Presbyterian Hymnal* (Louisville, Ky.: Westminster John Knox, 1990), #564.
3 See Walter Brueggemann, *Solomon: Israel's Ironic Icon of Human Achievement* (Columbia: University of South Carolina Press, 2005).
4 It is to be noted that in 1 Kings 11:12-13 there is a mitigation of the divine judgment "for the sake of your father David." In the end, however, even the exemption for the sake of David could not preclude the completion of divine judgment against Jerusalem and the Davidic monarchy.

5 Walter Brueggemann, *Biblical Perspectives on Evangelism: Living in a Three-Storied Universe* (Nashville: Abingdon, 1993), 103–9.
6 Michael Fishbane, *Sacred Attunement: A Jewish Theology* (Chicago: University of Chicago Press, 2008).
7 Norbert Lohfink, "Distribution of the Functions of Power," in *Great Themes from the Old Testament* (Edinburgh: T&T Clark, 1982), 55–75; S. Dean McBride Jr., "Polity of the Covenant People: The Book of Deuteronomy," in *Constituting the Community: Studies on the Polity of Ancient Israel in Honor of S. Dean McBride Jr.* (ed. J. T. Strong and S. S. Tuell; Winona Lake, Ind.: Eisenbrauns, 2005), 17–33.
8 On the introduction and consequences of the "laws of enclosure," see Karl Polanyi, *The Great Transformation* (Boston: Beacon Press, 1957).
9 On the "other" in relation to social power, see the remarkable study of Martha C. Nussbaum, *The Clash Within: Democracy, Religious Violence, and India's Future* (Cambridge, Mass.: Harvard-Belknap Press, 2007). Nussbaum concludes her study with this judgment: "The real 'clash of civilizations' is not 'out there,' between admirable Westerners and Muslim zealots. It is here, within each person, as we oscillate uneasily between self-protective aggression and the ability to live in the world with others" (337).
10 Martha C. Nussbaum, *Poetic Justice: The Literary Imagination and Public Life* (Boston: Beacon Press, 1995), explores the way in which the responsible judicial practice of justice requires uncommon imagination. See also James Boyd White, *Living Speech: Resisting the Empire of Force* (Princeton: Princeton University Press, 2006), with particular reference to his analyses of court opinions.
11 Michael Walzer, *Exodus and Revolution* (New York: Basic Books, 1985), 149. Waltzer is here quoting W. D. Davies, *The Territorial Dimension of Judaism* (Berkeley: University of California Press, 1982), 60.

CHAPTER TWELVE

1 See Donald E. Gowan, *Theology in Exodus: Biblical Theology in the Form of a Commentary* (Louisville, Ky.: Westminster John Knox, 1994); Terence E. Fretheim, *Exodus* (Interpretation; Louisville, Ky.: John Knox, 1991).
2 Norman K. Gottwald, *The Tribes of Yahweh: A Sociology of the Religion of Liberated Israel, 1250–1050 B.C.* (Maryknoll: Orbis Books, 1979), 609, nicely exposits the way in which Yahwism is a "function" of Israel's political community.
3 Patrick D. Miller, *The Ten Commandments* (Interpretation; Louisville, Ky.: Westminster John Knox, 2009), 117–18.
4 Pamela Constable, *Playing with Fire: Pakistan at War with Itself* (New York: Random House, 2011), 23–24, vividly characterizes the work of "brick-making" as she reports on the labor of the lowest ranking members of Pakistani society: "More than 200,000 migrant laborers work in kilns across Pakistan, earning a few hundred rupees a day. Small children squatted beside their fathers, rolling mud bricks on the quarry floor. Older boys loaded bricks on the little quarry donkeys, which trudged to the kilns and then trotted back on their own. Soot-streaked men shoveled coal into underground ovens, while chimneys overhead billowed trails of black smoke across the pale dawn sky. The kiln families live in

encampments of brick huts beside the quarries, cut off from schools and shops. . . . Kiln work is hot and dangerous, and many workers have old burn marks on their arms and legs. Baksh said . . . 'the worst part . . . is that I still haven't paid off my debt.' "

5 Terence E. Fretheim, "The Plagues as Ecological Signs of Historical Disaster," *Journal of Biblical Literature* 110 (1991): 385–96.

6 I have reference to 1 Peter 2:10, "Once you were no people, now you are God's people." Becoming God's people, I suggest, requires keeping Sabbath.

7 See George E. Mendenhall, *The Tenth Generation: The Origins of the Biblical Tradition* (Baltimore, Md.: Johns Hopkins University Press, 1973), 32–66.

8 See Peter J. Kearney, "Creation and Liturgy: The P Redaction of Ex 25–40," *Zeitschrift für die alttestamentliche Wissenschaft* 89 (1977): 375–87.

9 Joseph Blenkinsopp, "The Structure of P," *Catholic Biblical Quarterly* 38 (1976): 275–92, has observed this connection. He has gone further to suggest that the use of the same term in Joshua 19:51 with reference to the completion of the division of the land is an intentional parallel. To that might also be added the victorious cry of Jesus from the cross in John 19:30. Reference might also be made to the final verse of the great hymn of Charles Wesley, "Love Divine, All Loves Excelling," in *The Presbyterian Hymnal* (Louisville, Ky.: Westminster John Knox, 1990), #376:

Finish then, Thy new creation,
Pure and spotless let us be;
Let us see Thy great salvation
Perfectly restored in Thee;
Changed from glory into glory,
Till in heaven we take our place,
Till we cast our crowns before Thee,
Lost in wonder, love, and praise.

10 Charles Ferguson, *Predator Nation: Corporate Criminals, Political Corruption, and the Hijacking of America* (New York: Crown Business, 2012).

11 Michael Fishbane, *Sacred Attunement: A Jewish Theology* (Chicago: University of Chicago Press, 2008), 124.

12 Fishbane, *Sacred Attunement*, 126–27.

13 Fishbane, *Sacred Attunement*, 127.

CHAPTER THIRTEEN

* This chapter was originally delivered for a conference at Rochester College in 2012. The conference theme, "Mercy Not Sacrifice," is taken from Hosea 6:6, to which Brueggemann refers in several places throughout the chapter.

1 See Hans Walter Wolff, *Joel and Amos* (trans. Waldemar Janzen, S. Dean McBride Jr., and Charles A. Muenchow; ed. S. Dean McBride Jr.; *Hermeneia*; Philadelphia: Fortress, 1977), 218–19.

2 John Donahue, *The Gospel in Parables* (Philadelphia: Fortress, 1988), 189.

3 Donahue, *The Gospel in Parables*, 190.

4 This narrative is an early exemplar of the very land crisis of which Wendell Berry has written so compellingly in our own time.

5 Sandra Sanchez, "Has Nation Become Insane?," *Waco Tribune-Herald* (October 28, 2011), 10A, has written of our national insanity to which the Occupy Wall Street movement is an appropriate response. Her label of "insanity" is a close match to the disorder faced by Nebuchadnezzar.

6 On gradations of holiness, see Philip P. Jenson, *Graded Holiness: A Key to the Priestly Conception of the World* (JSOT Supp. 106; Sheffield: Sheffield Academic, 1992).

CHAPTER FOURTEEN

* A previous form of this chapter was presented to the Homiletics and Biblical Studies section at the 2010 annual meeting of the Society of Biblical Literature in Atlanta, Georgia, and published as "The Risk of Testimony," in *Preaching and the Personal* (ed. J. Dwayne Howell; Eugene, Ore.: Wipf & Stock, 2013), 44–55. Published with permission.

1 Elie Wiesel, "The Holocaust as Literary Inspiration," in *Dimensions of Holocaust* (Evanston, Ill.: Northwestern University Press, 1977), 9.

2 Walter Brueggemann, *Theology of the Old Testament: Testimony, Dispute, Advocacy* (Minneapolis: Fortress, 1997), 117–22.

3 For a novelistic presentation of the way in which utterance creates historical possibility, see Andre Brink, *A Chain of Voices* (Naperville, Ill.: Sourcebooks, 2007).

4 See Elie Wiesel, *The Jews of Silence: A Personal Report on Soviet Jewry* (New York: Schocken Books, 1987).

5 Andrew T. Lincoln, *Truth on Trial: The Lawsuit Motif in the Fourth Gospel* (Peabody, Mass.: Hendrickson, 2000).

6 I take my cue from Emmanuel Levinas, *Totality and Infinity: An Essay on Exteriority* (Pittsburgh, Pa.: Duquesne University Press, 1969).

7 It is not unimportant that the familiar adage, "Power corrupts and absolute power corrupts absolutely" was coined during the process through which the Roman Catholic hierarchy arrived at "papal infallibility" in 1870.

8 On the relation between the two texts, see Christopher R. Seitz, *Zion's Final Destiny: The Development of the Book of Isaiah: A Reassessment of Isaiah 36–39* (Minneapolis: Fortress, 1991), 197–99.

9 On this proposition, see Walter Brueggemann, *Finally Come the Poet: Daring Speech for Proclamation* (Minneapolis: Fortress, 1989).

10 James A. Sanders, *From Sacred Story to Sacred Text* (Philadelphia: Fortress, 1987), 70.

11 Paul Tillich, *Systematic Theology II: Existence and the Christ* (Chicago: University of Chicago Press, 1957), 125–37, 165–80.

CHAPTER FIFTEEN

* This chapter was originally delivered in January 2012 as the keynote address at Andrews University's weeklong celebration of Dr. Martin Luther King Jr.

1 Bruce Feiler, *America's Prophet: Moses and the American Story* (New York: HarperCollins, 2009).

2 See Feiler, *America's Prophet*, 252.

3 Lillian E. Smith, *Killers of the Dream* (New York: Norton, 1949, 1994).

4 See Walter Brueggemann, *Journey to the Common Good* (Louisville, Ky.: Westminster John Knox, 2010).

5 For the atrocity-producing power of totalizing systems, see Robert Jay Lifton, *Witness to an Extreme Century: A Memoir* (New York: Free Press, 2011), 67–68, 381.

6 Michael Walzer, *Exodus and Revolution* (New York: Basic Books, 1985).

7 Walzer, *Exodus and Revolution*, 149.

CHAPTER SIXTEEN

* This chapter was originally delivered as the Carl F. H. Henry lecture during the 2011 Baylor University Symposium on Faith and Culture, "Educating for Wisdom in the 21st Century."

1 Walter Isaacson and Evan Thomas, *The Wise Men: Six Friends and the World They Made* (New York: Simon & Schuster, 1986).

2 Kai Bird, *The Color of Truth: McGeorge Bundy and William Bundy, Brothers in Arms* (New York: Simon & Schuster, 1998), 149.

3 Terry Eagleton, *Reason, Faith, and Revolution: Reflections on the God Debate* (New Haven: Yale University Press, 2009) 10, 14.

4 On "slowness," see Walter Mosley, "Ten Things You Should Know about Slow," *The Nation* (December 13, 2010), 8. He lists the following:

Say no to fast food and join the Slow Food movement instead.
Slow down to the speed limit when driving.
Slow down your conversation.
Be slow to judge.
Tune in, not out.
Not so fast—do you really need a new [fill in the blank]?
Wouldn't you rather meditate than medicate?
Take the time to read poetry daily.
Take time to consider the children.
Don't rush through life.

5 Nicholas Wolterstorff, *Justice: Rights and Wrongs* (Princeton: Princeton University Press, 2008), 75–89, terms these four groups "the quartette of the vulnerable."

6 John McKnight and Peter Block, *The Abundant Community: Awakening the Power of Families and Neighborhoods* (San Francisco: Berrett-Koehler Publishers, 2010).

7 See Paul Hazard, *The European Mind: The Critical Years, 1680–1715* (New York: Fordham University Press, 1990).

8 For a narrative summary of Lifton's work, see Robert Jay Lifton, *Witness to an Extreme Century: A Memoir* (New York: Free Press, 2011).

9 Francis Fukuyama, *The End of History and the Last Man* (New York: Free Press, 1992).

10 See Walter Brueggemann, "Where Is the Scribe?," *The Anglican Theological Review* 93 (2011): 385–403.

11 Michael Walzer, *Exodus and Revolution* (New York: Basic Books, 1985).

12 Walzer, *Exodus and Revolution*, 149.

13 "We Are Marching in the Light of God," in *The New Century Hymnal* (Cleveland, Ohio: Pilgrim Press, 1995), #526.

14 Incidentally, in his analyses of the Iraq War, Slavoj Žižek focuses on the fourth term that Rumsfeld failed to include: the unknown knowns, the disavowed beliefs and unconscious commitments that Žižek identifies with the Freudian-Lacanian unconscious and views as driving forces behind U.S. foreign policy; see Žižek, *Iraq: The Borrowed Kettle* (London: Verso, 2004), 9–10.

15 See Walter Brueggemann, *Journey to the Common Good* (Louisville, Ky.: Westminster John Knox, 2010).

16 See Robert Fulgham, *All I Really Need to Know I Learned in Kindergarten* (New York: Villard Books, 1990).

CHAPTER SEVENTEEN

* Originally written in November 2008.

CHAPTER EIGHTEEN

* Originally written in June 2012.

RETROSPECT

1 See the remarkable poem by Jane Kenyon, "Otherwise," in *Collected Poems* (St. Paul, Minn.: Graywolf Press, 2005), 266.

INDEX OF SCRIPTURE REFERENCES

INDEX OF NAMES